OXFORD LEA

Grammar Finder

Oxford
LEARNER'S
GRAMMAR

Grammar
Finder

OXFORD
UNIVERSITY PRESS

Great Clarendon Street, Oxford OX2 6DP

Oxford University Press is a department of the University of Oxford.
It furthers the University's objective of excellence in research, scholarship,
and education by publishing worldwide in

Oxford New York

Auckland Cape Town Dar es Salaam Hong Kong Karachi
Kuala Lumpur Madrid Melbourne Mexico City Nairobi
New Delhi Shanghai Taipei Toronto

With offices in

Argentina Austria Brazil Chile Czech Republic France Greece
Guatemala Hungary Italy Japan Poland Portugal Singapore
South Korea Switzerland Thailand Turkey Ukraine Vietnam

OXFORD and OXFORD ENGLISH are registered trade marks of
Oxford University Press in the UK and in certain other countries

© Oxford University Press 2005

The moral rights of the author have been asserted

Database right Oxford University Press (maker)

First published 2005

2009 2008 2007 2006 2005
10 9 8 7 6 5 4 3 2 1

ISBN-13: 978 0 19 437593 1
ISBN-10: 0 19 437593 5

Printed in China

ACKNOWLEDGEMENTS

*The authors and publisher are grateful to those who have given permission to reproduce the following
extracts and adaptations of copyright material*: p34 from *Have you Heard…?* by Mary Underwood
© Mary Underwood. Reproduced by permission. p45 'Origins of the Universe' taken from
DK SCIENCE ENCYCLOPEDIA 2nd Edition (Dorling Kindersley, 2001) Copyright © Dorling
Kindersley 2001. p47 Extract from *Delia's How To Cook Book One* by Delia Smith reproduced
with the permission of BBC Worldwide Limited. Text copyright © Delia Smith 1998.
p171 'Joyriders treated to scare tactics' by Simon de Bruxelles, *The Times*, 10 March 2000
© *The Times* 10 March 2000. Reproduced by permission of NI Syndication. p197 'Hover
bovver for stowaway', Mail on Sunday, 17 July 1988 © Mail on Sunday. Reproduced by
permission of Atlantic Syndication. p199 *Animals and how they live* by FE Newing &
R Bowood, copyright © Ladybird Books Ltd, 1967, reproduced by permission of Ladybird
Books Ltd. p235 from *Have you Heard…?* by Mary Underwood © Mary Underwood.
Reproduced by permission. p238 From *Gallowglass* by Barbara Vine. Copyright © Barbara
Vine, 1990 and Kingsmarkham Enterprises, Ltd., 1990. Reprinted by permission of Penguin
Group (UK) and Penguin Group (Canada), a Division of Pearson Canada Inc. and PFD on
behalf of Kingsmarkham Enterprises Ltd. p322 J.Reid, *It Can't Be True*, Octopus Books Ltd.
Reproduced by permission of Hamlyn, a Division of Octopus Publishing Group Ltd

Although every effort has been made to trace and contact copyright holders before
publication, this has not been possible in some cases. We apologise for any apparent
infringement of copyright and if notified, the publisher will be pleased to rectify any
errors or omissions at the earliest opportunity.

Illustrated by: Trevor Dunton and Joanna Kerr

Contents

Sentence and text

Verb forms

Infinitive, gerund, and participle

The noun phrase

Adjectives, adverbs, and prepositions

Main clauses and sub-clauses

Endings and irregular forms

The Oxford Learner's Grammar website at www.oup.com/elt/olg contains
information on the following topics:

- Numbers and time   • Punctuation   • Stress
- Word formation   • American English

Introduction

Who is *Oxford Learner's Grammar* for?

Teachers:

Oxford Learner's Grammar can be used by teachers working with classes from intermediate to advanced level, including classes preparing for examinations such as the the Cambridge First Certificate or the Cambridge Certificate in Advanced English.

- for **grammar lesson** preparation
  - providing reference information on specific grammar topics
  - to help you teach specific grammar topics by using the detailed explanations and associated practice exercises.
- for **general lesson** preparation (e.g. alongside a main coursebook with its own grammar syllabus):
  - to anticipate grammar questions and problems likely to come up in class;
  - to provide extra explanation and practice of a grammar topic covered in the class coursebook;
  - to teach extra grammar topics not included in the class coursebook, but which may be part of a national or examination grammar syllabus.
- for **general reference**
  - to deal with problems which come up in class
  - to help you answer your own and your students' grammar questions.
- for **testing** of students' existing knowledge and for revision
  - The test questions on the *Grammar Checker* CD-ROM can be used to assess your students' level of grammar and to discover their strengths and weaknesses.
  - The *Grammar Builder* consists of practice exercises only – without accompanying explanation. This means you can use it to find out what your students know (and what they don't know) about a particular topic, as well as for revision.

Students:

If you are an intermediate or advanced level student, you will find *Oxford Learner's Grammar* useful to work with on your own, in class, or alongside a coursebook, to prepare for examinations such as the the Cambridge First Certificate or the Cambridge Certificate in Advanced English.

- for **self-study**
  - you can study the explanations and examples in the *Grammar Finder* and then practise using the *Grammar Builder* exercises and the *Grammar Checker* interactive CD-ROM.
- for **class study**
  - you can look up explanations of grammar topics in the *Grammar Finder*, especially when a topic is causing you problems;
  - you can use the *Grammar Builder* for extra practice in class or for homework as directed by your teacher.

What is the *Oxford Learner's Grammar* pack?

Oxford Learner's Grammar is a resource consisting of this *Grammar Finder* reference book including the *Grammar Checker* CD-ROM, and the *Grammar Builder* practice book.

The *Grammar Finder* is a reference book containing clear explanations and examples of English grammatical structures. Particular attention is paid to areas likely to cause difficulty, such as the gerund and infinitive, conditional sentence patterns, and the difference in use between the present perfect and the past simple. The *Grammar Finder* is designed to be as accessible as possible: as well as detailed explanations, it contains tip boxes which provide the learner with useful hints and guidelines. You can use the book to study grammar in detail or to sort out particular difficulties as they arise.

The *Grammar Checker* CD-ROM is inside the back cover of this book. It has three features. **Test Yourself** contains 200 test questions which enable you to identify problems and check progress. You can then move to the **Audio** feature, which lets you hear and then practise examples which illustrate grammar points where pronunciation plays an important part. There is also an **interactive index** to the *Grammar Finder*: its word search feature gives instant access to a **Grammar Hints** window which displays answers to your questions on grammar.

The *Grammar Builder* contains exercises on the grammar points dealt with in the main chapters of the *Grammar Finder*. There is a wide variety of exercise types, including some which are similar to those used in the Cambridge examinations. As well as exercises on individual points, there are contrastive exercises and review exercises covering the content of a whole chapter.

There is also an Oxford Learner's Grammar Website at www.oup.com/elt/olg.

How do I find my way around? Routes in ...

The first route into *Oxford Learner's Grammar* is through a contents overview at the beginning of this book. A second route is via the index. You can access a specific grammar point by means of the index at the back of this book or via the interactive index on the *Grammar Checker* CD-ROM. For example, to find an explanation of the difference between the question words *what* and *which*, you can look up either of these words and find a reference to 16B. This means that in part B of section 16 in the *Grammar Finder* you will find information on *who, what,* and *which*.

Practice material on a specific section can be found by referring to the section numbers at the head of each exercise in the *Grammar Builder*. For example, if you have studied 16B in the *Grammar Finder* and you need related practice material, you will find the reference ▶ Finder 16A-C in the *Grammar Builder* at Exercise 30, which practises *who, what,* and *which*. Answers can be checked in the key at the end of the *Grammar Builder*. Each answer has a reference back to a specific part of the *Grammar Finder*, which you can consult again if problems remain.

The **Test Yourself** feature on the *Grammar Checker* CD-ROM also has a key which either confirms that the answer is correct or takes you to a grammar hint which explains briefly why an answer is incorrect. There is also a reference to the relevant section of the *Grammar Finder* if you would like to study the topic further.

What kind of English are we talking about?

Oxford Learner's Grammar deals with modern standard British English. The examples are mainly neutral in style: not especially formal or informal. Usages that are formal, informal, literary, or non-standard are marked as such.

The website at www.oup.com/elt/olg covers in some detail the main grammatical differences between British and American English. Differences are also mentioned throughout the book.

How will I learn to communicate effectively?

Grammar and meaning
Grammar is a vehicle for expressing meaning, so there is little point in studying formal structure for its own sake. However, a poor knowledge of grammar can seriously hinder communication. As a student, you need to know the difference between *if I have time* and *if I had time* and between *So I do* and *So do I*. *Oxford Learner's Grammar* pays a good deal of attention to meaning. It also covers the use of grammatical forms in communicative functions, such as the use of modal verbs in requests and offers and the function of imperatives and question tags.

Grammar and context
Grammar consists of more than isolated sentences. There are many aspects of grammar which cannot be properly explained within the confines of a clause or sentence. Texts and dialogues are used to take account of discourse and the wider context whenever this is relevant. How answers relate to questions, how sentences are linked in a text, how emphasis depends on context – these are all examples of grammar going beyond the sentence.

Grammar and 'real world' English
Grammatical forms and structures underlie actual use of language in real situations. The *Grammar Finder* contains numerous examples to illustrate grammatical structures and bring them to life. Most of the texts and dialogues are authentic in that they are drawn from genuine conversations or book or newspaper articles. Some of the examples have been taken from or adapted from the British National Corpus. Many of the explanations and the lists of words occurring in particular patterns are also based on an analysis of the British National Corpus. Some examples are invented, especially where this is the best means of illustrating a point in the clearest possible way, but all the examples are realistic.

Is it necessary to learn rules?

The 'rules' in this book are explanations of how English is used. They are a means to understanding how English works, not a set of formulas to be learned by heart.

Modern descriptions of English are based on what people actually say and write. Language changes all the time and even grammar rules are subject to gradual change. However, there is a belief among some English speakers that there are unalterable rules which must always be obeyed. This has caused some controversy among English speakers over a small number of grammar points. For example, some people believe you should not split an infinitive or begin a sentence with the word *and*, despite the fact that English speakers frequently do so. The *Grammar Finder* draws attention to these prescriptive 'rules' and gives advice about usage.

What are the special problems of English grammar?

Unlike words in some other languages, English words do not have lots of different endings. Nouns have *-s* in the plural, but they do not have endings to show if they are the subject or the object. There are a few verb endings such as *-ed* for the past (*started*) but just one ending for person: *-s* in the third person singular of the present simple (*starts*). However, a verb phrase can still have a complicated structure such as *have started*, *will be seeing*, or *must have been waiting*.

Word order is very important in English. *The man bit the dog* means something different from *The dog bit the man*. The subject-verb word order in a statement is fixed, and we can change it only if there is a special reason.

A problem for the non-native-speaker is the use of prepositions, which have many idiomatic uses in phrases such as **on** *Friday* or **at** *two o'clock*. Both prepositions and adverbs combine with verbs in an idiomatic way: *wait* **for** *someone*, *turn the radio* **off**. There are many such expressions that need to be learned as items of vocabulary.

Good luck

The aim of the *Oxford Learner's Grammar* resource pack is to provide clear, accessible explanations and meaningful practice in order to facilitate learning. Author and publisher hope very much that teachers and students will benefit from the pack and enjoy working with it.

Editorial Team

Publishing Managers

David Baker

Glynnis Chantrell

CD-ROM Project manager

Mila Rendle

CD-ROM Project coordinator

Vicky Hawkins

Phonology Consultant

Dr Mark Gray, Université de Paris XII

American English consultant

Terra Brockman

Index consultant

Hilary Cooper

Thanks

I would like to thank the students and staff of the Oxford Intensive School of English and St Clare's International College, who kindly tried out the CD-ROM prototype. I am indebted to Dr Mark Gray and to Terra Brockman, who gave valuable advice on phonology and American English respectively. I am also grateful to those at Oxford University Press who worked on the project, in particular Mila Rendle for her work on the CD-ROM and Phil Hargraves for the design of the books. Special thanks are due to David Baker for his role in conceiving and instigating the whole project and to the editor Glynnis Chantrell, whose dedication and enthusiasm have been a great encouragement. Finally, as ever, thanks to my wife Sheila for her unfailing support.

Key to symbols

Phonetic symbols

These are usually inside slashes, e.g. /iː/.

iː	tea	ʌ	cup	p	put	f	first	h	house
ɪ	sit	ɜː	bird	b	best	v	van	m	must
i	happy	ə	away	t	tell	θ	three	n	next
e	ten	eɪ	pay	d	day	ð	this	ŋ	song
æ	had	əʊ	so	k	cat	s	sell	l	love
ɑː	car	aɪ	cry	g	good	z	zoo	r	rest
ɒ	dog	aʊ	now	tʃ	cheese	ʃ	ship	j	you
ɔː	ball	ɔɪ	boy	dʒ	just	ʒ	pleasure	w	will
uː	fool	ɪə	dear						
ʊ	book	eə	chair						
u	actual	ʊə	sure						

(r) four   linking r, pronounced before a vowel but (in standard British English) not
pronounced before a consonant:
four apples   /fɔːr 'æplz/
four bananas   /fɔː bə'nɑːnəz/

' = Stress follows, e.g. *about* /ə'baʊt/; *a* is unstressed, and *bout* is stressed.

ˌ = Secondary stress follows.

↘ = Falling intonation follows.

↗ = Rising intonation follows.

Other symbols

The symbol / (forward slash) between two words or phrases means that either is possible. *The shop may not/might not be open today* means that two sentences are possible: *The shop may not be open today* and *The shop might not be open today*.

We also use slashes around phonetic symbols, e.g. *tea* /tiː/.

Brackets ( ) around a word or phrase in an example mean that it can be left out. *I've been here (for) ten minutes* means that two sentences are possible: *I've been here for ten minutes* and *I've been here ten minutes*.

The symbol → means that two things are related. *Discuss → discussion* means that there is a relationship between the verb *discuss* and the noun *discussion*.

The symbol ~ means that there is a change of speaker.

The symbol > is a reference to another section and/or part of a section where there is more information. For example, >65 means 'see section 65'; > 225C means 'see part C of section 225; and >B means 'see part B of this section.'

The symbol → Audio is a reference to the audio feature on the *Grammar Checker* CD-ROM provided with this book.

Words and phrases

1 Word classes

Here is a piece of writing in English.

The Internet is, by far, one of the most amazing tools available to humans since the beginning of time. No, this is not an exaggeration. With some relatively inexpensive equipment (a computer, a modem and a telephone line) you can find information about practically anything, at any time, because the Internet is fast becoming a repository of the sum total of human knowledge.

No less incredible is the fact that, for people online, the world doesn't have borders. You can meet people from the most exotic corners of the earth, even develop meaningful relationships with people you'll never meet face to face. And with such global friendships comes the promise of peace and prosperity.

But enough of that pompous stuff. The truth is, the Internet is where you can find out all the latest gossip about Sandra Bullock or Kevin Costner. It's where you go shopping for hats or book airline flights. It's where you stay up all night chatting with strangers when you can't fall asleep. It's cool, fun, exciting, and, best of all, it's affordable.

(from *How to Use Microsoft Internet Explorer* by Hubert, SG/Schwerin, R, ©1996. Reprinted by permission of Pearson Education, Inc., Upper Saddle River, NJ.)

There are eight word classes in English, sometimes called 'parts of speech'. Here is a list with some examples from the passage above.

Word class	Examples
Verb:	*becoming, can, comes, develop, find, is, stay*
Noun:	*computer, Internet, night, people, time, world*
Adjective:	*amazing, cool, exotic, global, inexpensive*
Adverb:	*even, never, practically, relatively*
Determiner:	*a, any, some, such, the, that*
Pronoun:	*anything, it, you*
Conjunction:	*and, because, but*
Preposition:	*about, at, by, for, of, since, to, with*

NOTE
Most word classes can be divided into sub-classes. For example:

Verb ➔	Ordinary verb: *find, meet*	Determiner ➔	Article: *the, a*
	Auxiliary verb: *is, can*		Quantifier: *some, any*
Adverb ➔	Adverb of degree: *very, relatively*		Demonstrative: *this, that*
	Adverb of manner: *carefully, fast*		Possessive: *my, your*
	Adverb of frequency: *often, never*		
	etc		

1

2 Words belonging to more than one word class

Some words belong to more than one word class. Here are some examples.

promise	Verb:	*I **promise** I won't forget.*
	Noun:	*With such friendships comes the **promise** of peace.*
human	Noun:	*It's the most amazing tool available to **humans**.*
	Adjective:	*All **human** knowledge is there.*
fast	Adjective:	*Snail mail isn't as **fast** as e-mail.*
	Adverb:	*The Internet is **fast** becoming essential.*
that	Determiner:	*Enough of **that** pompous stuff.*
	Pronoun:	*It's something **that** people can afford.*
	Conjunction:	*It's a fact **that** the Internet doesn't have borders.*

In English there are lots of verbs that we can use as nouns.
*Have a **look** at the Help menu.*
*Can you make a **copy** of this document?*
*I'll do a **search** of the web.*

There are also nouns that we can use as verbs.
*Now you have to **name** the file.*
*Please **key** in your personal number.*
*Another means of communication is **texting** by mobile phone.*

3 Phrases

There are five kinds of phrase.

A Verb phrase: *is, can find, is becoming, doesn't have, comes, has been growing*

A verb phrase has an ordinary verb. There can also be one or more auxiliaries.

(Auxiliaries)	Ordinary verb
	is
can	*find*
is	*becoming*
doesn't	*have*
	comes
has been	*growing*

Be, have and *do* are both ordinary verbs and auxiliary verbs. > 64
*The Internet **is** amazing.* (*be* as an ordinary verb)
*The Internet **is becoming** essential.* (*be* as an auxiliary)

B Noun phrase: *the Internet, a computer, information, such global friendships*

A noun phrase has a noun. There is often a determiner and/or an adjective.

(Determiner)	(Adjective)	Noun
the		*Internet*
a		*computer*
		information
such	*global*	*friendships*

NOTE
A noun phrase can be replaced by a pronoun.
   The Internet is amazing. → ***It** is amazing.*

C Adjective phrase: *cool, most amazing*

An adjective phrase has an adjective, sometimes with an adverb of degree in front of it.

(Adverb)	Adjective
	cool
most	*amazing*

D Adverb phrase: *never, really quickly*

An adverb phrase has an adverb, sometimes with an adverb of degree in front of it.

(Adverb)	Adverb
	never
really	*quickly*

E Prepositional phrase: *at any time, of the earth, for hats*

A prepositional phrase is a preposition + noun phrase.

Preposition	Noun phrase
at	*any time*
of	*the earth*
for	*hats*
into	*it*

The simple sentence

4 Basic clause structure

This chapter is about sentences with just one clause. A clause which can stand alone as a sentence has a subject and a verb. It may also have other elements: an object, a complement, or an adverbial. Each element plays its part in the structure of a clause. We can put the elements together to form different kinds of clauses. Here are some examples of the different clause structures.

1

Subject	Verb
My friend	*is waiting.*
Nothing	*happened.*

2

Subject	Verb	Object
The company	*sells*	*mobile phones.*
The dog	*has eaten*	*my homework.*

3

Subject	Verb	Complement
This colour	*is*	*nice.*
The old cinema	*became*	*a nightclub.*

4

Subject	Verb	Adverbial
The concert	*is*	*tomorrow.*
The photos	*lay*	*on the table.*
The Olympics	*are*	*every four years.*

5

Subject	Verb	Object	Object
We	*should give*	*the children*	*some money.*
Sarah	*sent*	*me*	*a fax.*

6

Subject	Verb	Object	Complement
The project	*kept*	*everyone*	*very busy.*
The group	*made*	*Simon*	*their spokesman.*

7

Subject	Verb	Object	Adverbial
I	*put*	*my credit card*	*in my wallet.*
The police	*got*	*the car*	*out of the river.*

For more information about these clause elements, > GLOSSARY.

5 More details about clause structure

A Each of the clause structures in 4 begins with subject + verb. This is the normal word order in a statement. For inversion in questions, > 14B.

NOTE
For structures like *The police they got the car out of the river*, > 175D.

B The subject of a sentence is a noun phrase (e.g. *my friend*).
The object is also a noun phrase (e.g. *mobile phones*).
A complement usually gives information about the subject of the sentence. It can be an adjective phrase (e.g. *nice*) or a noun phrase (e.g. *a nightclub*). For object complement, > D
An adverbial expresses an idea such as when, how, or why something happens. It can be an adverb phrase (e.g. *tomorrow*), a prepositional phrase (e.g. *on the table*) or a noun phrase (e.g. *every four years*).

C Verbs which do not have an object (Structure 1 in 4) are called intransitive verbs, e.g. *wait, happen, sleep, go*. Verbs with an object (Structure 2 in 4) are called transitive verbs, e.g. *sell, eat, see, catch*. Verbs with a complement (Structure 3 in 4) are called linking verbs, e.g. *be, become, get, look, seem*.

NOTE
Some verbs can be used in more than one structure. Many can be either intransitive or transitive.
　　*The door **opened**.* (intransitive)　　*Someone **opened** the door.* (transitive)

D There are two different kinds of complement: subject complement and object complement. These two examples have a subject complement.
　　*Everyone was **very busy**.*　　*Simon became **their spokesman**.*
The subject complement relates to the subject of the clause (*everyone, Simon*).

These two examples have an object complement.
　　*The project kept everyone **very busy**.*
　　*The group made Simon **their spokesman**.*
The object complement relates to the object of the clause (*everyone, Simon*). In both pairs of examples, *very busy* relates to *everyone*, and *their spokesman* relates to *Simon*.

E We can add extra adverbials to any of the clause structures.
　　*My friend is waiting **outside**.*
　　***Unfortunately** the dog has eaten my homework.*
　　***A few months later** the old cinema **suddenly** became a night club.*
　　***According to the paper**, the concert is tomorrow **at the town hall**.*
　　***To my surprise**, Sarah **actually** sent me a fax **right away**.*
There are different places in the sentence where we can put an adverbial. For more details, > 190.

F We can link two or more words or phrases with *and* or *or*.
*The colour is **nice and bright**.*
***My friend and his brother** are here.*
*The work went **smoothly, quietly, and very efficiently**.*
*The concert is on **Wednesday or Thursday**.*

G We can use two noun phrases one after the other when they both refer to the same thing. We say that the phrases are 'in apposition'.
***My friend Matthew** is coming to stay.*
*Everyone visits **the White House, the home of the President**.*

6 *Give, send, buy*, etc

Give, send, buy, reserve, and similar verbs come in two different sentence structures. They can either have two objects, or they can have an object and a prepositional phrase.
*You give **the attendant your ticket**.*
*You give **your ticket to the attendant**.*

A Two objects

When the verb has two objects, the first is the indirect object, and the second is the direct object.

1

	Indirect object	Direct object
You give	*the attendant*	*your ticket.*
We'll send	*our teacher*	*a message.*
Nigel bought	*Celia*	*a diamond ring.*
I can reserve	*you*	*a seat.*

Here the indirect object refers to the person receiving something, and the direct object refers to the thing that is given.

B Object + prepositional phrase

Instead of an indirect object, we can use a prepositional phrase with *to* or *for*.

	Direct object	Phrase with *to* or *for*
You give	*your ticket*	***to** the attendant.*
We'll send	*a message*	***to** our teacher.*
Nigel bought	*a diamond ring*	***for** Celia.*
I can reserve	*a seat*	***for** you.*

The phrase with *to* or *for* comes after the direct object.

C *To* or *for*?

Some verbs go with *to* and some go with *for*. You give something *to* someone, but you buy something *for* someone.

> *You give your ticket **to** the attendant.*
> *Nigel bought a diamond ring **for** Celia.*

These verbs can go with *to*: *award, bring* (see Note b), *fax, feed, give, grant, hand, leave* (in a will), *lend, mail, offer, owe, pass, pay, post, promise, read, sell, send, show, take, teach, tell, throw, write.*

These verbs can go with *for*: *bring* (see Note b), *buy, cook, fetch, find, fix, get, keep, leave, make, order, pick, reserve, save.*

NOTE

a   *For* meaning 'to help someone', 'on someone's behalf' can go with very many verbs.
> *I posted a letter **to** Adam.* (a letter from me to him)
> *I posted a letter **for** Adam.* (a letter from Adam to someone else)

b   *Bring* goes with either *to* or *for*. We usually use *for* when we talk about giving things to people.
> *We've brought some flowers **for** our hostess.*
We use *to* when we talk about transporting things to places.
> *Lorries regularly bring coal **to** the power station.*
We also use *to* when *bring* has other more abstract meanings.
> *The news brought a smile **to** her face.*

D   Which structure to use?

In a clause with *go, send, buy*, etc, there is a choice between an indirect object and a prepositional phrase.

Indirect object:	*You give **the attendant** your ticket.*
Prepositional phrase:	*You give your ticket **to the attendant**.*

The choice depends on what is the new information in the clause. The new information usually goes at the end. Look at this conversation between two people on holiday who are buying postcards.

Emma: *I'm going to send this card to my brother.*
Lauren: *Yes, that's a nice one. And I like this one here with a photo of the cathedral. I might send it to Amy.*
Emma: *What about William?*
Lauren: *Oh, I'll send William this view of the harbour.*

Compare these sentences.
> *I'm going to send this card **to my brother**.*
My brother is the new information and so it comes at the end. *This card* is known information in the context. (They are looking at postcards.)
> *I'll send William **this view of the harbour**.*
This *view of the harbour* is the new information. *William* is known information. (Emma has just mentioned him.)

NOTE
For more details about information and sentence structure, > 31–32.

E Pronouns after *give, send,* etc

When there is a pronoun, it usually comes before a phrase with a noun.
*Mark lent **me** his umbrella.*
*I might send **it** to Amy.*
This is because the pronoun refers to known information. (*It* means the postcard just mentioned.)

When there are two pronouns after the verb, we normally use *to* or *for*.
*We'll send it **to** you straight away.*
*I've got a ticket for Wimbledon. Louise bought it **for** me.*

NOTE
In informal conversation you may hear two pronouns together.
*Louise bought **me it**./Louise bought **it me**.*

F *Describe, explain,* etc

Some verbs can occur in the structure with *to* or *for* but **not** with an indirect object.
Tim described the men to the police.
(NOT ~~Tim described the police the men.~~)
I'll explain everything to you.
(NOT ~~I'll explain you everything.~~)
My lawyer obtained a copy of the letter for me.
(NOT ~~My lawyer obtained me a copy of the letter.~~)

Such verbs include *announce, communicate, deliver, describe, donate, explain, obtain, propose, purchase, report,* and *suggest.*

TIP
It is safer to use an indirect object only with a short verb like *give* or *send* and **not** with a longer verb like *describe* or *explain*. Say *Can you give me the figures?* but *Can you explain the figures to me?*

NOTE
For structures with *say* and *tell,* > 260.

Sentence types

7 Introduction

A There are four sentence types: a statement, a question, an imperative, and an exclamation.

	Example	Main use
Statement	*You **took** a photo.*	giving information
Question	***Did** you **take** a photo?*	asking for information
Imperative	***Take** a photo.*	an order or a request
Exclamation	***What** a nice photo!*	expressing a feeling

A statement, a question and an imperative can be negative.
> *You **didn't take** a photo.*
> ***Didn't** you **take** a photo?*
> ***Don't take** photos, please.*

B Besides the main use, some sentence types have other uses. Here are some examples.

	Example	Possible use
Statement	*I'd like to know all the details.*	asking for information
Question	*Can you post this letter, please?*	a request
Imperative	*Have a nice time.*	expressing good wishes

This chapter is mainly about the use of statements, negative statements, the imperative, and exclamations. For word order in a positive statement, > 4. For questions and answers, > 13–19.

8 The use of statements

This conversation contains a number of statements.

A PROGRAMME ABOUT WILDLIFE

Stella: *There's a programme about wildlife on TV tonight.*
Adrian: *Uh-huh. Well, I might watch it.*
Stella: *I've got to go out tonight. It's my evening class.*
Adrian: *Well, I'll video the programme for you.*
Stella: *Oh, thanks. It's at eight o'clock on BBC 2.*
Adrian: *We can watch it together when you get back.*
Stella: *OK. I should be back around ten.*

The main use of a statement is to give information: *There's a programme about wildlife on TV tonight.* But some statements do more than that. When Adrian says *I'll video the programme for you,* he is **offering** to video it. His statement is an offer, which Stella accepts by thanking him. And *We can watch it together* is a suggestion to which Stella agrees.

There are many different uses (or 'communicative functions') of statements.

Expressing approval:	*You're doing the right thing.*
Expressing sympathy:	*It was bad luck you didn't pass the exam.*
Thanking someone:	*I'm very grateful.*
Asking for information:	*I want to know your plans.*
Giving orders:	*I want you to check these figures.*

9 Performative verbs

A Some present-simple verbs express what the use of the statement is. For example, we can say *I promise* when we promise to do something.

Promising:	*I **promise** to be good.*
Apologizing:	*It was my fault. I **apologize.***
Predicting:	*I **predict** a close game.*

In general, performative verbs are fairly emphatic. *I promise to be good* is a more emphatic promise than *I'll be good.* Some performative verbs are also rather formal. For example, *I apologize* is more formal than *I'm sorry.*

Examples of performative verbs are: *admit, advise, agree, apologize, disagree, guarantee, insist, object, predict, promise, protest, refuse, suggest, warn.*

NOTE

a   With a few verbs we can use the present continuous.
     *Don't come too close, I warn you/**I'm warning** you.*

b   Sometimes in formal situations the passive is used.
     *You **are requested** to vacate your room by 10.00 am.*

B Sometimes we use a modal verb or similar expression before a performative verb.

Advising:	*I'd **advise** you to see a solicitor.*
Insisting:	*I **must insist** we keep to the rules.*
Informing:	*I **have to inform** you that you have been unsuccessful.*

When we are telling people to do things, the modal verb makes the statement less direct and so more polite. It is also rather more formal to say *I'd advise you to see a solicitor* than *You should see a solicitor.*

Some typical examples are: *must admit, would advise, would agree, must apologize, must disagree, can guarantee, have to inform you, must insist, must object, can promise, must protest, would suggest, must warn.*

10 Negative statements

A Use

This text contains a number of negative statements.

FRANKENSTEIN

*In 1818 Mary Shelley wrote a famous book called 'Frankenstein'. But the monster **wasn't** called Frankenstein, as is popularly believed by people who have **never** read the book. Frankenstein is **not** the name of the monster but the name of the person who created it. People who haven't read the book sometimes talk about 'Doctor Frankenstein'. Frankenstein **wasn't** a doctor, and he did **not** study medicine. We **can't** be sure where Mary Shelley got the name from, but there is a place in Germany called Frankenstein, which might or might **not** have given her the idea.*

The negative statements correct a mistaken idea, such as the idea that the monster was called Frankenstein. In general, we use negative statements to inform someone that what they might think or expect is not so.

B *Not* with a verb

Compare the positive and negative forms.

Positive	Negative Full form	Negative Short form
was called	was **not** called	**wasn't** called
have read	have **not** read	**haven't** read
should be	should **not** be	**shouldn't** be
studied/did study	did **not** study	**didn't** study

In a negative statement, *not* or *n't* comes after the auxiliary. We write the auxiliary and *n't* together as one word.
  *Some people **have not** read the book.*
  *The monster **wasn't** called Frankenstein.*
If there is more than one auxiliary, *not* or *n't* comes after the first auxiliary.
  *That might or **might not have** given her the idea.*
  *We **shouldn't have** stayed so long.*
In simple tenses we use the auxiliary verb *do*.
  *I **don't** like horror films.* (NOT ~~I like not horror films.~~)
  *Frankenstein **did not** study medicine.* (NOT ~~Frankenstein studied not medicine.~~)

Be on its own has *not* or *n't* after it.
> *East London **is not** on most tourist maps.*
> *These shoes **aren't** very comfortable.*

We cannot use *no* to make a negative verb form.
> *The message did**n't** arrive.* (NOT ~~The message no arrived.~~)

NOTE

a   The negative forms of *can* are *cannot* and *can't.*

b   For the negative in a sentence with two clauses, e.g. *I **don't** think it's safe* or *I think it **isn't** safe,* > 253A.

C *Not* in other positions

Not can come before a word or phrase when the speaker is correcting something.
> *I ordered tea, **not coffee.***
> *That's a nice green.* ~ *It's blue, **not green.***

Not can also come before some expressions of quantity (e.g. *many, much, a lot (of), more, enough, everyone,* and *everything*) and before a phrase of distance (e.g. *far*) or time (e.g. *long*).
> ***Not many** people have their own aeroplane.*
> *Your call will normally be answered in **not more** than 30 seconds.*
> *There's an Internet Café **not far** from here.*
> *The business was explained to me **not long** afterwards.*

NOTE

a   *Not* can come before a negative prefix, e.g. *un-, in-,* or *dis-.*
> *Beggars are a **not unusual** sight on the streets of London.*

b   *Not* can stand for a whole clause, e.g. *I hope not.* > 28B

D Other negative words

There are other words besides *not* which have a negative meaning.

	No, none, etc	*Not/n't*
no	*There's **no** time.*	*There is**n't any** time.*
none	*We wanted tickets, but there were **none** left.*	*We wanted tickets, but there were**n't any** left.*
no one, nobody	*I saw **no-one** acting strangely.*	*I did**n't** see anyone acting strangely.*
nothing	*I saw **nothing** suspicious.*	*I did**n't** see **anything** suspicious.*
nowhere	*There was **nowhere** to park.*	*There was**n't anywhere** to park.*
few	***Few** people were interested.*	***Not many** people were interested.*
little	*There was **little** time.*	*There was**n't much** time.*
never	*I've **never** seen the film.*	*I have**n't ever** seen the film.*
seldom, rarely	*We **seldom** eat out.*	*We do**n't often** eat out.*

no longer	Adam **no longer** lives here.	Adam doesn't live here **any more**.
hardly, scarcely	We've **hardly** spoken to our neighbours.	We haven't **really** spoken to our neighbours.
neither, nor	I can't understand this ~ **Neither** can I.	I can't **either**.

NOTE

In standard English we do not normally use *not/n't* or *never* with another negative word.
  I didn't do anything. (NOT ~~I didn't do nothing.~~)
  That will never happen. (NOT ~~That won't never happen.~~)
  We've hardly started. (NOT ~~We haven't hardly started.~~)
But in non-standard English a double negative means the same as a single negative.
  I didn't see no one. (non-standard) (= I didn't see anyone./I saw no one.)
In Standard English two negatives are sometimes used together. The two negatives make a
positive. e.g. *I **didn't** do **nothing**. I did some work.* (= It isn't true that I did nothing.)

E The emphatic negative

We can stress *not* or an auxiliary with *n't*.
  I did NOT take your mobile phone.
  I DIDN'T take your mobile phone.
For emphatic stress, > 38B.

We can also use *at all* to emphasize a negative.
  *We don't like the town **at all**.*
  *In no time **at all**, the interview was over.*
At all usually goes at the end of a clause or after a negative phrase,
e.g *no time*.

Here are some other phrases which emphasize a negative.
  *The operation was not a success **by any means**.*
  *I'm not **in the least** tired.*
  *Her son's visits were **far from** frequent.*

We can use *absolutely* before *no, nobody, nowhere*, etc.
  *There was **absolutely** nowhere to park.*

We can use *whatever* or *whatsoever* after *nothing* or *none*, or after *no* + noun.
  *There's nothing **whatever/whatsoever** we can do about it.*
  *The people seem to have no hope **whatever/whatsoever**.*

F Inversion after a negative phrase

A negative phrase can come in front position. This can happen with phrases
containing the words *no, never, neither, nor, seldom, rarely, hardly,* and the
word *only*. There is inversion of subject and auxiliary.
  ***Under no circumstances** should you travel alone.*
  (Compare: *You should not travel alone under any circumstances.*)
  ***Never in my life** have I seen such behaviour.*
  (Compare: *I have never seen such behaviour in my life.*)

The telephone had been disconnected. **Nor** *was there any electricity.*
(Compare: *There wasn't any electricity either.*)
Only in summer *is it hot enough to sit outside.*
(Compare: *It is only hot enough to sit outside in summer.*)

The structure with inversion can sound formal and literary. It often adds emphasis to the negative.

Sometimes a phrase with *not* can come in front position.

Not since his childhood *had the old man been back to the village.*
Not until the following Monday *was I able to see a doctor.*

If the verb is in a simple tense, we use the auxiliary verb *do.*

Seldom do *we have any time to ourselves.*
(Compare: *We seldom have any time to ourselves.*)
Only once did *the company break the law.*
(Compare: *The company broke the law only once.*)

NOTE
No way is informal.
No way *am I going to let this happen.*
No way *can we get over there by six o'clock.*
(Compare: *There's no way we can get over there by six o'clock.*)
But *in no way* is more formal.
In no way *have I failed in my duty.*

11 The imperative

A Form

The imperative is the base form of the verb. The negative is *do not/don't* + base form, and for emphasis we use *do* + base form.

	Imperative form
Positive:	**Come** *here.*
	Please **read** *the instructions carefully.*
Negative:	**Do not remove** *this book from the library.*
	Don't make *so much fuss.*
Emphatic:	**Do be** *careful.*

NOTE
a   We can mention the subject *you* when it contrasts with another person.
   I'll wait here. **You** *go round the back.*
   You can also make an order emphatic or even aggressive.
   You *be careful what you're saying.*
   A few other phrases can be the subject.
   All of you *sit down!*   **Everyone** *stop what you're doing.*

b   We can use other negative words with an imperative.
   Never *touch electrical equipment with wet hands.*   *Leave* **no** *litter.*

c   In British English you may hear the emphatic *do* used as a polite form in offers and invitations.
   Do *have some cake.*   **Do** *come in.*

B Getting people to do things

There are many different ways of getting people to do things in English. Compare these sentences.

I'd be very grateful if you could translate this letter. (asking a favour)
Could you translate this letter, please? (a polite request)
Translate this letter. (an instruction on an exam paper)

The form we use for an order or request depends on the situation. It is usually necessary to use a polite formula such as *Could you ...?* rather than an imperative.

To be very polite when asking a favour, we need to use a longer formula.

Would you be so kind as to move into the other room, please?
I wonder if you'd mind dealing with the matter for me.

In most situations we use a question form.

Could you hold the door open for me, please?
Would you mind giving me a lift?

You should always take the trouble to put your request into a question form. It would not be polite to say simply *Give me a lift*. In such a situation, the imperative would sound abrupt and even rude.

Even people in positions of authority often use a polite formula rather than a simple imperative.

Can you get out your books, please?
I want you to just keep still a moment.
You mustn't spend too long on this.
I'd like you to move a bit closer together.
Would you like to come this way?

The imperative is sometimes used to give orders.

Teacher (to pupils):	*Open* your books at page sixty.
Doctor (to patient):	Just *keep* still a moment.
Boss (to employee):	*Don't spend* too long on this.
Traffic sign:	*STOP*

But it is unusual to begin a conversation with an imperative. Often a polite formula is used for the first request, followed by a series of imperatives.

Can you get out your books, please? *Open* them at page sixty and *look* at the photo. Then *think* about your reaction to it.

An imperative can also be used informally between equals.

Give me a hand with these bags.
Hurry up, or we're going to be late.

TIP
It's better not to say *Do it.*
Say *Could you do it please?*
or *Would you mind doing it please?*

C Asking for something

When we ask someone to give us something, we use *Can I/we have...?* or *Could I/we have...?*
> **Can we have** *our bill, please?*
> **Could I have** *one of those street plans, please?*

We do not say ~~*Give us our bill, please*~~.

In a shop or café we can simply name what we want, but we must add *please*.
> *A box of matches,* **please**.   *Two cappuccinos,* **please**.

We can also use *I'd like...* or *I'll have...*
> **I'd like** *an orange juice.*   **I'll have** *the fish, please.*

D Other uses of the imperative

Slogans and advertisements:
> **Save** *the rain forests.*   **Visit** *historic Bath.*

Suggestions and advice:
> *Why not take a year out before college?* **Travel** *around and* **see** *the world.*

Warnings and reminders:
> **Look** *out! There's a car coming.*   **Mind** *you don't fall.*
> *Always* **switch** *off the electricity first.*   **Don't** *forget your key.*

Instructions and directions:
> **Select** *the programme you need by turning the dial.* **Pull** *out the knob. The light will come on and the machine will start.*
> **Go** *along here and* **turn** *left at the lights.*

Informal offers and invitations:
> **Have** *a chocolate.*   **Come** *to lunch if you like.*

Good wishes:
> **Have** *a nice holiday.*   **Enjoy** *yourselves.*

E Imperative + question tag

We can use a positive tag after a positive imperative.
> *Get out your books,* **will/would/can/could** *you?*

The tag makes the imperative less abrupt.

The tag *can't you?* after an imperative expresses annoyance or impatience.
> *Keep still,* **can't** *you?*   *Hurry up,* **can't** *you?*

In warnings, reminders and good wishes, the tag is *won't you?* after a positive imperative and *will you?* after a negative.
> *Drive carefully,* **won't** *you?*
> *Don't forget your key,* **will** *you?*
> *Have a nice holiday,* **won't** *you?*

F *Let*

Let's + verb expresses a suggestion.
> *It's a lovely day. **Let's** sit outside.*

The full form is *let us*, but we normally use the short form *let's*.

We can use the tag *shall we?*
> *Let's have some coffee, **shall we**?*

The negative is *let's not* or *don't let's*.
> ***Let's not** waste/**Don't let's** waste any time.*

NOTE

a *Let me* means that the speaker is telling him/herself what to do.
> ***Let me** think. Where did I put the letter?*
> ***Let me** see what's in my diary.*

Let me see means 'I'm going to see.' Compare *let* meaning 'allow'.
> *Oh, you've got some photos. **Let** me see./May I see?*

b After *let* we can refer to another person or other people.
> *If Lauren doesn't want to come out with us, **let her** stay at home.*
> ***Let them** sort out their own problems.*

This means that I think they should sort out their own problems.

12 Exclamations

A An exclamation is any phrase or sentence spoken with emphasis and feeling.
> *Oh no!   Lovely!   You idiot!   Stop!   Oh, my God!*

In writing we use an exclamation mark (!).

B There are structures with *how* and *what* that can be used in an exclamation, although they do not always have an exclamation mark.

After *how* we can use an adjective or adverb.
> ***How** awful!   **How** nice to see you.   **How** brave you are.*

We can also use a subject + verb.
> *Look at the plants – **how** they've grown!*

After *what* there can be a noun phrase with *a/an* or without an article.
> ***What** a surprise!   **What** a good idea.*
> ***What** nonsense you talk.   **What** nice things you've got.*

C Some exclamations have the form of a negative question.
> ***Aren't** you lucky! (= You're lucky./How lucky you are!)*
> ***Wasn't** that fun! (= That was fun./What fun that was!)*
> ***Don't** you look smart! (= You look smart./How smart you look!)*

Questions and answers

13 The use of questions

BUYING A TRAIN TICKET

Travel agent: **Can I help you?**
Customer: **Do you sell rail tickets?**
Travel agent: *Yes, certainly.*
Customer: *I need a return ticket from Bristol to Paddington.*
Travel agent: **When are you travelling?**
Customer: *Tomorrow, Thursday. Coming back the same day.*
Travel agent: **Are you leaving before ten o'clock?**
Customer: *It's cheaper after ten, is it?*
Travel agent: *It's cheaper if you leave after ten and return after six.*
Customer: **What time is the next train after ten o'clock?**
Travel agent: *Ten eleven.*
Customer: *Oh, fine.* **And how much is the cheap ticket?**
Travel agent: *Thirty-two pounds.*
Customer: **Can I have one then**, *please?*

The most basic use of a question is to ask for information.
> *What time is the next train?* ~ **Ten eleven.**

But we can use questions in other ways, especially with modal verbs, e.g. *can*.

A request:	*Can I have one then, please?*
A suggestion:	*Shall we take the early train?*
Offering to help:	*Can I help you?*
Offering something:	*Would you like a brochure?*
Asking permission:	*May I take one of these timetables?*
Complaining:	*Why can't you listen when I'm talking to you?*

NOTE

There are also 'rhetorical questions', where an answer is not usually expected.
> *What do you think will happen?* ~ **Who knows?**
> *You're always criticizing me, but* **have I ever criticized you?**

14 Question forms

A Yes/no questions and wh-questions

There are two question types: a yes/no question and a wh-question.

A yes/no question can be answered by *yes* or *no*.
> *Do you sell rail tickets?* ~ **Yes, we do.**/*Certainly.*
> *Will I need to change?* ~ **No**, *it's a direct service.*

A yes/no question begins with an auxiliary verb (*do, will*).

Sometimes other expressions are used instead of *yes* or *no*.
*Are you leaving before ten o'clock? ~ **I expect so**.*

A wh-question begins with a question word.
***When** are you travelling? ~ Tomorrow.*
***What** shall we do? ~ I don't know.*
The question words are *who, what, which, whose, where, when, why,* and *how*. For more details, > 15–16.

NOTE
We can use *or* in a question.
*Are you coming back today **or** tomorrow? ~ Today.*
*Were you running **or** jogging? ~ I was running.*
Or can link two clauses.
*Are you coming back today, **or** are you staying overnight? ~ I'm coming back today.*
The second clause can be the negative of the first one.
*Are you coming back today, **or aren't you**?/**or not**?*
This stresses the need for a yes or no answer and can sound impatient.

B Inversion in questions

In most questions there is inversion of the subject and the auxiliary.

Statement	Question
***You are** leaving today.*	***Are you** leaving today?*
***The train has** stopped.*	*Why **has the train** stopped?*
***We can** sit here.*	*Where **can we** sit?*

If there is more than one auxiliary verb, then only the first one comes before the subject.

Statement	Question
***I could have** reserved a seat.*	***Could I have** reserved a seat?*
	(NOT *Could have I reserved a seat?*)

In simple tenses we use the auxiliary verb *do*.

Statement	Question
You like train journeys.	***Do** you like train journeys?*
They arrived at six.	***Did** they arrive at six?*

Be on its own as an ordinary verb can also come before the subject.

Statement	Question
***The train was** late.*	***Was the train** late?*
***My ticket is** somewhere.*	*Where **is my ticket**?*

NOTE
In simple tenses, *do* can be used for emphasis in a statement. > 38C Compare:

Statement with emphasis	Question
You do *like train journeys.*	**Do you** *like train journeys?*
They did *arrive at six.*	**Did they** *arrive at six?*

C Questions without inversion

In informal conversation a question can sometimes have the same word order as in a statement.

You're leaving tomorrow? ~ Yes.
The car was blue? ~ That's right.
The car was **what colour**? ~ Blue.
They went **which** *way? ~ That way.*

TIP
When you ask a question, say *Are you leaving tomorrow?* and not *You're leaving tomorrow?* A question without inversion is not as usual in English as in some other languages and can sometimes sound a little strange.

15 Wh-questions

A Question words

Here are some questions with the various question words. The sentence in brackets shows how each question relates to a statement.

Who did Luke take to the dance? (He took **someone** to the dance.)
What are you reading? (You're reading **something**.)
Which film shall we see? (We'll see **one of** the films.)
Whose bike is that? (It is **someone's** bike.)
Where do you live? (You live **somewhere**.)
When did the accident happen? (It happened **at some time**.)
Why is your friend so upset? (She is upset **for some reason**.)
How did you get a ticket? (You got a ticket **somehow**.)

For short questions, e.g. *Why?*, > 25A.
For *whom,* > 15C.

NOTE
a   In these examples, the question word relates to something in a sub-clause.
What did Emma think I said? (Emma thought I said something.)
When would you like to leave? (You would like to leave at some time.)

b   *Why (not)* can come before a noun phrase or a verb.
Why the panic? (= What is the reason for the panic?)
Look at our prices - why pay more? (= Why should you pay more?)
Why not stay for a while? (= Why don't you stay for a while?)

TIP
Do not confuse *who's* and *whose*.
Who's is a short form of *who is* or *who has*.
Who's *going to the party?*
Whose *party is it?*

B *Who, what,* etc as subject and object

When *who* or *what* is the subject of a question, there is no inversion. The word order is the same as in a statement. Compare these questions.

Subject	Object
Who invited *you to the party?* ~ *Laura did.* (**Someone** invited you.) **What caused** *the accident?* ~ *The driver of the lorry fell asleep.* (**Something** caused the accident.)	**Who did** *you* **invite** *to the party?* ~ *Oh, lots of people.* (You invited **someone**.) **What did** *the accident* **cause?** ~ *A 20-mile tailback.* (The accident caused **something**.)

*Who **saw** the detective?*
(Someone saw him.)

*Who **did** the detective **see?***
(He saw someone.)

Here are some more examples of a question word (or a question word + noun) as the subject.

    Who *is organizing the trip?*
    What *happens next?*
    Which *came first, the chicken or the egg?*
    Which coat *looks the best on me?*
    Whose car *has been stolen, did you say?*

We can also use *how many* and *how much*.
    How many people *know the secret?*
    How much of the money *goes to those who really need it?*

C *Whom*

When *who* is the object of a question, we can use *whom* instead.
> **Who/Whom** *did you invite?*

Whom is formal.

> **TIP**
> Use *who*, not *whom*. *Whom* is formal and rather old-fashioned.
> Say *Who can you see?* not *Whom can you see?*
> *Who* is more usual in everyday speech.

D Prepositions in questions

A question word can be the object of a preposition.
> **Where** *does Maria come* **from?**
> (Maria comes **from somewhere**.)
> **What** *are young people interested* **in** *these days?*
> (Young people are interested **in something** these days.)

Usually the preposition comes in the same place as in a statement (*come from*, *interested in*).

But in formal English the preposition can come before the question word.
> **On what** *evidence was it decided to make an arrest?*
> **In which** *direction did the men go?*

When *who/whom* is the object of a preposition, there are two possible structures.
> **Who** *were you talking* **to?**
> **To whom** *were you talking?* (formal)

When the question begins with a preposition, *whom* is used, not *who*.
> (NOT *To who were you talking?*)

NOTE
Since comes before *when* even in informal English. It often suggests disagreement.
> *I always help with the washing up ~ Oh yes,* **since when?**
> **Since when** *has this area been closed to the public?*

The second example might be used to challenge someone trying to bar people from a public place. The same question with *How long...?* would be more neutral.

16 More details about question words

A Question word + noun

What, *which* and *whose* can have a noun (or an adjective + noun) after them.

Without a noun	With a noun
What *will you do?*	**What action** *will you take?*
Which *is best, Thursday or Friday?*	**Which day** *is best?*
Whose *was this stupid idea?*	**Whose stupid idea** *was this?*

Which can come before *one/ones* or before an of-phrase.
>*We've got lots of suitcases.* **Which one** *shall we take?*
>**Which of the bands** *did you like best?*
We can also ask *Which one of ...?*
>**Which one of these boxes** *should I tick?*

B The use of *who*, *what*, and *which*

Who always refers to a human being.
Which can refer either to humans or to something non-human.
What refers mostly to something non-human, but it can refer to humans
when it comes before a noun.

	Human	Non-human
who	**Who** *is your maths teacher?*	
which	**Which** *teacher/***Which** *of the teachers do you have?*	**Which** *supermarket/***Which** *of the supermarkets is cheapest?*
what	**What** *idiot wrote this?*	**What** *book are you reading?*
		What *do you do in the evenings?*

Who cannot come before a noun or before an of-phrase.
>(NOT ~~Who teacher do you have?~~ and NOT ~~Who of the teachers do you have?~~)

There is a difference in meaning between *what* and *which*.
>**What** *do you do in your spare time?*   **What** *sport do you play?*
>**Which** *is the quickest route?*   **Which** *way do we go now?*
We use *what* when there is an indefinite (and often large) number of possible
answers. We use *which* when there is a definite (and often small) number of
possible answers.

>**What** *sport?*
>Tennis, or golf, or football, or ...
>**Which** *way?*
>Right or left?

The choice of *what* or *which* depends on how the speaker sees the number of
possible answers. In some contexts either word is possible.
>**What** *newspaper* / **Which** *newspaper do you read?*
>**What** *parts* / **Which** *parts of France have you visited?*
>**What** *size* / **Which** *size do you take?*

NOTE
We can use *what* to deny the existence of something just mentioned.
>*Why don't you invite a few friends?* ~ **What** *friends? I haven't got any friends.*

C Question phrases

What and *how* can combine with other words to form phrases that are often
used to begin a question.

23

What can come before a noun.
> **What time** *is the next train?* ~ *Ten eleven.*
> **What colour** *shirt was he wearing?* ~ *Blue, I think.*
> **What kind of/type of/sort of** *computer have you got?* ~ *Oh, it's a laptop.*
> **What make** *is your car?* ~ *It's a BMW.*

We use *what about* or *how about* to draw attention to something or to make a suggestion.
> **What about/How about** *this packaging? Are we going to throw it away?*
> **What about/How about** *some lunch?* ~ *Good idea.*

We use *what ... for* in questions about purpose or reason.
> **What** *are these screws* **for**? ~ *To fix the handles on.*
> **What** *did you make such a fuss* **for**? ~ *Sorry, but I was annoyed.*

How can come before an adjective or an adverb.
> **How old** *is this building?* ~ *About two hundred years old.*
> **How far** *did you walk?* ~ *Miles.*
> **How often** *does the machine need servicing?* ~ *Once a year.*
> **How long** *can you stay?* ~ *Not long, I'm afraid.*

It can also come before *many* or *much*.
> **How many** *people live in the building?* ~ *Twelve.*
> **How much** *is the cheap ticket?* ~ *Fifteen pounds.*

NOTE

How come is an informal phrase meaning 'why'. There is no inversion after *how come*.
> **How come** *all these papers are lying around?* ~ *I'm in the middle of sorting them out.*

D *How* and *what ... like?*

We can use *how* in friendly enquiries about someone's well-being, enjoyment or progress.
> **How** *are you?* ~ *Fine, thanks.*
> **How** *did you like the party?* ~ *Oh, it was great.*
> **How** *are you getting on at college?* ~ *Fine, thanks. I'm enjoying it.*

What ... like? asks about quality. Sometimes it has a very similar meaning to *How ... ?*
> **How** *was the film?* / **What** *was the film* **like**?

But *What ... like?* does not refer to well-being.
> **How**'s *your brother?* ~ *Oh, he's fine, thanks.*
> **What**'s *your brother* **like**? ~ *Well, he's much quieter than I am.*
> **What** *does he* **look like**? ~ *He's taller than me, and he's got dark hair.*

TIP

When you are introduced to someone, both of you say *hello*.

In a formal situation, you might say *How do you do?* (rather old-fashioned). If someone says *How do you do?* to you, you should reply in the same way. *How do you do?* is not a real question, so don't say *Very well, thank you.*

Americans say *How are you?* to each other when they are introduced.

When you meet someone you know, especially when you haven't seen them for some time, it is friendly to ask how they are.
How are you? ~ Very well, thank you. And you? ~ Oh, I'm OK, thanks.

E *What exactly ... ? About how many ... ?* etc

To ask for exact information we can use *exactly* or *precisely* after a question word.
*What **precisely** do you want to know?*
We can also put *exactly* or *precisely* in end position.
*When are you coming back **exactly**?*

To ask for approximate information, we can use *roughly* or *approximately*. They usually go in end position.
*How many people will there be **roughly**?*
*How big is the room **approximately**?*
They can also go before the question word or phrase.
***Roughly** how many people will there be?*

We can also put *about* before a question phrase such as *what time, how many, how much,* or *how long.*
***About** what time do you think you'll be ready?*
***About** how long would the journey take?*

F *Else*

Else means 'other'.
*What **else** do we need?* (What other things ...?)
*Who **else** did you invite?* (What other people ...?)

G Emphasizing a question

We can emphasize a question by using *on earth*.
*What **on earth** do you think you're doing?*
*Where **on earth** have I put that letter?*
On earth expresses the speaker's feelings. In the first example I am surprised or annoyed about what you are doing. In the second I am puzzled about the whereabouts of the letter.

We can also use *ever*.
*What **ever/Whatever** can the matter be?*
*How **ever/However** did you manage to find us?*
*Who **ever/Whoever** left that gate open?*

17 Indirect questions

We can ask a question indirectly by putting it into a sub-clause beginning with a question word or with *if/whether*. This makes the question sound less abrupt.

> *We need to know **what the rules are**.*
> *Can I ask you **how much you're getting paid for the job**?*
> *Could you tell me **where Queen Street is**, please?*
> *I'm trying to find out **who owns this building**.*
> *Do you know **when the train gets in**?*
> *I was wondering **if/whether you could give me a lift**.*

There is no inversion in the sub-clause.

> NOT ~~*We need to know what are the rules*.~~

NOTE

a   If the main clause is a statement (*We need to know*), then there is no question mark.

b   For question word + infinitive, > 108.
> *Could you tell me **how to get there**?*

18 Negative questions

POWER CUT

Claire: *Did you see 'Big Brother' last night?*

Anna: *No, we can't watch TV. Our electricity is still off.*

Claire: *What! **Haven't** they got the power back on yet?*

Anna: *No. It's an awful nuisance. It's over a week now.*

Claire: ***Isn't** there a deadline? **Don't** they have to do it within a certain time?*

Anna: *I don't know.*

Claire: ***Why don't** you refuse to pay your bill?*

Anna: *Yes, I might just do that.*

Claire: *And come to our place tonight.*

A Use

A negative yes/no question often expresses surprise.

> ***Haven't** they got the power back on yet?*

The context shows that the negative is true, because Anna has just explained that the electricity is still off. Claire is expressing her surprise at this.

A negative yes/no question or question with *why* can be a complaint.

> ***Can't** you be quiet? I'm trying to concentrate. ~ OK, sorry.*
> ***Why haven't** you done what you promised? ~ I didn't promise.*

We can use *Why don't/doesn't...?* or *Why not...?* for a suggestion.

> ***Why don't** you refuse to pay your bill?*
> ***Why not** use your credit card? We accept all major cards.*

Negative questions with *who, what,* or *which* usually ask for information.
> *Who hasn't returned this library book? ~ It must be Charlotte.*
> *What can't you understand? ~ This sentence here.*
> *Which of the guests doesn't eat meat? ~ Oh, that's Julia.*

We can use a negative question to ask the hearer to agree that something is true.
> *Isn't there a deadline? Don't they have to do it within a certain time?*
> *Haven't we met somewhere before?*

The meaning is similar to *We've met somewhere before, haven't we? > 20*

B Form

We make a question negative by putting *n't* after the auxiliary.

Positive	Negative
Are we a democratic people?	*Aren't we a democratic people?*
Have they got the power back on?	*Haven't they got the power back on?*

The negative of *am I* is *aren't I.*
> *Why aren't I getting paid for this?*

We do not use *not* after the auxiliary.
> (NOT *Are not we a democratic people?*)

In more formal English *not* can come after the subject.
> *Are we not a democratic people?*

We can use other negative words.
> *Are you never going to finish?*   *Is there no electricity?*

If the question word is the subject, *n't* or *not* comes after the auxiliary.

Positive	Negative
Who has filled in this form?	*Who hasn't/has not filled in this form?*
Which program works?	*Which program doesn't/does not work?*

We can also use other negative words in a wh-question.

Positive	Negative
Which of us has ever done anything dishonest?	*Which of us has never done anything dishonest?*

C Yes/no answers

The answer *no* agrees that the negative is true. The answer *yes* means that the positive is true.
> *Haven't they got the power back on yet? ~ No, not yet. It's a real nuisance.*
> *Haven't they got the power back on yet? ~ Yes, it's back, thank goodness.*

19 Answering questions

A How long should an answer be?

Some questions can be answered in a word or phrase, but for others you need one or more complete sentences. Here are some examples from real conversations.

Didn't you hear about the bank robbery? ~ **No.**
I've got a hat. ~ *What colour?* ~ **Brown.**
Do you like school? ~ **Yes, I do. It's OK.**
How long do you practise? ~ **About half an hour.**
How is Lucy? ~ **She's a lot better now. In fact I think she'll be back at school next week.**
Why did you sell the car? ~ **It was giving me too much trouble. I was spending more money on it than it was worth spending money on.**

It is usually enough to give the relevant piece of information without repeating all the words of the question. There is no need to say *No, I didn't hear about the bank robbery* or *The hat is brown* in answer to these questions.

NOTE
People sometimes give an indirect answer or avoid answering the question.
What time will you be back? ~ **Well, these meetings sometimes go on for hours.**
Are you a member of this club? ~ **Why do you ask?**

B Yes/no short answers

We can sometimes answer with a simple *yes* or *no*, but English speakers often use a 'short answer' like *Yes, I do* or *No, we haven't*. A short answer relates to the subject and auxiliary verb of the question. A positive answer is *yes* + pronoun + auxiliary. A negative answer is *no* + pronoun + auxiliary + *n't*.

	Positive	Negative
Is it raining?	*Yes, it is.*	*No, it isn't.*
Have you finished?	*Yes, I have.*	*No, I haven't.*
Can your sister swim?	*Yes, she can.*	*No, she can't.*

In simple tenses we use the auxiliary verb *do*.

	Positive	Negative
Do you play the piano?	*Yes, I do.*	*No, I don't.*
Did we do the right thing?	*Yes, we did.*	*No, we didn't.*

In this example, the question has *be* as an ordinary verb.

	Positive	Negative
Are you in a hurry?	*Yes, I am.*	*No, I'm not.*

We can sometimes use another phrase or clause instead of *yes* or *no*.
Am I in the team? ~ **Of course** *(you are).*
Were you late? ~ **I'm afraid** *I was.*
Does the jacket go with the shirt? ~ **I think** *it does.*

We often add information or comment after a simple *yes* or *no* or after a short answer.
Were you late? ~ *Yes,* **I missed the bus.**
Did Carl get the job? ~ *No, he didn't,* **unfortunately.**
Have you read this book? ~ *Yes, I have.* **I really enjoyed it.**

> **TIP**
>
> In some situations it can seem abrupt or unhelpful to simply answer
> *Yes* or *Yes, it is.* In a friendly conversation, it is better to add something
> relevant to keep the conversation going.
> *Is this CD player new.* ~ *Yes, it is. I bought it last week.*

NOTE
a   The full form *not* in a short answer is formal or emphatic.
    Was the scheme a success? ~ *No, it was* **not***. It was a complete failure.*

b   We can use a short answer to agree or disagree with a statement.

Agreeing:	*These photos are good.* ~ **Yes, they are.**
	It doesn't feel very warm. ~ **No, it doesn't.**
Disagreeing:	*I posted the letter.* ~ **No, you didn't.** *It's still on the table.*
	We can't afford a car. ~ **Yes, we can,** *if we borrow the money.*

c   We can use a pronoun + auxiliary when we answer a wh-question.
    Who filled this crossword in? ~ **I did.**

C Requests, offers, invitations, and suggestions

We cannot usually answer these with a short answer such as *Yes, you can* or
Yes, I would.
Can I use your phone, please? ~ **Sure./Of course.**
Would you like a chocolate? ~ **Yes, please. Thank you.**
Would you like to come to my party? ~ **Yes, I'd love to. Thank you very much.**
Shall we have a coffee? ~ **Good idea./Yes, why not?**

A negative answer to a request, invitation or suggestion needs some explanation.
Can I use your phone, please? ~ **Sorry, someone's using it at the moment.**
Would you like to come to my party on Saturday? ~ **I'm sorry. I'd like to, but I'm going to be away this weekend.**
Shall we have a coffee? ~ **I've just had one, but you go ahead.**

20 Question tags → Audio

A The form of a negative tag

The form of a tag depends on the subject and auxiliary of the main clause: *It's ..., isn't it?* The structure of a negative tag is auxiliary + *n't* + pronoun.

> *It's raining, **isn't it?***
> *You've finished now, **haven't you?***
> *The others can go, **can't they?***

In simple tenses we use the auxiliary verb *do*.

> *Louise works at the hospital, **doesn't she?***
> *You came home late, **didn't you?***

In these examples the main clause has the ordinary verb *be*.

> *It's colder today, **isn't it?***   *Those sausages were nice, **weren't they?***

After *I am* or *I'm* ... the tag is *aren't I?*

> *I'm late, **aren't I?***

NOTE

A negative tag occasionally has the full form *not* instead of *n't*. *Not* comes after the pronoun.
> *Progress is being made, **is it not?***

This structure is used in a formal style or to add emphasis.

B The form of a positive tag

A positive tag is like a negative one, but without *n't*.

> *It isn't raining, **is it?***   *You haven't finished, **have you?***
> *These beans don't taste very nice, **do they?***

C More details about the pronoun

We can use the subject *there* in a tag.

> *There were lots of people at the carnival, **weren't there?***

But we do not use *this, that, these* or *those* in the tag. We use *it* or *they* instead.

> *That was lucky, **wasn't it?***
> *These plates aren't very expensive, **are they?***

If the subject is a word ending in *-one* or *-body* (e.g. *anyone, nobody*), we use *they* in a tag.

> *Anyone could just walk in here, couldn't **they?***
> *Nobody likes going to the dentist, do **they?***

If the subject is a word ending in *-thing*, we use *it* in a tag.

> *Something fell out of your bag, didn't **it?***

D Summary of structures with tags

OFF TO AUSTRALIA

James: *It's colder today, **isn't it**?*

Tim: *Yes, it's not very warm, **is it**? But I'll be off to Australia soon, as usual.*

James: *Lucky you. You go there every year, **do you**?*

Tim: · *Yes, I always spend our winter in Sydney.*

James: *You get the best of both worlds, **don't you**?*

There are three main structures.

Positive statement + negative tag:	*It's your birthday, **isn't it**?* > E
Negative statement + positive tag:	*It isn't your birthday, **is it**?* > F
Positive statement + positive tag:	*It's your birthday, **is it**?* > G

NOTE

For tags with the imperative and *let's*, >11E–F.

E Positive statement + negative tag → Audio

This kind of tag asks the hearer to agree that the statement in the main clause is true. It is sometimes obvious that the statement is true. For example, in the conversation in D, both James and Tim know that it is colder today. In the sentence *It's colder today, isn't it?* the tag is not really a request for information. It is an invitation to the hearer to respond.

*It's cold, **isn't it**? ~ It's freezing. I should have put a coat on.*
*You're Italian, **aren't you**? ~ Yes, I come from Milan. I'm staying here with some friends.*

We can use a tag in a reply.

*It's not so warm today. ~ No, it's freezing, **isn't it**?*

Here the tag expresses agreement. We do not need to reply to it.

When the statement is clearly true, a falling intonation is used on the tag.

*It's cold, ➘ **isn't it**?*   *Coal fires are nice, ➘ **aren't they**?*

But when the speaker is not sure if the statement is true, the voice can rise on the tag.

*You'll be back in the spring, ➚ **won't you**?*
*We're going the right way, ➚ **aren't we**? ~ I hope so.*

In the second example the speaker can choose a rising intonation in order to ask for reassurance.

NOTE

Sometimes a tag with a rising intonation can express surprise.
*They have central heating, **don't they**? Everyone has central heating nowadays.*
Compare *Don't they have central heating?,* which also expresses surprise. > 18A

31

F Negative statement + positive tag → Audio

This structure is used mostly in the same way as the examples in E. The tag invites the hearer to respond. Compare these sentences.

> *It's colder, **isn't it**?*
> *It isn't so warm, **is it**?*

With both negative and positive tags, the voice falls when it is obvious that the statement is true.

In these examples with a rising intonation, the speaker expresses suspicion or disapproval by inviting the hearer to confirm or deny something.

> *You didn't make a scene, **did you**? ~ No, of course I didn't.*
> *You aren't staying in bed all day, **are you**?*

The second example means 'I hope you aren't staying in bed all day.'

We can also use the structure with a rising intonation to ask a tentative question or make a tentative request.

> *You haven't heard the test results, **have you**? ~ No, sorry, I haven't.*
> *You couldn't lend me ten pounds, **could you**? ~ Yes, OK.*

A negative statement can have a negative word other than *not*.

> *There's been **no** news yet, has there?*
> *You **never** tell me anything, do you?*

G Positive statement + positive tag → Audio

This structure has a different meaning to the examples with a negative statement or a negative tag. Look at this part of the conversation in D.

James: *I'll be off to Australia soon, as usual.*
Tim: *You go there every year, **do you**?*

Tim realizes from James's words (*as usual*) that James goes every year. The information is new to him. He is expressing interest and inviting James to continue the conversation and give him more details. Tim's words mean 'Oh, so you go there every year.'

Here are some more examples.

> *I've got no time at the moment. ~ You're busy, **are you**?*
> *~ Very busy, I'm afraid.*
> *Vicky doesn't live here any more. ~ Oh, she's moved, **has she**?*
> *~ She moved out about a month ago.*

In the second example *she's moved, has she?* means that I realize she has moved but I would like you to confirm this and perhaps tell me more.

Compare the positive and negative tags.

> *We can't move this cupboard. ~ It's heavy, **isn't it**? I tried to lift it, but I couldn't.*

Here the second speaker already knows that it is heavy. But in the following example, the information that it is heavy is new to the second speaker.

> *We can't move this cupboard. ~ It's heavy, **is it**? I was afraid it might be.*

NOTE
a   In informal speech a statement tag is sometimes used after a positive statement.
      *You're crazy, **you are**.   That was great, **that was**.   It makes me mad, **it does**.*
      The tag adds emphasis to the statement.

b   A positive statement + positive tag is not used in American English.

21 Echo questions and echo tags

A Echo questions

We can use an echo question when we do not understand what someone
says, or we find it hard to believe.
  *I often eat bits of wood. ~ **What** do you eat?/You eat **what**?*
  *My father knew Bill Clinton. ~ **Who** did he know?/He knew **who**?*
  *Did you see the naked lady? ~ Did I see the **what**?*
The second speaker is asking the first to repeat the important information.

The voice rises on the question word.
  ↗ What have they done?   They've done ↗ what?

NOTE
We can use a statement with rising intonation to check that we heard correctly.
  I often eat bits of wood. ~ You eat bits of wood?

B Echo tags → Audio

We form an echo tag like a question tag. A positive statement is followed by a
positive tag, and a negative statement is followed by a negative tag.
  *We're moving house soon. ~ Oh, **are you**?*
  *The team played brilliantly. ~ **Did they** really?*
  *My sister isn't very well. ~ **Isn't she**? I'm sorry to hear that.*
  *The children can't swim. ~ **Can't they**?*
These tags express interest in what someone has just said. The voice rises.
  Oh, ↗ are you?   Did they ↗ really?

Now look at these examples.
  *We're moving house soon. ~ **You aren't, are you**?*
  *The children can't swim. ~ **They can, can't they**?*
  *Max won the prize. ~ **He didn't, did he**?*
The last example expresses surprise or disbelief. The speaker didn't expect
Max to win the prize.

We can use a negative tag in reply to a positive statement.
  *That was great. ~ Yes, **wasn't it**?*
  *It's a lovely day. ~ It is, **isn't it**?*
  *The team played brilliantly. ~ Yes, **didn't they**?*
In the last example, both speakers saw the team and agree that they played
very well.

Leaving out and replacing words

22 Avoidance of repetition

A   In this conversation Mary's friends are talking about her new glasses.

MARY'S GLASSES

Sarah: *Mary's got a new pair of glasses, look. Does she look different to before?*

Tom: *No, I wouldn't say so.*

Simon: *They're very nice. I like them.*

Tom: *I rather like them, yes.*

Simon: *I think they suit you extremely well.*

Susan: *I think they're good.*

Simon: *Very nice.*

Tom: *Yes, are they a bit bigger than your previous ones?*

Mary: *Mm, quite a lot.*

Susan: *I prefer them to the last ones.*

Tom: *Yes, I think they're nice.*

Simon: *They're a different shape, definitely. Yes, they're very circular. The other ones were a bit more - were they a bit more square?*

Mary: *Yes, that's right. And these are photochromic.*

In many of these sentences, some words are left out or replaced by a pronoun. We do this to avoid repeating a word when it is not necessary to repeat it. For example, the topic of the conversation is Mary's glasses, so there is no need to keep repeating the word *glasses*.

Sentence	Meaning
I like them.	I like **the glasses**.
And these are photochromic.	And these **glasses** are photochromic.
Very nice.	**The glasses are** very nice.
I wouldn't say so.	I wouldn't say **that she looks different**.
That's right.	**That the other ones were a bit more square** is right.

NOTE
Sometimes we can leave out or replace words that come later in the sentence.
  If you want to, you can pay by credit card.
  (= If you want to **pay by credit card**, ...)
  After he had been given oxygen, the patient recovered.
  (= After **the patient** had been given oxygen, ...)
Here *he* refers forwards to *the patient*, which comes later in the sentence.

B It is not always possible to avoid repetition. We sometimes need to repeat a
word to make the meaning clear.
  *I bought a book and a CD yesterday. I've got **the book** here, but I can't
  remember where I put **the CD**.*
We cannot use *it* instead of *the book* or *the CD* because we need to make clear
which one we are talking about.

It is sometimes more helpful to repeat things because it makes the meaning
easier to understand.
  *After about half a mile you'll see a school on the left. Turn right just after
  the school.*

We can also repeat words for emphasis.
  *This jacket is cotton, the best **cotton** you can get.*
It is possible here to say *the best you can get*, but the speaker chooses to
emphasize the fact that the jacket is made of cotton.

23 Replacing and leaving out nouns

We often replace a noun phrase with a pronoun to avoid repeating the noun,
as happens with *glasses* in MARY'S GLASSES in 22.
  *Mary's got some new glasses. **They**'re very nice.*
  *Have you seen Mary? **She**'s got some new glasses.*
For more details about pronouns, > 175.

We can also leave out a noun after certain words.

A number:	*There's only one CD in here.* ~ *No, there are **two**, look.*
A quantifier:	*I've got some chocolate here. Would you like **some**?*
This, that, these, or *those*:	*My old glasses weren't photochromic, but **these** are.*
A superlative adjective:	*Which question was the **most difficult**?*

We cannot leave out the whole noun phrase.
  (NOT *I've got some chocolate here. ~~Would you like?~~*)

24 Leaving out words after the auxiliary

A A sentence can end with an auxiliary if the meaning is clear from the context.

*I'm doing this wrong. ~ Yes, it looks as if you **are**.*
*Kate hadn't brought an umbrella. She was pleased to see that Lauren **had**.*
*I don't want to answer this letter, but perhaps I **should**.*
*Can you get cable TV? We **can**.*

If the verb is in a simple tense, we use the auxiliary verb *do*.

*I don't enjoy parties as much as my wife **does**.*
*Don't laugh. If you **do**, I'll kill you.*

We can also end a sentence with the ordinary verb *be*.

*This piece isn't long enough. ~ This one **is**.*

We often use this kind of sentence when we are expressing a comparison or contrast.

*The meeting went on longer **than I thought it would**.*
*I'm not a student, but **my girlfriend is**.*

NOTE

The stress can be on the auxiliary or the subject, whichever is the new information.
I've made a mistake. ~ Yes, I'm afraid you HAVE. (focus on the fact)
Someone's made a mistake. ~ Yes, I'm afraid YOU have. (focus on the person)

B The auxiliary can be positive or negative. A positive auxiliary cannot be a short form.

*Am I too late? ~ Yes, I'm afraid **you are**.* (NOT ~~I'm afraid you're.~~)

But an auxiliary can be followed by *not* or by the short form *n't*.

*Am I too late? ~ Of course **you aren't/you're not**.*

We can use a negative auxiliary to contradict someone.

*What did you have for breakfast? ~ I **didn't**. I never have breakfast.*

C Usually everything after the auxiliary is left out.

*Can you see now? ~ Yes, I **can**.*

After *can* we leave out *see now*. But in some contexts we put a word or phrase after the auxiliary, for example, a tag or an adverbial.

*This is a nice colour. ~ It is, **isn't it**?*
*Is there a market today? ~ I don't know. There was **yesterday**.*

In the second example *a market* is left out of the answer, but *yesterday* is new information.

D Sometimes we have to use two auxiliary verbs. When the first auxiliary is a new word in the context, we cannot leave out the second.

*Have the team won? ~ Everyone's smiling, so they **must have**.*
*I don't know if Tom is still waiting. He **might be**.*
*When is the fence going to be repaired? ~ It already **has been**.*

In these examples *must*, *might*, and *has* are new in the context, so we use both verbs.

But when the two auxiliaries are both in the previous sentence, then we can leave out the second auxiliary.

*The gate hasn't been repaired, but the fence **has (been)**.*
*You could have hurt yourself, jumping off there. ~ I suppose **I could (have)**.*

In British English, *do* is sometimes used after an auxiliary.

*I don't want to answer this letter, but perhaps I **should (do)**.*
*Have we won the contract? ~ Everyone's smiling, so we **must have (done)**.*

Here *do* means 'answer the letter', and *done* means 'won the contract'.

25 Other structures where words are left out

A Short questions

A short yes/no question consists of an auxiliary + subject.

*I've been to New York before. **Have you**? ~ No, I haven't.*
*I wanted Karen to pass her test. ~ And **did she**? ~ Yes, fortunately.*

Here it is clear from the context that *And did she?* means 'And did she pass her test?'

In a short wh-question, we simply use a question word or question phrase.

*I think I'm going to give up my course. ~ Really? **Why**?*
*I've got a hair appointment this afternoon. ~ **What time**?*

When the question word is the subject, the auxiliary can come after it.

*Something rather strange has happened. ~ What **(has)**?*

A sub-clause can also end with a question word if the meaning is clear from the context.

*The road is closed to traffic. No one knows **why**.*
*I put the letter somewhere, and now I can't remember **where**.*

NOTE
For *why* in structures such as *Why the hurry?* and *Why bother?*, > 15A Note b.

B Leaving out a to-infinitive clause

When there is no need to repeat a to-infinitive clause, we can sometimes leave out the words after *to*.

*Would you like to join us for lunch? ~ Yes, I'd love **to**.*
*Jane got the job, although she didn't expect **to**.*
*We need people to serve refreshments. Are you willing **to**?*
*I didn't take any notes because I didn't feel the need **to**.*
*You've switched the computer off. I told you not **to**, didn't I?*

This happens most often when *to* follows a verb, adjective, or noun, e.g. *love to, willing to, need to*.

But we repeat an auxiliary after *to*.

*Jane was chosen for the job, although she didn't expect to **be**.*
*I'm not sure if the system has crashed, but it seems to **have (done)**.*

Sometimes we can leave out *to*. This happens especially after the verbs *like*, *try*, and *want*.

> *You can stay as long as you **like**.*
> *Take one of these brochures if you **want**.*

We often leave out *to* after an adjective or noun.

> *You can come through now if you're **ready**.*
> *I'd love to ask that question, but I haven't got the **nerve**.*

C Leaving out the main verb

The main verb can sometimes be left out.

> *The boys sat on the wall and the girls on the seat.*
> (... and the girls **sat** on the seat.)
> *America has won twelve medals and Australia ten.*
> (... and Australia **has won** ten medals.)

We do not need to repeat the verb when there are two clauses with the same structure and the same verb.

26 Leaving out the first word

A In conversational English certain kinds of words can be left out at the beginning of a sentence if the meaning is clear without them.

> A: *Ready?*
> B: *Sorry, no. Can't find my car keys.*
> A: *Doesn't matter. We can go in my car. Better get going, or we'll be late.*

It is clear in this situation that *Ready?* means 'Are you ready?' and that *Doesn't matter* means 'It doesn't matter.'

B The pronoun *I* can be left out at the beginning of a statement.

> *Can't find my keys.* (= I can't find my keys)

We can leave out *I* and a positive auxiliary.

> *Sorry I was late.* (= **I'm** sorry I was late.)
> *Talk to you soon.* (= **I'll** talk to you soon.)

It, *it's*, or *there's* can also be left out.

> *Feels colder today.* (= **It** feels colder today.)
> *Colder today.* (= **It's** colder today.)
> *A cold wind today.* (= **There's** a cold wind today.)

We can sometimes leave out *a/an* or *the* before a noun at the beginning of the sentence.

> *Cup of coffee is what I need.* (**A** cup of coffee ...)
> *Television's broken down.* (**The** television ...)

C   We can leave out the auxiliary or the ordinary verb *be* from a yes/no question.
   Your problem been sorted out? (= **Has** your problem been sorted out?)
   Everything all right? (= **Is** everything all right?)

We can sometimes leave out the subject as well, especially if the subject is
you or *there*.
   Tired? (= **Are you** tired?)
   Any free seats in here? (= **Are there** any free seats in here?)
   Need a loan? Just give us a ring. (= **Do you** need a loan?)
The last example is from an advertisement which is written in a
conversational style.

D   We can sometimes leave out an imperative verb, especially *be* or a verb which
expresses movement.
   Careful. (= **Be** careful.)
   This way, please. (= **Come** this way, please.)

27 *Too, either, so,* and *neither/nor*

A *Too* and *either*

After a clause there can be a short addition with *too* or *either*. It expresses the
idea that what is true of one thing is also true of another. These are the
patterns.

Positive: subject + auxiliary + *too*
   You're yawning. ~ **You are, too.** *We're both tired.*
Negative: subject + auxiliary + *n't* + *either*
   *My sister can't drive, and **her husband can't either**.*

In simple tenses we use the auxiliary verb *do*.
   I like chocolate. ~ **I do, too.**
   That calculator doesn't work. ~ **This one doesn't either.**

We can also use *be* on its own as an ordinary verb.
   I'm tired. ~ **I am, too.**

In informal English we can say *Me too* or *Me neither*.
   I'm tired. ~ *I am, too.*/**Me too.**
   I haven't got any money. ~ *I haven't either.*/**Me neither.**

B *So* and *neither/nor*

We can also form a short addition with *so* and *neither* or *nor*. Here *so* means
'too', 'also'.

Positive: *so* + auxiliary + subject
> *I like chocolate.* ~ **So do I.**
> *You're beautiful.* ~ **So are you.**
> *Children should behave themselves, and* **so should adults.**

Negative: *neither/nor* + auxiliary + subject
> *My sister can't drive, and* **neither/nor can her husband.**
> *We haven't got a colour printer.* ~ **Neither/Nor have we.**
> *The apples don't taste very nice.* ~ **Neither/Nor do the oranges,** *I'm afraid.*

So do I means the same as *I do too,* and *neither/nor do I* means the same as *I don't either.*

NOTE
For *Children should behave themselves,* **as** *should adults,* > 233D Note.

C Negative after positive; positive after negative

In these examples, a negative addition follows a positive statement, and vice versa. This kind of addition is used to express a contrast. What is true of one thing is not true of another.
> *I'm tired.* ~ *Well,* **I'm not.**
> *We don't go bowling.* ~ WE **do.**

The stress is on the subject *I* and *we.*

We can also use a short statement to contradict what someone says.
> *You're tired.* ~ *No,* **I'm** NOT.
> *You don't go bowling.* ~ **We** DO.

The stress is on *not* or on the auxiliary.

28 *So* and *not*: *I think so, I hope not,* etc

A *So* replacing a clause

The word *so* has a number of different uses. In these examples, it replaces a whole clause.
> *Will you be going out?* ~ *Yes, I expect* **so.**
> (= I expect **I will be going out.**)
> *I'm not sure if this is the right answer, but I think* **so.**
> *Is your luggage insured?* ~ *I don't know. I hope* **so.**
> *Has the committee reached a decision?* ~ *Well, it seems* **so.**

We cannot leave out *so,* and we cannot use *it* in these contexts.
> (NOT *Yes, I expect.*) and (NOT *Yes, I expect it*)

In this structure with *so* replacing a clause, we can use these verbs and expressions: *be afraid, it appears/appeared, assume, believe, expect, guess, hope, imagine, presume, say, it seems/seemed, suppose, suspect, tell (someone), think.* For *do so,* > 29A.

We do not use *know* or *be sure* in this structure.
> *The flight has been cancelled.* ~ *Yes, I know.* (NOT ~~*Yes, I know so.*~~)
> *The flight has been cancelled.* ~ *Are you sure?* (NOT ~~*Are you sure so?*~~)

NOTE
We can use *so* with the verb *be*.
> *I'm travelling around the world.* ~ *Is that so?*
Here *Is that so?* (= Is that true?) expresses interest.

B *So* or *not* in the negative

There are two negative structures.
Negative verb + *so*: *Will you be going out?* ~ *I don't expect so.*
Positive verb + *not*: *Is this watch broken?* ~ *I hope not.*

With the verbs *expect*, *imagine*, and *think*, we usually form the negative with
n't ... so.
> *Is it a public holiday on Monday?* ~ *I don't think so.*
I think not is possible but rather formal.

There are some verbs and phrases which always form the negative with *not*.
> *It's no use waiting any longer.* ~ *I guess not.*
> *Is this picture worth a lot of money?* ~ *I'm afraid not.*
These verbs include *assume, guess, hope, presume*, and *suspect*. We also use
not after *afraid*.

Some verbs can be used in either structure.
> *Will they give us a day off?* ~ *I don't suppose so.*
> *We can't just leave without telling anyone.* ~ *I suppose not.*
These verbs are *appear, believe, say, seem*, and *suppose*.

The two structures with *say* have different meanings.
> *Is the illness serious?* ~ *I don't know. The doctor didn't say so.*
> *Is the illness serious?* ~ *No, it isn't. The doctor said not.*

C *So* at the beginning

With a few verbs, *so* can come at the beginning of the clause. We use this
structure to comment on the truth of a statement.
> *Is there going to be an extra day's holiday?* ~ *Well, so I've heard.*
> *The exam has been postponed. Or so I understand.*
These verbs include *assume, believe, hear, say*, and *understand*.

We can use *so they say* to express the idea that a piece of information may be
just a rumour.
> *They're giving away free tickets. Or so they say.*
So you say expresses doubt or disbelief about what someone says.
> *You're bound to get a nice welcome.* ~ *So you say. I rather doubt it myself.*

We can also use *appear* and *seem* after *it*.
> *Mark and Laura are good friends.* ~ *So it appears. / So it seems.*

D *If so* and *if not*

So and *not* can replace a clause after *if*.
> *Looking for a higher rate of interest?* **If so**, *you need our Super Savers account.*
> *Have you got transport?* **If not**, *I can give you a lift.*

E *Not* after an adverb

We can also use *not* after certain adverbs.
> *Will your friend be fit to travel?* ~ *No,* **definitely not**.
These adverbs include *certainly, definitely, maybe, of course, perhaps, possibly, presumably,* and *probably.*

29 More patterns with *so*

A *Do so, do it,* and *do that*

We can use *do so* or *do it* to avoid repeating an action verb and the words that follow it. *Do so* is a little formal.
> *If you have not already paid this bill, please* **do so** *immediately.*
> *She had always wanted to fly a plane, and now at last she was* **doing so**/*it.*
The stress is on *do,* not on *so* or *it.*

When *do* has a different subject from the verb it replaces, we cannot use *so.*
> *Everyone else jumped. Why couldn't you* **do it**?
Here the subjects *everyone else* and *you* are different.

When we use *do that,* we usually stress *that.*
> *We need someone to serve drinks.* ~ *I'll* **do** THAT *if you like.*
> *I might tell the boss exactly what I think of her.* ~ *Oh, I wouldn't* **do** THAT *if I were you.*
In this last example, *that* is stressed to express surprise or shock at the kind of action that is mentioned.

B *So* in short answers

A short answer with *so* can express agreement. The structure is *so* + pronoun + auxiliary or *be.*
> *You can't go this way. This is a one-way street.* ~ *Oh,* **so it is**.
So it is means that the speaker agrees that it is a one-way street. He/She is noticing or remembering it.

Compare these two structures.
> *You've made a mistake.* ~ **So I have**. (I agree that I have made a mistake.)
> *I've made a mistake.* ~ **So have I**. (I have made a mistake, too.)

C *So* and *that way*

So can replace an adjective after *become* and *remain*.
> *The situation is not yet serious, but it may become **so**.*
> (= It may become **serious**.)

So is rather formal here. In informal English we use *get/stay that way*.
> *The situation isn't serious yet, but it may get **that way**.*

We can also use *so* after *more or less*.
> *It's usually quite busy here – more **so** in summer, of course.*

D *The same*

The same can replace words just mentioned, such as a complement or an object.
> *Monday was beautiful, and Tuesday was **the same**.*
> *What are you having? ~ Steak and chips. ~ I think I'll have **the same**.*

We can use *do the same (thing)* to refer to an action just mentioned.
> *The actor forgot his lines at a vital moment. The next night he **did the same** (thing)*. (= The next night he **forgot his lines again**.)

We can also use *say the same (thing)* or *think the same* to report words or thoughts that have just been mentioned.
> *The first person I asked said they disagreed with the idea, and everyone else **said the same (thing)**.* (= Everyone else said **they disagreed with the idea**.)
> *The others think we should take part, and I **think the same**.*
> (= I think **we should take part**.)

Note the expression *feel the same* or *feel the same way*.
> *The others think we should take part, and I feel **the same (way)**.*

We can use *The same is true of* ... or *The same goes for* ... to show that information about one thing also applies to another.
> *The Labour Party is divided on the issue, and **the same is true of** the Conservatives.* (= The Conservatives **are also divided on the issue**.)
> *There is a shortage of cheap housing here, but **the same goes for** other places.* (= **There is also a shortage of cheap housing** in other places.)

NOTE
We can use *(The) same to you* to return good wishes.
> *Happy New Year! ~ Thank you. **(The) same to you**.*

30 Special styles

In some special styles of English, words are left out to save space.

A Signs and labels

A sign or label usually gives the necessary information in as few words as possible, e.g. *Office, No entry, Airmail, Sold*.

B Newspaper headlines

A/an, the, and the verb *be* are often left out of headlines.

> *Stone circle discovery* (= **The** discovery of **a** stone circle)
>
> *PM on holiday* (= **The** Prime Minister **is** on holiday.)

The simple present is often used to refer to recent events, where normally the present perfect would be used.

> *Actor dies* (= An actor **has died**.)
>
> *Bomb kills boy.* (= A bomb **has killed** a boy.)

A passive participle on its own is often used instead of the present perfect passive.

> *Six arrested in raid* (= Six people **have been arrested** in a raid.)

A to-infinitive is sometimes used with a future meaning.

> *Factory to close* (= A factory **is going to close**.)

C Instructions

The is sometimes left out of instructions.

> *Open battery compartment cover by pushing in direction of arrow.*
>
> (= ... **the** battery compartment cover ... **the** direction ... **the** arrow)

When an instruction is on the thing it refers to, there is often no need for the verb to have an object.

> *Handle with care.* (on a parcel)
>
> *Do not cover.* (on a heater)

D Note style

English can be written in note style when information needs to be given as briefly as possible, for example on a postcard.

> *Arrived safely Saturday. Hotel OK, weather marvellous, sun shining. Lots to do here. Going on excursion tomorrow.*

However, this style would not be polite in a letter, where there is space for full sentences.

This example is from a guidebook.

> *French-style café on two floors, just off Bridge St. Nice pastries and delicious coffee downstairs. Some hot food served upstairs. Trendy late-night hangout; office crowd during the day.*

The words left out include *I* and *we*, *a/an* and *the*, auxiliary verbs, the verb *be* and *there is/are*.

Text messages often use note style and abbreviations.

> *Arrive in 30 mins. CU soon.*
>
> (= I will arrive in thirty minutes. See you soon.)

Word order and emphasis

31 Introduction

A Imagine you are sitting in a café with a friend drinking a cup of coffee when one of you makes this comment.

This coffee tastes awful.

This statement begins with the subject (*This coffee*) and the verb (*tastes*). This is the normal word order in a statement. Here a complement (*awful*) follows the verb. For details of what can follow the verb, > 4.

We can also look at the sentence from the point of view of the information it communicates. The first phrase (*This coffee*) is the topic, what the sentence is about. The last phrase (*awful*) is the important information about the topic. This coffee is 'old information' because it is naturally in our thoughts in the situation. *Awful* is 'new information', the point of the message. The sentence starts with old information and then tells us something new about it. This is a typical way of communicating information, although it is certainly not an absolute rule.

B Sometimes there are different ways of saying the same thing. Compare these pairs of sentences.

The Studio Café does better coffee than this.	*This coffee isn't as good as at the Studio Café.*
A group of us went to the Studio Café last week.	*Last week a group of us went to the Studio Café.*
I like the atmosphere in this place.	*What I like about this place is the atmosphere.*

Each pair of sentences orders the information in a different way. The choice of one or the other will depend on the context and what information is old or new. The rest of this chapter is about how we make such choices.

32 Linking the information in a text

ORIGIN OF THE UNIVERSE

Many scientists think that the universe was born in a colossal explosion called the Big Bang. In this explosion, 15,000 million years ago, all matter, energy, space and time were created. Of course no one was there to tell us what happened. But discoveries in physics and astronomy have enabled scientists to trace the Universe's history to its first fraction of a second. They believe at that time the Universe was squashed into a tiny volume, and it has been expanding ever since. The Big Bang Theory was put forward in 1933. Another idea, called the Steady State Theory, was suggested in 1948. This said that new material was continuously being created, and so overall the Universe would not change. The Steady State Theory has now been discounted. More recently, scientists have been looking into the future of the Universe. What happens next?

(from *The Dorling Kindersley Science Encyclopedia*)

When we are writing a text we usually try to start each sentence with something known or expected in the context. Usually it relates to something just mentioned. The new information comes later in the sentence. For example, in the sentence *The Steady State Theory has now been discounted*, the theory is already in our thoughts because it has just been mentioned. The new and important information is that scientists no longer believe it.

Here are some ways in which the starting-point of a sentence can link to something mentioned in the previous sentence.

Type of link	Just mentioned in the previous sentence	Starting-point of the new sentence
Repeating a word	*in a colossal **explosion***	← *In this **explosion**, …*
Using a pronoun	*have enabled **scientists***	← ***They** believe …*
Expressing something in different words	***the Universe was squashed into a tiny volume, and it has been expanding ever since***	← *The **Big Bang Theory** was …*
Making a contrast	*has **now** been discounted*	← *More recently, scientists …*

Most of the sentences in ORIGIN OF THE UNIVERSE take as their starting-point an idea which is already familiar or which links to something earlier in the text. This helps the reader to see how one sentence follows on from another.

> **TIP**
> When writing a composition, try to link your sentences by starting each one with known information and then saying something new about it.

33 Linking the subject

We often use the subject to link with what has gone before.
*The men are in prison. **They** raided five banks.*
*There was a series of robberies. **Five banks** were raided.*
*The girls did well. **Celia** won the first prize.*
*There were lots of prizes. **The first prize** went to Celia.*
*We can't get all the furniture in. **The sofa** is too big to go through the door.*
*There's a problem. **The door** isn't wide enough to get the sofa through.*

We can often express an idea in different ways, e.g. *They raided five banks./ Five banks were raided.* In these examples the subject relates to the previous sentence and the new information comes at the end of the sentence.

In these examples, *the garage* and *September* would typically come after a preposition (*in*). Here they are the subject of the second clause or sentence.

*The house was empty, but **the garage** contained some old chairs and tables.* (= There were some old chairs and tables **in the garage**.)
*This has been an eventful year for the company. **September** saw our move to new offices.* (= We moved to new offices **in September**.)

Garage links to *house* because it is next to the house, and *September* links to *year* because it is part of the year. Note that in the second example the structure *September saw ...* is rather formal.

Sometimes we can use an abstract noun to refer back to the idea in the previous sentence.

*Someone threw a stone through the window. **This incident** upset everyone.*
*Lucy had finally made up her mind. But **the decision** had not been easy.*
*The people here have nothing. **Their poverty** is extreme.*

34 Front position

The subject often comes in front position (at the beginning of a sentence). But it does not always do so. We can put another phrase in front position before the subject. We sometimes do this to emphasize a phrase or to contrast it with phrases in other sentences. Putting a phrase in front position can make it more prominent than in its normal position.

A An adverbial in front position

Most kinds of adverbial can go in front position, for example truth adverbs, comment adverbs, and linking adverbs > 200–202.

*I'm not sure why we're in this traffic jam. **Maybe** there's been an accident.*
*I left the car unlocked. **Luckily** it was still there when I got back.*
*The weather wasn't very good. **Despite that**, we had a good day out.*

Adverbials of time often go in front position. Look at these instructions.

***First of all** sift the flour and salt into a large, roomy bowl. **Then** put a grater in the bowl and coarsely grate the parsnips into the flour, **then** toss them around. **After that**, add the cubes of Parmesan and chopped sage and toss that in. **Now** lightly beat the eggs and milk together.*

(from D. Smith *Delia's How to Cook*)

Here the position of the adverbials of time makes it easier for the reader to see the sequence of events.

Adverbs of place and frequency can come in front position for contrast or emphasis.

> *It was warm and comfortable in the little cottage.* **Outside**, *it was getting dark.* (*Outside* contrasts with *in the cottage.*)
> *Everyone shops at the big supermarket now.* **Quite often** *the little shop is completely empty.* (emphasis on *quite often*)

An adverb of manner can also come in front position.

> **Slowly** *the sun sank into the Pacific.*

This can be rather literary.

B Inversion after an adverbial

This sentence has the normal word order: subject + verb + adverbial.

> *A furniture van was outside the house.*

Now look at this same information in a written context where the adverbial of place (*outside the house*) is in front position to link with the information (*number sixteen*) in the previous sentence.

> *Alan walked along Elmdale Avenue and found number sixteen without difficulty.* **Outside the house was a furniture van**.

After the adverbial of place there is inversion of the subject (*a furniture van*) and the ordinary verb *be*. (NOT *Outside the house a furniture van was.*)
A furniture van is the new information and comes at the end of the sentence.

We can do the same with other verbs of place and movement, e.g. *come, go, lie, sit, stand*.

> *The room contained a table and four chairs.* **On the table lay a newspaper**.
> *Detectives were watching the house when* **out of the front door came a man in a black coat**.

The important information (*a newspaper, a man in a black coat*) comes at the end of the clause or sentence.

There is no inversion with other verbs,

> *Outside the house* **two women were talking**.
> (NOT *Outside the house were talking two women.*)

NOTE
We can also use the structure *there + be*. > 35

> *There was a furniture van outside the house.*

C Inversion after *here* and *there*

We can use *here* and *there* in front position to draw attention to something in the situation.

> **Here** *is an announcement for passengers on flight TW513 to Miami.* (an airport announcement)
> *And* **there** *goes Williams! Into the lead!* (a sports commentary)

In this structure we can use *be, come*, or *go* in the present simple. There is inversion of the subject and verb. The subject, the new information, goes at the end.

> *Here is an* **announcement**.

But when the subject is a pronoun, there is no inversion.
> *And there goes Williams! There **he goes**, look!*
> *Where are my keys? ~ Here **they are**.*

D An object or complement in front position

We can sometimes put an object in front position, especially when it is in contrast with something else, or when it makes a link with what has gone before.

> *Do you prefer cats or dogs? ~ **Dogs** I love, but **cats** I can't stand.*
> *His possessions from his previous address had been delivered to her door that same morning: two boxes of personal effects and an ancient iron bicycle. **The bicycle** she wheeled into the back yard. **The boxes** she carried upstairs.*

(from R. Harris *Enigma*)

We can also sometimes put a complement in front position.
> *They enjoyed the holiday. **Best of all** was the constant sunshine.*
> *The scheme has many good points. **One advantage** is the low cost.*

There is inversion. The subject (*the low cost*) is the important new information and comes after the verb *be*.

35 The empty subject *there*

A The use of *there*

Imagine that two people are discussing where to eat, and one of them wants to mention a Chinese restaurant which is just round the corner. In this situation a sentence like *A Chinese restaurant is round the corner* would be possible but unusual. A phrase with *a/an* is usually new information, and so would not usually come at the beginning of such a sentence. Instead we use a structure with *there + be*.

> *Where can we eat? ~ **There's** a Chinese restaurant round the corner.*

There + be expresses the idea that something exists.

> **TIP**
> To point out the existence of something, use *there*.
> > ~~*A message is for you.*~~ → *There's a message for you.*
> > ~~*A big parade was yesterday.*~~ → *There was a big parade yesterday.*

NOTE
The subject *there* is not stressed and is normally spoken in its weak form /ðə/, like *the*. The subject *there* is not the same as the adverb *there* meaning 'in that place'. The adverb is pronounced /ðeə(r)/.
> ***There** /ðə/ was a restaurant **there** /ðeə/, almost hidden from view.*

B Adverbials with *there + be*

In structures with the empty subject *there*, we often use an adverbial in end position.

> *There was a roof **over the stadium**.*
> *There's a concert **next week**.*
> *There are some letters **for you**.*

But we can use *there + be* without an adverbial. This can happen especially with nouns expressing a situation or an event.

> *I'm afraid there's a problem.* (= A problem **exists**.)
> *There's been an accident.* (= An accident **has happened**.)

C Noun phrases after *there + be*

We normally use *there + be* before a noun phrase which is new information. The noun phrase has an indefinite meaning – it can have *a/an, some, any, no,* or a number, or it can be a noun on its own or with an adjective. It can also have a quantifier such as *a lot of, many, much,* or *several* or a pronoun such as *something*.

> *There's **a calculator** in the drawer.*
> *There was **no time** to look round properly.*
> *There must have been **twenty people** at least in the queue.*
> *There's **hot water** if you'd like a bath.*
> *There can't be **much memory** in this computer.*
> *There's **something** I ought to tell you.*

We do not usually use a noun phrase with *the, this/that* etc or *my/your* etc, except when we remind someone of the existence of something specific.

> *We haven't got anything we could sell.*
> *~ Yes, we have. There's **your jewellery**.*

The verb *be* agrees with the noun phrase that comes after it.

> *There **is a letter** for you.   There **are some letters** for you.*

But in informal speech you may hear *there's* before a plural.

> *There's **some letters** for you.*

D Negatives, questions, and tags

We form negatives and questions with *there* in the normal way.

> *There **wasn't**/There was **not** a single thing to eat in the house.*
> ***Are there** any letters for me?*
> *What **is there** to do in this place?*

We often use *no* + noun to form a negative.

> *There was **no food** in the house.*

We can use *there* in a question tag.

> *There's a concert next week, isn't **there**?*

E *There* + infinitive or ing-form

There can also be the subject of an infinitive (*to be*) or an ing-form (*being*).
*I didn't expect **there to be** such a big crowd.*
*The village is very isolated, **there being** no bus service.*

But this structure is rather literary. A finite clause is more usual.
*I didn't expect **there would be** such a crowd.*
*The village is very isolated because **there's** no bus service / **there isn't** a bus service.*

F *There* + *be* with relative clauses

We can put an active or a passive participle after the noun phrase.
***There's** someone **waiting** for you.*
(= Someone **is waiting** for you.)
***There was** a van **parked** outside the house.*
(= A van **was parked** outside the house.)

But we do not use a participle for a single complete action.
***There was** a noise **that woke** me up.*
(= A noise **woke** me up.)
(NOT *There was a noise waking me up.*)

In the following example the relative pronoun (*which*) is the object of the relative clause.
***There's** a small matter **which we need** to discuss.*
When the relative pronoun is not the subject, we cannot replace it with a participle.
NOT *There's a small matter needing to discuss.*

G *There* with other verbs

We use the subject *there* mostly with the verb *be*. Some other verbs are possible but only in a formal or literary style.
*On top of the hill **there stands** an ancient tower.*
*There now **follows** a party political broadcast.*
*The next day **there occurred** a strange incident.*
Verbs in this structure include: *appear, arise, arrive, come, emerge, enter, exist, follow, lie, live, occur, remain, result, sit, stand, take place.*

We can sometimes use another verb between *there* and *be*.
***There don't seem to be** enough chairs.*
***There proved to be** no truth in the rumour.*
***There appears to have been** an accident.*
Verbs in this structure are: *appear, chance, happen, prove, seem, tend, turn out, use.*

NOTE
We can sometimes leave out *to be* after *seem*, especially before a phrase with *little* or *no*.
***There seemed** (to be) **little difference** in the prices.*
***There seems** (to be) **no reason** for alarm.*

36 The empty subject *it*

A *It* for time, distance, etc

We can use *it* to refer to the time, distance, the environment, or the weather.

It's quarter past ten. *How far is **it** to the beach?*
It'll be getting dark soon. *It was cold yesterday.*

B *It* referring to a clause

Look at these sentences. Each has a clause as its subject.

***To make new friends** is difficult.*
***That so few people came to the meeting** was a pity.*
***How much money some people earn** amazes me.*

This word order is possible but not very usual. Instead, we normally use *it* as the subject, and the clause comes later in the sentence.

It's difficult to make new friends.
It was a pity so few people came to the meeting.
It amazes me how much money some people earn.

Because the clause is long, it comes more naturally at the end of the sentence than at the beginning.

With a gerund clause we use both structures.

***Making new friends** is difficult.*
It's difficult making new friends.

We can also use *it* as the object.

subject + verb	*it*	complement	clause
I find	*it*	*difficult*	*to make new friends.*
We all thought	*it*	*a pity*	*so few people came to the meeting.*
The Board has made	*it*	*clear*	*that no money will be available.*

This structure is the most natural way of expressing the meanings in these examples. It would be a little awkward to say *I find making new friends difficult* and impossible to say ~~We all thought that so few people came to the meeting a pity~~.

C *It seems*, etc

It can also be an empty subject before *appear, happen, seem,* and *turn out.*

***It seems** the phone is out of order.*
(= The phone seems to be out of order.)
***It** just so **happened** that I had my camera with me.*
(= I happened to have my camera with me.)

There is also a structure with *it looks as if / as though* and *it seems as if / as though*.

> **It looks as if** *it's going to rain.*
> **It seems as though** *we'll never manage to save enough money.*

NOTE
For *It is said that ...,* > 92A.

37 *There* or *it*?

there	it
There + be expresses the fact that something exists or happens.	*It + be* identifies or describes something.

We use *there* with a noun phrase of indefinite meaning, e.g. *a young man*, *any* classes.
   There's *a young man at the door.*
   (= **A** young man is at the door.)
   There's *a strong wind today.*
   (= **A** strong wind is blowing.)
   There *weren't any classes.*
   (= **No** classes took place.)
	It refers to something definite, e.g. *the young man*, *the day*, something known in the situation.
	   It's Jonathan.
	   (= **The** young man is Jonathan.)
	   Yes, it's windy.
	   (= **The** weather is windy.)
	   It was Saturday.
	   (= **The** day was Saturday.)

Compare the structure with *there* and the structure with *have*.
   There *isn't* **any truth** *in the story.*
   The story **has no** *truth in it.*
	It can also refer forward to a clause.
	   It isn't true what they say.
	   (=**What they say** isn't true.)

38 Emphasis → Audio

A Introduction

In this conversation, emphasis is laid on a number of words and phrases.

MUSIC PRACTICE

Chloe: *Why weren't you at the music practice yesterday?*

Emma: *I didn't know there was one. How did you find out about it?*

Chloe: **It was you** *who told me. Don't you remember?*

Emma: *Oh, yes, I* **do remember** *now. I'd forgotten. I've got a* TERRIBLE *memory. Anyway, I thought it was* THURSDAY, *not Tuesday.*

Chloe: **What** *you need is* **your own personal secretary**.

Chloe uses structures with *it* and *what* to emphasize *you* and *your own personal secretary*. Emma emphasizes the fact that she remembers, and she emphasizes the words *terrible* and *Thursday*.

B Emphatic stress → Audio

When we put emphatic stress on a word, we speak it with greater force than usual. We do this to make it more prominent and often to contrast it with something else.

> *Is the practice on Tuesday?* ~ *No, I told you. It's on* THURSDAY.
> *I wanted a* LARGE *packet, not a small one.*

Here the stressed word is in capital letters to show that it is spoken emphatically. You may also see *italics*, **bold** or <u>underlining</u> used to emphasize a word in print.

When a word has more than one syllable, we write the whole word differently, e.g. *on '*THURSDAY. But in speech only one syllable has extra stress, e.g. *on '*THURS*day*. We stress *Thurs-* but not *-day*.

We can also use emphatic stress to give extra force to a word expressing an extreme quality or feeling.

> *I've got a* TERRIBLE *memory.*   *It's a* HUGE *building.*
> *The talk was* EXTREMELY *interesting.*   *I'd* LOVE *a cup of coffee.*

NOTE
Some words can be repeated for emphasis. They are *very*, *really*, and words expressing extreme feelings, quantity, or length of time.

> *I've been **very very** busy.*   *This has happened **many many** times before.*
> *What a **terrible, terrible** tragedy!*   *We had a **long, long** wait.*

The use of commas to separate repeated words is optional.
Sometimes we use *and*, especially with verbs and particles.

> *We **waited and waited**, but no one came.*
> *The noise just went **on and on**.*

C Emphasis in the verb phrase → Audio

We can stress the auxiliary or the ordinary verb *be*.

> *You* CAN *download the software. Someone told me you couldn't.*
> *I* HAVEN'T *taken your calculator. I haven't touched it.*
> *You aren't tired surely!* ~ *Yes, I* AM. *I'm exhausted.*

In a simple tense we use the auxiliary *do* to emphasize the verb.

> *I really* DO *want to be a doctor. It's my ambition in life.*
> *Oh, your garden* DOES *look nice.*
> *I* DID *post the letter. I'm absolutely certain.*
> *Do you want to fly in a balloon?* ~ *No, I* DON'T. *The idea terrifies me.*

When a positive form of *do* is used for emphasis, we do not need to mark the emphasis in writing.

> *I really do want to be a doctor.*

When we emphasize the auxiliary, we are usually emphasizing the positive or negative meaning of the sentence. *I did post the letter* means that **yes**, I posted it. But sometimes emphasis on the auxiliary contrasts with another kind of meaning.

We MIGHT go away for the weekend. We haven't decided definitely.
(It is POSSIBLE, not definite.)
I DID have a mobile phone, but it was stolen.
(in the PAST, not now)

We can stress an ordinary verb to emphasize its meaning.
I've BORROWED your calculator. I haven't stolen it.
Did you deliver the letter? ~ Well, I POSTED it.
Here *borrowed* and *posted* are emphasized in contrast to *stolen* and *delivered*.

NOTE
We can also add emphasis by using adverbs such as *really, indeed,* and *certainly*.
*Your garden **really** does look nice.*
*You can **indeed** download the software.*

D Emphasis with *it*

In the conversation MUSIC PRACTICE in A, Chloe wants to emphasize the
identity of the person who told her about the practice.
It was you *who told me.*
The structure is *it + be +* phrase + relative clause. The phrase that we want to
emphasize (*you*) comes after *be*.

Look at this statement.
Amundsen reached the South Pole in 1911.
We can emphasize the subject, object or adverbial.
It was Amundsen *who reached the South Pole in 1911.*
It was the South Pole *that Amundsen reached in 1911.*
It was in 1911 *that Amundsen reached the South Pole.*
For details about the use of *who, which,* and *that,* > 268A.

When a pronoun comes after *be,* it is usually in the object form.
*It was **me** who told you, remember?*
For *It was I,* > 175B Note.

We can also emphasize a prepositional object.
*How do you like the choir? ~ **It's the orchestra** I'm in.*
We can even emphasize a whole clause.
It's because I was in such a hurry *that I forgot my ticket.*

We can include a phrase with *not*.
*It was Amundsen, **not Scott**, who reached the South Pole in 1911.*
*It was the South Pole, **not the North Pole**, that Amundsen reached in 1911.*

E Emphasis with *what*

In the conversation MUSIC PRACTICE in A, Chloe wants to emphasize that Emma
needs her own personal secretary (and nothing else).
What *you need is **your own personal secretary**.*
We can use a what-clause + *be* to emphasize a part of the sentence. The thing
we need to emphasize comes after *be*.

Look at these statements.

A technical fault caused the delay.
The guests played mini-golf after tea.

We can emphasize different parts of the sentence.

What *caused the delay was* **a technical fault**.
What *the guests played after tea was* **mini-golf**.
What *the guests did after tea was* **(to) play mini-golf**.
What *happened after tea was that* **the guests played mini-golf**.

We can sometimes emphasize a prepositional object.

What *I long for is* **a little excitement**.

We cannot use *who* in this structure. We use it only with a noun in front of it.

The people who *played mini-golf were the guests.*
(NOT ~~Who played mini-golf were the guests.~~)

NOTE

a   We can emphasize an action: **What** *the guests did was* **(to) play mini-golf**. Here are
     some examples with other verb forms.
     What *the guests are doing is* **playing mini-golf**.
     What *I've done is* **sent**/*is* **(to) send** *a letter of complaint.*
     What *we could do is* **(to) hire** *a car.*

b   We can reverse the order of the what-clause and a noun phrase. Compare the word
     order in the following two examples.
     The train was two hours late. What caused the delay was **a technical fault**.
     There have been problems with new signalling equipment. **A technical fault** *was what
     caused the delay.*

Verb tenses

39 Introduction

These are the tenses of the English verb *play*.

Present simple:	*We **play** card games every week.* > 40
Present continuous:	*We **are playing** now.* > 41
Present perfect:	*We **have played** two games.* > 44
Present perfect continuous:	*We **have been playing** cards.* > 48
Past simple:	*We **played** tennis yesterday.* > 43
Past continuous:	*We **were playing** with some friends.* > 47
Past perfect:	*We **had played** the day before.* > 49
Past perfect continuous:	*We **had been playing** for ages.* > 50

The verb phrases *play, are playing,* etc are the main verb of a clause. Each verb phrase is either present or past. It can also be continuous (*be* + ing-form) or perfect (*have* + past participle), or it can be both continuous and perfect (*have* + *been* + ing-form).

Some verbs are not normally used in the continuous form. These are state verbs like *know, belong,* and *seem.* For example, we can say *I'm playing tennis* (an action), but we say *I like tennis* (a state). For more details about state verbs and action verbs, > 51.

In this chapter we look at tenses, but they are not the only possible verb forms. A verb phrase can begin with a modal verb, > 70. It can also be passive, > 86.

NOTE

a   The forms above are usually called 'tenses'. But strictly speaking, there are only two tenses in English – present and past. The two tenses can combine with the two 'aspects' – continuous aspect and perfect aspect.

b   Another word for the continuous is the 'progressive'.

c   For ways of talking about the future, > 53.

40 The present simple

A Form

The present simple is the base form of a verb, e.g. *play, know, take.*
    *You **know** the answer.*   *I usually **take** the bus.*
In the third person singular we add *-s* or *-es.*
    *Tom **knows** the answer.*
    *My sister usually **takes** the bus.*
    *This colour **matches** my jacket.*

	Present simple	Short forms
Positive:	*I/you/we/they* **play** *he/she/it* **plays**	
Negative:	*I/you/we/they* **do not play** *he/she/it* **does not play**	*I/you/we/they* **don't play** *he/she/it* **doesn't play**
Questions:	*do I/you/we/they* **play?** *does he/she/it* **play?**	

There are some spelling rules for the s-form.
We add *-es* after a sibilant sound, e.g. *push* → *pushes*. > 276.
y changes to *ie*, e.g. *hurry* → *hurries*. > 280A.

For the pronunciation of the ending, > 276B.

Note also the forms *does* /dʌz/, *goes* /gəʊz/, *has* /hæz/, and *says* /sez/.

The verb *be* is irregular. > 65A.
  *I **am** / You **are** / Simon **is** the oldest.*

In the negative we use *do not* or *don't* and the base form of a verb.
  *I just **do not know** the answer.*
  *The neighbours **don't take** any notice.*
In the third person singular we use *does not* or *doesn't* and the base form.
  *Tom **does not know** the answer.*
  *The journey **doesn't take** long.* (NOT *The journey no takes long.*)

In questions we use *do* and the base form of a verb.
  ***Do** you **know** the answer?*   *What **do** we **take** with us?*
In the third person singular we use *does* and the base form.
  ***Does** Tom **know** the answer?*
  *How long **does** the journey **take**?* (NOT *How long takes the journey?*)

We do not use *do* with *be*.
  ***Are** you the oldest?*
For *have*, > 66C.

B Basic uses of the present simple

We use the present simple for a present state. This might be a feeling, an opinion, or the fact that something belongs to someone.
  *My girlfriend **likes** hiphop.*
  *I **think** it's a good idea.*
  *This bike **belongs** to my brother.*

For the difference between a state and an action, > 51A.

We also use the present simple for facts such as what or where things are.

*Silicon **is** a chemical element.*
*York **lies** on the River Ouse.*

We use the present simple for repeated actions such as routines and habits, jobs and hobbies, things that happen again and again.

*The old man **walks** his dog every morning.*
*Tom **works** in Oxford. He usually **drives** to work.*
*We **do** lots of things in our spare time. We **play** volleyball.*
*I **don't** often **see** my cousins.*

Typical time expressions with the present simple are *always, often, usually, sometimes, ever/never; every day/week*, etc; *once/twice a week*, etc; *on Friday(s)*, etc; *in the morning(s)/evening(s), at ten o'clock*, etc.

We also use the present simple for things that always happen.

*Food **gives** you energy.*
*Paint **dries** quicker in summer.*

NOTE
We can also use the present simple for future events seen as part of a timetable. > 56B
*The flight **gets** in at eight tomorrow morning.*

41 The present continuous

A Form

The present continuous is the present of *be* + ing-form.

*It's **raining** now, look.*   *Is that boy **throwing** stones at your car?*
*I'm not **making** a noise.*   *Where **are** you **calling** from?*

	Present continuous	Short forms
Positive:	I **am** play**ing**	I'm play**ing**
	you/we/they **are** play**ing**	you're/we're/they're play**ing**
	he/she/it **is** play**ing**	he's/she's/it's play**ing**
Negative:	I **am not** play**ing**	I'm **not** play**ing**
	you/we/they **are not** play**ing**	you're/we're/they're not play**ing**
		you/we/they **aren't** play**ing**
	he/she/it **is not** play**ing**	he's/she's/it's **not** play**ing**
		he/she/it **isn't** play**ing**
Questions:	**am** I play**ing**?	
	are you/we/they play**ing**?	
	is he/she/it play**ing**?	

There are some spelling rules for the ing-form.
We normally leave out *e* before *-ing*, e.g. *lose → losing.* > 278A
We double some consonants, e.g. *stop → stopping.* > 279

B Basic use of the present continuous

We use the present continuous for a present action over a period of time, something that we are in the middle of now. The action has started but it hasn't finished yet.

> The train **is leaving** Victoria now.
> Hurry up. Your friends **are waiting** for you.
> What **are** you **reading**? ~ It's called 'White Teeth'.
> I won't be long. I'm just **ironing** this shirt.
> The earth **is getting** warmer, scientists tell us.

Some typical time expressions with the present continuous are *now, at the moment, at present, just, already,* and *still.*

The action does not need to be going on at the moment of speaking, as long as it has started but not finished.

> **I'm reading** a really interesting novel, but I can't remember what it's called.
> **Is** anyone **sitting** in this seat? ~ No, it's free.

42 Present simple or present continuous?

A The basic difference

Present simple	Present continuous

A routine or habit:
    We **eat** in the canteen most days.
	Something we're in the middle of:
	    We**'re eating** lunch at the moment.

A state or fact:
    My dad **loves** cheeseburgers.
    We **need** a new car.
    Two and two **makes** four.
For states, > 51A.	

These are the most basic uses of the two tenses. For more details about the use of the two tenses, > B–I.

B Routines and habits

Present simple	Present continuous

We use the present simple for a permanent routine or habit.
    I **travel** to work by car.
	We use the present continuous for a temporary routine.
	    My car's off the road. I'm **travelling** to work by bus this week.

My friends **live** in Manchester.	They**'re living** in a rented flat until they find somewhere to buy. Some typical time expressions are *this week, these days, nowadays, at/ for the moment, at present,* and *still.*

NOTE

a   We use the present continuous to say that we are regularly in the middle of something.
   *At seven we're usually **having** supper.*
   (= At seven we're usually in the middle of supper.)
   Compare the use of the present simple.
   *At six thirty we usually **have** supper.*
   (= Six thirty is our usual time for supper.)

b   We can use the following pattern to talk about two things happening at the same time.
   *Whenever I **see** Matthew, he's **wearing** a tracksuit.*
   *I usually **listen** to music when I'm **driving**.*

C *Always*

There is a special use of *always* with the continuous.
   *They're **always giving** parties, those people next door.*
   *I'm **always losing** things. I can never find anything.*
In this pattern *always* means 'very often'. It sometimes expresses annoyance.
In the second example I am annoyed at losing things so often.

Compare these sentences.
   *Our teacher **always gives** us a test.* (every lesson)
   *Our teacher **is always giving** us tests.* (very often)

D States

We normally use the present simple for a state.
   *I **prefer** classical music to pop.*   *These colours **look** lovely.*
For states, > 51A.

There are some verbs which can be either simple or continuous when referring to a temporary state.
   *The weather **looks**/The weather **is looking** better today.*
For more details, > 51D.

E Present actions

The present simple is sometimes used to describe actions as they happen, for example in a sports commentary or a demonstration.
   *Hacker **passes** the ball to Short, but Burley **wins** it back for United.*
   *I **add** the onions, and then I **turn** down the heat.*
The speaker sees these actions as completed in an instant. For actions over a period we use the continuous.
   *United **are** really **playing** well now. The crowd **are cheering** them on.*

We can use the present simple with a performative verb, e.g. when we suggest something by saying *I suggest*.
   *I **suggest** we all pay a pound a week. ~ Yes, I **agree**.*
For performative verbs, > 9.

NOTE
We can also use the present simple for actions in expressions like *Here it **comes*** and *There they **go**.* > 34C

F Past actions

We normally use the past tense to talk about things in the past. But we sometimes use present tenses for the important parts of a story. This makes the action seem more immediate and helps bring it to life.

*You'll never guess what happened yesterday. I'm **standing** there in the street, and a man **comes** up to me and **grabs** me by the arm...*

We use the present continuous to set the scene (*I'm standing there*) and the present simple for actions (*a man comes up to me*).

We also use the present tenses to talk about what happens in a novel, play or film.

*The film is about a waitress who **wins** the lottery.*
*Macbeth **murders** the King of Scotland, who **is staying** at his castle.*

NOTE
The present simple is used in headlines for a recent event.
*England **win** 5–1 in Germany*

G The written word

We can report the written word with a present-simple verb. We see the written statement as existing in the present.

*It **says** in the paper that the factory will close.*
*The notice **warns** passengers to take care.*
*The letter **explains** everything.*

We can also do this with what people have said recently.

*Laura **says** she doesn't feel very well.*

H Instructions

We can use the present simple to give instructions or to say what is the right way to do something.

*You **put** your money in here.*
*You **pull** down the File menu and **choose** Print.*

I The future

We can use the present simple for future events which are seen as part of a timetable. > 56B.

*The flight **leaves** Los Angeles at six tomorrow morning.*

We can also use the present simple in some sub-clauses of future time. > 59.

*If you **need** any help tomorrow, let me know.*

We can use the present continuous to talk about what someone has arranged to do in the future. > 56A.

*A friend of ours **is coming** to stay with us next week.*

43 The past simple

A Form

With most verbs, we add *-ed* to form the past simple.
> *We **walked** back to the hotel.*
> *I just **stayed** in and **watched** television.*

The form is the same in all persons.

	Past simple	Short forms
Positive:	*someone played*	
Negative:	*someone **did not play***	*someone **didn't play***
Questions:	***did** someone **play?***	

There are some spelling rules for the ed-form.
We just add *d* after *e*, e.g. *close → closed.* > 277A
We double some consonants, e.g. *stop → stopped.* > 279
y changes to *ie*, e.g. *hurry → hurried.* > 280

For the pronunciation of the *-ed* ending, > 277B.

But some past forms are irregular.
> *The campers **left** at six in the morning.*
> *Someone **saw** the smoke and **rang** the fire brigade.*

Many common verbs have an irregular past form. For a list, > 286.

The past form is the same in all persons (*she left, we left*, etc). The only exception is the verb *be.* > 65A.
> *I **was**/You **were** late this morning.*

In the negative we use *did not* or *didn't* and the base form of a verb.
> *The old people **did not walk** all the way.*
> *I **didn't see** any smoke.* (NOT ~~I no saw any smoke.~~)

In questions we use *did* and the base form of a verb.
> ***Did** you **see** any smoke?*
> *How far **did** the old people **walk?*** (NOT ~~How far walked the old people?~~)

We do not use *did* with *was* or *were.* > 65A.
> ***Were** you late this morning?*

B Basic use of the past simple

We use the past simple for an action in the past.
> *I **bought** this jacket yesterday.*
> *The earthquake **happened** in 1905.*
> *I **saw** the film three weeks ago.*
> *When **did** the first Winter Olympics **take** place?*

The time of the action (e.g. *yesterday, in 1905*) is over.

The verb can refer to a number of actions in the past.
> We **went** to clubs every weekend when we were at college.
> I **saw** my career advisor several times.

We can also use the past simple for states.
> I **was** a beautiful baby.
> The Romans **had** a huge Empire.
> I **believed** everything my teachers told me.

For states and actions, > 51A.

The past is the normal tense in stories.
> Once upon a time a Princess **went** into a wood and **sat** down by a stream.

Some typical time expressions with the past simple are *yesterday, this morning/evening, last week/year, a week/month ago, that day/afternoon, the other day/week, at eleven o'clock, on Tuesday, in 1990, just, recently, once, earlier, then, next, after that.*

NOTE

a   With the past simple we often say when the action happened. But the information about the time does not need to be in the same sentence.
> I went to town **yesterday** and had a look round the shops. I **bought** this jacket.

Here it is clear from the context that I bought the jacket yesterday.
Sometimes there is no phrase of time, but we understand a definite time in the past.
> My sister **took** this photo.   I **didn't eat** any breakfast.

b   Besides the past simple, there are other ways of expressing repeated actions or states in the past. > 82A
> We **used to go** to clubs every weekend when we were at college.

c   The past tense refers to things which are distant from us. These are usually things that happened in the past. But we can also use the past tense to make something in the present sound less direct.
> I **wanted** to ask you something.

This is a more tentative request than *I want to ask you something.*

d   We can also use the past for something unreal. > 232B, 246
> I wish I **was** rich. If I **had** some money, I could buy a nice house.

Here the past expresses the idea that being rich and having money is distant from our experience.

44 The present perfect

A Form

The present perfect is the present tense of *have* + past participle.
> I'**ve finished** with the computer now.
> The train is late. It **hasn't** even **reached** Swindon yet.
> **Has** Sarah **passed** her exams?
> How long **have** you **worked** here?

Most verbs have a past participle ending in *-ed.*

	Present perfect	Short forms
Positive:	*I/you/we/they* **have** *played* *he/she/it* **has** *played*	*I've/you've/we've/they've played* *he's/she's/it's played*
Negative:	*I/you/we/they* **have not** *played* *he/she/it* **has not** *played*	*I/you/we/they* **haven't** *played* *he/she/it* **hasn't** *played*
Questions:	**have** *I/you/we/they played?* **has** *he/she/it played?*	

There are some spelling rules for the *ed*-form.
We just add *d* after *e*, e.g. *close* → *closed*. > 277A
We double some consonants, e.g. *stop* → *stopped*. > 279
y changes to *ie*, e.g. *hurry* → *hurried*. > 280

For the pronunciation of the *-ed* ending, > 277B.

But some past participles are irregular.
  I haven't **seen** *this programme before.*
  The children have **spent** *all their money.*
Many common verbs have an irregular past participle. For a list of these verbs, > 286.

We always use *have* in the present perfect, not *be*.
  The bus **has** *already left.* (NOT ~~The bus is already left.~~)

NOTE
For *gone to* and *been to*, > 65D.

B The use of the present perfect

The present perfect tells us about the past and about the present. When we use the present perfect, we look back from the present. For example, we can use the present perfect for an action in a period leading up to the present.
  The café **has** *just* **opened**. (The café is open **now**.)
  The visitors **have arrived**. (The visitors are here **now**.)

The period of time referred to by the present perfect can be very long. It can cover the whole of history or the whole of someone's life up to the present.
  I wonder if anyone **has** *ever* **said** *that before.*
  Have *you ever* **ridden** *a horse?* ~ *Yes, but not since I was about twelve.*

We can also use the present perfect for repeated actions before now.
  I've **ridden** *horses lots of times.*
  We've often **talked** *about emigrating to Australia.*

We can also use the present perfect for a state lasting up to the present.

> *The café **has been open** for about ten minutes.*
> *I've **had** these skis for years.*

Some typical time expressions with the present perfect are *just, recently, lately, already, before, so far, still, ever/never, today, this morning/evening, for weeks/years, since 1998.*

NOTE

Americans can use either the present perfect or the past simple for a recent action.

> *I've just **met** an old friend. / I just **met** an old friend.*

45 Past simple or present perfect?

A Actions

Past simple – in the past	Present perfect – linked to the present
*The new bridge **opened** last week.* *The car **broke** down yesterday.*	*The new bridge **has just** opened.* (So it is open **now.**) *The car **has broken** down.* (So it is out of action **now.**)

The choice of tense depends on whether the speaker sees something as in the past or as linked to the present. The past simple means a finished time and does not tell us about the present.

> *The car **broke** down yesterday. It's still off the road.*
> *The car **broke** down yesterday. But luckily we got it going again.*

The car broke down does not tell us whether it is all right now. But *The car has broken down* tells us that the car is out of action now.

When we refer to a specific time in the past (e.g. *last week, yesterday*), we use the past simple rather than the present perfect.

B States

Past simple	Present perfect

If a state is over, we use the past.
    *I **had those** skis for years. (Then I sold them.)*
    *I **was there** from three o'clock to five. (Then I left.)*
	If the state still exists now, we use the present perfect.
	    *I've **had these** skis for years.*
	    *I've **been here** since three o'clock.*

C Repeated actions

Past simple	Present perfect
When we use the past simple for repeated actions, it means that the series of actions is over. *Gayle **acted** in more than fifty films.* (Her career is over.)	When we use the present perfect for repeated actions, it means that the action may happen again. *Gayle **has acted** in more than fifty films.* (Her career has continued up to the present and may or may not go on in the future.)

D Reporting news

We often use the present perfect when we first give some news, and then we use the past simple for the details such as when and how it happened.

*There **has been** a serious accident on the M6. It **happened** at ten o'clock this morning when a lorry **went** out of control and **collided** with a car.*

The same thing happens in conversation.

*I've **just been** on a skiing holiday. ~ Oh, where **did** you **go?***
*The new furniture **has arrived**. It **came** yesterday.*

46 Adverbials of time with the past simple and present perfect

Some adverbials of time can be used with either tense.

A *Just, recently*, and *already*

With *just* and *recently* there is little difference in meaning between the tenses.

*I've **just heard** the news. / I **just heard** the news.*
*We've **recently moved** house. / We **recently moved** house.*

Compare these examples with *already*.

*I've **already heard** the news.* (before now)
*I **already knew** before you told me.* (before then)

B *Once, twice*, etc and *ever, never*

Once, twice, etc with the present perfect means the number of times the action has happened up to now.

*We've **been** to Scotland **once**. ~ Oh, we've **been** there **lots of times**.*
*I've **rung** about **five times**, but no one is answering.*
With the past simple *once* usually means 'on one occasion in the past'.

*We **went** to Scotland **once**. I think it was about five years ago.*

Ever or *never* with the present perfect means 'in all the time up to now'.
>   *I've **never done** white water rafting.*
>   ***Have** you **ever visited** our showroom?*
With the past simple it refers to a finished period.
>   ***Did** you **ever visit** our old showroom?*

C *This morning, today,* etc

We can use *this morning, this afternoon,* and *today* with the present perfect when *this morning* etc includes the present time.
>   *It **has been** windy this morning.* (The morning is not yet over.)
When *this morning* etc is over, we use the past.
>   *It **was** windy **this morning**.* (It is now afternoon or evening.)

With *today* there is little difference in meaning.
>   *It **has been** windy **today**.*   *It **was** windy **today**.*
Both sentences are spoken late in the day.

We usually use the present perfect with *this week/month/year* when we mean the period from its beginning up to now.
>   *I've **watched** a lot of television **this week**.*
The past simple is also possible if the period is almost over.
>   *I **watched** a lot of television **this week**.*

We use the past simple for one time during the period.
>   *I **watched** an interesting programme **this week**.*
We might say this on Friday about something two or three days earlier.

We use the past simple with *last week/month/year*.
>   *I **watched** a lot of television **last week**.*

We often use the negative with phrases referring to an unfinished time.
>   *It **hasn't been**/It **wasn't** very warm **today**.*
>   *I **haven't watched** /I **didn't watch** much television **this week**.*

D *For* and *since*

We often use *for* or *since* with the present perfect to talk about a state.
>   *My sister **has been** ill **for** three days/**since** Tuesday.*

We also use *for* with the past simple to say how long something went on in the past.
>   *The man **stood** there **for** a moment.*   *We **skied for** hours that day.*
Compare these sentences.
>   *I've **been** here **for** a month now.* (I arrived a month ago.)
>   *I'm here **for** a month.* (I'm staying here for a month in total.)

We also use *for* and *since* with the negative present perfect to talk about the last time when an action happened.
>   *I **haven't skied for** years. / I **haven't skied since** about 1998.*
We can also use *since* with a clause.
>   *I **haven't skied since** I was twelve.*

Compare the positive past simple.

*I last **skied** years **ago**/**in** 1998/**when** I was twelve.*
*It was **in** about 1998 that I last **skied**.*

E *Since I did it / I've done it*

We can use *since* in the pattern *it + be +* length of time + *since* + clause. We can use either the past simple or the present perfect.

*It's years since I (last) **skied**.*
*It's years since I've **skied**.*
*It's a month since the President (last) **appeared** in public.*
*It's a month since the President **has appeared** in public.*

47 The past continuous

A Form

The past continuous is the past of *be* + ing-form.

*It **was getting** dark.*
*People **were going** home from work.*
*The coffee machine **wasn't working**.*
*What **were** you **thinking** about?*

	Past continuous	Short forms
Positive:	*I/he/she/it **was** playing* *you/we/they **were** playing*	
Negative:	*I/he/she/it **was not** playing.* *you/we/they **were not** playing*	*he/she/it **wasn't** playing* *you/we/they **weren't** playing*
Questions:	***was** I/he/she/it playing?* ***were** you/we/they playing?*	

B Basic uses of the past continuous

We use the past continuous for an action over a period of past time. It expresses the idea that at a time in the past we were in the middle of something.

*At three o'clock in the morning I **was lying** there wide awake.*
*The room was full of old people who **were** all **watching** television.*
*We stood there horrified. Water **was pouring** through a hole in the ceiling.*

Compare the present continuous and past continuous.
Present: *I'm travelling around the world.*
(I **am** in the middle of my journey.)
Past: *I was travelling around the world.*
(I **was** in the middle of my journey.)

But remember that for a complete action in the past we use the past simple.
I travelled round the world last year. It was a marvellous experience.

We sometimes use the past continuous to talk about an action going on over a whole period.
I was travelling from February to December.
The rescue services were working all night.
The phrases of time show the length of the period. We could also use the past simple here.
The rescue services worked all night.

C Past continuous and past simple

An action in the past continuous can happen around a specific time, such as the time of day.
It was raining at ten o'clock.

The past continuous can also happen around another action.
It was raining when I left the house.
The past continuous is the longer action (the rain falling), and the past simple is the shorter, complete action (my leaving the house). The shorter action can 'interrupt' the longer one.
Debbie was washing her hair when the doorbell rang.
When/While/As we were waiting in a traffic queue, a man ran to our car and tried to pull the door open.
We use the past simple for the main action and past continuous to describe things in the background.
We walked along the beach. People were lying in the sun. Children were playing football.
The sun was shining when the campers woke.

When we mention two actions that went on at the same time, we can use the past continuous in both clauses.
Debbie was washing her hair while Tim was tidying up the flat.
We can also use the past simple for either or both of the actions.
Debbie washed her hair while Tim was tidying up the flat.
Debbie was washing her hair while Tim tidied up the flat.
Debbie washed her hair while Tim tidied up the flat.

When one complete action followed another, we use the past simple for both.
When the doorbell rang, Tim went to the door.
(The doorbell rang and then Tim went to the door.)

D Past states

For a past state we normally use the past simple.
*My grandmother **loved** this house.*
(NOT *My grandmother was loving this house.*)
*The woman **had** long dark hair.*
*I **didn't know** what to do next.*

There are some verbs which can be either simple or continuous when referring to a temporary state.
*The men **were wearing** masks. / The men **wore** masks.*
For more details, > 51D.

E Other uses of the past continuous

Just as we can use the present continuous for a temporary routine in the present, so we can use the past continuous for a temporary routine in the past.
Present continuous: *I'm **using** the manager's office while she's away.*
Past continuous: *I **was using** the manager's office while she was away.*

Just as we can use the present continuous for a present arrangement, so we can use the past continuous for a past arrangement.
Present continuous: *I'm on my way to the club. I'm **meeting** someone there.*
Past continuous: *I was on my way to the club. I **was meeting** someone there.*

With the continuous, *always* means 'very often'.
Present continuous: *Those children **are always getting** into trouble.*
Past continuous: *When I was younger, I **was always getting** into trouble.*

NOTE
The past continuous is sometimes used to report what someone said. > 262A Note
*Fiona **was saying** she really likes her new job.*

48 The present perfect continuous

A Form

The present perfect continuous is the present of *have* + *been* + ing-form.
*The war **has been going** on for two years now.*
*You **haven't been doing** enough revision.*
*How long **have** you **been using** a wheelchair?*

	Present perfect continuous	Short forms
Positive:	*I/you/we/they **have been** playing* *he/she/it **has been** playing*	*I've/you've/we've/they've **been** playing* *he's/she's/it's **been** playing*

Negative:	*I/you/we/they* **have not been** *playing* *he/she/it* **has not been** *playing*	*I/you/we/they* **haven't been** *playing* *he/she/it* **hasn't been** *playing*
Questions:	**have** *I/you/we/they* **been** *playing?* **has** *he/she/it* **been** *playing?*	

B Use of the present perfect continuous

We use the present perfect continuous for an action over the period of time leading up to the present.

*Where have you been? **I've been waiting** here for half an hour.*
*Opposition to the regime **has been growing** recently.*
*The carpet's wet. The roof **has been leaking**.*

We do not use the present simple or the present continuous.

(NOT ~~I wait here for half an hour.~~)
(NOT ~~I'm waiting here for half an hour.~~)

The action can be continuing in the present.

*Where is he? **I've been waiting** half an hour.* (I am still waiting.)

Or the action may have ended recently.

*I'm hot because **I've been running**.* (I stopped running a short time ago.)

We often use *for* and *since*. > 213B.

*We've **been living** here **for** six months/**since** April.*

We can also use the present perfect continuous for a series of repeated actions in the period leading up to the present.

***I've been going** to evening classes in Arabic.*
*My brother **has been writing** letters of protest.*

C Present perfect or present perfect continuous?

Present perfect	Present perfect continuous
This tense focuses on the result of the action. *I've **washed** the car, so it looks a lot cleaner now.*	This tense focuses on an action that has been going on up to the present. *I've **been washing** the car, so I'm rather wet.*
When we say how much or how many, we do not use the continuous. *Tina **has written** twelve pages of her report.*	When we say how long, we normally use the continuous form. *Tina **has been writing** her report since two o'clock.*

When we say how many actions, we do not use the continuous.

> *I've tried to phone the hotline at least twenty times.*

We can use the continuous for repeated actions.

> *I've been trying to phone the hotline all day.*

We use the present perfect for a state up to the present.

> *My friend has been in a wheelchair for two years now.*
> *I've always hated hospitals.*

We do not use the continuous for a state.

> (NOT ~~I've always been hating hospitals.~~)

Now look at these examples.

> *We've been living here since May. / We've lived here since May.*
> *I've been working there for six weeks. / I've worked there for six weeks.*

With *live* and *work*, either form is possible, but the continuous is more usual.

49 The past perfect

A Form

The past perfect is *had* + past participle.

> *James apologized for the trouble he had caused.*
> *I didn't travel to the match because I hadn't bought a ticket.*
> *How long had the animals been without food or water?*

We use *had* in all persons.

	Past perfect	Short forms
Positive:	*someone had played.*	*they'd played.*
Negative:	*someone had not played.*	*they hadn't played.*
Questions:	*had someone played?*	

B Use of the past perfect

We use the past perfect for an action or a state before a past time.

> *Miranda lay on her bed and stared at the ceiling. She was depressed. Her boyfriend Max **had gone** on holiday with his brother the day before. He **hadn't invited** Miranda to go with him. He **hadn't** even **said** goodbye properly. They **had been** friends for six months, and everything **had seemed** fine. What **had** she **done** wrong?*

This paragraph begins in the past simple. The situation is that Miranda *lay* on her bed. The writer looks back from this situation to a time before.

Compare the present perfect and past perfect.

> Present perfect: *The floor is clean. I **have** just **washed** it.*
> Past perfect: *The floor was clean. I **had** just **washed** it.*

NOTE
For the past perfect in if-clauses, > 247.

C Past simple and past perfect

To talk about a single action in the past we use the past simple.
*This lamp is new. I **bought** it last week.*
(NOT *I had bought it last week.*)

We also use the past simple when one action comes immediately after another.
*When the shot **rang** out, everyone **threw** themselves to the floor.*

To say that someone finished one action and then did something else, we use either *when ... had done* or *after ... did/had done.*
*When Miranda **had typed** the message, she mailed it to Max.*
*After Miranda **typed**/**had typed** the message, she mailed it to Max.*
(NOT *When Miranda typed the message, she mailed it to Max.*)

Sometimes the choice of past simple or past perfect makes a difference to the meaning.
*When the boss arrived, the meeting **began**.*
(= The boss arrived and then the meeting began.)
*When the boss arrived, the meeting **had begun**.*
(= The meeting began before the boss arrived.)
*When Max **spoke**, Miranda put the phone down.*
(= When Max started speaking, ...)
*When Max **had spoken**, Miranda put the phone down.*
(= When Max finished speaking, ...)

We can use the past perfect after *before* or *until.*
*The printer went wrong before it printed / it **had printed** a single sheet.*
*We didn't want to stop until we finished / we **had finished** the job.*

50 The past perfect continuous

A Form

The past perfect continuous is *had been* + ing-form.
*Someone **had been using** my office.*
*Things **hadn't been going** very well for some time.*
***Had** the police already **been investigating** the matter?*
We use *had* in all persons.

	Past perfect continuous	Short forms
Positive:	someone **had been** playing	they**'d been** playing
Negative:	someone **had not been** playing	they **hadn't been** playing
Questions:	**had** someone **been** playing?	

B Use of the past perfect continuous

We use the past perfect continuous for an action that went on over a period before a past time.

I was delighted when I found a second-hand copy of the book. I'd been looking for one for some time.
The driver who died in the accident had been drinking.

In the second example, the action (*drinking*) went on over a period before the driver's death.

C The past perfect continuous and other tenses

Compare the present and past perfect continuous.

Present perfect continuous:	*My hands are wet. I have been washing the floor.*
Past perfect continuous:	*My hands were wet. I had been washing the floor.*

Compare the past perfect and past perfect continuous.

Past perfect:	*The volunteers had collected hundreds of pounds.*
Past perfect continuous:	*The volunteers had been collecting money all morning.*

The past perfect focuses on the result of the action. The continuous form focuses on the action going on.

Compare the past continuous and past perfect continuous.

Past continuous:	*When I saw Alice, she was playing golf.* (I saw her in the middle of the game.)
Past perfect continuous:	*When I saw Alice, she'd been playing golf.* (I saw her after the game.)

51 Action verbs and state verbs

A Actions and states

Actions	States
Jane went to bed.	*Jane was tired.*
I'm buying a new briefcase.	*I need a new briefcase.*
I lent Jeremy ten pounds.	*Jeremy owes me ten pounds.*
An action is something happening. Action verbs are verbs like *do, go, buy, play, stop, take, decorate, tell, ask, realize,* etc. Most refer to physical actions, but some are verbs of reporting (e.g. *say*) or verbs of thinking (e.g. *decide*).	A state is something that stays the same. State verbs are verbs like *be, exist, seem, depend, consist, include, contain, belong, own, need, matter, intend, cost, owe, know, understand, believe, love, like, hate, want,* etc. They express meanings such as existing, having an opinion, and thinking.

We can use action verbs in the continuous, but state verbs are not usually continuous.

We are decorating the flat. (NOT ~~We are owning the flat.~~)
They were guessing the answers. (NOT ~~They were knowing the answers.~~)

B Verbs with more than one meaning

Some verbs have more than one meaning. One meaning can be an action, and another meaning can be a state.

Actions (can be continuous)	States (cannot be continuous)
We're having lunch now. (action – 'eating')	*We have a big kitchen.* (state – 'own')
We're thinking about the offer. (action – 'deciding')	*I think we should accept it.* (state – 'believe')
They're expecting trouble. (action – 'waiting for it')	*I expect so.* (state – 'believe')
Can you imagine the result? (action – 'picture in your head')	*I imagine so.* (state – 'believe')
Nurses care for the sick. (action – 'look after')	*I don't care what happens.* (state – 'have no feelings about it')
We stopped to admire the view. (action – 'look at with pleasure')	*I admire your courage.* (state – 'approve of')
He was looking at a picture. (action – 'directing his eyes at')	*It looks lovely.* (state – 'has a lovely appearance')
Would you like to taste the soup? (action – 'eat a little')	*It tasted like water.* (state – 'had a flavour')
Smell these flowers! (action – 'sniff', 'use your nose')	*It smells very strange.* (state – 'has a strange smell')
She's appearing in a film. (action – 'playing a part')	*He appeared perfectly calm.* (state – 'seemed')
He needs to measure the door. (action – 'find out the size')	*It measured two metres.* (state – 'was two metres long')
We must weigh the luggage. (action – 'find out the weight')	*It weighed ten kilos.* (state – 'was ten kilos in weight')
Someone has to cost the project. (action – 'find out the cost')	*A ticket costs ten pounds.* (state – 'has a price of ten pounds')
I was fitting a new switch. (action – 'putting in place')	*The jacket fits perfectly.* (state – 'is the right size')

C State verbs in the continuous

With some state verbs, we can use the continuous when we are talking about feelings at a particular time, rather than a permanent attitude.

I love holidays. (permanent attitude)
I'm loving every minute of this holiday. (around the present time)

Here are some more examples of continuous verb forms referring to a particular time.

*How **are** you **liking** the play? ~ Well, it's all right so far.*
*This trip **is costing** me a lot of money.*

Enjoy is an action verb.

*I'm **enjoying** this party. I always **enjoy** parties.*
(NOT ~~I enjoy this party.~~)

NOTE

a   *Be* can be an action verb meaning 'behave', > 65C.
      *The dog **was being** a nuisance, so we shut him out.*

b   *Know* is a state verb, but *get to know* expresses an action.
      *I **know** the town quite well now.*
      *I'm **getting** to know the town quite well.*

D Verbs which can be simple or continuous

There are some verbs which can be either simple or continuous when referring to a temporary state. There is almost no difference in meaning.

*I **feel** depressed. / I'm **feeling** depressed.*
*She **hopes** to get a job./She's **hoping** to get a job.*
*My arm **hurt**. / My arm **was hurting**.*

These verbs include *feel, hope, hurt, lie, look* (= appear), *stand, wear*, and *wonder*.

But *feel* meaning 'believe' is a state verb.

*I **feel** it's the right thing to do.*
And for other meanings of *feel*, > E.

E Verbs of perception

When we are talking about perception (seeing, hearing, etc), we often use *can* (present) and *could* (past) rather than a present or past tense.

*I **can see** something under the sofa.*
*We **could hear** music.*
*I **can smell** something burning.*
*Sam **could feel** the weight of the rucksack.*

We do not normally use the continuous.

We can use the past simple when what we saw, heard, or felt was a complete action.

*We **saw** a magnificent sunset.*
*Tom **heard** the whole story.*
*They **felt** the building shake.*

See (= meet) is an action verb.

*I'm **seeing** the doctor this afternoon.*
See (= understand) is a state verb.

*You put the CD in here, like this. ~ Oh, I **see**. Thank you.*

Look (at something), *watch*, and *listen* are action verbs.
> We **looked** at / We **were looking** at the sunset.

Smell, taste, and *feel* as action verbs mean a deliberate action, > B.
> I picked up the carton and **smelled** the milk.
> When we arrived, people **were** already **tasting** the wine.
> Judy **was feeling** her way in the dark.

52 Overview: the main uses of the tenses

Present simple: > 40	A present state or fact	*I **like** old films.* *Atlanta **is** in Georgia.*
	A permanent routine	*I **work** late most days.*
Present continuous: > 41	In the middle of an action A temporary routine	*I'm **watching** this film.* *I'm **working** late this week.*
Past simple: > 43	An action in the past A series of past actions	*I **wrote** the letter yesterday.* *I **played** basketball regularly at one time.*
	A past state	*I **was** there for a week.*
Present perfect: > 44	An action in the period up to the present A series of actions up to the present	*I've **written** the letter.* *I've **played** basketball a few times.*
	A state up to the present	*I've **been** here for a week.*
Past continuous: > 47	An action over a period of past time	*It **was raining** when I got up.*
Present perfect continuous: > 48	An action over a period up to the present	*It **has been raining** all day.*
Past perfect: > 49	An action before a past time A state before a past time	*By that time the rain **had stopped**.* *The weather **had been** awful for days.*
Past perfect continuous: > 50	An action over a period up to a past time	*By that time it **had been raining** for hours.*

The future

53 Introduction

A This news item is about a teacher who is going to run the length of Britain.

BOB'S RECORD CHALLENGE

*32-year-old Bob Brown, a teacher from Cornwall, **is about to set** off on a run of more than 800 miles. Tomorrow morning at four o'clock he **leaves** John O'Groats, the most northerly point in Scotland, on a journey to Land's End, the south-western tip of England. He is hoping to beat the record of ten days and two hours. It **won't be** easy. Each day he **will run** 84 miles – 28 miles before breakfast, 28 miles before lunch and 28 miles before dinner.*
*But Mr Brown has had lots of practice; he once ran 3,000 miles across Australia in 60 days. His personal chef **is travelling** with him in a camper van and **will be cooking** lots of pasta, rice and potatoes. In spite of a large intake of high-energy foods, Mr Brown **will** probably **have lost** ten kilos by the end of the run. 'I've put on a few kilos in preparation,' he says, 'but I'm going to burn it off pretty quickly.' Mr Brown also expects to wear out four pairs of running shoes.*

In the last chapter we looked at verb forms referring to the present and the past. For example we use the past simple for an action in the past.
   *Mr Brown once **ran** across Australia.*
But we cannot be as definite about the future as we can about the present or the past. There are different ways of talking about the future depending on how we see a future event. We may see something as certain to happen, or it may be a plan or an intention, or it may be something we think will happen but can't be sure about.

B There is no single 'future tense' in English. Here are some examples of the different ways of talking about the future.

Form	Example
will:	*Each day he **will run** 84 miles.*
be going to:	*He **is going to burn** off the extra weight.*
Present continuous:	*His personal chef **is travelling** with him.*
Present simple:	*He **leaves** John O'Groats at four tomorrow morning.*
be to:	*Mr Brown **is to appear** on a chat show next Saturday.*
be about to:	*He **is about to set** off on his run.*
will be doing:	*His chef **will be cooking** lots of pasta, rice, and potatoes.*
will have done:	*Mr Brown **will have lost** ten kilos by the end of the run.*
may, might, could:	*It all **might go** horribly wrong.*
	*He **could get** injured.*

| To-infinitive after *aim, expect, hope, intend*, or *plan*: | *Mr Brown is **hoping to beat** the record.* *Each day he **plans to run** 84 miles.* |

Often there is more than one possible form in a particular context.
*Each day he **will run** 84 miles.*
*Each day he**'s going to run** 84 miles.*
*Each day he **will be running** 84 miles.*

C To show how sure or unsure we are about the future, we can use an adverb like *definitely, certainly, probably, perhaps, maybe*, or *possibly*.
*He**'ll probably lose** about ten kilos.*
Or we can use *I know, I'm sure, I think, I expect*, or *I suppose*.
***I think** he**'s going to break** the record.*

54 *Will* and *shall*

A Form

After *will* we put an infinitive without *to*. *Will* has a short form *'ll*, and *will not* has a short form *won't* /wəʊnt/.
*This book **will change** your life.*   *We **will not get** another chance.*
*I**'ll know** soon if I've got the job.*   *We **won't get** another chance.*
***Will** you still **love** me tomorrow?*

We use *will* in all persons. In the first person we can use either *will* or *shall*. The meaning is the same, but *shall* is a little formal.
*I **will be/shall be** at home tomorrow.*
*We **will have/shall have** lots of fun.*

NOTE
a   *Shall not* has a short form *shan't* /ʃɑːnt/.
      *I **shan't** be here tomorrow.*
   Shan't is old-fashioned. *Won't* is more usual.

b   In the US *shall* is less usual than *will*, and *shan't* is not used.

B *Will* for the future

Will is often used to talk about things in the future that we can be fairly certain about. The future is seen as fact, something we cannot control.
*Southern England **will stay** dry and sunny over the weekend.*
*My father **will** definitely **be** in hospital for at least two weeks.*
*I**'ll be** twenty-five next year.*
Here there is no sense of a wish or intention.

We can also use *will* for a prediction.
*I think United **will win**.*

We can use *will* with *have to*, *be allowed to*, and *be able to*.
> *It's getting late. We'll **have to** hurry.* > 71A
> *Competitors **will not be allowed** to use mobile phones.* > 75C
> *Now you've got some funding, you'll **be able to** continue your studies.* > 80B

C An instant decision

We can sometimes use *I'll/we'll* for an instant decision.
> *It's raining. **I'll take** an umbrella.*
> *I think **I'll** just **sit** down for a minute.*
Will expresses the idea that we decide at the moment of speaking. Compare *be going to*.
> *What else do I need? Oh, I know. **I'll buy** some postcards.*
> (I'm deciding now to buy some.)
> ***I'm going to buy** some postcards, so let's walk past the shops, shall we?*
> (I've already decided to buy some.)

We also use *I'll/we'll* when ordering food or drink.
> ***I'll have** the soup, please.*

Do not confuse *will* and *want*.
> Action: *I think **I'll buy** some postcards.* ~ *OK, **I'll wait** for you.*
> Wish: *I **want to buy** some postcards, but I haven't got any money.*

D Willingness

Will sometimes expresses willingness.
> *I expect my friend **will translate** it for you. She speaks Italian.*
> ***I'll sit**/I'm willing to sit on the floor. I don't mind.*
I'll sit on the floor means that I am willing to sit on the floor.

Won't or *will not* can express unwillingness or an emphatic refusal.
> *The doctor **won't come** out at this time of night.*
> *I **won't put** up with this nonsense.*
> *The minister **will not agree** to the plan.*
The subject can be a thing rather than a person.
> *I'm late already, and now the car **won't start**.*

E Other uses of *will* and *shall*

In an offer we can use *I'll/we'll* and *shall I/we*.
> ***I'll hold** the door open for you.* ~ *Oh, thanks.*
> ***Shall I hold** the door open for you?* ~ *Oh, thanks.*
We do not use *be going to* to make an offer.

In a promise we can use *I'll/we'll*.
> *(I promise) **I'll do** my best to help you.*

In an invitation we can use *won't you*, but *would you like to* is more usual.
> ***Won't you sit** down? / **Would you like to** sit down?*

When we can't decide, we use *shall I/we* to ask for advice or a suggestion.
> *Where **shall I put** these flowers? ~ I'll get a vase.*
> *What **shall we do** this weekend?*

We can use *shall we* to make a suggestion.
> ***Shall we go** to the seaside this weekend?*

This means the same as *Let's go* ... , > 11F.

NOTE

a   *Will* can express an assumption, > 76.
> *James left this morning. He**'ll be** in London now.*

b   When *will* is stressed, it can express determination.
> *I WILL succeed.* (= I am determined to succeed.)

c   *Will* is sometimes used in formal orders. It emphasizes the authority of the speaker.
> *You **will** leave the building immediately.*

d   We generally use *shall* only with *I* or *we*, but we can use *you shall* in a promise.
> ***You shall** be the first to know, (I promise).*

e   *Shall* is also sometimes used for formal rules.
> *The employee **shall give** two weeks' notice in writing.*

55 *Be going to*

A Form

The form is *be going* + to-infinitive.
> ***I'm going to watch** television.*
> *It **isn't going to rain**, is it?*
> *Are you **going to buy** a newspaper?*

NOTE

In informal speech *going to* is often pronounced /ˈɡʌnə/.

B *Be going to* for the future

We can use *be going to* for something in the future.
> *It**'s going to stay** dry and sunny over the weekend.*
> *My father **is** definitely **going to be** in the hospital for at least two weeks.*

We can use *be going to* to make a prediction.
> *I think United **are going to win**.*

Will is also possible in the three examples above, > 54B.
For a comparison of *will* and *be going to*, > 57.

When we use *be going to*, there is a sense of something in the present pointing to the future.
> *It's ten already. We**'re going to be** late.*
> *This fence **is going to fall** down soon.*

These predictions are based on something we can see in the present. We can see from the time now that we are going to be late, and we can see from the condition of the fence that it is going to fall down. The present evidence points to the future.

C Intentions

We can also use *be going to* for a plan or an intention.
> *I'm **going to start** my own business.*
> *They're **going to build** some new flats here.*

In the first example, *I'm **going to start*** means that I intend to start/I have decided to start.

With verbs of movement, especially *go* and *come*, we often use the present continuous rather than *be going to*.
> *I'm **going** out in a minute. I've got some shopping to do.*
> *I'll pop in and see you. I'm **coming** past your place in any case.*

NOTE
Going to go and *going to come* can sound awkward and are often avoided.

56 Present tense forms for the future

A The present continuous

We use the present continuous for what someone has arranged to do.
> *I'm **meeting** Kate at the club tonight.*
> *What **are** you **doing** tomorrow?*
> *Julie **is going** to Florida next month.*
> *I'm **doing** some shopping this afternoon.*

Julie is going to Florida suggests that Julie has made arrangements such as buying her ticket. *I'm doing some shopping* means that I have planned my day so that I can do the shopping.

The meaning is similar to *be going to* for an intention, and in many contexts we can use either form.
> *We're **visiting**/We're **going to visit** friends at the weekend.*

B The present simple

We can sometimes use the present simple for the future, but only for what we see as part of a timetable.
> *The meeting **is** on May 13.*   *We **change** at Birmingham.*
> *The train **leaves** in five minutes.*   *What time **do** you **arrive** in Chicago?*

We do not use the present simple for decisions or intentions.
> (NOT *I carry that bag for you.*)
> (NOT *They build some new flats here soon.*)

For the present simple in a sub-clause, > 59A.
For *be due to* + to-infinitive referring to a timetable, > 58D.

57 *Will*, *be going to*, or the present continuous?

A We use both *will* and *be going to* to talk about the future.

> *It'll probably **rain**. It usually rains at weekends.*
> *It's **going to rain**. Look at those clouds.*

The prediction with *going to* is based on the present situation.

We use be *going to* (not *will*) when the future action seems certain to happen and is very close.

> *Help! I'm **going to fall**!*   *I'm **going to be** sick!*

Sometimes we can use either form with little difference in meaning.

> *One day the sun **will cool** down/**is going to cool** down.*
> *City **won't beat**/**aren't going to beat** United.*

When we talk about intentions, plans and arrangements, we use *be going to* or the present continuous, but not *will*.

> *We're **going to eat** out tonight.* (= We intend to eat out.)
> *We're **eating** out tonight.* (= We have arranged to eat out.)

We use *will* for an instant decision.

> *I'm too tired to cook. I think I'll **get** a take-away.*

We do not use the ordinary verb *be* in the present continuous.

> *We'll **be** in South Africa for a month.*
> (NOT ~~We're being in South Africa for a month.~~)

B This conversation takes place at the end of work on Friday afternoon.

A FEW DAYS OFF

> Emma: *I'll **see** you on Monday then.*
>
> Polly: *Oh, I **won't be** here. Didn't I tell you? I'm **taking** a few days off. I'm **going** on holiday. I'll **be** away for a week.*
>
> Emma: *No, you didn't say. Where **are** you **going**?*
>
> Polly: *The Lake District. I'm **going to do** some walking.*
>
> Emma: *Oh, that'll **be** nice. Well, I hope you have a good time.*
>
> Polly: *Thanks. I'll **see** you the week after.*

Polly gives the news of her plans by using the present continuous and *be going to*.

> *I'm **taking** a few days off.*   *I'm **going** to do some walking.*

We cannot use *will* in this context. But after first mentioning a plan or intention, we often use *will* for further details and comments.

> *I'm **going** on holiday. I'll **be** away for a week.*
> *I'm **going to do** some walking. ~ Oh, that'll **be** nice.*
> *They're **going to build** some new flats. The work **will take** about six months.*

84

TIPS

When you're talking about the future...

1 Remember that *be going to* can be used for both predictions and intentions, so it is often the safest choice, especially in conversation.
    *It's **going to be** a nice day. We're **going to have** a picnic.*
2 Use *will* for instant decisions.
    ***I'll go** and switch the computer off.*
3 Use the present continuous for arrangements.
    ***I'm acting** in a play next week.*
4 Do not use the present simple for plans or intentions.
    (NOT ~~I act in a play next week~~)

58 *Be to, be about to*, etc

A *Be to* for an arrangement

We can use *be* + to-infinitive for an official arrangement.
    *The Prime Minister **is to visit** Budapest.*
    *The two companies **are to merge** at the beginning of next year.*

Be is often left out of *be to* in news headlines.
    *Prime Minister **to visit** Budapest.*

B *Be to* for an order

Be to can also express a rule or an order by a person in authority.
    *The teacher says we **are to wait** here.*
    *You're **not to stay** up late.*
    *No one **is to leave** this building.*
    *This trolley **is not to be removed** from the station.*

C *Be about to* and *be on the point of*

We can use *be about* + to-infinitive for an action in the near future.
    *The audience are in their seats, and the performance **is about to start**.*
    *Hurry up. The bus **is about to leave**.*
We do not usually give a time with *about to*. We say *The bus leaves in ten minutes* but NOT ~~The bus is about to leave in ten minutes~~.

We can use *just* with *be about to* and *be going to*.
    *The bus **is just about to leave**/**is just going to leave**.*
This means that the bus is leaving in the very near future.

Be on the point of means the same as *be about to*. It is followed by an ing-form.
    *The government **is on the point of announcing** a decision.*

D *Be due to*

We can sometimes use *be due* + to-infinitive when we are talking about a timetable.

*The meeting **is due to take** place on May 13.*
*The train **is due to leave** in five minutes.*

E *Be set to*

Be set + to-infinitive is used in news reports about things that are expected to happen soon.

*The player **is set to move** to an Italian club.*
*The oil companies **are set to raise** prices once more.*

F *Be bound to* and *be sure/certain to*

We use these forms to say that something will definitely happen in the future.

*There**'s bound to be** trouble.*
*The President **is sure/certain to** resign.*

59 The present tense in a sub-clause

A

We often use the present simple for future time in a clause with *if, when, as, while, before, after, until, by the time,* or *as soon as.* This happens when both clauses are about the future.

*If we **meet** at seven, we'll have plenty of time.*
*My parents are going to move to the seaside when they **retire**.*
*Let's wait until the rain **stops**.*
*Call me as soon as you **have** any news.*
(NOT *Call me as soon as you'll have any news.*)

The same thing happens in other kinds of sub-clauses, such as a relative clause or a noun clause.

*There will be a prize for the person who **scores** the most points.*
*Can you make sure that the place **is** left tidy?*

B

In a sub-clause we also use the present continuous or present perfect for future time, rather than the future continuous or future perfect.

*I'll think of you here when **I'm lying** on the beach next week.*
(NOT *I'll think of you here when I'll be lying on the beach next week.*)
*Let's carry on until we**'ve finished**.*
(NOT *Let's carry on until we'll have finished.*)

C

But if the main clause has a present-tense verb (e.g. *I expect*), then we do not use another present-tense verb for the future.

*I expect the rain **will stop** soon.*
*I keep reminding myself that **I'll be lying** on the beach next week.*

NOTE

After *hope* we can use either a present or a future form.

> *I hope you **have**/**you'll have** a lovely time.*

60 The future continuous: *will be doing*

A Form

The future continuous is *will be* + ing-form.

> *The committee **will be discussing** the matter next month.*
> *We **won't be doing** much at the weekend.*
> ***Will** you **be staying** here long?*

NOTE

a   In the first person we can also use *shall*.
> *I **will**/**shall be visiting** customers all day.*

b   We can use *be going to* as well as *will*.
> *We **aren't going to be doing** much at the weekend.*

B Action over a future period

We can use the future continuous for an action over a period of future time. It means that we will be in the middle of an action.

> *Mike can't come tonight. He**'ll be working**.*
> *How will I recognize you?*
> *~ I'm fair, quite tall, and I**'ll be wearing** a blue coat.*

Compare the past, present, and future.

> Past: *I've just had a holiday. This time last week I **was lying** in the sun.*
> Present: *I'm phoning from Crete. I'm on the beach. I**'m lying** in the sun.*
> Future: *I'm going on holiday. This time next week I**'ll be lying** in the sun.*

Compare these sentences:

> *The crowd **will cheer** when the Queen arrives.*
> (She will arrive and then the crowd will cheer.)
> *The crowd **will be cheering** when the Queen arrives.*
> (The crowd will start cheering and then she will arrive.)

We sometimes use the future continuous with a phrase of time to talk about an action going on over a whole period.

> *I**'ll be working** all day tomorrow.*

NOTE

We can also use the future continuous for an assumption about what is happening now.
> *I expect Lisa is busy. She**'ll be revising** for her exam.*

C A routine or arrangement

We can also use the future continuous for an action which will result from a routine or arrangement.

*I'll **be phoning** my mother tonight. I always phone her on Fridays.*
(The phone call will be the result of my regular routine.)
*The Queen **will be arriving** in ten minutes' time.*
(Her arrival in ten minutes is part of her schedule.)
*We are centralizing our operations, so this office **will be closing** next month.*
(The closure will be a result of the centralization.)

Other forms are also possible in the above contexts.
*I'm **going to phone** my mother tonight. > 55*
*I'm **phoning** my mother tonight. > 56A*

We can use the future continuous to ask about someone's plans to see if they fit in with our wishes.
***Will** you **be going** past the post office this morning? ∼ Yes, why? ∼ Could you post this for me, please?*
*How long **will** you **be using** the tennis court? ∼ We've booked it until three.*
*When **will** you **be marking** our test papers? ∼ Next week, probably.*
We could use the present continuous in these examples. > 56A

61 The future perfect and future perfect continuous

A The future perfect

The future perfect is *will have* + past participle.
*When we get to York, we'**ll have done** half the journey.*
*Seven is too early. I **won't have got** home from work by then.*
*How long **will** the spaceship **have been** in orbit?*

We can use the future perfect to talk about something being over at a time in the future.
*I'**ll have finished** this book soon. I'm nearly at the end.*
*We don't need all day for the museum. I expect we'**ll have seen** enough by lunch time.*
*Sarah **won't have completed** her studies until she's twenty-five.*

NOTE
a   In the first person we can also use *shall*.
     *When we get to York, we **will/shall have done** half the journey.*

b   We can sometimes use *be going to* as well as *will*.
     *They **aren't going to have finished** the repairs until next week.*

c   The future perfect can express an assumption about the past. > 76C
     *You'**ll have met** my boss – he was at the meeting you went to.*

B The future perfect continuous

The future perfect continuous is *will have been* + ing-form.
*It's Mike's party in October. He'**ll have been working** here for ten years.*

We use this form when we imagine ourselves looking back from a time in the future, e.g. October. We look back at an action that will continue up to that time, e.g. Mike working.

Here are some more examples.
> *If I manage to finish this book by Friday, I'll **have been reading** it for eight weeks.*
> *Our neighbours are moving soon. They'll **have** only **been living** here a year.*
> *How long **will** the spaceship **have been orbiting** the earth?*

C Future perfect or future perfect continuous?

Future perfect	Future perfect continuous
This tense focuses on the result of the action.	This tense focuses on the action going on.
*I'll **have written** the report by six, so it'll be on your desk tomorrow morning.*	*This report is taking ages. I'll **have been writing** it for a week by the time I finish.*

62 *Was going to, would, was to*, etc

We use these forms when we are talking about a past situation, for example when we are telling a story. We use the forms to refer forward to later events.

A *Was/were going to*

We can use *was/were going to* for a prediction in the past.
> *Alice felt so relieved. Everything **was going to be** all right after all.*

We can also use *was/were going to* for an intention in the past.
> *I **was going to buy** some presents, so I took my credit card with me.*
I was going to buy some presents means that I intended to buy some presents. Sometimes the intended action does not actually happen.
> *The bus pulled away just as we **were going to get** on it.*
We did not get on the bus because it pulled away too soon.

Compare the past continuous referring to a past arrangement. > 47E
> *We were on our way to the gym. We **were playing** basketball at three.*

B *Would*

We can use *would* as a past form of *will*. This use can be rather literary.
> *George Washington was the first President of a nation that **would become** the richest and most powerful on earth.*
> *They set off at daybreak. They **would reach** the camp before nightfall.*
Here a past action (reaching the camp) is seen from a time when it had not yet happened.

For *would* as a past form of *will* in indirect speech, > 262E.
> *They thought they **would reach** the camp before nightfall.*

89

We can use *would not* for unwillingness or a refusal in the past.
> *The spokesperson **wouldn't answer** any questions.*
> *The car **wouldn't start** this morning.*

Compare *won't* for a refusal in the present. > 54D

C *Was to, was about to,* and *was on the point of*

We can also use *be to, be about to,* and *be on the point of* in the past tense.
> *The workers were arriving for their last shift. The factory **was to close** the next day.* (There was an arrangement for the factory to close.)
> *We had to hurry. The bus **was about to** leave.*
> *Max **was on the point of saying** goodbye to everyone when he suddenly noticed an attractive girl looking across the room at him.*

NOTE

a   We can use *was to* with the perfect.
> *The factory **was to have closed** the next day, but it was decided to keep it going for another few weeks.*

This means that the arrangement was changed. The factory did not close the next day.

b   Sometimes *was to* has the same meaning as *would.*
> *George Washington was the first President of a nation that **was to become** the richest and most powerful on earth.*

This means that the nation later became the richest and most powerful on earth.

63 Overview: the future

These are some of the main ways of talking about the future.

Use	Form
The future:	*The problem **will get** worse.* > 54B
	*The problem **is going to get** worse.* > 55B
The near future:	*The shop **is about to** close.* > 58C
An instant decision:	*I'll just **put** the kettle on.* > 54C
A plan or intention:	*We're **going to move** house soon.* > 55C
	*We're **moving** house soon.* > 56A
A timetable:	*We **land** at 10.25.* > 56B
An official arrangement:	*The conference **is to take** place in November.* > 58A
A future action which is part of a routine:	*I'll **be seeing** my boss tomorrow morning.* > 60C
A future action over a period:	*We'll **be driving** all through the night.* > 60B
Looking back from the future:	*You'll **have eaten** all those chocolates by tea time.* > 61A
Looking forward from the past:	*I **was going to wash** up, but I forgot to.* > 62A

Be, have, and *do*

64 Auxiliary verbs and ordinary verbs

A In these sentences, *be* and *have* are auxiliary verbs. They combine with ordinary verbs.

> *I'm surfing the Net.*
> *The information **is** updated daily.*
> *The computer **has** crashed.*

Here *be* is used to form the continuous (*am surfing*) and the passive (*is updated*). *Has* is used to form the perfect (*has crashed*).

We use the auxiliary verb *do* in simple-tense negatives and questions.

> *How often **do** you surf the Net?*

But in a simple-tense positive statement we do not normally use an auxiliary.

> *I often **surf** the Net.*

We also use auxiliaries in short answers, in short additions, and for emphasis.

> *Are you using the computer? ~ Yes, I **am**.*
> *Sarah has done a computer course, and so **have** I.*
> *Yes, I **did** download the file. I'm quite sure of that.*

We sometimes use two auxiliary verbs together.

> *I've **been** surfing the Net.* (present perfect continuous)
> *Petrol **had been** leaking from the tank.* (past perfect continuous)

B *Be, have,* and *do* can also be ordinary verbs. We can use them on their own as the main verb of a sentence.

> *The weather **was** beautiful.*
> *We **had** some sandwiches.* (*had* = ate)
> *I **did** the crossword this morning.* (*did* = completed)

Like other ordinary verbs, *be, have,* and *do* can be perfect or continuous.

> *The weather **has been** beautiful.*
> *We **were having** some sandwiches.* (*were having* = were eating)
> *I've **done** the crossword.* (*have done* = have completed)

Sometimes we use the same auxiliary and ordinary verb together.

> *I **was being** lazy.* (continuous of *be*)
> *I've **had** a sandwich.* (perfect of *have*)
> *I **did do** the crossword.* (emphatic form of *do*)

We can also use *be, have,* or *do* after a modal verb such as *might* or *can*.

> *I **might be** a bit late tomorrow.*
> *You **can do** this crossword if you like.*

65 The ordinary verb *be*

A Form

Present simple	
	Short forms
I **am**	*I'm*
you/we/they **are**	*you're/we're/they're*
he/she/it **is**	*he's/she's/it's*

Present continuous	
	Short forms
I **am being**	*I'm* **being**
you/we/they **are being**	*you're/we're/they're* **being**
he/she/it **is being**	*he's/she's/it's* **being**

Past simple
I/he/she/it **was**
you/we/they **were**

Past continuous
I/he/she/it **was being**
you/we/they **were being**

Present perfect	
	Short forms
I/you/we/they **have been**	*I've/you've/we've/they've* **been**
he/she/it **has been**	*he's/she's/it's* **been**

Past perfect	
	Short forms
someone **had been**	*I'd/you'd/he'd/we'd/they'd* **been**

We do not use the auxiliary verb *do* in simple tenses.
> *This pizza* **isn't** *very nice.* (NOT ~~*This pizza doesn't be very nice.*~~)
> **Were** *your friends there?* (NOT ~~*Did your friends be there?*~~)

In the other tenses, we form negatives and questions with the auxiliary in the normal way.
> *The weather* **has been** *nice.*
> *The weather* **hasn't been** *very nice.*
> *How* **has** *the weather* **been**?

B Uses of *be*

Here are some contexts where we use the ordinary verb *be*.

Identity: *Those girls **are** my cousins.*
Nationality: *We're Swedish. We're from/We come from Sweden.*
Job: *My sister **is** a doctor.*
Interests: *I'm a keen cyclist.*
Place: *The Science Museum **is** in South Kensington.*
Time: *The match **was** last Saturday.*
Early/late: *We **were** late for the show.*
Age: *I'll **be** eighteen in November.*
Qualities: *That building **is** really ugly.*
Feelings: *How **are** you? ~ I'm fine, thanks.*
We're cold and we're hungry.
Behaviour: *Please **be** careful.*
Right/wrong: *That **isn't** right. I think you're mistaken.*
Possession: *Are these bags yours?*
Cost: *How much **is** this CD/does this CD cost?*

NOTE
When we say where something is, we can sometimes use *lie* or *stand* instead of *be*.
*The island **is/lies** off the coast of Scotland.*
*The church **was/stood** at a busy crossroads.*
In these contexts *lie* and *stand* are more formal and literary than *be*.
We can also use *be located* or *be situated*.
*Our head office **is located** on the outskirts of Northampton.*
*The hotel **is situated** in lovely gardens with magnificent views.*

C *Be* in the continuous

We can use *be* in the continuous for temporary behaviour.
*The neighbours **are being** very noisy today.*
*I told the children off because they **were being** silly.*

Compare these two sentences.
You're being stupid. (= At present you are behaving stupidly.)
You're stupid. (= You are always stupid. / You are a stupid person.)

D *Gone* or *been*?

Compare these two sentences.
*Tom has **gone** to town, but he'll be back soon.*
*Tom has **been** to town. He got back half an hour ago.*
Here *gone* means 'gone and still away'. *Been* means 'gone and come back'.

Sometimes we use an ing-form after *gone* or *been*.
*The girls have **gone swimming**. They're at the pool.*
*The girls have **been swimming**. They've just got back.*

In questions about what places people have visited, we use *been*.
*Have you (ever) **been** to Egypt?*

66 *Have* and *have got*

A Use

The basic use of *have* and *have got* is to express possession.
   *Our friends **had** a dog.*   *We**'ve got** a balcony.*
This includes temporary possession.
   *I think you**'ve got** a book that belongs to me.*

In the above examples, *have* and *have got* cannot be used in the continuous.
For *have* as an action verb with a continuous form, > 67.
   *We**'re having** a picnic.*

For some other related meanings of *have* and *have got*, > F.

B Form

have	*have got*
Present simple	
I/you/we/they **have**	*I/you/we/they* **have got**
he/she/it **has**	*he/she/it* **has got**
Past simple	
someone **had**	*someone* **had got**
Present perfect	
I/you/we/they **have had**	
he/she/it **has had**	
Past perfect	
someone **had had**	

The word *got* is informal and typical of everyday conversation. We can use it
in simple tenses, but it is more common in the present than in the past. And
it is more common in Britain than in the US.

C Short forms of *have* and *have got*

have	*have got*
With *have* on its own, we prefer full forms to short forms.	Before *got* we can use the short forms *'ve*, *'s*, or *'d*.
Present simple	
*I **have** the key.*	*I **have got** the key.*
*I**'ve** the key.* (infrequent)	*I**'ve got** the key.*
Past simple	
*I **had** the key.*	*I **had got** the key.*
*I**'d** the key.* (infrequent)	*I**'d got** the key.*

NOTE
In very informal speech, you may hear *got* without *have.*
> *I **got** lots of time.* (= I've got lots of time.)
> *You **got** any money?* (= Have you got any money?)

TIP
Say *I've got ...* for the present.
Say *I had ...* for the past.

D Negatives and questions

In negatives and questions we can use *do* or *have* as the auxiliary.

have	*have got*
Present simple	
*I **don't have** a key.*	*I **haven't got** a key.*
***Do** you **have** a key?*	***Have** you **got** a key?*
*I **haven't** a key.* (less frequent)	
***Have** you a key?* (less frequent)	
*Amy **doesn't have** a key.*	*Amy **hasn't got** a key.*
***Does** Amy **have** a key?*	***Has** Amy **got** a key?*
*Amy **hasn't** a key.* (less frequent)	
***Has** Amy a key?* (less frequent)	
Past simple	
*I **didn't have** a key.*	*I **hadn't got** a key.*
***Did** you **have** a key?*	***Had** you **got** a key?*
*I **hadn't** a key.* (less frequent)	
***Had** you a key?* (less frequent)	

In the present *I don't have* and *I haven't got* are both possible, although Americans prefer *I don't have.* In the past we usually use *did* in negatives and questions.

In perfect tenses we form negatives and questions in the usual way.
> *I **haven't had** a chance to talk to you.*
> ***Had** you **had** any symptoms before yesterday?*

TIP
Ask *Do you have ...?* or *Have you got ...?* for the present.
Ask *Did you have ...?* for the past.

E More details about *got*

There are some structures where we do not normally use *got*.

Perfect: *I've **had** these shoes for years.*
            (NOT *I've had got*)

Short answer:	*Have you got your ticket?* ~ **Yes, I have.**
	(NOT ~~*Yes, I have got.*~~)
Infinitive:	*It would be nice **to have** more time together.*
	(NOT ~~*to have got*~~)
Ing-form:	*It's pretty depressing **having** no job.*
	(NOT ~~*having got*~~)
After a modal verb:	*You **can have** these books if you like.*
	(NOT ~~*You can have got*~~)

Have got can sometimes be the present perfect of *get*.
> *I left my books outside. They**'ve got** wet.* (= They have become wet.)

Compare these examples.
> *I**'ve got** this newspaper from one of the neighbours.* (= I have obtained/ borrowed it.)
> *I**'ve got** a newspaper somewhere. I just can't find it.* (= I have one.)

When *have got* expresses an action, we can use it in these structures.

Infinitive:	*We're grateful **to have got** somewhere to live.*
	(= to have found)
Ing-form:	*I can't help **having got** a cold.*
	(= having caught)
After a modal verb:	*They must **have got** our letter by now.*
	(= must have received)

We can leave out *got* from the above examples.
> *We're grateful **to have** somewhere to live.*

Here *have* expresses possession.
But when *have got* means 'have become', we cannot leave out *got*.
> *They must **have got** wet in all this rain.*

F Other uses of *have* and *have got*

As well as possession, *have* and *have got* can express other related meanings.

Qualities:	*Those soldiers certainly **had** courage.*
Features:	*Kate **has got** blue eyes.*
Parts:	*The house **has** five bedrooms.*
Relationships:	***Have** you **got** any brothers or sisters?*
Position:	*He **had** both his hands in his pockets.*
Thoughts:	*I**'ve got** an idea.*
Availability:	*We **don't have** time to hang around.*
Necessity:	*I**'ve got** a lot of work at the moment.*
Illness:	*I**'ve got** a terrible headache.*

G *With* and *there*

We can also use *with* to express possession.
> *We saw a man **with** a gun.* (= a man who had a gun)
> (BUT NOT ~~*The man was with a gun.*~~)

There is a structure with *have* or *have got* which means the same as one with *there + be*.

> *The T-shirt **had** a slogan on it.*
> (= **There was** a slogan on the T-shirt.)
> *Their house **has got** a filling-station right next to it.*
> (= **There is** a filling-station right next to their house.)

67 The ordinary verb *have*

Have can be an ordinary verb with all the usual tenses, including the continuous. It has a number of different meanings.

> *The children **are having** a wonderful time.* (= are experiencing)
> *I'**ve had** a letter.* (= have received)
> *We'**ll be having** a late lunch.* (= will be eating)
> *I always **have** orange juice at breakfast.* (= drink)
> *My father **has** a sleep after lunch.* (has a sleep = sleeps, > 69)

Here *have* is an action verb.

We use the auxiliary verb *do* in simple-tense negatives and questions.

> *We **don't have** breakfast on Sundays.*
> ***Did** you **have** a good journey?*

We cannot use *got* with the ordinary verb *have*.

> (NOT ~~The children have got a wonderful time.~~)

68 The ordinary verb *do*

A Form

Present simple	Present continuous
*I/you/we/they **do***	*I **am doing***
*he/she/it **does***	*you/we/they **are doing***
	*he/she/it **is doing***

Past simple	Past continuous
*someone **did***	*I/he/she/it **was doing***
	*you/we/they **were doing***

Present perfect	Present perfect continuous
*I/you/we/they **have done***	*I/you/we/they **have been doing***
*he/she/it **has done***	*he/she/it **has been doing***

Past perfect	Past perfect continuous
*someone **had done***	*someone **had been doing***

We form negatives and questions in the same way as with other verbs.

> *I **haven't done** anything wrong.*
> *What subjects **are** you **doing**?*

In simple tenses we use the auxiliary verb *do*.
> *I **don't do** a Saturday job any more.*
> *How many miles **did** you **do** on your run?*

We can also use the negative imperative and the emphatic form with the ordinary verb *do*.
> ***Don't do** anything dangerous, will you?*
> *Your sister **did do** well in the competition!*

B Uses of *do*

The ordinary verb *do* has a number of uses.

We use *do* for an action when we do not say what the action is.
> *What are you **doing**? ~ I'm drawing a plan of the garden.*
> *You can **do** lots of exciting things at Adventure World!*
> *Guess what we **did** yesterday.*

We may not know what the action is, or we may not want to be specific.

We also use *do* to mean 'carry out' or 'complete'.
> ***Have** you **done** your exercises?*
> *They're **doing** some repairs to the roof.*
> *We **did** the job in less than an hour.*

Do can replace another verb in the context of a task or a service.
> *There's something wrong with the car. They're **doing** it today.* (= repairing)
> *I've **done** the report.* (= written)
> *The restaurant **does** Sunday lunches.* (= serves)

We can also use *do* with an ing-form. > 124B
> *What course have you chosen? ~ I'm going to **do marketing**.*
> *Someone ought to **do some cleaning** in here.*
> *I **did a lot of skiing** last year.*

C *Do* and *make*

We use the ordinary verb *do* to stand for any action, or when we talk about doing a task.
> *I'm afraid I've **done** something silly.*
> *We're just **doing** the washing-up.*

The basic meaning of *make* is 'produce' or 'create'.
> *I was just **making** a cup of tea.*
> *They've **made** a new Harry Potter film.*
> *The company **makes** a small profit.*

We use *make* in these structures.
> *Tom **made this table**.* (*made* = created)
> *Tom **made me this table**.* (*made* = created)
> *Tom **made this table for me**.* (*made* = created)

*A week in Portugal would **make a nice break**. (make = be)*
*The music **made me sad**. (made me sad = caused me to become sad)*
*The music **made me cry**. (made me cry = caused me to cry)*

There are many idiomatic uses of *do* and *make*. For example, you **do** your homework, you **do** a course or a subject, you **do** your best, and you **make** sure you don't **make** a mistake.

A common idiom is the phrase *to do with* meaning 'connected with'.
*The boss wants to see you. It's something **to do with** an e-mail.*

69 *Have a look, make a start*, etc

A Compare these sentences.
*We often **swim** in the pool.*
*We often **have a swim** in the pool.*
The two sentences have a very similar meaning. We can express some actions as a verb (*swim*) or as an idiom consisting of a verb + object (*have a swim*).

Have is often used in these idioms, but with some we use a different verb such as *make*.
*One of the guests **complained**.*
*One of the guests **made a complaint**.*

The verb in the idiom is an ordinary verb and can be continuous.
*Someone **is having** a swim.*
*One of the guests **was making** a complaint.*

NOTE
Compare these sentences.
*Chloe jumped in the water and **swam** a few strokes.*
*Chloe went to the pool and had **a swim**.*
*We missed the bus, so we **walked**.*
*It was a lovely day, so we went for **a walk**.*
With some physical actions, the noun suggests a leisure activity going on for a period of time. *A swim* is a period of swimming from start to finish. *A walk* is a complete journey on foot.

B Here are some *verb + object* idioms of this kind.

Verb	Idiom
act	*take action*
affect	*have an effect on*
announce sth	*make an announcement*
argue	*have an argument*
choose	*make a choice*
comment	*make a comment*
complain	*make a complaint*
contact	*make contact with*
contribute	*make a contribution*
control	*have/take control of*

decide	*take/make a decision*
describe	*give a description of*
discuss	*have a discussion about*
drink	*have a drink*
	have something to drink
eat	*have a meal*
	have something to eat
feel	*have a feeling*
guess	*have a guess*
hold	*take/have/keep hold of*
indicate	*give an indication of*
look	*have/take a look*
move	*make a move*
predict sth	*make a prediction (of/about)*
rest	*have a rest*
revise	*do some revision*
ride	*have a ride*
	go for a ride
sleep	*have a sleep*
start	*make a start*
suggest sth	*make a suggestion*
suspect sth	*have a suspicion*
swim	*have a swim*
	go for a swim
talk to	*have a talk with*
think	*have a think*
try	*have a try/have a go*
	make an effort
use	*make use of*
walk	*have/take a walk*
	go for a walk
wash	*have a wash*
work	*do some work*

C Compare the use of the adverb and the adjective in these sentences.

Adverb	Adjective
*I washed **quickly**.*	*I had a **quick** wash.*
*They argued **passionately**.*	*They had a **passionate** argument.*

TIP
The structure with the adjective is usually neater. For example,
*James made **good** use of the computer* sounds much better than
James used the computer well.

Modal verbs

70 Introduction

A The modal verbs are *can, could, must, should, ought, may, might, will, would,* and *shall*. A modal verb always has the same form and never has an ending such as *-s*, *-ing*, or *-ed*. Modal verbs express meanings such as necessity and possibility. We can use them to tell or allow people to do things; or we can use them to say how certain or uncertain we are. There is an overview of meanings in G.

There are two verbs which we use either as a modal verb or as an ordinary verb. They are *need* (> 73) and *dare* (> 83).

B After a modal verb we put an infinitive without *to*.
> *We **can park** here.*   *It's getting late. I **must go.***
> *The government **should do** more to help.*   *It **will be** windy tomorrow.*

The only exception to this is *ought*, which has a to-infinitive.
> *The government **ought to do** more to help.*

NOTE
When there is an adverb, it usually comes between the modal verb and the infinitive.
> *We **can probably park** here.*

C To form the negative we use *not* or *n't* with the modal verb.
> *The plan **might not** work.* (NOT ~~The plan doesn't might work.~~)
> *You **shouldn't** be so untidy.* (NOT ~~You don't should be so untidy.~~)

But note the spelling and pronunciation of *won't* (> 54A), *shan't*, (> 54A), *mustn't* > (73D), and *can't/cannot* > (80A).

To form questions we put the modal verb before the subject.
> ***Can** we park here?* (NOT ~~Do we can park here?~~)
> *How **should** I organize my work?* (NOT ~~How do I should organize my work?~~)

We also use modal verbs in short answers and in question tags.
> ***Can** we park here? ~ Yes, we **can**.*
> *We can park here, **can't** we?*

D The same modal verb form can refer to the present or the future.
> Present: *I'm looking for the letter. It might be somewhere in this
>   pile of papers.*
> Future: *I posted the letter today. It might get there **tomorrow**.*

The context shows whether the present or the future is meant. For example, *tomorrow* is in the future.

To talk about the past we can use a modal verb + *have* + past participle.
*I posted the letter two days ago. It **might have** arrived yesterday.*
We can also use a phrase like *had to, was able to,* or *was allowed to.*
*We all **had to** work late yesterday.*

Could sometimes expresses ability in the past.
*I can't remember names very well. When I saw Simon's sister on Friday, I **couldn't** remember her name at all. It was quite embarrassing.*

E A modal verb is followed by an infinitive without *to.* The infinitive can be simple, perfect, continuous, or passive.

Form	Example
Simple	*They **may show** us their holiday photos.*
Perfect	*I **may have shown** you this before.*
Continuous	*They **may be showing** the film on television soon.*
Passive	*We **may be shown** the results later.*
Perfect + continuous	*You **must have been dreaming**.*
Perfect + passive	*The car **must have been stolen**.*

F There are some phrases like *have to, be allowed to,* or *be able to* which have the same meanings as modal verbs.

Modal verb	Phrase
*You **must** fill in this form.*	*You **have to** fill in this form.* > 71C
*The man **couldn't** board the plane.*	*The man **wasn't allowed to** board the plane.* > 75C
*We **can** cancel the order.*	*We **are able to** cancel the order.* > 80B–C

But there are differences in use between the phrases and the modal verbs.

G Here is an overview of the kind of meanings expressed by modal verbs and phrases.

Use	Example
Necessity	*I **must** clean my shoes.* > 71B
	*We **have to** wait here.* > 71B
	*We**'ve got to** turn left here.* > 72
No necessity	*You **needn't** wear a tie.* > 73A
	*You **don't have to** wear a tie.* > 73A
Necessity to avoid something	*You **mustn't** break anything.* > 73D

Use	Example
The right thing to do	*You **should** complain.* > 74A *You **ought to** complain.* > 74A *We**'d better** get ready now.* > 74B *You**'re supposed to** make your own bed.* > 74C
Permission	***Can** I go/**May** I go now?* > 75A *We**'re allowed to** walk on the grass.* > 75C
Certainty	*The game **will** be over now.* > 76A *This place **must** be crowded in summer.* > 76B
Impossibility	*This **can't** be real gold.* > 76B
Probability	*Things **should** start to get better.* > 77
Possibility	*We **may** go/**might** go out later.* > 78A *We **could** go out later.* > 79A
Ability	*I **can** ski.* > 80A *I **could** ski when I was a child.* > 80A *We **were able to** ski all afternoon.* > 80B,C
Hypothesis	*A million pounds **would** be very useful.* > 81B
Past habits	*My friend **would** always call on me after school.* > 82A *We **used to** play together every day.* > 82B
Having courage	*No one **dare** speak openly.* > 83

71 *Must* and *have to*

A Form

Must has just one form, and it is followed by an infinitive without *to*.
   *You **must** wear something smart.*

We often use *have to* in the present simple or past simple.

Present simple:	*We **have to** wear smart clothes.* *David **has to** work on Sundays.*
Past simple:	*I **had to** get up early today.*

We form negatives and questions with *do*.
   *We **don't have to** wear smart clothes.*
   ***Does** David **have to** work on Sundays?*
   *What time **did** you **have to** get up?*
   *We **didn't have to** get up early.*

The short forms *'ve, 's,* and *'d* are used much less often than the long forms
have, has, and *had*. Sentences like *We've to wear smart clothes* and *I'd to get
up early* are unusual. But we can say *We**'ve got** to wear smart clothes.* > 72A

Must has no past tense, perfect, or continuous form. We use *have to* instead.

Past simple:	I **had to** queue for hours for these tickets.
Present perfect:	We**'ve had to** make a few changes.
Present continuous:	I**'m having to** spend a lot of time travelling.
Past continuous:	At that time we **were having to** survive on very little money.

We also use *have to* (not *must*) in the infinitive or ing-form and after *will*.

To-infinitive:	I wasn't expecting **to have to** look after the children.
ing-form:	It's no fun **having to** stand the whole journey.
Future with *will*:	You **will have to** pay the full standard fare.

B Basic use

We use *must* and *have to* to talk about what is necessary now or in the near future.

> I'm really sweaty. I **must** have a shower.
> We **must** make the arrangements soon.
> We **have to** turn left here. It's one-way.
> Mark **has to** take an exam at the end of his course.

When we talk about things we have to do in the near future, we can use *have to* either in the present or with *will*.

> I **have to** go out soon. / I'**ll have to** go out soon.

NOTE
Here are some other ways of expressing necessity. They are more formal than *must* or *have to* and more likely to be used in writing than in speech.
> It's **essential**/**vital** you keep me informed. (= You **must** keep me informed.)
> You are **obliged to**/**required to** return the form within thirty days.
> It was **necessary** to change the arrangements. (= The arrangements **had to** be changed).

C *Must* or *have to*?

There is a difference in meaning between *must* and *have to*. Look at this information for rail passengers.

> You **must** buy your ticket before starting your journey, unless you join the train at a station where ticket purchase facilities are not available.

Now look at this conversation.

> Emily: There isn't much time to spare. You'd better buy your ticket on the train.
> Steve: I can't do that. I **have to** buy the ticket before I get on.

We normally use *must* when the speaker or writer decides what is necessary, and we use *have to* when the necessity comes from the situation.

You must … is a way of telling someone to do something. *You have to* … is a way of explaining what is necessary in the situation.

> *You **must** fill in a form.* (I'm telling you.)
> *You **have to** fill in a form.* (That's the rule.)
> *I **must** go on a diet. I'm getting overweight.*
> *I **have to** go on a diet. Doctor's orders.*

TIP

In general it is safer to use *have to* than to use *must*. *Have to* is much more common in speech. Sometimes *must* can sound strange if you use it in the wrong way.

D *Must* to recommend things

We sometimes use *must* to recommend something enjoyable.

> *You really **must** watch this new soap opera. It's fascinating.*
> *We **must** have lunch together some time.* ~ *Yes, that would be nice.*

Have to is less usual in this context.

72 *Have got to*

A Both *have to* and *have got to* express necessity.

> *I **have to** take an exam in June.*
> *I **have got to** take / I've **got to** take an exam in June.*
> *Lucy **has to** do some work.*
> *Lucy **has got to** do / Lucy's **got to** do some work.*

Have to is used in both formal and informal English. *Have got to* is informal.

B We use *have got to* mostly in the present simple. In the past simple *had to* is more usual than *had got to*.

> *I couldn't go to the party. I **had to** finish my project.*

We cannot use *have got to* with perfect or continuous forms or in the infinitive or ing-form.

> *Day after day Karen **was having to** do the work of two people.*
> (NOT *Karen was having got to do* …)
> *It's a nuisance **to have to** wait so long.*
> (NOT *It's a nuisance to have got to wait so* …)

TIP

It is generally safer to use *have to* than to use *have got to*.

C We form negatives and questions like this.

	have to	*have got to*
Negative:	We **don't have to** *pay.*	We **haven't got to** *pay.*
	Tom **doesn't have to** *wait.*	Tom **hasn't got to** *wait.*
Question:	**Do** *we* **have to** *pay?*	**Have** *we* **got to** *pay?*
	Does Tom **have to** *wait?*	**Has** Tom **got to** *wait?*

In the past simple we form negatives and questions with *did.*
> We **didn't have to** *pay.*   **Did** Tom **have to** *wait?*

73 *Needn't, don't have to,* and *mustn't*

A *Needn't* and *don't have to*

We use *needn't* and *don't have to* to say that something is not necessary.
> You **needn't** *apologize. It's not your fault.*
> You **don't have to** *apologize. It's not your fault.*

The modal verb *needn't* is normally used only in the negative.

> **TIP**
> There is little difference in meaning between *needn't* and *don't have to,* but it is usually safer to use *don't have to.*

B *Need to*

There is an ordinary verb *need,* which we can use in positive and negative sentences and in questions. *Need to* means the same as *have to.* To form negatives and questions we use *do.*

have to	*need to* (ordinary verb)	*needn't* (modal verb)
The colours **have to** *match.*	*The colours* **need to** *match.*	
The figure **doesn't have to** *be exact.*	*The figure* **doesn't need to** *be exact.*	*The figure* **needn't** *be exact.*
Do *we* **have to** *book in advance?*	**Do** *we* **need to** *book in advance?*	

NOTE

a   The verb *need* can have an object.
> *I really* **need** *a calculator.*

b   We can also use an object + to-infinitive after *need.*
> *We* **need you to fax** *us a copy.*

c   For *need* + gerund, e.g. *This carpet* **needs cleaning,** > 96A.

d   We can also use *need* as a noun, for example in the phrase *no need.*
> *There's* **no need** *to book in advance.*

C *Needn't have done* and *didn't need to do*

We use these forms to talk about an unnecessary past action. If someone didn't do something because it wasn't necessary, we use *didn't need to*.

> We **didn't need to** *make any sandwiches. We knew no one would be hungry.*
> *There wasn't a queue, so I* **didn't need to** *wait.*

If someone did something which we now know was unnecessary, we can use either *needn't have done* or *didn't need to*.

> *We* **needn't have made** / **didn't need to make** *these sandwiches.*
> *No one's eaten any.*
> *It's a beautiful day. I* **needn't have brought** / **didn't need to bring**
> *this umbrella.*

NOTE
Didn't have to means the same as *didn't need to*.
> *Fortunately we* **didn't have to pay**/**didn't need to pay** *for the repairs.*

D *Mustn't*

We use *mustn't* to tell someone not to do something, or to say that it is necessary to avoid something.

> *You* **mustn't** *forget your keys or you'll be locked out.*
> *We* **mustn't** *lose this game. It's really important that we win.*

Mustn't is pronounced /ˈmʌsnt/.

Mustn't or *may not* can be used to forbid something.

> *Students* **must not** *use*/**may not** *use dictionaries in the examination.*

Mustn't has a different meaning from *needn't* or *don't have to*. Compare these examples.

> *I* **needn't** *run. / I* **don't have to** *run. I've got plenty of time.*
> *I* **mustn't** *run. I've got a weak heart.*

74 *Should, ought to, had better,* and *be supposed to*

A *Should* and *ought to*

Should and *ought to* mean the same thing. We use them to say what is the right thing or the best thing to do.

> *There aren't enough hospitals. They* **should build** / *They* **ought to build**
> *more of them.*
> *You* **should go**/**ought to** *go to York. It's an interesting place.*

In negatives, questions, and short answers we normally use *should*.

> *People* **shouldn't** *leave litter all over the place,* **should** *they?*
> *Who* **should** *we invite to the wedding?*
> **Should** *I apologize, do you think? ∼ Yes, you* **should.**

We can use the continuous or perfect after *should* and *ought to*.

Continuous: *I **should be doing** some work instead of drinking coffee.*
*We **ought to be going** soon or we'll be late.*
Perfect: *You **should have planted** these potatoes last month.*
*After all the help you've given Guy, he **ought to have
thanked** you.*

B *Had better*

We also use *had better* to say what is the best thing to do in a particular
situation. It is used more in speech than in writing.
*These letters **had better** go today. They're quite urgent.*
*You're ill. You'**d better** see a doctor.*
*This room is in a mess. I'**d better** tidy up, **hadn't** I?*
Had better is stronger than *should* or *ought to*. *I'd better tidy up* means that I
am going to tidy up because it is the best way to deal with the problem.

We sometimes use *had better* to suggest unpleasant consequences if the
action is not taken.
*That car's in the way. Someone **had better** move it or I won't be able
to get out.*
*You'**d better** do what you're told or you'll be in trouble.*

The negative is *had better not*.
*Come on. We'**d better not** waste any time.*

NOTE
You may hear *best* instead of *better*.
*You're ill. You'**d best** see a doctor.*

C *Be supposed to*

Be supposed to has a number of different meanings.

We use it when we say what **should** happen because it is the rule, or it is the
normal way of doing things, what people are expected to do.
*When you've paid, you'**re supposed to** take your receipt to the counter over
there and collect what you've bought. ~ Oh, I see.*
*You'**re supposed to** be working, not sitting around chatting.*

We also use *be supposed to* for something that is arranged or intended.
*I'm not going to phone the office. I'**m supposed to** be on holiday, aren't I?*
*How **is** this bottle-opener **supposed to** work?*

We can also use it when we talk about what people in general say or believe.
*Too much sugar **is supposed to** be bad for you.*
(= People say too much sugar is bad for you.)

We also use *be supposed to* in the negative when something isn't allowed.
*We'**re not supposed** / We **aren't supposed to** keep pets in the flat.*
We can use *wasn't supposed to* for something that happened without
permission.
*You **weren't supposed to** mention my secret, you know.*

75 *Can, could, may*, and *be allowed to*

A Asking permission

We use *can, could,* or *may* to ask permission.
> **Can** *I take your umbrella?* ~ *Of course you can.*
> **Could** *I borrow this calculator, please?* ~ *Well, I need it actually.*
> **May** *we come in?* ~ *Yes, of course.*

Here *could* is less direct than *can* and so often sounds more polite. *May* is rather formal.

NOTE
For *can* and *could* in requests, > 79B.

B Giving and refusing permission

We use *can* or *may* to give permission. *May* is more formal.
> *You* **can** *use my phone if you like.*
> *May I read the letter?* ~ *Yes, of course you* **may**.

We use *cannot/can't* to refuse permission.
> *These rooms are private. I'm afraid you* **can't** *just walk in here.*

NOTE
a   *May* is sometimes used in formal written rules.
> *Any person over the age of 18* **may** *apply to join the club.*
> *You* **may not** *vote for more than one candidate.*

b   Here are some other ways of refusing permission.
> *Outdoor shoes* **must not** *be worn on this floor.* > 73D
> *The use of mobile phones* **is not allowed/permitted** *in the library.*
> *Smoking* **is prohibited** *on school premises.*
> **No** *picnics.* (mainly written)

C Talking about permission

We sometimes talk about permission when we are not giving it or asking for it. To do this, we can use *can* referring to the present or the future and *could* referring to the past.
> *I* **can** *stay up as late as I like. My parents don't mind.*
> *These yellow lines mean that you* **can't** *park here.*
> *At one time anyone* **could** *go and live in the US.*

We do not normally use *may* here. A sentence such as *I may stay up late* is less usual.

We can also use *be allowed to*.
> *I'm* **allowed to** *stay up as late as I like. My parents don't mind.*
> *Did Tina get permission from her boss?* **Was** *she* **allowed to** *leave work early?*
> *You* **won't be allowed to** *take photos in the museum.*

Compare these two sentences.

May we leave early, please? (Will you allow it?/I'm asking for permission.)
Are we allowed to leave early? (What is the rule?/I'm asking about permission.)

We use *be allowed to* (not *can* or *may*) in these forms.

Future:	No one **will be allowed to** leave the building until they have been questioned by the police.
Present perfect:	Since the beginning of the conflict, the media **have not been allowed to** report what is going on.
Present continuous:	No one without a ticket **is being allowed to** go near the stadium.
To-infinitive:	I didn't expect **to be allowed to** look round the factory.
Ing-form:	It's great **being allowed to** do whatever I like.

To talk about general permission in the past, we use *could* or *was/were allowed to*.

*Years ago visitors to Stonehenge **could go/were allowed to** go right up to the stones.*

But for a specific action done with permission, we use *was/were allowed to*.

*The five students **were allowed to** go right up to the stones.*

76 *Will, must,* and *can't* expressing certainty

A We can use *will* for an assumption.

*It's no good ringing Luke now. He'**ll** be at work.*
*There's someone at the door. It'**ll** be the postman.*

In the last example, the speaker assumes that the postman is at the door because this is the time when he normally calls. *It'll be the postman* is a kind of prediction about the present.

B *Must* can express certainty.

*You saw the film last week, so you **must** know what it's about.*
*Jane got up at four o'clock! Well, she **must** be tired then.*

The speaker sees it as necessarily and logically true that Jane is tired.

We use *can't* for something we see as impossible.

*This **can't** be Roland's textbook. He doesn't do physics.*

Must and *can't* are opposites.

*The bill **can't** be so much. There **must** be a mistake.*
(= There is certainly a mistake.)

NOTE

a   We also use *have (got) to* with the same meaning as *must*.
   *There **has to** be a mistake.*

b   We can also use *be sure to* or *be bound to*.
   *My brother **is sure to** be late. / My brother **is bound to** be late.*

c   In questions about what is possible we normally use *can*.
Who **can** that be at the door?   **Can** it really be true?

d   Americans say *That must not be Roland's textbook.*

C After *will*, *must*, and *can't* expressing an assumption or certainty, we can use the continuous, the perfect, and the passive.

Continuous:	*Where's Carl?* ~ *He'll be sitting in a café somewhere, I expect.*
	*The bus is late. It **must be coming** soon.*
Perfect:	*This glass is cracked. Someone **must have dropped** it.*
	*I **can't have gone** to the wrong house. I checked the address.*
Perfect passive:	*The best seats **will have been sold** by now.*
	*The bike **must have been stolen** while we were having lunch.*

NOTE

a   Compare *must have done* and *had to*.
  *The washing-machine is working again. Paul **must have repaired** it.*
  *The washing-machine broke down. Paul **had to repair** it.*
  Here *must have repaired* expresses certainty about the past and *had to repair* expresses a past necessity.

b   Compare *must do* and *must be doing*.
  *You've got exams soon. You **must work**.* (I'm telling you to work.)
  *Paul isn't at home. He **must be working**.* (So I'm sure he's working.)

D We can use *had to* and *couldn't* when something seemed certain in the past.
*The fingerprints were the husband's, so he **had to** be the murderer.*
*Harold stared in amazement. It **couldn't** be true!*

77 *Should* expressing probability

We can use *should* to say what is the right thing to do. > 74A
*You broke Vicky's camera, so you **should** buy her a new one.*

We can also use *should* to say that something is probable, either in the present or the future.
*I posted the letter ages ago. They **should** have it by now.*
*The journey normally takes four hours, so we **should** get there about six.*

In the negative we use *shouldn't*.
*We're nearly at the front of the queue. We **shouldn't** have to wait much longer.*

Should has the additional meaning of 'if all goes well'.
*There are no reports of delays. The train **should** be on time.*
But we cannot use it to predict that something will go wrong.
*There are reports of delays. The train **will probably be** late.*
(NOT *The train should be late.*)

111

NOTE
a   *Ought to* has the same meaning as *should*.
   *The journey normally takes four hours, so we **ought to** get there about six.*

b   We can also use *be (un)likely to* to express probability.
   *I'm afraid the train **is likely to** be late.*
   *Don't worry. There **are unlikely to** be any problems.*

78 *May* and *might*

A   We use *may* and *might* to say that something is possibly true.
   *This old picture **may/might** be valuable.*
   *The shop **may not/might not** be open today.*
   It may not be open means that possibly it isn't open.

We can also use *may* and *might* for an uncertain prediction or intention.
   *You **may/might** get stuck in traffic if you don't leave early.*
   *I'm not sure, but I **may/might** go away somewhere next weekend.*

We do not often use *may* or *might* in questions. Instead we can use a phrase like *Do you think …?*
   ***Do you think** you'll get the job?*

NOTE
a   *Might not* has a short form *mightn't*.
   *I **mightn't** be at home tomorrow.* (= Possibly I won't be at home tomorrow.)

b   We can use *may well/might well* to express a strong possibility.
   *This picture **may well / might well** be valuable.*
   (= It is very possible that this picture is valuable.)

c   We can also use *could* to express possibility.
   *This picture **could** be valuable.* > 79

d   There are other ways of being less than certain in English.
   ***Perhaps/Maybe** the picture is valuable.*
   *It's **possible**/There's a **possibility** (that) the picture is valuable.*
   *I **think** this is the right answer, but I'd better check.*

B   We can use the continuous after *may* and *might*.
   *Tina hasn't come home yet. She **may be working** late.*
   *I **might be playing** badminton tomorrow if I can book a court.*

We can also use the perfect.
   *I don't know where the letter is. I **may have thrown** it away.*
   *I'm not very good at typing, so I **might have made** some mistakes.*
   *I suppose the flight **might have been delayed**.*

C   We can use a statement with *might* to make a suggestion.
   *If you're going to the post office, you **might** get some stamps.*

Might can also express criticism that something is not done.
   *You never do anything to help. You **might** wash up occasionally.*
   *Someone **might** have thanked me for all my trouble.*
   We can also use *could* here.

D   We use *may as well* or *might as well* to say that something is the best thing to do because there is no better alternative.

*You're not going to finish that crossword. You **may as well** give up.*
*This lamp is no good. I **might as well** throw it away.*
*Do you want to go to this party? ~ Well, I suppose we **might as well**.*

79 *Can* and *could* expressing possibility

A   We use *could* to suggest possible future actions.

*We **could** go for a walk this afternoon.*
*As we're short of money, I **could** sell my jewellery.*

Compare the use of *may* or *might* for an uncertain intention.

Suggestion: *We **could** have a party. ~ Yes, why not?*
Uncertain intention: *We **may/might** have a party. ~ Oh, really? When?* > 78

B   We use *can* and *could* in requests.

***Can/Could** I have one of those leaflets, please?*
***Can/Could** you wait a moment, please?*

We can use the imperative: ***Wait** a moment, please*, but this is less polite. By using *can* or *could*, we ask if it is possible for someone to wait a moment.

We also use *can* in an offer of help.

***Can** I give you a lift? ~ Yes, please.*
*The upstairs lights aren't working. ~ Oh, I **can** fix them for you.*

> **TIP**
>
> Ask people to do things – don't tell them. Say *Could you carry this for me, please?* not *Carry this for me.* In general it is safer to use *could* in requests because it is less direct than *can* and usually more polite.

C   We can use *could* for something that is possibly true, or for an uncertain prediction.

*I'm not sure where the timetable is. It **could** be in the drawer.*
*The asteroid **could** hit the earth. It's not impossible.*

We can also use *may* or *might* here > 78A. But we do not use *can*.

We can use the continuous after *could*.

*Tina isn't home yet. She **could be working** late.*

We can also use the perfect to talk about possible actions in the past.

*You **could have forgotten** to post the letter.*
(= It is possible you forgot.)
*The flight **could have been delayed**.*
(= It is possible the flight has been/was delayed.)
*He **could have been having** a shower.*
(= It is possible he was having a shower.)

We can also use this structure for a possible action when we know that the action did not happen.

> *You were mad to drive here on these icy roads. You **could have had** an accident.*

NOTE

a   For *could have done* meaning a chance not taken, > 80C.

b   We can use *could have* + perfect to express criticism.
> *You **could have done** a bit more to help instead of leaving everything to me.*
We can also use *might* here. > 78C

D   We sometimes use *can* to say that something is generally possible.
> *You **can** make wine from bananas.*
> *Smoking **can** damage your health.*

In these sentences *can* means 'sometimes'.
> *The motorway **can** get busy.* (= It sometimes gets busy.)
> *This computer **can** drive me mad.* (= It sometimes drives me mad.)
Here *can* refers to a possible situation, one that we know sometimes happens.

E   *Can't* expresses logical impossibility. > 76B,C
> *She **can't** be very nice if no one likes her.*
> *You **can't** have switched the TV off. It's still on.*

Compare *can't* with *may not/might not*.
> *This answer **can't** be right. It must be wrong.*
> (= It is impossible for this answer to be right.)
> *This answer **may not/might not** be right.*
> (= It is possible that this answer isn't right.)

80 *Can, could*, and *be able to*

A *Can* and *could*

We use *can* to express ability.
> *Nicola **can** play chess. I taught her.*
> ***Can** you draw a perfect circle?*
> *We **can't** move this piano. It's too heavy for us.*
The negative of *can* is *cannot* /ˈkænɒt /, written as one word. It has a short form *can't* /kɑːnt /.

We use *could* for ability in the past.
> *Nicola **could** play chess when she was six.*
> *My grandfather **could** walk on his hands.*

As well as physical or mental ability, we also use *can* and *could* for an opportunity to do something.
> *We **can** sit in the garden when it's sunny.*
> *When we lived in a flat, we had so little space we **couldn't** keep a dog.*

NOTE
a   We do not use *can* + object. We always use a verb.
     *He **can** speak Italian.* (NOT *He can Italian.*)

b   For *can/could* with verbs of perception, e.g. *I **can see** a light,* >51E.

B Be able to

Be able to in the present tense means the same as *can* for ability or
opportunity.
    *The pupils **can** already read./The pupils **are** already **able to** read.*
    ***Can** you drive with that injured knee?/**Are** you **able to** drive with that
    injured knee?*

To form the negative of *be able to*, we can use either *not able to* or *unable to*.
    *The company **cannot** supply / **is not able to** supply / **is unable to**
    supply the information.*

We use *be able to* (not *can*) in the following forms.

Present perfect:	*Mr Fry has been ill. He **hasn't been able to** work for some time.*
Past perfect:	*I arrived late because I **hadn't been able to** find a taxi.*
To-infinitive:	*I'm having a wonderful holiday. It's nice **to be able to** relax.*
Ing-form:	***Being able to** speak the language is a great advantage.*
After *will*:	*Take this course and you **will be able to** impress others with your sparkling conversation.*
After *would*:	*I **wouldn't be able to** do your job. I'd be hopeless at it.*

C Could and was/were able to

We can use these forms to talk about a general ability in the past.
    *Andrew **could** walk when he was only eleven months old.*
    *Andrew **was able to** walk when he was only eleven months old.*

But we use *was/were able to* (and not *could*) for an action in a particular
situation.
    *Firemen **were able to** bring the blaze under control.*
    *The injured man **was able to** walk to a phone box.*
    (NOT *The injured man could walk to a phone box.*)
He was able to walk there means that he had the ability to walk there, and he
did actually walk there.

The phrases *succeeded in doing* and *managed to do* mean the same as *was/
were able to do*.
    *Detectives **managed to** identify / **succeeded in** identifying the murderer.*

In negatives and questions we can use either form.
    *Detectives **couldn't** identify / **weren't able to** identify the murderer.*
    ***Could** you get / **Were you able to** get tickets for the show?*

We normally use *could* (not *was/were able to*) with verbs of perception and verbs of thinking.

> *I **could see** smoke on the horizon.*
> *We **could understand** that Emily was feeling upset.*

To say that someone had the ability or the chance to do something but didn't do it, we use *could have done*.

> *He **could have walked** there, but he was too lazy.*
> *I **could have got** tickets, but there were only very expensive ones left.*

For an action that possibly happened in the past, e.g. *She could have missed the flight,* > 79C.

Could can also mean 'would be able to'. > B

> *The factory **could** produce a lot more if it was modernized.*
> *I **couldn't** do your job. I'd be hopeless at it.*

81 *Would*

A Form

The modal verb *would* has a short form *'d*.

> *Anyone **would** look silly in a shirt like that.*
> *I**'d** look ridiculous wearing that.*

We form negatives, questions, and short answers in the usual way.

> *This colour **wouldn't** suit me, **would** it?*
> *When **would** I wear it?*
> ***Would** you buy it?* ~ *No, I **wouldn't**.*

B Use

Compare these two replies.

> *We're going to have a barbecue.* ~ *Oh, that**'ll** be nice.* (*'ll* = *will*)
> *We're thinking of having a barbecue.* ~ *Oh, that**'d** be nice.* (*'d* = *would*)

Here *will* refers to a future situation, a barbecue which will definitely take place. *Would* refers to a possible situation, a barbecue which may or may not take place.

With *would*, there is often a phrase or clause explaining the situation that the speaker is imagining.

> *It **would** be nice to **have a barbecue.***
> *You **wouldn't** be much use **in a crisis.***
> *No one **would** pay taxes **if they didn't have to.*** > 246

We often use *would* in combinations such as *would like, would mind,* and *would rather.* > C–E

NOTE
For *would* looking forward from the past, > 62B.

C *Would like*

Would like means the same as *want*.

*Fiona **would like** to work in television.* (= Fiona wants to work in television.)
*We**'d like** a place of our own.* (= We want a place of our own.)

When we ask for something, we use *would like*, not *want*.
*I**'d like** a drink, please.*
As a request, *I want a drink* is impolite.

We also use *Would … like …?* in offers and invitations.
***Would anyone like** a drink?*
***Would you like** to join us for lunch?*

Compare *like* and *would like*.
*I'm a great clubber. I **like** going/I **like** to go to clubs.*
(= I go to clubs and enjoy it.)
*Let's go out somewhere. I**'d like** to go to a club.*
(= I want to go to a club.)

We can also use *would* with verbs such as *love, hate,* and *enjoy* when we are talking about things we want (or don't want) to do.
*My sister **would love** to do deep-sea diving.*
*I**'d hate** to live out in the country where nothing ever happens.*
*We**'d enjoy** a trip to Las Vegas. We've never been there before.*

D *Would mind*

We use *would mind* in negatives and questions.
*I **wouldn't mind** watching this film.* (= I want to watch this film.)
***Would** you **mind** changing places with me? ~ OK.*
(a polite request to change places)

E *Would rather*

Would rather means 'prefer' or 'would prefer'.
*I**'d rather** walk than hang around for a bus.*
*The guide **would rather** we kept together.*
***Would** you **rather** eat now or later?*
Would rather is followed by an infinitive without *to* (*walk*) or by a clause (*we kept together*).

The negative is *would rather not*.
*I'm a cautious person. I**'d rather not** take any risks.*

NOTE
We can also use *would sooner*.
*I**'d sooner** walk than hang around for a bus.*

82 *Would* and *used to* for past habits

A *Would*

In rather formal or written English, *would* is sometimes used to talk about past habits.

117

> *Before we had television, people **would** make their own entertainment.*
> *Every morning my father **would** leave the house before I woke.*

In general it is safer to say *used to*. > B

B Used to

Used to expresses the idea that something happened regularly or continued over a period of time in the past.

> *I **used to** come here when I was a child.*
> *Emma **used to** have a bicycle, but then she sold it.*
> *Before we had television, people **used to** make their own entertainment.*

I used to come here means that at one period I came here regularly, but then I stopped. *Used to* is pronounced /ˈjuːst tə/.

There is no present-tense form.

> (NOT *I use to come here now.*)

We use *did* in negatives and questions.

> *There **didn't use to** be so much crime as there is today.*
> *What kind of books **did** you **use to** read as a child?*

NOTE

We can use *never* in the negative.
> *There **never used to be** so much crime.*

Used not to is rather formal.
> *There **used not to be** so much crime.*

C Used to and be / get used to

Compare *used to do* and *be used to doing*.

> *We **used to live** in the country. But then we moved to London.*
> (= At one time we lived in the country.)
> *We're **used to living** in London now. But at first it was quite a shock, after life in the country.*
> (= Living in London no longer feels strange to us.)

We can also say *get used to* to talk about becoming more familiar with something.

> *I still find driving in Britain quite difficult. I'll never **get used to driving** on the left.*
> *Sarah had never seen herself as a manager, but she soon **got used to being** in charge.*

83 Dare

Dare is a mixture of forms. We sometimes use it as an ordinary verb and sometimes as a modal verb. It takes an infinitive with or without *to*.

> *Not many people **dare (to) walk** along here at night.*
> *No one **dares (to) protest/dare protest**.*
> *Only four of us had **dared (to) accept** the challenge.*

If you *dare* to do something, you are brave enough to do it. If you *daren't*, then you are too afraid to do it.

Dare is more common in negatives and questions than in positive statements. The negative forms are *don't/doesn't/didn't dare* or *daren't/dare not* (present) and *dared not* (past).

> *This place is so expensive. I **don't dare (to) look**/I **daren't look** at the bill.*
> *The police **didn't dare (to) approach**/**dared not approach** the building with the gunman inside.*

In questions we can use *do*, or we can use *dare* as a modal verb.

> ***Do** you **dare (to) say**/**Dare** you say what you're thinking?*

We can also use *would* with *dare*.

> *I **wouldn't dare (to) take** the risk.*
> ***Would** enough people really **dare (to) resist** armed troops?*

We use *How dare ...?* for an angry protest.

> *Just get lost, will you? ~ What! **How dare** you speak to me like that?*

NOTE

Americans normally use a to-infinitive with *dare*.

84 Modal verb + phrase

We cannot use two modal verbs together.

> (NOT ~~I might can get the day off.~~)

Instead we use a phrase like *be able to*, *be allowed to*, or *have to* after a modal verb.

> *I **might be able to** get the day off. I'll have to ask my boss.*
> *We aren't children, are we? We **ought to be allowed to** decide for ourselves.*
> *It won't be busy, so we **shouldn't have to** queue.*
> *In the old days people **used to have to** wash clothes by hand.*
> ***Will** you **be able to** find your way without a map?*

85 Overview: the use of modal verbs

Verb	Use	Example
can	Ability > 80A	*I **can** play the piano.*
	Opportunity > 80A	*We **can** watch TV in the evenings.*
	Request > 79B	***Can** you help me, please?*
	Offer of help > 79B	***Can** I help you?*
	Permission > 75	*You **can** go now.*
	Asking permission > 75A	***Can** I ask a question?*
	General possibility > 79D	*Maths **can** be fun.*
	Impossibility > 76B	*The story **can't** be true.*

Modal verbs

Verb	Use	Example
could	Past ability > 80	*I **could** play the piano when I was five*
	Possible ability > 80C	*If I had a camera, I **could** take a photo.*
	Suggestion > 79A	*We **could** meet later.*
	Request > 79B	***Could** you help me please?*
	Asking permission > 75A	***Could** I ask a question?*
	Past permission > 75C	*You **could** park here years ago.*
	Possibility > 79	*The plan **could** go wrong.*
must	Necessity > 71	*You **must** be careful.*
	Logical certainty > 76B,C	*You **must** be tired.*
need	When something is not necessary > 73	*We **needn't** hurry.*
should	The right thing to do > 74	*You **should** revise before the exam.*
	Probability > 77	*It **should** be fine tomorrow.*
ought	The right thing to do > 74	*You **ought to** revise before the exam.*
may	Possibility > 78	*The plan **may** go wrong.*
	Uncertain intention > 78A	*We **may** move house.*
	Permission > 75	***May** I ask a question?*
might	Possibility > 78	*The plan **might** go wrong.*
	Uncertain intention > 78A	*We **might** move house.*
	Request/criticism > 78C	*You **might** help me.*
will	The future > 54	*The post **will** be here soon.*
	Assumption > 76A	*The letter **will** be somewhere in this file.*
would	A possible situation > 81	*A holiday **would** be great.*
	A past refusal > 62B	*The doorman **wouldn't** let us in.*
	Looking forward from the past > 62B	*No one knew what **would** happen next.*
	Past habits > 82A	*Every weekend we **would** go to the cinema.*
shall	Asking what to do > 54E	*What **shall** we do?*
	The future > 54A	*I **shall** be away next week.*
dare	Being brave enough > 83	*I **didn't dare** climb up.*

The passive

86 Introduction

Compare the active and passive sentences.

>Active: *My brother **faxed** the document.*
>Passive: *The document **was faxed** by my brother.*

We can choose to talk about *my brother* and what he did, or about *the document* and what happened to it. The two structures have the same meaning but the focus is different. The choice between active and passive often depends on what is old or new information in the context. > 88A And the passive is sometimes more impersonal in style. > 88B

In the active sentence, the person doing the action (*my brother*) is the subject, and we use an active verb. In the passive sentence, the subject is what the action is directed at (*the document*), and we use a passive verb. A passive verb has a form of the auxiliary verb *be* (*was*) and a passive participle (*faxed*). Note that *the document* is the object of the active sentence and the subject of the passive sentence.

The person doing the action is called the agent. In a passive sentence, the agent can be added in a phrase with *by*.

>*The document was faxed **by my brother**.*

We can end a sentence with the passive verb and not mention the agent.

>*The document **was faxed**.*

The important information here is the method of sending the document. It was faxed, not sent through the post.

Although the passive is more typical of an impersonal style, it can also occur in conversation.

>*This house must be really old. ~ Yes, it **was built** in 1720.*

87 Passive verb forms

A Tenses

A passive verb has a form of *be* and a passive participle, e.g. *killed, cut.*

>*Lots of people **are killed** on the roads.*
>*The budget for the project **has been cut**.*
>*The drugs **will be destroyed**.*

Be is in the same tense as the equivalent active form.

>Active: *Accidents **kill** lots of people.* (present simple)
>Passive: *Lots of people **are killed**.* (present simple of *be* + participle)
>Active: *They**'ve cut** the budget.* (present perfect)
>Passive: *The budget **has been cut**.* (present perfect of *be* + participle)

The following verb tenses and future forms can be passive.

Active	Passive
Present simple	
*They **play** the game.*	*The game **is played**.*
Present continuous	
*They **are playing** the game.*	*The game **is being played**.*
Present perfect	
*They **have played** the game.*	*The game **has been played**.*
Past simple	
*They **played** the game.*	*The game **was played**.*
Past continuous	
*They **were playing** the game.*	*The game **was being played**.*
Past perfect	
*They **had played** the game.*	*The game **had been played**.*
Future	
*They **will play** the game.*	*The game **will be played**.*
*They **are going to play** the game.*	*The game **is going to be played**.*

We can use short forms.
> *Football is a very popular game. It's played all over the world.*
> *The prisoners are free. They've been released.*

B Negatives and questions

We use the auxiliary verb in the same way as we do in active sentences.
In the negative *not* comes after the first auxiliary.
> *Motorists **are not killed** by cyclists.*
> *The money still **hasn't been found**.*

In a question there is inversion of the subject and the (first) auxiliary.
> *__Has__ the money **been found**?*
> *When **was** the fax **sent**?*

C Modal verbs in the passive

We can use the passive with a modal verb (or a phrase like *used to* or *have to*).
The pattern is modal verb + *be* + passive participle.
> *Stamps **can be bought** at any post office.*
> *Animals **should** really **be seen** in their natural habitat.*
> *Many things that **used to be done** by hand are now done by machine.*

Negatives and questions are formed in the usual way.
> *Animals **shouldn't be kept** in cages.*
> *__Must__ everything always **be done** at the last minute?*
> *__Do__ meals **have to be prepared** every day?*

A modal verb can also go with the perfect and the passive together. The pattern is modal verb + *have been* + passive participle.
> *I can't find that leaflet. It **must have been thrown** away.*
> *They've found a play that **might have been written** by Shakespeare.*
> *This bill **ought to have been paid** weeks ago.*

For modal verbs, > 70.

D Phrasal and prepositional verbs in the passive

Some phrasal verbs and prepositional verbs can be used in the passive.
> *The building was **knocked down** last year.*
> *Has the doctor been **sent for**?*

The adverb or preposition (e.g. *down, for*) comes after the participle.

Note also verb + adverb + preposition, and verbal idioms with prepositions.
> *Such out-of-date practices should be **done away with**.*
> *The poor child is always being **made fun of**.*

E *Was broken*: action or state?

Was broken can be a passive verb form.
> *The vase **was broken** by a guest. He knocked it over.*

Here *the vase was broken* expresses an action. It is equivalent to *Someone broke the vase.*

We can sometimes use a participle such as *broken* before a noun, like an adjective.
> *There was a **broken** vase on the floor.*

We can also put the participle after *be*.
> *The vase **was broken**. It lay in pieces on the floor.*

Here *the vase was broken* expresses a state, not an action.

Compare these two examples.
> *The drugs **were hidden** in containers and then loaded onto the ship.*
> (passive verb expressing an action: someone hid the drugs)
> *The drugs **were hidden** in the ship, but the police didn't know where.*
> (be + participle expressing a state: the drugs were in a secret place)

88 The use of the passive

A Ordering information

One of these paragraphs is about the scientist J.J. Thomson, and the other is about the electron.

THOMSON, SIR JOSEPH JOHN
(1846-1940)
British physicist and mathematician and head of a group of researchers at the Cavendish Laboratory in Cambridge. Thomson discovered the electron. He is regarded as the founder of modern physics.

ELECTRON
A subatomic particle and one of the basic constituents of matter. The electron was discovered by J.J. Thomson. It is found in all atoms and contains the smallest known negative electrical charge.

Compare these two sentences, one from each paragraph.
  Thomson *discovered the electron.*
  The electron *was discovered by Thomson.*

The sentences have the same meaning, but they are about different things. The topic of the first sentence is *Thomson*, and the new information is that he discovered the electron. The topic of the second sentence is *the electron*, and the new information is that its discoverer was Thomson.

Here the choice of active or passive verb depends on the context. We usually structure the sentence in a way that enables us to start with old information and end with new. > 31–32 In the second sentence, we need to start with *the electron*, and so we use the passive.

B Typical contexts for the passive

We sometimes use the passive in speech, but it is more common in writing, especially in the impersonal style of textbooks and factual information.
  The paint is then pumped into a large tank, where it is thinned.
  Large numbers of slaves were transported to the New World.
  If sulphur is heated, a number of changes can be seen.
  Thousands of new jobs have been created.
Here we focus on the process of paint-thinning, the destination of the slaves, and so on, rather than on the people carrying out the actions.

The passive is also sometimes used in rules and to describe procedures.
  The service is provided under a contract.
  Your prize must be claimed by 31 December.
  Application should be made in writing.
The active equivalent *We provide the service* ..., *You must claim your prize* ..., *You should apply* ... is more friendly and less impersonal.

The passive also occurs in news reports.

A new health tax will be introduced next year.
Two people were killed in the accident.

TIP

Do not overuse the passive. Use it only when it fits the context and the
style. Remember that even in formal writing most clauses are active,
not passive.

C Verbs which cannot be passive

An intransitive verb (a verb without an object) cannot be passive. These
sentences have no passive equivalent.

*Something **happened**.*
*The problem will **become** more urgent.*
*We **stayed** at home.*
*The streets **seemed** empty.*

There are also some transitive verbs which cannot be passive, e.g. *have*
(= own), *lack, resemble,* and *suit* (= be right for). These are all state verbs.

*My friend **had** a sports car.* (NOT *A sports car was had by my friend.*)
*The player **lacks** ability.* (NOT *Ability is lacked by the player.*)
*That colour **suits** you.* (NOT *You're suited by that colour.*)

But other state verbs can be passive, e.g. *believe, contain, include, intend,*
know, like, love, mean, need, owe, own, understand, want.

*The business **is owned** by an American company.*
*These old postcards **are wanted** by collectors.*

Some verbs can be either action verbs or state verbs, e.g. *cost, fit, measure,*
weigh, > 51B. They can be passive only when they are action verbs.

Action & active: *The decorator **measured** the wall.*
Action & passive: *The wall **was measured** by the decorator.*
State: *The wall **measured** three metres.*
                  (BUT NOT *Three metres was measured by the wall.*)

D The passive and *you, we, they,* etc

The passive is used less in informal English than in formal or written contexts. In informal English we often use an active sentence with a vague subject like *you, we, they, people,* or *someone.*

Active: ***You** can't do anything about it.* (*you* = people in general > 176)
Passive: *Nothing can be done about it.*
Active: ***We/People** use electricity for all kinds of purposes.*
Passive: *Electricity is used for all kinds of purposes.*
Active: ***They**'re building some new houses.*
Passive: *Some new houses are being built.*
Active: ***Someone** has taken down the poster.*
Passive: *The poster has been taken down.*

In the passive sentences we do not need to mention *you, we,* etc when they have this vague meaning.

NOTE
We can also use *one,* although its use is limited. > 176A
*   ***One** can't do anything about it.*

89 The agent in passive sentences

A

When we need to mention the agent in a passive sentence, we use a phrase with *by.*

*Hercule Poirot was created **by Agatha Christie.***
*The land has been bought **by a property developer.***
*The submarine is powered **by nuclear energy.***

Here the agents – *Agatha Christie, a property developer* and *nuclear energy* – are the new information we are focussing on.

B

But often we do not need to include the agent in a passive sentence. Other kinds of information can come at the end of the sentence.

*The dark side of the moon was first seen **in 1959.***
*The reception will be held **at the Manor Hotel.***
*Plugs should be wired **correctly.***

We mention the agent only if we need to mention it. We do not mention it if it is not relevant.

A large number of Sherlock Holmes films have been made.
The atom was regarded as solid until the electron was discovered in 1897.
The drugs were destroyed.

The people who made the films, discovered the electron and destroyed the drugs are not relevant to the message. The first two examples are about the **number** of films and the **time** of the discovery. The last example is about what happened to the drugs, not when or where it happened or who did it.

Sometimes we do not know the identity of the agent.

My car was stolen.

The phrase *by a thief* would add no information.

Sometimes we do not need to mention the agent because it is obvious.

A new government has been elected.

The phrase *by the voters* would add no information because we know that governments are elected by voters.

Sometimes we do not mention the agent because we do not want to.

Mistakes have been made.

This use of the passive without an agent is a way of not saying who is responsible. Compare the active *I/We have made mistakes.*

90 The passive with *get*

A We sometimes form the passive with *get* rather than with *be*.

*We **get paid** monthly.*

*The booklet **got thrown** out with the rubbish.*

*The leaves **were getting blown** about by the wind.*

We use the passive with *get* mainly in informal English, and it has a more limited use than *be*. We can use it to talk about good or bad things happening to someone or something.

*Luckily I **got accepted** at art school.*

*The flower display **got vandalized**.*

'Bad things' can be accidents.

*Lots of people **get killed** on the roads, unfortunately.*

*The vase **got broken** when we moved house.*

This pattern with *get* can also refer to something happening incidentally, as part of a larger operation.

*The dustbin **gets emptied** once a week.*

*Everyone **got moved** to a new office during the reorganization.*

But we do not use *get* for a major, planned action.

*The railways **were privatized** 20 years ago.*

(NOT *The railways got privatized 20 years ago.*)

In simple tenses we use *do* in negatives and questions.

*I forgot to leave the dustbin out, so it **didn't get emptied**.*

*How often **do** people **get injured** playing rugby?*

B We also use *get* + passive participle in some idiomatic expressions.

*We didn't even have time to **get washed**. (= wash ourselves)*

*Simon **got married** last year. (= married someone)*

Such expressions include *get washed, get shaved, get (un)dressed, get changed* (= change your clothes); *get engaged, get married, get divorced; get started* (= start); and *get lost* (= lose your way).

We can also use some of these verbs in the active without an object.

*There wasn't much time to **wash** and **change**.*

Here *wash* means the same as *get washed*. Verbs that occur in both patterns are *wash, shave, (un)dress, change; marry, divorce;* and *start*.

NOTE
a   *Get* can be followed by a participle used as an adjective.
> *After a while I **got interested** in the film, but then the doorbell rang.*
> (= After a while I **became interested** in the film.)
> Other words in this pattern are *bored, confused, fed up, involved, stuck,* and *tired.*

b   With *engaged,* we can use either *get* or *become.*
> *We've just **got/become** engaged.*

91 The passive with *give, send,* etc

A In the active, *give* can have two objects. > 6
> *The nurse gives **the patient a sleeping pill**.*

Either of these objects can be the subject of a passive sentence.
> ***A sleeping pill** is given to the patient.*
> ***The patient** is given a sleeping pill.*

We can use other verbs in these patterns, e.g. *send, offer, award.* > C

B Compare these two sentences.
> *£5 million damages were awarded to a recent accident victim.*
> *A recent accident victim was awarded £5 million damages.*

The choice of structure depends on the context – for example, whether we are talking about a sum of damages and who received it, or about an accident victim and how he/she was compensated. > 88A

C It is quite usual in English for the person receiving something to be the subject. Here are some more examples.
> ***The chairman** was handed a note.*   *I've been offered a job.*
> ***We** were told all the details.*   ***The residents** will be found new homes.*

Here are some verbs that we can use in this pattern.

allow	*feed*	*leave*	*pay*	*show*
ask	*find*	(in a will)	*promise*	*teach*
award	*give*	*lend*	*refuse*	*tell*
charge	*grant*	*offer*	*sell*	
deny	*hand*	*owe*	*send*	

92 The passive with verbs of reporting

With verbs of reporting there are two special passive patterns.

Active: ***People say** / **They say** that elephants have good memories.*
Passive with *it*:   *It is said that elephants have good memories.*
Passive with
to-infinitive: *Elephants **are said to** have good memories.*

A *It is said* ...

Some verbs can occur in the pattern *it* + passive verb + that-clause.
It is thought that the stone houses are 5,000 years old.
It was reported that the army was crossing the frontier.
It has been shown that the theory is correct.
It is proposed that the industry should be privatized.

We often use these verbs:

accept	believe	estimate	imply	propose	say
agree	claim	expect	intend	realize	see
allege	conclude	feel	know	recognize	show
announce	consider	fear	note	recommend	state
anticipate	decide	find	notice	report	suggest
argue	discover	hold	observe	reveal	think
assume	envisage	hope	predict	rumour	understand

B ... *said to be* ...

We can also use the pattern: subject + passive verb + to-infinitive.
The stone houses are thought to be 5,000 years old.
United were expected to win easily, but they lost.
The film was felt to lack excitement.

We can use these verbs:

allege	declare	find	presume	say	think
assume	discover	intend	prove	see	understand
believe	estimate	know	report	show	
claim	expect	mean	reveal	state	
consider	feel	observe	rumour	suppose	

The to-infinitive can also be continuous, perfect, or passive.
The army was reported to be crossing the frontier.
The prisoner is known to have behaved violently in the past.
The disease was thought to be spread by mosquitoes.
It can be both perfect and passive.
Twelve people are believed to have been killed in the accident.

We can use the subject *there* with *to be*.
There is considered to be no chance of the bill becoming law.

The passive verb can have a modal verb, e.g. *can, must.*
The company can hardly be said to be prospering.
The rumour must be assumed to be false.

NOTE
Agree, decide, and *propose* can come in pattern A with *it* and a that-clause.
It was agreed that the committee should appoint a press secretary.
A typical use is to report what was said in a meeting.
We can also use the same three verbs in the pattern *it* + passive verb + to-infinitive.
It was agreed to appoint a press secretary.
We can use this pattern only with *agree, decide,* and *propose.*

C The agent with verbs of reporting

In both the patterns A and B, we can include the agent in a phrase with *by*.
*It was reported **by CNN** that the army was crossing the frontier.*
*The film was felt **by audiences** to lack excitement.*
Here the agent comes next to the verb it relates to (*reported by CNN, felt by audiences*).

93 Passive verb + to-infinitive or active participle

A Infinitive

Some patterns with a verb + object + to-infinitive have a passive equivalent.
Active: *Police advise drivers to use an alternative route.*
Passive: *Drivers **are advised to use** an alternative route.*

We can use this passive pattern with verbs like *tell, ask, persuade, warn,* and *advise,* > 105B; and verbs like *force* and *allow,* > 105C.

Now look at this pair of sentences.
Active: *The terrorists made the hostages lie down.*
Passive: *The hostages **were made to lie** down.*

In the passive we always use a to-infinitive (*to lie*) even if in the active the infinitive is without *to*. This happens after *make* and after verbs of perception such as *see*.
Active: *The detective saw the woman put the jewellery in her bag.*
Passive: *The woman **was seen to put** the jewellery in her bag.*

We can use *let* in the active pattern but not in the passive, where we use *allow* instead.
Active: *They **let** the hostages **rest**./They **allowed** the hostages **to rest**.*
Passive: *The hostages **were allowed to rest**.*

We can also use a finite clause after *is told, was asked,* etc, but not after *make* or after verbs like *force* or *allow*.
Drivers are advised that an alternative route should be used.
BUT *Drivers are forced to use an alternative route.*
(NOT ~~Drivers are forced that an alternative route should be used.~~)

NOTE
For the passive to-infinitive, > 95.
*There is an alternative route **to be used** by goods vehicles.*

B Participle

Some patterns with a verb + object + active participle have a passive
equivalent.

Active: *The detective saw the woman putting the jewellery in her bag.*
Passive: *The woman **was seen putting** the jewellery in her bag.*
Active: *The officials kept us waiting for half an hour.*
Passive: *We **were kept waiting** for half an hour.*
Active: *We spend too much time arguing over little details.*
Passive: *Too much time **is spent arguing** over little details.*

We can use the passive pattern with verbs of perception (e.g. *see*) and with
catch, discover, find, keep, leave, lose, spend, and *waste.*

NOTE
For *I saw the jewellery **being put** in the bag,* > 125C.

94 Some patterns with *have* and *get*

A The active: *have/get* + object + infinitive

This pattern means 'cause someone to do something'.
  *I **had** the garage **service** my car.*
  *I **got** the garage **to service** my car.*
After *have* we use an infinitive without *to*, and after *get* we use a to-infinitive.
This active pattern with *have* is more common in the US than in Britain,
where it is rather formal. *Get* is informal.

B The passive: *have/get something done*

This pattern means 'cause something to be done'.
  *I **had** my car **serviced**.*
  *I **got** my car **serviced**.*
This means that I arranged for someone, for example a garage, to service my
car; I did not service it myself. We use this pattern mainly to talk about
professional services to a customer. Both forms are used in Britain and in the
US. *Have* is neutral, and *get* is a little informal.
  *You should **have/get** the job **done** professionally.*
  *I **had/got** the machine **repaired** only last week.*
  *We**'re having**/We**'re getting** a new kitchen **fitted**.*
  *Where did you **have/get** your hair **cut**?*
Both *have* and *get* are ordinary verbs which can be continuous (*are having/
are getting*). In simple-tense negatives and questions we use *do*
(*did ... have/get ...?*).

Compare the two patterns with *had*.
  *Have something done: We **had** a burglar alarm **fitted** (by a security
                      company) last year.*
  Past perfect: *We **had fitted** a burglar alarm (ourselves) some
                      time previously.*

131

We can also use *get* informally when we are talking about a job we do ourselves.

*I must **get** my homework **done**.* (= I must do my homework.)
*We finally **got** everything **packed** into suitcases.* (= We packed the suitcases.)

C *Have something happen*

This pattern has the same form as *have something done* in B. We use it to say that we experience something, often something unpleasant.

*We **had** a window **broken** in the storm.*
*My sister **has had** some money **stolen**.*

95 The passive to-infinitive and gerund

Look at these forms of the verb *play*.

	Active	Passive
To-infinitive:	*to play*	*to be played*
Perfect to-infinitive:	*to have played*	*to have been played*
Gerund:	*playing*	*being played*
Perfect gerund:	*having played*	*having been played*

Each passive form ends with a passive participle (*played*).

Here are some examples of the passive forms.

To-infinitive:	*I expect **to be invited** to the wedding.*
	*It's awful **to be criticized** in public.*
	*I want this place **to be tidied** up by the time I get back.*
Perfect to-infinitive:	*The fire seems **to have been caused** by an electrical fault.*
	*I want this place **to have been tidied** up by the time I get back.*
Gerund:	***Being searched** by customs officers is unpleasant.*
	*Let's not risk **being arrested** for spying.*
Perfect gerund:	*I'm annoyed at **having been made** a fool of.*
	*There is no record of any message **having been sent**.*

After a preposition we can use a gerund but not an infinitive. > 114

NOTE
We can sometimes use *get* instead of *be* with the passive forms.
*I don't expect **to get invited** to the wedding.*
*Let's not risk **getting arrested** for spying.*

96 Active forms with a passive meaning

A Gerund

The active gerund can sometimes have a passive meaning. This happens after *need* or *want* (= need).

> *The room needed **decorating**.* (= The room needed to be decorated.)
> *This bike wants **cleaning**.* (= This bike needs to be cleaned.)

Want in this sense of 'need' is informal.

We cannot use the passive gerund here.

> (NOT *The room needed being decorated*.)

B To-infinitive

We sometimes use an active to-infinitive when we are talking about jobs we have to do.

> *We had the living-room **to decorate**.*
> *I've got some homework **to do**.*

When the subject of the sentence (*We, I*) is the agent (the person doing the job), then we use the active infinitive, not the passive.

If the subject of the sentence is NOT the agent, we use the passive infinitive.

> *The living-room had **to be decorated**.*
> *The homework is **to be done** by tomorrow.*

After the subject *there*, we can use either an active or a passive infinitive.

> *There were several rooms **to decorate** / **to be decorated**.*
> *There's quite a lot of homework **to do** / **to be done**.*

But when we talk about leisure activities, we normally use the active.

> *There are lots of exciting things **to do** here.*

After an adjective, the infinitive is usually active.

> *This machine isn't **safe to use**.*
> *The piano is too **heavy to move**.*
> *That box isn't **strong** enough **to sit on**.*

If we use a phrase with *by* and the agent, then the infinitive is passive.

> *The piano is too heavy **to be moved by one person**.*
> (=The piano is too heavy for one person to move.)

C Main verbs

A few verbs can be used in the active form with a passive meaning.

> *Her latest record **is selling** in huge numbers.* (= It is being sold...)
> *This sentence **doesn't read** quite right.* (= When it is read, it isn't right.)
> *This sweater **washes** all right in warm water.* (= It can be washed ...)

The infinitive

97 Introduction

A There are two kinds of infinitive – with *to* and without *to*.
Infinitive with *to*: *I'd prefer **to sit** at the back.*
Infinitive without *to*: *I'd rather **sit** at the back.*
Whether we use *to* or not depends on the grammatical structure. For
example, we use *to* after *prefer* but not after *would rather.*

The most common use of an infinitive without *to* is after a modal verb,
e.g. *can.* > 70B
*I **can sit** at the back.*
For more on the infinitive without *to*, > 110. The rest of this chapter is about
infinitives with *to*, often referred to as to-infinitives.

B A to-infinitive can have a perfect or continuous form.
Simple: *to play*
Perfect: *to have played*
Continuous: *to be playing*
Perfect and continuous: *to have been playing*

We use a perfect infinitive for something that happened (or possibly
happened) earlier.
*I seem **to have left** my umbrella behind.*
*The man was relieved **to have survived** the accident.*
In this last example the man's survival happened before his feeling of relief.
We cannot use a past form.
(NOT ~~I seem to left it behind.~~)

We use a continuous infinitive for something happening over a period.
*You're lucky **to be living** in such a nice place.*
*We were happy **to be starting** on a new adventure.*
*The man was unsteady on his feet. He appeared to **have been drinking**.*

In the negative, *not* comes before the infinitive.
*I'd prefer **not to sit** at the front.*
*The two lovers pretended **not to have met** before.*

NOTE
a   In some contexts we can use a simple to-infinitive as well as a perfect or continuous
form.
*We expect **to complete/to have completed** the work by the summer.*
*We hope **to make/to be making** a start soon.*

b   With some expressions such as *would like, would hate,* and *would be nice/awful,* we
can also use the perfect in either or both clauses when talking about the past.
*I'd **like to have seen** the show last week.*
*I'd **have liked to see** the show last week.*
*I'd **have liked to have seen** the show last week.*

c   For the passive infinitive, e.g. *to be played,* > 95.

98 Infinitive clauses

A An infinitive can be followed by an object or complement and/or by one or more adverbials. The infinitive together with such phrases is called an infinitive clause.

*A sightseeing tour is the best way **to see the city**.* (infinitive + object)
*I'd prefer **to sit at the back**.* (infinitive + adverbial)

An infinitive clause can be just an infinitive without an object or adverbial.

*We decided **to leave**.*

NOTE
An adverbial usually goes after the infinitive or after the object if there is one.
*I didn't expect you to change your mind **suddenly**.*
Often a one-word adverb can also go before the to-infinitive or between *to* and the verb.
*I didn't expect you **suddenly** to change your mind.*
*I didn't expect you to **suddenly** change your mind.*
This last example is sometimes called a 'split infinitive' because the infinitive *to change* is split by the word *suddenly*. A few people think this is incorrect, but in fact it has become common usage, and there is no need to avoid it.
*At last we've got a chance to **really** relax.*
*Remember to **always** keep your design simple.*

B In an infinitive clause, a preposition comes in its normal place, often after a verb or adjective.

*It isn't enough money to live **on**.*
*There's nothing to get excited **about**.*
*I need a vase to put these flowers **in**.*

NOTE
In more formal English we can sometimes begin a clause with a preposition and relative pronoun.
*It is hardly enough money **on which** to live.*

99 The to-infinitive with *it*, as subject, and as complement

A We often use a pattern with *it* as the subject and an infinitive clause at or near the end of the sentence.

*It seems rude **to turn down the invitation**.*
*It is a great mistake **not to take a holiday now and then**.*
*It takes ages **to defrost this fridge**.*

We can sometimes use a to-infinitive clause as a subject, but this is less frequent than the pattern with *it*.

***To turn down the invitation** seems rude.*
***Not to take a holiday now and then** is a great mistake.*

NOTE
A gerund as subject is more usual than an infinitive.
***Defrosting this fridge** takes ages.*

135

B A to-infinitive clause can be a complement after *be*.
> *My great ambition is **to emigrate to Australia**.*
> *The important thing is **not to panic**.*
> *The idea was **to give everyone a nice surprise**.*

100 The to-infinitive used as an adverbial

A to-infinitive clause can function as an adverbial. It can express ideas such as purpose or outcome.

A Purpose

A to-infinitive clause can express purpose.
> *My friend has gone to town **to do some shopping**.*
> *I am writing **to enquire about activity holidays**.*
> ***To get a good seat** you need to arrive early.*

For other ways of expressing purpose, > 240.

In the negative we cannot use a simple to-infinitive.
(NOT *We came in quietly not to disturb you.*)

Instead we use *so as* or *so that*.
> *We came in quietly **so as not to** disturb you*
> *We came in quietly **so that** we **wouldn't** disturb you.*

After *so that* we use a finite clause.

NOTE
In informal British English we use *go and/come and* rather than *go to/come to* before a verb.
> *Let's **go and have** a cup of coffee.*
> ***Come and take** a look at this.*

Americans say *Let's go have a cup of coffee.*

B Outcome

We can sometimes use a to-infinitive clause to express the outcome of an action or process.
> *Laura came home **to find her house on fire**.*
> *The prince grew up **to be a handsome young man**.*

We can put *only* before the to-infinitive to express the idea that effort has been wasted.
> *We all arrived for the concert **only to find** it had been cancelled.*
> *Smith beat the goalkeeper **only to see** his shot hit the post.*

C Comment

An infinitive clause can also express a comment on the speaker's honesty.
> ***To be frank**, you didn't make a very good impression.*
> *I'm a bit tired of sightseeing, **to tell you the truth**.*

We can also use *to be (perfectly) honest* and *to put it bluntly*.

D *To hear ... / To see ...*

We can use a clause with *to hear* or *to see* to explain why something could give you the wrong idea.

> **To hear him talk**, *you'd think he was God's gift to women.*
> **To see her walking around in her old clothes**, *you'd never guess she owned a multi-million pound business.*

101 Verb + to-infinitive or verb + gerund?

A We can use a to-infinitive after certain verbs.

> *I* **decided to take** *a bus.*
> *People will* **refuse to pay** *the new tax.*
> *I'm* **planning to visit** *India next year.*
> *We* **hope to be moving** *into our new flat soon.*
> *We* **expect to have completed** *the work by the summer.*

Other verbs take a gerund,

> *I* **suggested taking** *a bus.*
> *People will* **resent paying** *the new tax.*
> *I'm* **considering visiting** *India next year.*

There are some verbs which take both forms: they can be followed by either a to-infinitive or a gerund, > 103. But many verbs can be followed by only one of the forms. It is difficult or impossible to give rules about which verbs take a to-infinitive and which take a gerund; they all have to be learned individually.

B We can use more than one to-infinitive or gerund together, or a combination of the two.

> *You need* **to prepare to answer** *some awkward questions.*
> *I refuse* **to risk losing** *so much money.*
> *Jane was considering* **offering to help** *the refugees.*

For more information about infinitives and gerunds with other clauses, > 229.

C Here is a list of some common verbs + to-infinitive.

afford > 102G	*consent* (= agree)	*hesitate*	*prove* > 102A
agree > 102E	*dare* > 83	*hope*	*refuse*
aim	*decide*	*learn*	*seek* (= try)
appear > 102A	*decline* (= refuse)	*long* > 102B	*seem* > 102A
arrange	*demand*	*look* > 102C	*tend* > 102A
ask > 102F	*desire* > 102B	*manage*	*threaten*
attempt (= try)	*be dying* > 102B	*need* > 104I	*turn out* > 102A
be > 58A–B	*expect*	*offer*	*used* > 82
beg	*fail*	*ought* > 74A	*volunteer*
care (= like) >102H	*be going* > 55	*plan*	*vote*
choose	*happen* > 102A	*prepare*	*can't wait*
claim	*have* > 71	*pretend*	*want* > 102B
come > 102A	*help* > 102D	*promise*	*wish* > 102B

Here is a list of some common verbs + gerund.

admit	*enjoy*	*justify*	*resist*
allow > 102I	*can't face*	*keep*	*report* > 102F
avoid	*fancy* > 102B	*keep on*	*resent*
consider	*finish*	*mind* > 102H	*resume*
delay	*give up*	*miss*	*risk*
deny	*can't help*	*postpone*	*suggest*
detest (= hate)	*imagine*	*practise*	
dislike	*involve*	*quit*	

NOTE
Sometimes a to-infinitive comes after a passive verb.
*You **were warned to take** care.*
The equivalent active pattern is verb + object + to-infinitive.
*I **warned you to take** care.*
For more details about these patterns, > 105.

102 Verb + to-infinitive or gerund: more details

A A special group of verbs which take a to-infinitive are *appear, come, happen, prove, seem, tend,* and *turn out.*
*The plane **seemed to be losing** height.*
(The plane was **apparently** losing height.)
*We **happened to meet** in the street.*
(We met **by chance** in the street.)
*The couple **came to accept** the death of their son.*
(The couple **finally** accepted the death of their son.)
*Rich people **tend to live** longer.*
(Rich people **usually** live longer.)
Here the to-infinitive expresses what happened, and the verb before it says something about the truth of the statement (e.g. how sure we are that the plane is losing height) or about the manner or time of the action (e.g. how quickly the couple accepted the death of their son).

The object of the to-infinitive can be the subject of a passive sentence.
Active: *Someone seems to have stolen **my computer**.*
Passive: ***My computer** seems to have been stolen.*

We can use an empty subject *it* before *appear, happen, seem, turn out.* > 36C
***It seemed** that the plane was losing height.*
We use a that-clause after *it* + verb.

B *Want* + to-infinitive is a common pattern. *Wish* and *desire* are more formal.
 *Does anyone **want to say** anything?*
 *Does anyone **wish to make** a comment?*
Be dying to and *long to* are more emphatic.
 *I'm **dying to open** this parcel. I can't wait.*
Fancy + gerund is informal.
 *Do you **fancy going** out somewhere?*

C *Look* + to-infinitive can mean the same as 'seem' or 'appear'.
 *With profits sharply down, the company **looks to be** in trouble.*
In the continuous form it can mean 'aim to'.
 *United are **looking to return** to the top of the table.*

D After *help* we can leave out *to*.
 *We all **helped** (**to**) **put** up the tent.*

E We can use *agree* with a to-infinitive but not *accept*.
 *My friend **agreed to pay** half the cost.*
 *My friend **accepted that he should pay** half the cost.*
 (NOT *My friend accepted to pay half the cost.*)

F We can use a to-infinitive after *ask*.
 *The customer **asked to see** the manager.*
Usually there is an object between *ask* and the to-infinitive. > 105B
 *The customer **asked the manager to sort** the problem out.*

We use a gerund after *report*.
 *Witnesses **reported seeing** the aircraft burst into flames.*

G We use *afford* (= have enough money or time for) after *can/could* or *be able to*,
often in a negative sentence or a question.
 *I **can't afford to buy** a house.* *Will we **be able to afford to go** to Peru?*

H We use *mind* + gerund and *care* + to-infinitive mainly in a negative sentence
or a question.
 *I don't **mind walking** if it's fine.*
 *Would you **care to come** along with us?*
Would you care to …? is a formal way of saying *Would you like to …?*

I *Allow* takes a gerund.
 *They don't **allow sunbathing** here.*
But when it has an object, *allow* takes a to-infinitive.
 *They don't **allow you to sunbathe** here.*
And *be allowed* takes a to-infinitive.
 *You aren't **allowed to sunbathe** here.*

103 Verbs taking either a to-infinitive or a gerund

A Sometimes the choice of to-infinitive or gerund after a verb depends on the meaning, > 104. But some verbs can take either a to-infinitive or a gerund with almost no difference in meaning.

*I **hate to leave**/**hate leaving** everything to the last minute.*
*We **intend to take**/**intend taking** immediate action.*
*It suddenly **started to rain**/**started raining**.*

These verbs are: *begin, bother, can't bear, cease, commence, continue, hate, intend, like, love, prefer, propose, can't stand,* and *start*.

But with these verbs we normally avoid using two ing-forms together.

*The spectators were already **beginning to arrive**.*
(NOT *The spectators were already beginning arriving*.)

After *begin, continue,* and *start,* a state verb usually has the to-infinitive form.

*I soon **began to understand** what the problems were.*

NOTE

a *Cease* (= stop) and *commence* (= begin) are formal.

b We normally use *bother* in a negative sentence or a question.
   ***Don't bother to wash** up. | **Don't bother** washing up.*
   ***Why** should we **bother** to call / **bother** calling a meeting if no one will come to it?*

B *Like, love,* and *hate* take either a to-infinitive or a gerund.

*I **like to cook**. / I **like cooking**.*
*Kate **hates to travel** / **hates travelling** on buses.*

The gerund is more usual when we are talking about the pleasure or displeasure we feel when doing something.

Like takes a to-infinitive when it means that we do something because it is a good idea rather than a pleasure.

*I **like to keep** all these papers in order.*

Would like, would love, and *would hate* normally take a to-infinitive.

*Our guest **would like to say** a few words to you.*
*We'**d love to go** on a cruise.*

TIP
Use *like* + gerund to talk about the things people enjoy.
***Do** you **like playing** tennis? ∼ Yes, I do. I really enjoy it.*
Use *would like* + to-infinitive to say what you want to do or to make suggestions or invitations.
***Would** you **like to play** tennis? ∼ Yes, OK. Let's have a game.*

104 Verb + to-infinitive/gerund with a change in meaning

The to-infinitive and gerund have different meanings after these verbs: *remember, forget* (> A), *regret* (> B), *dread* (> C), *try* (> D), *stop* (> E), *mean* (> F), *get* (> G), *go on* (> H), *need, want,* and *deserve* (> I).

A We use *remember* and *forget* with a to-infinitive to talk about necessary actions and whether we do them or not.
> Did you **remember to turn** off the computer?
> You **forgot to sign** the cheque. ~ Oh, sorry.

We use a gerund with *remember* and *forget* to talk about memories.
> I can **remember waking** up in the middle of the night.
> I'll never **forget breaking** down on the motorway. It was awful.

B We use *regret* + to-infinitive when we are giving bad news.
> We **regret to inform** you that your application has been unsuccessful.

We use a gerund to express regret about the past.
> I **regret wasting** / I **regret having wasted** so much time last year.

C We use *dread* + to-infinitive mainly in *I dread to think* / *I dread to imagine.*
> I **dread to think** what might happen to you all alone in the big city.

We use a gerund for something that makes us afraid.
> I always **dreaded being kissed** by my aunts.

D *Try* + to-infinitive means to do your best to achieve something.
> I'm **trying to light** a fire, but the wood won't burn.

Try + gerund means to do something to see if it will solve the problem.
> You could **try pouring** some petrol on to make it burn.

NOTE
In informal English we can use *try and* instead of *try to.*
> Let's **try and move** the cupboard away from the wall.

E After *stop* we can use a to-infinitive of purpose. > 100A
> At the services the driver **stopped to buy** a newspaper.

Stop + gerund means to end an action.
> You'd better **stop dreaming** and get on with some work.

F *Mean* + to-infinitive has the sense of 'intend' or 'plan'.
> I'm sorry. I didn't **mean to step** on your foot.

Here *mean* has a personal subject (*I*).

Mean + gerund means 'involve'. It expresses the idea that a situation creates the need for a particular action.
> I have to be at the airport by eight o'clock. It **means getting** up early.

Here *mean* has an impersonal subject (*it*).

141

G *Get* + to-infinitive means to get an opportunity to do something or to succeed in doing it.

> *I hope I can **get to speak** to the President.*
> *The kids **got to ride** on a steam engine.*

But *get* + gerund means 'start'.

> *It's half past seven. We'd better **get going**.*
> *Once you two **get talking**, no one else can get a word in.*

Get is rather informal.

H *Go on* + to-infinitive means to do something different, to do the next thing.

> *After receiving the award, the actor **went on to thank** all the people who had helped him in his career.*

Go on + gerund means to continue doing something.

> *The band **went on playing** even after everyone had left.*

We can also say *The band **kept** on playing*.

I We can use *need*, *want*, and *deserve* with a to-infinitive.

> *We **need to leave** at eight.*
> *Amy **wants to use** the computer.*
> *After all your hard work you **deserve to succeed**.*

A gerund after these verbs has a passive meaning. > 96A

> *All these figures **need/want checking**.*

105 Verb + object + to-infinitive

A Introduction

Some verbs can take an object and a to-infinitive.

> *Simon **wants you to ring** him on his mobile.*
> *We **asked the teacher not to give** us any homework.*
> *I **expected Tim to meet** me at the airport.*

The object of the verb (*you*, *the teacher*, *Tim*) also functions as the subject of the to-infinitive. For example, *Tim* is the subject of *to meet*.

NOTE
Compare the infinitive with and without a subject.

> *I **expected Tim to meet** me.* (= I expected that Tim would meet me.)
> *I **expected to meet** Tim.* (= I expected that I would meet Tim.)

In the sentence *I expected to meet Tim*, the subject of the to-infinitive is understood to be the same as the subject of the sentence (*I*).

B Verbs meaning 'order', 'request', etc

*The doctor **told** Julie to stay in bed.*
*We **persuaded** our neighbours to turn the music down.*
*Why did you all **leave** me to clear up on my own?*
These verbs include: *advise, ask, beg, challenge, command, encourage, instruct, invite, leave, order, persuade, remind, request, tell, trust, urge, warn.*

We cannot use *suggest* in this pattern. We have to use a finite clause.
We suggested (to our neighbours) that they should turn the music down.

With verbs meaning 'order', 'request', etc, the main clause can be passive.
***Our neighbours were persuaded** to turn the music down.*

C Verbs meaning 'cause', 'help', etc

*The crisis has **forced** the government to act.*
*My laptop **enables** me to work on the train.*
We can use these verbs: *allow, assist, authorize, cause, compel, drive, enable, entitle, forbid, force, get, help, inspire, intend, lead, mean, oblige, pay, permit, provoke, require, teach, tempt, train.*

The main clause can be passive.
***The government has been forced** to act.*
But *cause* and *get* cannot be passive before an infinitive.

After most verbs we can use *there* as the subject of the to-infinitive clause. It is rather formal.
*The regulations **permit there to be** no more than 200 people in the hall.*

For *get* in this pattern, > 94A.
*I **got** someone to lend me an electric drill.*

After *help* we can leave out *to*.
*I'm **helping** my friend **(to) find** a flat.*

D Verbs meaning 'say', 'think', 'show', etc

*A brief examination **revealed** the picture to be a fake.*
*The police **believed** a rival drugs gang to have committed the crime.*
We can use these verbs: *announce, assume, believe, consider, declare, discover, estimate, expect, feel, find, imagine, judge, know, presume, prove, reveal, show, suppose, suspect, take (= assume), understand.*

This pattern is rather formal. A finite clause is more usual.
*The police believed that a rival drugs gang **had committed** the crime.*

If we use a to-infinitive, the passive pattern is more common.
*A rival drugs gang **was believed** to have committed the crime.*
*The theory **has been proved** to be incorrect.*
The verb *say* is used only in the passive pattern.
*The party **is said** to be split on the issue.*
For more details about verbs of reporting in this pattern, > 92B.

We can sometimes leave out *to be*, especially after *believe, consider, declare,* and *find*.

> *The country declared itself (**to be**) independent.*

We can use *consider* but not *regard*.

> *We consider ourselves (**to be**) a separate nation.*
> *We regard ourselves **as** a separate nation.*

We can use *there* as the subject of the to-infinitive clause. It is rather formal.

> *We understood **there to be** money available for the project.*

E Verbs meaning 'want', '(dis)like', 'need', etc

> *We **want** everyone to enjoy themselves.*
> *I'd **like** you to tell me the whole story.*

We can use these verbs: *can't bear, (would) hate, (would) like, (would) love, need, (would) prefer, want, wish.*

We cannot use a finite clause after *hate, like, love,* or *want*.

> (NOT *We want that everyone enjoys themselves.*)

But after *can't bear, hate, like, love,* and *prefer,* we can use *it when* or *it if* and a finite clause.

> *I **hate it when** you ignore me.*
> *My aunt would **love it if** we took her out for a drive.*

Some of these verbs can take an object + gerund. > 113E

> *I **hate you looking** at me like that.*

The main clause cannot be passive.

> (NOT *Everyone is wanted to enjoy themselves.*)

We can use *there* as the subject of the to-infinitive clause. It is rather formal.

> *We'd prefer **there to be** an adult in charge.*

106 Adjective + to-infinitive

A The pattern *It is easy to answer the question*

A common pattern is *it* + linking verb + adjective + to-infinitive clause.

> *It was **good to see** you again.*
> *It is **difficult to describe** colours precisely.*
> *It felt **strange to be watched** by so many people.*
> *It'll be **safer to copy** the data to disk.*

There are many different adjectives that we can use in this pattern. They include: *convenient, correct, dangerous, difficult, easy, exciting, expensive, foolish, good, great, hard, important, impossible, interesting, necessary, nice, possible, right, safe, silly, simple, strange,* and *wrong.*

B The pattern *The question is easy to answer*

Here we understand *the question* as the object of *to answer*.
*Colours are **difficult to describe** precisely.*
*Is gas **cheaper to cook** with than electricity?*

The adjectives that we can use in this pattern are fewer than those in pattern A. They include *cheap, dangerous, difficult, easy, expensive, hard, impossible,* and *safe*.

We can use *impossible* but not *possible*.
*It is **impossible to solve** the puzzle. / The puzzle is **impossible to solve**.*
*It is **possible to solve** the puzzle.*
(BUT NOT *The puzzle is possible to solve*).

We do not use an object in the to-infinitive clause.
(NOT *Colours are difficult to describe them.*)
(NOT *Is gas cheaper to cook with it than electricity?*)

C The pattern *It is an easy question to answer*

In this pattern the to-infinitive comes after an adjective + noun.
*It's a **difficult** colour **to describe**.*
*That was a **silly** thing **to do**, wasn't it?*
We can use most of the adjectives listed in A.

D *Too* and *enough*

We can use *too* or *enough* in patterns A and B.
*It would be **too expensive to stay** in a hotel.*
*The streets aren't **safe enough to walk** along at night.*
Too comes before the adjective, and *enough* comes after it.

There are many other adjectives we can use with *too* and *enough*, besides those listed in A and B.
*The coffee was **too hot to drink**.*
*This rucksack isn't **big enough to get** everything in.*

When we use *too* in pattern C, we put *a* after the adjective.
*It was simply **too good an** opportunity **to miss**.*
But when we use *enough*, we put *a* in its usual place, before the adjective.
*It's **a big enough** vehicle **to get** a whole volleyball team in.*

E The pattern *I am happy to answer the question*

Here the subject of the main clause is often a person, e.g. *we, the boss*.
*We were **sorry to hear** your bad news.*
*The boss seems **reluctant to make** a decision.*
*You were **lucky to win** that game.*
*The goods are **ready to be collected**.*

The adjectives that we can use in this pattern include: *able, afraid, anxious, ashamed, content, delighted, desperate, determined, eager, foolish, fortunate, free, glad, happy, horrified, impatient, interested, keen, lucky, pleased, prepared, proud, quick, ready, reluctant, slow, sorry, surprised, unable, unwilling, willing,* and *wise.*

Quick and *slow* express the manner in which an action is carried out.
> *The government has been **quick to act**.*
> (= The government has acted **quickly**.)

F The pattern *He is unlikely to answer the question*

In this pattern the adjective expresses a degree of probability or makes a comment on the truth of what is said.
> *The peace talks are **likely to last** several weeks.*
> *Adrian is **liable to lose** his temper if you say the wrong thing.*
> *The party is **sure to be** a great success.*

We can use the adjectives *bound, certain, due, liable, likely, sure,* and *unlikely.*

With *certain, likely,* and *unlikely,* we can use this pattern with the subject *it* and a finite clause.
> *It is **likely that** the peace talks will last several weeks.*

107 Noun phrase + to-infinitive

A The pattern *the need to answer*

We can use a to-infinitive clause after certain verbs and adjectives.
> *I **need to answer** these e-mails.* > 101
> *Laura is **determined to succeed** in her career.* > 106E

We can also use a to-infinitive after nouns which are related to such verbs and adjectives. As well as *I need to answer*, we can say *the need to answer*; as well as *determined to succeed*, we can say *her determination to succeed*.
> *Is there really any **need to answer** every single e-mail?*
> *You have to admire Laura's **determination to succeed**.*
> *The **decision to raise** taxes has proved unpopular.*
> *Everyone laughed at Mark's **attempt to impress** the girls.*

Here are some nouns that we can use in this pattern.

ability	deal	move	proposal
agreement	decision	need	refusal
aim	demand	obligation	reluctance
anxiety	desire	offer	request
arrangement	determination	permission	tendency
attempt	eagerness	plan	threat
choice	failure	preparations	willingness
confidence	intention	promise	wish

There are a number of other nouns which can take a to-infinitive. They include: *ambition, chance, effort, idea, opportunity, power, race, reason, right, scheme, time,* and *way.*

>*There will be an **opportunity to ask** questions.*

NOTE
Some nouns take a preposition + gerund, not a to-infinitive. > 117
>*There's no **hope of getting** there in time.*

B The pattern *a question to answer*

In this pattern the to-infinitive expresses necessity or possibility.

>*You've got some **questions to answer**.* (= questions that you **have to answer**)
>*Take **something to read** on the train.* (= something that you **can read**)

The to-infinitive clause here is neater than the finite clause with *have to* or *can.*

Compare these sentences.

>*I have some **work to do**.* (= I have/There is some work that I need to do.)
>*I **have to do** some work.* (= I must do/I need to do some work.)

NOTE
For *questions to answer/to be answered,* > 96B.
For *an easy question to answer,* > 106C.
For patterns with *for* and *of,* e.g. *It's time for people to choose,* > 109.
For *the first person to leave,* > 275A.

108 Question word + to-infinitive

A We can use a question word or phrase before a to-infinitive.

>*I just don't know **what to say**.* (= what I **should** say)
>*We weren't sure **how much to add** to the bill.* (= how much we **should** add)
>*No one told Tom **where to meet** us.* (= where he **should** meet us)
>*Can you give me any tips on **what to wear**?* (= what I **should** wear)

The pattern expresses an indirect question about what the best action is.

We can also use a to-infinitive after *whether.*

>*I was wondering **whether to ring** you.*
>*We'll have to decide **whether to go** or not.*

We cannot use *if* here.

>(NOT *I was wondering if to ring you.*)

After *what, which, whose, how many,* and *how much,* we can use a noun.

>*I didn't know **what size to buy**.*
>*The driver wasn't sure **which way to go**.*

B Here are some of the words and expressions that can come before the question word.

Verb:	*choose, decide, explain, find out, know, learn, remember, say, see, understand, wonder, work out*
Verb + indirect object:	*advise someone, show someone, teach someone, tell someone*
Verb + preposition:	*think about, worry about*
Noun + preposition:	*decision on, guidance on/about, information about, instructions on, problem of, tips on*
Adjective:	*obvious, not sure*
Idioms:	*have an idea, not have a clue*

When we talk about teaching and learning, we can use *learn (how) to, tell/show someone how to* and *teach someone (how) to.*
> Students need to **learn (how) to plan** and organize their work.
> The instructor **showed us how to give** the kiss of life.

Compare these examples with *tell.*
> Lucy **told me how to** turn on the heating. You just turn this switch.
> Lucy **told me to** turn on the heating. She felt cold.

109 *For* and *of* with a to-infinitive

A Here are some examples of the pattern *for* + noun phrase + to-infinitive clause.
> I'll wait **for you to finish your breakfast.**
> It's important **for the company to expand into new markets.**
> Here's a printout **for us to have a look at.**

The noun phrase (e.g. *you*) is the object of the preposition *for.* It also functions as the subject of the to-infinitive.

B The pattern with *for* can be the subject of a sentence.
> **For a newspaper to publish such lies** is disgraceful.

But more often we use *it* as the subject.
> It is disgraceful **for a newspaper to publish such lies.**

The pattern with *for* can also be the complement of the sentence.
> My dream is **for the world to be at peace.**

It can also express purpose.
> There are telephones **for drivers to call for help** if they break down.
> **For plants to grow properly,** you have to water them regularly.

C We can use the pattern after a verb which combines with *for.*
> We've arranged **for a photographer to take** some photos.
> It took ages **for everyone to check** in.

Such verbs are *arrange for, ask for, call for, look for, pay for, send for, take (time) for,* and *wait for.*

NOTE
The verb *hate* can take the pattern with *for* in American English but not in British English.
  *I'd **hate for everyone to be** disappointed.*

D Many adjectives and nouns which take a to-infinitive can also take the pattern with *for*. For example, we can say that something is *easy to do* and that it is *easy for someone to do.*
  *It's easy **for people to criticize**.*
  *It's dangerous **for someone with a heart condition to sky-dive**.*
  *There's no need **for you to leave so early**.*
  *I've brought some photos **for everyone to look at**.*

E We use the pattern with *of* after adjectives that say what people are like or how they behave.
  *It's kind **of you to help me**.*
  *It was rude **of your friend not to shake hands**.*

The adjectives include *arrogant, brave, careless, clever, foolish, generous, good, kind, mean, nice, rude, selfish, silly, stupid, thoughtless, typical, unfair, unreasonable, unwise,* and *wrong.*

Some of these adjectives can take the pattern with *for*. They include *good, nice, silly, unfair, unreasonable,* and *wrong.* Compare these sentences.
  *It was nice **of** Tom to take the dog for a walk.*
  (It was a kind action by Tom.)
  *It was nice **for** Tom to take the dog for a walk.*
  (It was a pleasant experience for Tom.)

110 The infinitive without *to*

An infinitive without *to* is the simple form of the verb, e.g. *play*. It can also have a perfect or continuous form.

Simple:	*play*
Perfect:	*have played*
Continuous:	*be playing*
Perfect and continuous:	*have been playing*

We use an infinitive without *to* in the following patterns.

A After a modal verb > 70B

  *Nothing **will go** wrong.*
  *You **could have** phoned me.*
  *They **must be** having a party next door.*
  *I **should have** been working, not playing computer games.*

But note *be able to, be allowed to, be going to, have to,* and *ought to.*
*You **ought to be** more careful.*

B After *had better, would rather/would sooner,* and *rather than*

*We'd **better not be** late.* > 74B
*I didn't enjoy the show. I'd **rather have stayed** at home.* > 81E
*They decided to accept the offer **rather than take/taking** their case to court.*

C *Make/let/have* + object + infinitive without *to*

Make, let, and *have* can take an object and an infinitive without *to.*
*The official **made me fill** out a form.*
*The head teacher **let the pupils go** home early.*
*I'll **have the porter bring** up your bags.* > 94A

Here are some more examples with *let.*
*I can **let you have** a copy.* (= give you)
*I'll **let everyone know** my new address.* (= tell everyone)
***Let me go** or I'll scream.* (= release me)

Compare *force, allow,* and *get,* which all take a to-infinitive.
*The gunman **forced the pilot to land** at Miami.*
*The head teacher **allowed the pupils to go** home early.*
*I'll **get the porter to bring** up your bags.* > 94A

NOTE
In the passive pattern with *make,* we use a to-infinitive. > 93A
*I **was made to fill** out a form.*

D *See/hear,* etc + object + infinitive without *to*

Verbs of perception can take an object and an infinitive without *to.* > 125B
*Someone **saw the men leave** the building.*
*I thought I **heard someone knock** on the door.*

E After *except* and *but* (= except), we normally use an infinitive without *to.*

*As for the housework, I do everything **except cook**.*
*You've done nothing **but grumble** all day.*

F We sometimes put an infinitive after *be* when we are explaining what kind of action we mean.

*The only thing I can do is **(to) apologize**.*
*What the police did was **(to) charge** into the crowd.*
The infinitive can be with or without *to.*

The gerund

111 Introduction

A A simple gerund is a verb with the ending *-ing*, e.g. *meeting, buying*.
> *It was nice **meeting** you.*
> *Save money by **buying** online.*

There are some spelling rules for the ing-form.
We normally leave out *e* before ing, e.g. *lose* → *losing*. > 278A
We double some consonants, e.g. *stop* → *stopping*. > 279

NOTE

a   A gerund is sometimes referred to as an ing-form. But not all ing-forms are gerunds. An ing-form can also be an active participle.
   Gerund: ***Jogging** isn't my idea of fun.*
   Participle: *A man was **jogging** along the street.*
   The gerund and participle both end in *-ing*, but a gerund is used like a noun. There are some contexts where it is difficult to say whether an ing-form is a gerund or a participle. But it is more important to use the form correctly than to name it.

b   In some contexts we can use either a gerund or a to-infinitive.
   *It was nice **meeting** you./It was nice **to meet** you.*
   But there are also patterns where only one of the forms is possible.
   *Save money by **buying** online.*

B These are the forms of the gerund.

	Active	Passive
Simple:	*playing*	*being played*
Perfect:	*having played*	*having been played*

A perfect gerund refers to something before the time of the main clause.
> *The man gave no sign of **having understood**.*

It is often possible to use a simple gerund instead of a perfect gerund.
> *We remembered **having visited** the place before.*
> *We remembered **visiting** the place before.*
> *The prisoners were compensated for **having been interned** without trial.*
> *The prisoners were compensated for **being interned** without trial.*

For more examples of the passive gerund, > 95.

C In the negative, *not* comes before the gerund.
> *It was frustrating **not hearing** any news for so long.*
> *I regret **not having learned** the language.*

112 Gerund clauses

A A gerund can have an object or complement, and it can have one or more adverbials. The gerund together with such phrases is called a gerund clause.

*No one likes **cleaning shoes**.*
***Being a doctor** means you're always busy.*
***Going on holiday** always makes me feel nervous.*

A gerund clause can be just a gerund on its own.
*Do you like **dancing**?*

B A gerund clause can have a subject. It comes before the gerund.

*We rely on **our friend watering** the plants while we're away.*
*I dislike **people asking** me personal questions.*

The subject can be possessive, especially *my, your*, etc or a name with *'s*.
*It's a bit inconvenient **you/your** coming in late.*
*Do you mind **me/my sitting** here?*
*I'm fed up with **Sarah/Sarah's laughing** at my accent.*
Both forms have the same meaning here. But the possessive is more formal, and it is less usual in everyday speech.

A possessive is more likely at the beginning of a sentence.
***Your coming** in late is a bit inconvenient.*
***Sarah's laughing** at my accent is getting on my nerves.*

113 Some patterns with the gerund

A Gerund clause as subject

The gerund clause can be the subject of a sentence.
***Digging** is hard work.*
***Keeping a copy of your letters** is a good idea.*
***Choosing the colour** won't be easy.*

In subject position, the gerund is much more usual than the to-infinitive. *To choose the colour ...* is possible but less likely.

We can also use *it* as the subject and put the gerund clause at or near the end of the sentence.
*It won't be easy **choosing** the colour.*
But the to-infinitive is more usual after *it*.
*It won't be easy **to choose** the colour.*
*It's a good idea **to keep** a copy of your letters.*

> **TIP**
> Say ***Booking** in advance was a good idea.* or
> *It was a good idea **to book** in advance.*

B *It, there*, and *have*

After the subject *it* we generally use a to-infinitive rather than a gerund, > A.
But there are certain expressions where a gerund is commonly used.
> *It's no* **good arguing**. *I've made up my mind.*
> *It might be* **worth taking** *the guided tour.*
> *It wouldn't be* **much use trying** *to stick the pieces together again.*
> *It was quite an* **experience working** *abroad.*
> *It's a* **nuisance being** *without electricity.*
> *It's* **fun skiing** *down a mountain.*

After *experience, fun*, and *use* we can sometimes use a to-infinitive.
> *It was quite an* **experience to work** *abroad.*
> *It's* **fun to ski** *down a mountain.*

We can use a gerund after *there ... problem/difficulty* and *there ... point*.
> **There** *won't be any* **problem parking**.
> **There's** *no* **point starting** *something we aren't going to finish.*

We can also say *There's no point* **in** *starting.*

There is also a pattern with *have* = 'experience' where we can use a gerund.
> *You won't* **have** *any* **problem parking**.   *We* **had fun skiing**.

C Gerund clause as complement

The gerund clause can be a complement after *be*.
> *A more recent crime is* **hacking into computer systems**.
> *What I suffer from is* **not being able to sleep**.

D Verb + gerund

There are certain verbs which take a gerund (rather than a to-infinitive).
> *These people* **keep sending** *me e-mails.*
> *Would you* **mind waiting** *a moment?*

For a list of verbs taking a gerund or to-infinitive, > 101C.

Some verbs take either form. > 103
> *The band* **began playing/began to play**.

E Verb + object + gerund

We can use a gerund after a verb + object.
> *I can't* **imagine anyone buying** *a thing like that.*
> *How can they* **justify lives being put** *at risk?*
> *The arrangements* **involve you giving** *two other people a lift.*

In the last example, *you* is the object of the verb *involved*. It also functions as
the subject of *giving*.

We can use a possessive form. > 112B
> *The arrangements involve* **your** *giving two other people a lift.*

These are some of the verbs that we can use before an object + gerund.

avoid	enjoy	involve	resent
celebrate	excuse	justify	risk
defend	experience	mention	save
delay	fancy	mind	can't stand
detest	forget	miss	stop
discuss	forgive	necessitate	tolerate
dislike	can't help	prevent	understand
dread	imagine	remember	

Some verbs can take either an object + gerund or an object + to-infinitive.
They are *hate, like, love, prefer,* and *can't bear.* > 105E

We use *imagine* and *understand* with a gerund.
   *I just couldn't **imagine Chloe dancing** in a club at two in the morning.*
   *I can **understand people feeling** upset.*
We use them in a to-infinitive pattern when they mean 'believe'. > 105D
   *I **imagined Chloe to be** a quiet, reserved person.*
   *We **understand the decision to be** final.*

114 Preposition + gerund

A We sometimes use a gerund after a preposition.
   *I drove all the way **without stopping**.*
We cannot use a to-infinitive after a preposition.
   (NOT *I drove all the way without to stop.*)
And we cannot use a that-clause.
   (NOT *I drove all the way without I stopped.*)

Here are some more examples.
   ***Instead of landing** at Heathrow, we had to go to Manchester.*
   *She succeeded **by being** completely single-minded.*
   ***How about coming** round this evening?*
   *I feel tired **in spite of having slept** eight hours.*
   ***Far from being** the end of the story, it was only the beginning.*
   *Please switch off the lights **before leaving**.*
   *The drug was approved **after being tested**.*

We can use a gerund after these prepositions.

after	by	in addition to	since
against	by means of	in favour of	through
as a result of	despite	in spite of	what about
as for	far from	in the process of	with
as well as	for	instead of	without
because of	from	on	
before	how about	on account of	
besides	in	on the point of	

NOTE
We can use the conjunctions *before*, *after*, and *since* in a finite clause.
> *Please switch off the lights **before you leave**.*
> *The new drug was put on the market **after it was approved** by the government.*

B With most of these prepositions, the gerund can have a subject.
> *The picture was hung upside down **without anyone noticing**.*
> ***Despite you/your reminding** me, I completely forgot.*

C *On* and *in* have special meanings in this pattern.
> ***On turning** the corner, I saw a most unexpected sight.*
> (= As soon as I had turned the corner, ...)
> ***In building** a new motorway, they attracted new industry to the town.*
> (= As a result of building a new motorway, ...)
> This use of *on* and *in* is a little formal.

For often expresses purpose.
> *These pages are **for making** notes on.*
> We can also use a to-infinitive of purpose.
> *These pages are **to make** notes on.*

D We can also use a gerund after *than*, *as*, and *like* expressing comparison.
> *A holiday is nicer **than sitting** at a desk.*
> *Walking isn't as good for you **as swimming**.*
> *Getting information from the company is **like getting** blood out of a stone.*

NOTE
We usually use an infinitive after *than* in this pattern with *it*.
> *It is better to discuss your worries **than (to) keep** them to yourself.*

115 Verb + preposition + gerund

A We can use a gerund after a prepositional verb such as *think of* or *insist on*.
> *My friend is **thinking of selling** his motor-bike.*
> *Paul **insists on getting** there early.*
> *I **apologized for making** a mess.*

The gerund can sometimes have a subject. It comes after the preposition and before the gerund.
> *Paul **insists on everyone getting** there early.*
> *You were **talking about your cousin going** to South America.*

The prepositional verbs that we can use in this pattern include the following.

admit to	complain about	forget about	resort to
aim at	concentrate on	get on with	settle for
(dis)agree with	confess to	guard against	succeed in
apologize for	cope with	insist on	talk about
(dis)approve of	count on	look forward to	think about/of
assist in	deal with	object to	vote for
believe in	depend on	protest at/about	worry about
benefit from	dream about/of	put up with	
boast of	escape from	refrain from	
care for	feel like	rely on	

For more details about prepositional verbs, > 222.

B A gerund can also follow a verb + object + preposition.
*I'd like to **congratulate you on breaking** the world record.*
*Please **forgive me for interrupting**.*

The verbs that we can use include the following.

accuse ... of	discourage ... from	save ... from
admire ... for	forgive ... for	stop ... from
arrest ... for	inform ... about	suspect ... of
assist ... in	involve ... in	tell ... about
blame ... for	keep ... from	thank ... for
charge ... with	praise ... for	use ... for
congratulate ... on	prevent ... from	warn ... about
criticize ... for	punish ... for	
deter ... from	remind ... of	

In the passive, the preposition comes directly after the verb.
*The government is **accused of concealing** important information.*
*The man was **charged with resisting** arrest.*

116 Adjective + preposition + gerund

A gerund can follow an adjective + preposition.
*She's **keen on riding**.*
*I'm **nervous of saying** the wrong thing.*
*What's **wrong with borrowing** a little money?*

The adjectives that we can use include the following.

accustomed to	*content with*	*intent on*	*satisfied with*
afraid of	*different from*	*interested in*	*sorry for*
angry at	*engaged in*	*involved in/with*	*successful at/in*
annoyed at	*excited at*	*keen on*	*surprised at/by*
anxious about	*famous for*	*known for*	*tired of*
ashamed of	*fed up of/with*	*nervous about/of*	*unhappy about/at*
aware of	*fond of*	*opposed to*	*used to > 82B*
bad at	*good at*	*pleased about*	*worried about*
bored with	*grateful for*	*ready for*	*wrong with*
capable of	*guilty of*	*resigned to*	
close to	*happy about/at*	*responsible for*	

In this pattern the gerund can sometimes have a subject. It comes after the preposition and before the gerund.

> I was **aware of people staring** at me.
> I'm **surprised at Anna failing** her exam.

117 Noun + preposition + gerund

A gerund can follow a noun + preposition.

> We're looking into the **possibility of renting** a flat.
> I had no **sense of being** in danger.
> It's just a **question of getting** yourself organised.
> What's your **excuse for being** late?

Of is the most common preposition in this pattern.

The nouns that we can use include the following.

advantage in/of	*effect of*	*intention of*	*purpose in/of*
aim of	*excuse for*	*interest in*	*question of*
anger at	*experience of*	*job of*	*reason for*
appearance of	*fact of*	*matter of*	*reputation for*
awareness of	*fear of*	*objection to*	*risk of*
benefit of	*feeling of*	*opportunity for/of*	*sense of*
business of	*habit of*	*part of*	*success in*
case of	*honour of*	*pleasure in/of*	*task of*
chance of	*hope of*	*point in/of*	*way of*
danger of	*idea of*	*possibility of*	
difference between	*importance of*	*problem of*	
difficulty in	*insistence on*	*prospect of*	

In this pattern the gerund can sometimes have a subject. It comes after the preposition and before the gerund.

> I don't like the **idea of someone looking** over my shoulder all the time.
> What's the **point of you/your waiting** around here all afternoon?

For the choice between *you* and *your*, > 112B.

118 *For joining* and *to join*

A After some verbs and adjectives we can use either a preposition + gerund or a to-infinitive with no difference in meaning.

*The people voted **for joining/to join** the European Union.*
*I was annoyed **at finding/to find** the office closed.*

These are some of the words we can use in both patterns.

aim at doing / to do
annoyed at finding / to find
content with being / to be
excited at seeing / to see
grateful for having / to have

ready for printing / to print
satisfied with being / to be
surprised at finding / to find
vote for joining / to join

B Sometimes the two patterns have a different meaning, or their uses are partly the same and partly different. Compare the examples.

---

agree

I don't **agree with dumping** waste in the sea. (= I don't think it is right.)	We all **agreed to meet** the next day (= We decided to meet)

---

tell

I **told you about losing** my credit card, didn't I? (*told* = informed)	I **told you to keep** that card safe. (*told* = advised/requested)

---

remind

This **reminds me of skiing** in the Alps years ago. (an impersonal subject)	Why didn't you **remind me to listen** to the weather forecast. (a personal subject)

---

interested

Simon is **interested in gardening**. (= He likes gardening.)	Simon would be **interested to see/ interested in seeing** your garden. (= He would like to see your garden,) Simon was **interested to see** your garden. (= He found your garden interesting.)

---

pleased

Karen was **pleased about winning/pleased to win** a prize. (pleased about something in the past)	I'm **pleased to meet** you. (pleased about something in the present)

---

afraid

He's **afraid of being hit** by a car. (= He is afraid because he might be hit.)	The old man is **afraid to cross/ afraid of crossing** the road. (= He won't cross because he is afraid.)

ashamed

I'm **ashamed of making** mistakes in my English. (= I'm ashamed because I make mistakes.)	I'm **ashamed to open** my mouth. (= I won't open my mouth because it makes me feel ashamed.)

anxious

Jane was **anxious about making** a mistake. (= She was worried.)	Jane was **anxious to get** home as soon as possible. (= She wanted to get home.)

sorry

I'm **sorry for making** / **sorry to have made** such a fuss. (an apology for a past action)	**Sorry to disturb** you / **Sorry for disturbing** you, but can I have a word? (an apology for a present action)
	I'm **sorry to tell** you this, but your work is not of the required standard. (regret when you say something unwelcome)
	I was **sorry to hear** about your mother. (regret about bad news)

119 *To* + gerund and the to-infinitive

To can be a preposition, or it can be part of a to-infinitive.
I'm looking forward **to seeing** you soon. (**look forward to** + gerund)
I hope **to see** you soon. (**hope** + to-infinitive)

After the preposition *to*, we can put a noun phrase instead of a gerund clause.
I'm looking forward **to next weekend**.
We cannot do this with a to-infinitive.

We can use a gerund (but not an infinitive) after these combinations with *to*:
admit to, close to, confess to, look forward to, object to, objection to, opposed to, resigned to, resort to.

For *be used to doing* and *used to do*, > 82C.

120 Determiner + gerund

A We can sometimes put a determiner such as *the* before a gerund.
> *Nancy likes her new job, but **the driving** makes her tired.*

Compare the two sentences.
> ***Driving** makes her tired.* (= all driving, driving in general)
> ***The driving** makes her tired.* (= the driving she does in her job)

The + gerund is specific rather than general.

We can also use *this, that, some, no, a lot of, a little, a bit of,* and *much.*
> ***This** constant **arguing** gets on my nerves.*
> *I'd like to find time for **some fishing** at the weekend.*
> ***No parking**.* (= Parking is not allowed.)
> *I'd better do **a bit of tidying** up.*

We can also use a possessive.
> ***Your driving** always terrifies me.*

NOTE

a   Compare these examples.
> ***Your driving** always terrifies me. You go so fast.*
> (= the way you drive)
> ***Your driving** the car wouldn't be sensible. You're too tired.*
> (= the idea of you driving)

b   For the pattern *do the washing,* > 124B.

c   There are some words formed from verb + -ing which are used as ordinary nouns and can be plural.
> *There's another **meeting** next week.*
> *The square is surrounded by tall **buildings**.*

B A gerund clause can have an object. > 112A
> *An important part of our work is **keeping records**.*
> ***Playing ball games** is prohibited.*

Sometimes we can use the pattern *the* + gerund + *of* + object.
> *An important part of our work is **the keeping of records**.*
> ***The playing of ball games** is prohibited.*

The pattern with *of* can be rather formal and is typical of an official, written style.

NOTE

a   Sometimes the noun phrase after *of* is the understood subject.
> *I was disturbed by **the ringing of the telephone**.*
> (The telephone was ringing.)

b   Instead of a gerund, we often use other abstract nouns in this pattern. > 257
> *the **management** of the economy* (more usual than *the managing of the economy*)
> *the **education** of young children* (more usual than *the educating of young children*)

Participles

121 Introduction

A The most common kinds of participle are the active participle, the past participle, and the passive participle.

Form	Example
Active participle:	*I fell asleep **watching** television.* *We're **taking** a short break now.*
Past participle:	*I've **watched** all these videos.* *The job had **taken** a long time.*
Passive participle:	*The game was **watched** by a handful of spectators.* ***Taken** by surprise, he didn't know* *what to say.*

An active participle is a verb with the ending *-ing*, e.g. *watching*, *taking*, sometimes called the 'present participle'. It is the same form as a gerund. For spelling rules for the ing-form, > 111A. For information about the difference between a gerund and a participle, > 111A Note a.

The past participle and the passive participle have the same form. A regular verb has a past/passive participle ending in *-ed*, e.g. *watched*, *played*. For spelling rules for the ed-form, > 44A. For irregular participles, e.g. *taken*, *caught*, > 286.

We can put *not* before a participle.
*I sat there **not listening** to a word.*

NOTE
Most verbs have the same past/passive participle and past tense form.
    Past participle: *We've **walked** all the way.*
    Past tense: *We **walked** all the way.*
But some irregular verbs have different forms. > 286
    Past participle: *We've **run** all the way.*
    Past tense: *We **ran** all the way.*

B An active or passive participle can combine with *be*, and a past participle can combine with *have* in the following verb forms.
Continuous tenses
(*be* + active participle):   *The train **was stopping**.*
The passive
(*be* + passive participle):   *We **were stopped** by a policeman.*
Perfect tenses
(*have* + past participle):   *My watch **has stopped**.*

This chapter deals with other uses of the participles.

*We heard you **creeping** up the stairs.*

***Abandoned** by its owners, the house fell into disrepair.*

In these examples the participle is not a main verb.

C As well as the main participles, there are three more complex forms.

Form	Example
Perfect participle: (*having* + past participle)	***Having cleared** the snow, they were able to drive on.*
Perfect passive participle: (*having been* + passive participle)	*The snow **having been cleared**, they were able to drive on.*
Continuous passive participle: (*being* + passive participle)	*They watched the snow **being cleared** away.*

In the negative *not* usually goes before the whole participle.

*The snow **not having been cleared**, they were unable to drive on.*

NOTE

Compare the passive participle and the continuous passive participle.

Passive: *They wanted the snow **cleared** away.*

Continuous passive: *They watched the snow **being cleared** away.*

122 Participle clauses

A A participle can have an object or complement, and it can have one or more adverbials. The participle together with such phrases is called a participle clause.

*We saw a policeman **chasing someone**.*

*My sister is good at arguing, **being a lawyer**.*

***Cut above the right eye**, the boxer was unable to continue.*

The object comes after the participle.

(NOT ~~We saw a policeman someone chasing.~~)

A participle clause can be just a participle on its own.

*I just lay there **thinking**.*

For expressions such as *heat-seeking missile* and *rapidly-rising inflation*, > 123C.

B A participle can sometimes have a subject.

***The lights having gone out**, we couldn't see a thing.*

***Everything being in a complete mess**, it took me an hour to tidy up.*

If there is no subject, then it is normally understood to be the same as in the main clause.

*The men sat round the table **playing** cards.*

(The men were playing cards.)

NOTE
Try to avoid writing sentences like this one.
(NOT ~~Walking along the street, a fire-engine raced past.~~)
This 'hanging participle' makes it sound as if the fire engine was walking, which doesn't make sense. The subject of the main clause should be the people who were walking.

Walking along the street, we saw a fire-engine race past.

Here the subject of the main clause is the same as the understood subject of the participle. But this doesn't always have to be so. The main thing is that there should be a clear connection between the two clauses.

Knowing how little time she had, this new delay infuriated her.
(= Because **she** knew how little time she had, **she** was infuriated by this new delay.)
When adjusting the machine, the electricity should be switched off.
(= When **you** adjust the machine, **you** should switch off the electricity.)

123 Participle + noun

A We can use an active or passive participle before a noun.

*The team was welcomed by **cheering crowds**.*
(= crowds who were cheering)
***Boiling water** turns to steam.*
(= water which is boiling)
*The experiment must be done under **controlled conditions**.*
(= conditions which are controlled)
*The terrorists used a **stolen car**.*
(= a car which had been stolen)

In these examples the participle functions rather like an adjective. Compare *cheering* crowds/*noisy* crowds, *boiling* water/*hot* water. See also Note a.

It is often neater to use a participle + noun than to use a clause such as *crowds who were cheering*. But we cannot always use a participle before a noun. For example, we can talk about *a barking dog* but NOT ~~an eating dog~~.

Sometimes we use a participle with a prefix.

a **rewritten** version	**underfed** children	an **overflowing** drain
a **misspent** youth	an **unsmiling** face	a **disconnected** telephone

> **TIP**
> Use only those participle + noun combinations that you have already heard or seen, like *cheering crowds* or *controlled conditions*. There are no rules about which verbs can be used in this way and which cannot.

NOTE
a   Some words with the form of a participle are regarded as adjectives, e.g. *interesting, confused.* > 187

b   For *be* + passive participle expressing a state or an action, > 87E.
*The terrorists' car **was stolen** – it didn't belong to them.*
*The car **was stolen** two days before the incident.*

B There are a few past participles that we can use before a noun.
> *The road is blocked by a **fallen** tree.*
> (= a tree which **has fallen**)
> *The leaders of the **failed** uprising attempted to flee the country.*
> (= the uprising which **had failed**)

Compare the past and passive participles.
> Past: *The **escaped** prisoner was soon recaptured.*
> (=the prisoner who **had escaped**)
> Passive: *The **injured** prisoner was treated in hospital.*
> (=the prisoner who **had been injured**)

C Sometimes we put an adverb before the participle.
> ***fanatically cheering** crowds* (= crowds who are cheering fanatically)
> ***properly trained** staff* (= staff who have been properly trained)

We can also form a compound by combining another element with the participle.
> *a **fast-growing** economy*
> (= an economy which is **growing fast** – verb + adverbial)
> ***earth-moving** equipment*
> (= equipment which **moves earth** – verb + object)
> *a **nice-looking** jacket*
> (= a jacket which **looks nice** – verb + complement)
> *an **oil-fired** central heating system*
> (= a central heating system which **is fired by oil** – verb + by-agent)
> *a **newly-married** couple*
> (= a couple who **have recently married** – verb + adverbial)

We do not use longer phrases before the participle.
> (NOT *~~written in pencil notes~~*)
> (NOT *~~at the tops of their voices cheering crowds~~*)

But we can say *notes written in pencil.* > 274

D We can add *-ed* to some nouns.
> *a **walled** city* (= a city with a wall)

This happens mostly with compounds.
> *a **dark-haired** man* (= a man with dark hair)
> *a **short-sleeved** shirt* (= a shirt with short sleeves)

124 Verb + participle

A The pattern *They stood watching*

We can use a participle after *go, lie, run, sit,* and *stand* to refer to two actions happening at the same time.

*Everyone **stood watching** the aircraft.*
*The girl **lay trapped** under the wreckage for three days.*
*People **ran screaming** for help.*

We can put an adverbial between the verb and participle.
*Everyone **stood there watching** the aircraft.*
*Karen **sat at the table reading** a newspaper.*

B Go swimming, do the washing, etc

We use *go* + active participle to talk about activities that we go out to do, especially leisure activities.
*I'd love to **go swimming**.*
*We **went riding** yesterday.*
*Simon has **gone fishing**.*

We use *do the* + gerund for some types of work, especially routine housework.
*I usually **do the washing** at the weekend.*
*Someone comes in to **do the cleaning** for us.*

We can use *do some ...*, *do a bit of/a lot of ...*, etc for both leisure and work activities.
*I once **did some surfing** in California.*
*James **does a lot of cooking**, doesn't he?*
*Luckily I haven't got **much ironing to do**.*

We can also use *do* + gerund.
*I can't **do sewing**. I always make a mess of it.*
*We **did trampolining** every day on holiday.*

NOTE
a   With verbs of movement we can also use the pattern *go for a swim/ride*, etc.
        *I'd love to **go for a swim**.*

b   The expression *go clubbing* is formed from the noun *club*.
        *They spend all their spare time **going clubbing**.*

125 Verb + object + participle

A The pattern *I saw you doing it*

We can use an object + active participle after certain verbs.
*I **saw two men cutting** down a tree.*
*We **heard you arguing** with your brother.*
*Can you **smell something burning**?*
We can use verbs of perception, including: *feel, hear, listen to, notice, observe, see, smell, watch.*

B *I saw you doing it* or *I saw you do it*?

After a verb of perception there is also a pattern with an object + infinitive without *to*.

> *I **saw two men cut** down a tree.*
> *We didn't **notice anyone leave** the building.*

An infinitive without *to* means the complete action.

> *I saw them **cut** the tree down. It didn't take long.*
> (I saw them. They cut it down.)

The participle means that the action goes on over a period of time.

> *I saw them **cutting** the tree down as I went past.*
> (I saw them. They were cutting it down.)

When we talk about a short action, we can use either form.

> *They watched the horse **jump/jumping** the fence.*
> *We didn't notice anyone **leave/leaving** the building.*

C *I saw it being done* and *I saw it done*

The patterns in B can be used with a participle clause in the passive.

	Complete action	Action over a period
Active:	*I saw them **cut** down the tree.*	*I saw them **cutting** down the tree.*
	*We heard someone **fire** a shot.*	*We heard people **firing** shots.*
Passive:	*I saw the tree **cut** down.*	*I saw the tree **being cut** down.*
	*We heard a shot **fired**.*	*We heard shots **being fired**.*

D The pattern *I kept you waiting*

We can use an object + participle after certain verbs. The participle means action over a period of time.

> *The doctor is very slow. He often **keeps his patients waiting**.*
> *They **caught a student cheating** in the exam.*
> *We soon **got the machine working** again.*

The verbs we can use include: *catch, find, get, have, keep, leave, need, start.*

In the following pattern *have* can mean 'cause someone to be doing something'.

> *The trainer **had the players running** round the field.*

Not have can also mean 'refuse to accept'.

> *I won't **have people treating** this house like a hotel.*
> (= I won't allow people to treat this house like a hotel.)

NOTE

For other patterns with *have* and *get*, e.g. *He had the players **run** round the field* and *We soon got the machine **to work** again*, > 94A.

E The pattern *I spent some time waiting*

We can use an active participle after *spend*, *waste*, or *lose* and an expression of time or money.

*I've **spent half an hour looking** for that letter.*
*The company **wasted millions of pounds investing** in out-of-date technology.*

F The pattern *You were seen doing it*

We can sometimes use the passive before an active participle.

*The men **were seen cutting** down a tree.*
*A student **was caught cheating** in the exam.*

We can use some of the verbs in pattern A (*hear, observe, see*) and some of the verbs in pattern C (*catch, find, keep, leave*).

G The pattern *I want it done*

We can use an object + passive participle (or passive to-infinitive) after certain verbs.

*Polly **wanted the carpet (to be) cleaned**.*
*I'd **like this map (to be) photocopied**, please.*
*We **prefer the lights (to be) turned** down.*

We can use these verbs: *(would) hate, (would) like, (would) love, need, (would) prefer, want.*

In informal English we can also use an ing-form.

*Polly **wanted the carpet cleaning**.*
*I'd **like this map photocopying**, please.*

We can also use an object + passive participle with *find, get, have*, and *leave*.

*The police **found a body buried** in the garden.*
*We decided to **have the tree cut** down.*

For *have/get something done*, > 94B.

126 Conjunction + participle

We can use an active or passive participle after some conjunctions.

*You should wear gloves **when using** an electric saw.*
(= ... when you use an electric saw.)
***Once opened**, the contents should be consumed within three days.*
***Although expecting** the news, I was greatly shocked by it.*
***If not claimed** within one month, the prize will be donated to charity.*

The pattern is used mainly in writing and is common in instructions.
We can use these conjunctions: *although, if, once, unless, until, when, whenever, while.*

Conjunction + participle is a similar pattern to preposition + gerund. > 114A
> ***Despite expecting** the news, I was greatly shocked by it.*
> *I always have a shower **after working** out in the gym.*

127 Participle clauses of time

A We can use a clause of time with an active participle.
> *Mike hurt his hand **playing volleyball**.*
> *We were rushing about **serving tea to everyone**.*
The two actions take place at the same time.

Sometimes the participle clause can come first.
> ***Coming up the steps**, I fell over.*
This is used more in writing than in speech. It is more neutral to say *I fell over (when I was) coming up the steps.*

B We can also use a participle clause to talk about two short, connected actions which happen one after the other.
> ***Taking a note from her purse**, she slammed it down on the counter.*
> ***Opening the file**, the detective took out a newspaper cutting.*
This pattern is rather literary. It is more neutral to use *and*.
> *She took a note from her purse **and** slammed it down on the counter.*

With two short actions, we mention the actions in the order they happen. The participle usually comes in the first clause, but it can sometimes come in the second.
> *She took a note from her purse, **slamming it down on the counter**.*

C When a short action comes before another connected one, we can use a perfect participle for the first action.
> ***Having sealed the envelope**/**Sealing the envelope**, the lawyer locked it in the safe.*
But when the first action is not short, we must use the perfect.
> ***Having read the document**, the lawyer locked it in the safe.*
> ***Having dug a hole in the road**, the men just drove away.*
> (NOT *Digging a hole in the road, the men just drove away.*)

The clause with the perfect participle can come after the main clause.
> *They left the restaurant, **having spent two hours over lunch**.*

D A passive participle can be simple, continuous or perfect.
> *The old woman walked slowly to the lift, **assisted by the porter**.*
> *I don't want to stay out here **being bitten by insects**.*
> *A **hole having been dug**, the men just disappeared.*

E Compare these ways of saying that one thing happened after another.
1   *The man **left** the building **and (then)** hailed a taxi.*
2   ***After he had left** the building, the man hailed a taxi.*
3   ***After leaving** the building, the man hailed a taxi.*
4   ***After having left** the building, the man hailed a taxi.*
5   ***Having left** the building, the man hailed a taxi.*
6   ***Leaving the building**, the man hailed a taxi.*

Sentence (1) is the simplest way of expressing the idea. (2) makes more explicit the order in which the two things happened. (3) is shorter and neater and a little formal. (4) is less usual because there is no need to use both *after* and *having* to express the same idea. (5) and (6) are both rather formal. (6) means that the two actions happened close together.

128 Participle clauses of reason

A A participle clause can express reason.
*Crowds were waiting at the airport, **hoping to see Madonna arrive**.*
(= ... because they hoped/they were hoping to see Madonna arrive.)
***Being rather busy**, I completely forgot the time.*
(= Because I was rather busy, ...)
***Not feeling very well**, Emma decided to lie down.*
***Having lost my passport**, I have to apply for a new one.*
*The **restaurant having closed**, there was nowhere to eat.*
This type of participle clause can be rather formal.

NOTE
For other ways of expressing reason, > 239.

B We can use *with* before a participle clause with a subject.
***With the restaurant having closed**, there was nowhere to eat.*
(= Because the restaurant had closed, ...)
***With prices going up so fast**, there's no point in trying to save money.*
*I can't concentrate **with you talking all the time**.*
This pattern is neutral in style. ***With** the restaurant having closed, ...* is less formal than *The restaurant having closed,...*

C A passive participle in a clause of reason can be simple, continuous, or perfect.
*He died at thirty, **struck** down by a rare disease.*
*In summer the ducks have it easy, always **being fed** by tourists.*
***Having been renovated** at great expense, the building looks magnificent.*

129 Other participle clauses

A Result

An active participle after the main clause can express result, whether this happens by accident or deliberately.

*They pumped waste into the river, **killing all the fish**.*
(= ... and killed all the fish.)
*The film star made a dramatic entrance, **attracting everyone's attention**.*
(= ... and attracted everyone's attention.)

B Conditions

A participle clause can express a condition.

*We plan to eat outside, **weather permitting**.*
(= ... if the weather permits it.)
***Taken daily**, vitamin pills can improve your health.*
(= If they are taken daily, ...)

C *With* in a participle clause

These examples have *with* and a subject at the beginning of the clause.

*There were scenes of celebration, **with people dancing in the streets**.*
*It was a large room, **with bookshelves covering most of the walls**.*

A typical use of this pattern is to add details to a description. Compare the use of *with* to express reason. > 128B

D *Following, considering*, etc

There are some participle forms which function rather like a preposition.

***Following** the reception, there will be a talk by the professor.*
(= After the reception, ...)
***Considering/Given** the awful weather, our Open Day was a great success.*
(= In view of the awful weather, ...)
*No action has been taken **regarding** your complaint.*
(= ... about your complaint.)
***Judging by** all the noise, it must have been a pretty good party.*
(= All the noise makes me think that ...)

E Idioms

We use a participle clause in some idiomatic phrases which comment on a statement or relate it to a previous one.

***Strictly speaking**, you can't come in here unless you're a club member.*
*Things don't look good. But **having said that**, I'm still optimisitic.*
*I'm going on a computer course. ~ **Talking of** computers, ours are all down.*
***All being well**, we should get there about six.*

Nouns

130 Introduction

A This news report contains a number of nouns.

JOY RIDERS TREATED TO SCARE TACTICS

*Ten **teenagers** on a **youth project outing** stumbled from their **minibus** to be confronted by the **sight** of a horrific **car accident**. **Debris** from the head-on **crash** was strewn across the **road**. Injured **people**, covered in **blood** and trapped inside the wrecked **vehicles**, were pleading for **help** from the **police**, **fire-fighters**, and **ambulance crews** struggling to free them.*

*But the '**crash**' was an elaborate **stunt** set up by the South **Wales Police** and **youth workers** to give potential **joyriders** an **idea** of the **consequences** of their **actions**. The '**crash**' was so realistic that several of the **youngsters**, aged between 14 and 17, broke down in **tears**. Yesterday the **shock tactic** was being hailed an unqualified **success** after several of the **youngsters** swore never to travel in stolen **vehicles** again.*

(from *The Times*)

Nouns have many different kinds of meaning. There are concrete nouns like *minibus* and *blood* and abstract nouns like *consequences* and *success*. Nouns can also refer to events like *accident* and to roles like *worker*. A noun can also be a name like *Wales*.

Some nouns can have a plural ending, e.g. *youngsters, tears*. > 131
The only other ending that we put on a noun is the possessive form with *'s* or *s'*, e.g. *the ambulance crew**'s** task*. > 132

NOTE
We can sometimes add *-ed* to a noun, e.g. *a left-**handed** golf club*. > 123D

B A noun phrase is sometimes a noun on its own.
*   **Debris** *was strewn across the road.*
    The injured people were covered in **blood***.*

But more often a noun combines with other words to form a noun phrase.
*   *an idea   the road   their actions   several of the youngsters*

A noun phrase can be the subject, object, or complement of a sentence, or it can come after a preposition.
*   *The stunt was* ***a great success***.
    It gave them ***an idea*** *of* ***the consequences*** *of* ***their actions***.

C These kinds of word can combine with a noun to form a noun phrase.

Articles:	*a road accident*	*the police* > 150
Possessives:	*his first reaction*	*their minibus* > 164
Demonstratives:	*this project*	*those shock tactics* > 165
Quantifiers:	*a lot of accidents*	*several of the youngsters* > 166–173
Adjectives:	*a horrific accident*	*a clever, very elaborate stunt* > 181
Other nouns:	*a car accident*	*a youth project outing* > 141

A phrase or clause can come after the noun and modify it.

Prepositional phrase:	*Debris **from the head-on crash** was strewn across the road.* > 143
To-infinitive clause:	*It was a plan **to shock the teenagers**.* > 107A
Participle clause:	*It was a stunt **set up by the police**.* > 274
Relative clause:	*The people **who were pleading for help** weren't really injured.* > 266

131 The plural of nouns

A Form

A countable noun has both a singular and a plural form. To form the plural we usually add *-s* or *-es*.

Singular	Plural
the road	*the roads*
a minibus	*two minibuses*

There are some spelling rules for the plural with *-s/-es*.
We add *es* after a sibilant sound, e.g. *dish* → *dishes*. > 276A
Y changes to *ie*, e.g. *baby* → *babies*. > 280A

For the pronunciation of the *s/es* ending, > 276B.

But some nouns have an irregular plural, e.g. *man* → *men*. > 281–284

B The plural of compound nouns

To form the plural of a compound noun or of two nouns together, we add *-s/-es* to the end.

weekends   motorways   fire-fighters   car crashes   shock tactics

We do the same with a noun formed from a verb + adverb.

pile-ups   breakdowns   handouts

When a prepositional phrase comes after the noun, we add *-s /-es* to the first noun.

Doctors of Philosophy   mothers-in-law

And when an adverb comes after a noun in *-er*, we add *-s* / *-es* to the noun.
> *passers-by   runners-up*

In expressions with *man* / *woman* + noun, both parts change to the plural.
> *women jockeys* (women who are jockeys)

C The use of plural nouns

We use the singular to talk about one thing.
> *The **door** was closed.   We waited for an **hour**.*
> *There was only one **passenger**.   I've lost my **job**.*

We use the plural to talk about more than one.
> *The **doors** were all closed.   We waited for one and a quarter **hours**.*
> *There were hundreds of **passengers**.   I've got one or two **jobs** to do.*

For a negative or unknown quantity, we normally use the plural.
> *There were no **passengers** on the bus.*
> *Have you read any good **books** lately?*

We can use the singular after *no* meaning 'not a single ...'.
> *No **passenger(s)** came to the driver's help when he was attacked.*
> (= Not a single passenger ...)

NOTE
We can also use an uncountable noun with *no* or *any*. > 172
> *There's **no milk** in the fridge.   Have you got **any money**?*

132 The possessive form

A Form

This is how we form the possessive.
Singular noun + *'s*	*my friend**'s** name*
S-plural + *'*	*my friends**'** names*
Other plurals + *'s*	*the children**'s** names*

We add an apostrophe + *s* to a singular noun (*friend's*); we add an apostrophe to a plural noun ending in *-s* (*friends'*); and we add an apostrophe + *s* to a plural NOT ending in *-s* (*children's*).

Pronouns ending in *-one* / *-body* and the pronouns *one, each other*, and *one another* can be possessive.
> *I found **someone's** coat here.*
> *They looked into **each other's** eyes.*

For pronunciation of the possessive ending, > 276B.

NOTE
a   After a surname ending in *s*, we can add *'s* or we can just add an apostrophe.
> *Mr **Perkins's** room*/*Mr **Perkins'** room   **Yeats's** poetry*/***Yeats'** poetry*
> When we just add an apostrophe, we do not need to pronounce an extra syllable. We can pronounce *Yeats'* /jeɪts/ or /ˈjeɪtsɪz/.

b   If there is a short phrase before the noun, then the possessive ending comes after the phrase.
   the people next door's *cat*
   You may hear this in informal speech, but it is rather awkward. More neutral is *the cat belonging to the people next door.*

c   We can add an apostrophe + *s* to a phrase with *and.*
   *Did you go to **Tom and Julie's** party?* (= the party given by Tom and Julie)
   This is much more usual than *Tom's and Julie's party.*

B   Use

We use the possessive form to express a connection, often the fact that someone has something or that something belongs to someone.
   Sam's coat   Lucy's idea   my brother's friend   people's jobs

The possessive usually has a definite meaning. *Sam's coat* means '**the** coat that belongs to Sam'. So we do not put *the* before a singular name.
   (NOT *the Sam's coat*)
But we can say ***a coat of Sam's.*** > 164D

We can leave out the noun after the possessive if the meaning is clear.
   Is this your umbrella? ~ *No, I think it's **Peter's**.*

We can sometimes use two possessive forms together.
   *Anita is my cousin – my **mother's brother's** daughter.*

133   Possessive form or *of*?

A   These two structures have the same meaning.
   Possessive form: ***my friend's** name*
   Of-structure: *the name **of my friend***

Sometimes we can use either form. But often only one form is possible.
   ***your father's** car* (NOT *the car of your father*)
   *the beginning **of the term*** (NOT *the term's beginning*)

B   We normally use the possessive with people and animals.
   ***my uncle's** address   **the dog's** bed   **the Atkinsons'** car*

The of-structure is sometimes possible for relations between people.
   the young man's** mother/the mother **of the young man

When there is a long phrase or clause describing the person, we use the of-structure.
   *It's the house **of a wealthy businessman from Saudi Arabia.***
   *I was looking after the coats **of all the people attending the reception.***

C   We generally use the of-structure with things.
   *the middle **of the night**   the colour **of the walls***
   *the results **of the inquiry**   the size **of the problem***

But we can use both structures with nouns that do not refer directly to people but suggest human activity or organization, for example nouns referring to places, companies or newspapers.

Scotland's rivers   *the rivers **of Scotland***
the company's** head office*   *the head office **of the company
the magazine's** political views* *the political views **of the magazine

But there are no absolute rules about when to use which pattern. We can sometimes use the possessive form with things even when there is no human connection.

*the **water's** temperature*   *the temperature **of the water***
*the **meteor's** speed*   *the speed **of the meteor***

> **TIP**
> Use the possessive form with people and the of-structure with things. Say *my friend's address* but *the address of the website.*

134 Some other uses of the possessive

We often use the possessive form to express the idea that something belongs to someone > 132B. Here are some other uses of the possessive form. Sometimes the of-structure is also possible.

A Who something is intended for

*You can use **the customers' car park**.* (= the car park for customers)
*There's **a children's playground** in the park.* (= a playground for children)

B Classifying

*We found **a bird's nest** in the hedge.* (= the kind of nest made by a bird)
*It was **a man's voice** that I heard.* (= a male voice)

C The person doing the action

***The man's reply** surprised us.*
(The man replied.)
***The teacher's actions** / **The actions of the teacher** were criticized.*
(The teacher acted.)

D The person who the action is directed at

***Emma's promotion** is certainly well deserved.*
(They are promoting Emma.)
***The prisoner's release** / **The release of the prisoner** has been welcomed.*
(They have released the prisoner.)

NOTE
With things we generally use the of-structure.
The release of the information *has caused a sensation.*
(NOT ~~the information's release~~)

E Qualities

The man's stupidity / *The stupidity of the man* *is unbelievable.*
(The man is stupid.)
There are doubts about *the player's fitness.*
(Is the player fit?)

NOTE
For more examples like those in C–E, where a noun phrase has a similar meaning to a clause, > 257.

135 *Today's weather, an hour's journey,* etc

A The possessive form can express time.
Have we still got *yesterday's newspaper?*
Next month's figures *are expected to show an improvement.*
Next month's figures means 'the figures for next month', 'the figures relating to next month'.

We cannot use a time of day.
the three o'clock race (NOT ~~three o'clock's race~~)

NOTE
Sunday's newspaper is a newspaper on one specific Sunday, such as last Sunday. *A Sunday newspaper* (without an apostrophe) is a type of newspaper, one that appears on Sundays.

B The possessive form can also express length of time.
The coast is *half an hour's drive* *away.*
There's *a whole year's work* *on this disk.*

We sometimes use a plural noun in the possessive form.
I would like *a few minutes' rest.*
We get just *three weeks' holiday* *a year.*

NOTE
a   People whose first language is English sometimes leave out the apostrophe, especially with plural nouns, e.g. *a few minutes rest, three weeks holiday.* But some people regard this as a mistake, so it is safer to write the apostrophe.

b   We can also say *a four-hour journey.*

136 *At Sophie's, to the doctor's*, etc

We can use the possessive form without a following noun when we talk about someone's home or about a particular kind of shop or office.

*We're all meeting at **Dave's** (house/flat).*

*There's a police car outside **the Hardings'** (house/flat).*

*Is there a **baker's** (shop) near here?*

*I was sitting in the waiting-room at the **dentist's**.*

We can also use company names.

*I'm just going into **Tesco's** to buy some milk.*

But many companies leave out the apostrophe from their names.

*There's a **Barclays Bank** on the university campus.*

137 Countable and uncountable nouns

A Countable nouns can be singular or plural: *boat(s), book(s), bus(es), day(s), friend(s), man/men, photo(s), problem(s), team(s), town(s)*. We use countable nouns for separate, individual things that we can count: *a boat, some books, three buses*, etc. Many countable nouns are concrete, e.g. *car(s), chair(s), shop(s)*. But some are abstract, e.g. *idea(s), situation(s)*.

Uncountable nouns are neither singular nor plural: *air, butter, electricity, health, money, music, peace, water*. We use uncountable nouns for things that do not naturally divide into separate units. Many uncountable nouns are abstract, e.g. *violence, happiness, security*. But some are concrete, e.g. *sand, glue*.

An uncountable noun takes a singular verb, and we use *this/that* and *it*, not *these/those* or *they*.

***This** milk **is** off. I'll pour **it** down the sink.*

Many nouns can be either countable or uncountable, depending on how they are used, e.g. *Is ice-dancing **a sport**?/I like **sport**.* > 140

B There are grammatical differences between countable and uncountable nouns. For example, we can use an uncountable noun on its own, but a singular noun has to have a word like *a* or *the*.

Uncountable: ***Water** is essential for life.*

Countable: ***The boat** leaves at ten o'clock.*

(NOT ~~Boat leaves at ten o'clock.~~)

Some words go with both countable and uncountable nouns: ***the** boat* or ***the** water*. But some words go with only one kind of noun: ***a** boat* but NOT ~~*a water*~~, *how **many** boats*, but *how **much** water*.

These are the possible combinations.

	Countable		Uncountable
	Singular	Plural	
the	*the* boat	*the* boats	*the* water
no	*no* boat	*no* boats	*no* water
Possessives	*our* boat	*our* boats	*our* water
a/an	*a* boat		
one	*one* boat		
each/every	*each/every* boat		
these/those		*these/those* boats	
few		*few* boats	
many		*many* boats	
Plural numbers		*two/three* boats	
much			*much* water
little			*little* water
some	(> 172F)	*some* boats	*some* water
any	(> 172E)	*any* boats	*any* water
a lot of		*a lot of* boats	*a lot of* water
all		*all* boats	*all* water
this/that	*this/that* boat		*this/that* water

NOTE

a   We can use a plural or uncountable noun on its own without a determiner.
   Boats *are supposed to float on* ***water***.
   But we do not use a singular noun on its own except in special cases such as news headlines.
   Boat *sinks in storm.*
   For other contexts where we use a singular noun on its own, > 159.

b   We often use *all* with another determiner such as *the*, e.g. *all the boats*, > 169.

138 The of-structure expressing quantity

A Here are some examples of the of-structure.
   a **packet of** *flour*   *two* **pieces of** *wood*
   a **box of** *matches*   *a* **kilo of** *tomatoes*
We use this pattern to say how much flour or wood or how many matches or tomatoes. We cannot leave out *of* (NOT *a packet flour*).

We use the of-structure with uncountable nouns (*flour, wood*) because we cannot say *a flour* or *two woods*. We use it with plural nouns (*matches, tomatoes*) because it is more convenient to express the quantity in boxes or kilos.

NOTE

   A box of matches means something different from *a matchbox*. > 142B

B Before *of* + uncountable/plural noun we can use these types of noun.

Containers: *a **cup of** coffee, a **carton of** milk, a **bottle of** wine,*
*a **jar of** honey, a **tin of** biscuits, a **bag of** potatoes*
Measurements: *three **metres of** material, thousands of **litres of** water,*
*a **pint of** beer, **two kilos of** apples*

C Before *of* + uncountable noun we can also use *piece* and nouns of similar meaning.
*a **piece of** land   a **sheet/piece/bit of** paper   a **lump/piece of** earth/coal*
*a **drop of** water/milk/oil   no **trace of** blood*

For more examples with *piece, bit,* and *item,* > 139.

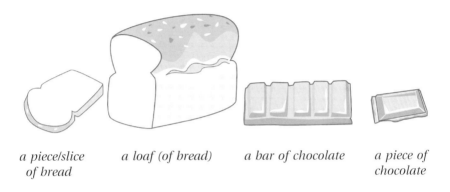

a piece/slice   a loaf (of bread)   a bar of chocolate   a piece of
of bread   chocolate

NOTE
For *a bit of,* > 167C , and for *an amount of,* > 166.

D There are a number of nouns we can use with *of* + plural noun but not with *of* + uncountable noun.
*a **crowd of** people   a **group of** tourists*
*a **bunch of** flowers   a **series of** concerts*

139 *Information, news,* etc

A It is not always clear from the meaning whether a noun is countable or uncountable. For example, *information, news,* and *furniture* are uncountable.
*I've found out **some information** for you.* (NOT *an information*)
*There **was** no **news** of the missing child.* (NOT *There were no news*)
*They had **very little furniture**.* (NOT *very few furnitures*)

But we can often use *pieces(s) of*, *bit(s) of*, and *item(s) of* with such nouns.
> *I've found out **a piece of information** for you.*
> *They had very **few items of furniture**.*

B Here are some uncountable nouns whose equivalents may be countable in
other languages. Sometimes there is an alternative countable expression.

	Uncountable	Countable
accommodation	*looking for* **accommodation**	*looking for a place to stay/live*
advice	*I got some **advice***	*I got a piece of advice*
baggage/luggage	*we lost some **baggage/ luggage***	*we lost some bags/cases* *we lost some items of baggage/luggage*
cash/money	*I had some **cash/money***	*I had some notes/coins*
clothing	*take some warm **clothing***	*take some warm clothes* > Note a
country/ countryside/ scenery	*through lovely **country/ countryside/scenery*** > Note b	*through a lovely bit of country/countryside/scenery*
damage/harm	*it did some **damage/harm*** > Note c	
equipment	*we needed some **equipment***	*we needed a piece of equipment*
English	*he speaks good **English** (the language)*	
evidence	*they found some **evidence***	*they found a piece of evidence*
fun	*have some **fun***	*have a good time*
furniture	*we bought some **furniture***	*we bought some pieces/ items of furniture*
health	*I enjoy good **health***	
homework	*students with **homework** to do*	*students with a task/ a project to do*
housework	*doing **housework** all day long*	*doing chores all day long*
jewellery	*I bought some **jewellery***	*I bought some pieces of jewellery*
land	*we own some **land** > Note d*	*we own a piece/bit of land*
leisure	*I have little **leisure***	

	Uncountable	Countable
litter/rubbish	he dropped some **litter/ rubbish**	he dropped a bit/piece of litter/rubbish
lightning	there was **lightning**	There was a flash of lightning
luck	I had some good **luck**	I had a piece/bit/stroke of luck
machinery	installing some **machinery**	installing a machine/a piece of machinery
news	I heard some **news**	I heard one piece/bit/item of news
permission	they left without **permission**	
pollution	increasing **pollution**	
progress	I've made some **progress**	
publicity	receiving lots of **publicity**	seeing lots of adverts
rain	we've had some **rain**	we've had a shower (of rain)
research	doing **research**	doing a piece of research
stuff	my **stuff** is in the car	my things are in the car
thunder	there was **thunder**	there was a clap of thunder
traffic	a queue of **traffic**	a queue of cars/vehicles
travel	work involving **travel** around the country	work involving journeys/ trips around the country
weather	we had nice **weather**	
work	do some **work** > Note e	do a job

NOTE

a   We cannot use *clothes* in the singular or with a number. We can say *some clothes* but NOT ~~four clothes~~. We say *four items of clothing* or *four garments*.

b   *Country* is countable when it means 'nation', e.g. *all the **countries** of the world*.

c   *Damages* in the plural means 'money paid in compensation'.
      *He received **damages** of £500,000 for his injuries.*

d   *Land* can be used as a countable noun meaning a country or region.
      *For the immigrants, America was a **land** of opportunity.*
    This use is rather literary.

e   *Work* can be countable in certain meanings, e.g. *a **work** of art, the **works** of Shakespeare. Works* can also mean 'factory', e.g. *a steel **works**.* > 147C

140 Nouns that can be either countable or uncountable

A Some nouns are countable when they mean something separate and individual, but they are uncountable when they mean a kind of material or substance.

Countable	Uncountable
*They had **a** nice **carpet** in the living-room.*	*We bought ten square metres of **carpet**.*
*The mob threw **stones** at the police.*	*The church was rebuilt in **stone**.*

B Animals, vegetables, and fruit are uncountable when we cut or divide them.

Countable	Uncountable
*buy **a** (whole) **chicken***	*put **some chicken** in the sandwiches*
*pick **three tomatoes***	*a pizza with **tomato***

C The following nouns can be countable or uncountable depending on the meaning. The countable noun often means a specific example, but the uncountable noun has a more general meaning.

Countable	Uncountable
*a small **business*** (= a company)	***Business** is booming.* (= economic activity)
*having **an** interesting **conversation***	*the art of **conversation***
*The US is **a democracy**.*	*the idea of **democracy***
*a **drawing/painting*** (= a picture)	*good at **drawing/painting*** (the activity)
*a girl in **a** red **dress***	*wearing evening **dress***
*an interesting **experience*** (= something that happens to you)	*having **some experience** in the job* (= having done the job for a time)
*a **glass/some glasses** of water* *glasses for reading* > 148	***some glass** for the window.*
*a **hair/some hairs** on your sweater*	*comb your **hair***
*an **iron*** (for pressing clothes)	*tablets containing **iron*** (a metal)
*He led **a** good **life***	***Life** just isn't fair, is it?*
*a bedside **light*** (= a lamp)	*at the speed of **light***
*I just heard **a noise**.*	***Noise** can cause stress.*

Countable	Uncountable
a daily paper (= a newspaper) *my papers* (= documents)	*some writing paper*
a property (= a building)	*some property* (= what you own)
Chess is a game, not a sport.	*There's always sport on television.*
The meeting was a success.	*I'm longing for fame and success.*
a tin of beans	*where tin was mined* (a metal)
I've been here lots of times before.	*I'm busy. I haven't got much time.*
It was a long and bloody war.	*I've always been against war.*

NOTE
We can use *a/an* with *knowledge* and *education* when the meaning is specific.
  Specific: *A knowledge of computers would be useful.   I had an excellent education.*
  General: *Knowledge is power.   The government should spend more on education.*
But *knowledge* and *education* cannot be plural.

D Nouns for feelings are usually uncountable.
  · *The animal was trembling with fear.*
  Where there's life, there's hope.
But some can be countable, especially when the feeling is about something specific.
  a fear of dogs   our hopes for the future   having doubts about the decision
  an intense dislike of quiz shows   a longing to get away

Some nouns for feelings are singular as complement.
  Thanks very much. ~ It's a pleasure.
  It seemed a pity to break up the party.
These nouns are *delight, pity, pleasure, relief, shame,* and *wonder*.

E Some abstract nouns can be used after *a/an* or in the plural, but they can also be used as uncountable nouns after *some, any, a lot of, much,* or *little*.
  We should have a choice / some choice in the matter.
  I haven't noticed any changes / any change in the situation.
  There have been some criticisms. / There's been some criticism of the behaviour of the officials.
  We didn't get many responses / much response to the questionnaire.
  The story failed to make an impact / made little impact on public opinion.
Such nouns include: *advantage, benefit, chance, choice, change, comment, criticism, detail, difference, difficulty, effect, effort, idea, impact, point, reason, response*.

F When we order food or drink or talk about portions, we can use phrases like *a juice* and *three coffees*.

> *I'll have **an orange juice**.* (= a glass of orange juice)
> ***Three coffees**, please.* (= three cups of coffee)
> ***Two sugars** for me.* (= two spoonfuls of sugar)

Some nouns can be countable with the meaning 'kind(s) of'.

> *This is **a cheese** I really like.* (= a kind of cheese)
> *There are lots of different **grasses**.* (= kinds of grass)

141 Two nouns together

A We often use one noun before another.

> *a tennis club   money problems   a microwave oven*

The first noun modifies the second. It tells us something about it – what kind it is or what it is for.

a tennis club	a club where you can play tennis
vitamin pills	pills containing vitamins
a phone bill	a bill for using the phone
a train journey	a journey by train

For more details about meanings, > 142.
For combinations with the possessive form, e.g. *the train's speed*, > 133–134.

B When two nouns come together, there are three different ways of writing them.

As two separate words: *address book, television programme*
With a hyphen: *waste-bin, water-bottle*
As one word: *armchair, website*

There are no exact rules about whether we join the words or not or whether we put a hyphen.

C The stress is usually on the first noun. → Audio

> *the 'tennis club   a ma'chine gun   the 'car park   the 'fire alarm*

But there are also combinations where the stress is on the second noun.

> *a cardboard 'box   the town 'hall*

There are no exact rules about stress, but for more details, > 142.

D The first noun is usually singular, even if it refers to more than one.

> *a **vegetable** garden   a **picture** gallery   an **eye** test   a **bookcase***

A *vegetable garden* is a garden where **vegetables** are grown.

But there are exceptions.

> ***careers** information   the **sales** office   a **sports** shop*

These include nouns with a plural-only form. > 147A
*an **arms** dealer   a **clothes**-brush   **customs** regulations   a **goods** train*

E There are more complex structures with nouns. For example we can use more than two nouns.
credit card charges
a motorway service station
the Customer Helpline number

We can build up phrases like this.
an air accident (= an accident in the air)
an investigation team (= a team that investigates)
an air accident investigation team (= a team that investigates accidents in the air)
Here *air accident* modifies *investigation team*.

We can use adjectives in complex noun structures.
*a **comprehensive** road atlas   **handy** keyboard shortcuts*
*a 'Sunuser' **solar** heating system   **domestic** violence statistics*

142 More details about two nouns together

A Here are some examples of different kinds of meaning with noun + noun combinations.

Purpose: *a milk bottle* (= a bottle for putting milk in)
a car park   a coffee table   security cameras   hand cream

Means: *a car journey* (= a journey by car)
a petrol engine (= an engine that uses petrol)
a fax message   an oil lamp   a coal fire   a phone link

Topic: *a war film* (= a film about war)
a crime story   peace talks   a computer magazine   science fiction

Object: *a chess player* (= someone who plays chess)
a taxi driver   music lovers   a professional dog walker
a food mixer (= a machine that mixes food)
a lawnmower   a bottle opener   a bread maker
car theft (= the stealing of cars)
steel production   home contents insurance

With these kinds of meaning the stress is usually on the first noun:
*a '**milk** bottle.* → Audio

NOTE
a   We can use a gerund before a noun to express purpose.
*a **sleeping** bag   **washing** powder*

b   Compare these two phrases.
Noun + noun: *an '**English** teacher* (=someone who teaches English)
Adjective + noun: *an English '**teacher*** (=a teacher who is English)

B There is a difference in meaning between *a milk bottle* and *a bottle of milk*.

a milk bottle

A *milk bottle* is a bottle for putting milk in.

a bottle of milk

A *bottle of milk* is a bottle full of milk.

Here are some more examples.

an empty wine glass	*an old jam jar*	*a teapot*
a nice glass of wine	*a jar of strawberry jam*	*a pot of tea*

C Here are some more noun + noun combinations.

Time: *a summer holiday* (= a holiday in summer)
        the morning rush   *a future date*
        breakfast television   *an evening paper*

Place: *a country cottage* (= a cottage in the country)
        a motorway bridge   *Swindon station*   *a world recession*

Material: *a plastic bag* (= a bag made of plastic)
          a paper cup   *a brick wall*   *a glass vase*   *a cardboard box*

With these kinds of meaning the stress is usually on the second noun: *a summer 'holiday.* → Audio But there are many exceptions.
    'evening classes   *a 'Glasgow woman*
We stress the first noun when it is more important in the context. For example, we talk about an evening class to distinguish it from a class in the daytime.

D We also use the noun + noun pattern to refer to something which is part of something else.
    the car door (= the door of the car)
    a bicycle wheel   *the TV screen*   *the town centre*   *the river bank*

The stress is often on the second noun: *the car 'door.* But sometimes we stress the first noun: *a 'bicycle wheel.* We can talk about *the river 'bank* or *the 'river bank.* It depends which word is more important in the context.

With *top, bottom, side, back,* and *end* we normally use the of-structure.
the end of the motorway (NOT ~~the motorway end~~)
the side of the house (NOT ~~the house side~~)

NOTE
There are some combinations with noun + *top,* noun + *bottom,* etc.
*They stood by the **roadside**/the **side of the road**.*
These combinations include: *a **cigarette end**, along the **cliff top**, on a **hillside**, by the
roadside, over the **rooftops**, the **valley bottom**, at the **waterside**, profits at the **year end**.*

143 Phrases after a noun

A We can use a phrase after a noun to modify it.
*all these papers **here**   every day **of the week**   a meal **for two***

We can use these kinds of phrase.

Prepositional phrase:	*When will I meet the girl **of my dreams**?*
Adverb phrase:	*We don't talk to the people **upstairs**.*
Adjective phrase:	*The police found parcels **full of cocaine**.*
Noun phrase:	*The weather **that day** was awful.*

The prepositional phrase is the most common.
*The period **just after lunch** is always quiet.*
*I'd love an apartment **on Fifth Avenue**.*
*The idea **of space travel** has always fascinated me.*
*What are the prospects **for a peaceful solution**?*
For noun + preposition, e.g. *prospects for,* > 226.

B We can sometimes use two or more phrases together after a noun. Here are
some examples from newspapers.
*Passengers **on some services from King's Cross, Euston, and Paddington**
will need a boarding pass.*
*They meet the Turkish champions Galatasary, having drawn three-all in
the first leg **of their second round tie at Old Trafford**.*
*The ideas for changing the lifestyle of the British soldier were developed at a
brain-storming conference **between an army team and experts from the
Henley Centre think-tank in Berkshire**.*

We can also use a mixture of phrases and clauses.
*The baffling case **of a teenage girl who vanished exactly twenty years ago**
has been re-opened by police.*

Agreement

144 Introduction

A It is sometimes said that there is no subject-verb agreement in English. Although English has fewer verb endings than many other languages, there are times when the verb has to agree with the subject. Here is an example.

*The **house is** empty.*
*The **houses are** empty.*

Here we use the verb *is* with a singular subject (*house*) and the verb *are* with a plural subject (*houses*). The verb 'agrees with' the subject. Agreement is sometimes called 'concord'.

An uncountable noun takes a singular verb.

*The **grass is** growing.*

B There is agreement when we use a present-tense verb in the third person.

*The **window is** broken.*   *The **windows are** broken.*
*The **house has** a garden.*   *The **houses have** gardens.*
*This **jacket looks** nice.*   *These **jackets look** nice.*

The singular verb ends in *-s*.

But a modal verb does not have singular and plural forms. > 70

*The **house must** have a garden.*   *The **houses must** have gardens.*

NOTE
In the present tense of *be*, the first-person singular form is *am*, e.g. ***I am** ready.* > 65A

C With a past-tense verb, there is agreement only with *be*.

*The **window was** broken.*   *The **windows were** broken.*

Other verbs do not have singular and plural forms.

*The **house had** a garden.*   *The **houses had** gardens.*
*The **room looked** nice.*   *The **rooms looked** nice.*

NOTE
In the past tense of *be*, *was* is both the first-person singular (***I was** ready*) and the third-person singular form (***He was** ready*). > 65A

145 Singular and plural subjects

It is usually easy to decide if a subject is singular or plural. But there are some problem areas, and these are dealt with in 146–149. Here are some basic points about singular and plural subjects.

A Two or more phrases linked by *and* take a plural verb.
Simon and Chloe go sailing at weekends.
Both the kitchen and the dining-room face due south.
Wheat and maize are exported.
But when the two together are seen as a single idea, then we use a singular verb.
Bread and butter was all we had.
(= bread with butter on it)

A phrase in apposition (see GLOSSARY) does not make the subject plural.
Simon, my neighbour, goes sailing at weekends.

B When two phrases are linked by *or*, the verb usually agrees with the nearest.
Either Thursday or Friday is OK by me.
Either the Internet or these books are where you'll find the information.

C A phrase of measurement usually takes a singular verb.
Ten miles is too far to walk.
Thirty pounds seems a reasonable price.
Here we are talking about **a distance** of ten miles and **a sum** of thirty pounds, not the individual miles or pounds.

D Titles and names take a singular verb when they refer to one thing.
'Star Wars' was a very successful film.
The Rose and Crown is that old pub by the river.

Plural place names referring to a single country usually take a singular verb.
The United States wants to increase the permitted pollution levels.
The Netherlands is a member of the European Union.

NOTE
The name of an island group usually takes a plural verb.
The Seychelles lie in the middle of the Indian Ocean.

But we can use a singular or plural verb when talking about the group as a political unit.
The Solomon Islands is/are a nation-state.

E A phrase with *as well as* or *with* does not make the subject plural.
The kitchen, as well as the dining-room, faces due south.
Paul, together with some of his friends, is buying a racehorse.

A phrase with *and* in brackets does not usually make the subject plural.
The kitchen (and of course the dining-room) faces due south.

After *not only ... but also*, the verb agrees with the nearest phrase.
Not only Paul but also some of his friends are buying the horse.
Not only his friends but also Paul himself has a share in the horse.

F If a phrase comes after the noun and modifies it, the verb agrees with the first noun.

> The **house** between the two bungalows **is** empty.

G A phrase or clause as subject takes a singular verb.

> **Through the trees is** the quickest way.
> **Opening our presents was** exciting.

146 *One of, a number of, every,* etc

A After a subject with *one of*, we use a singular verb.

> **One** of these letters **is** for you.

B When a plural noun follows *a lot of*, *number of*, or *majority of*, we normally use a plural verb.

> A lot of **people have** complained.
> A large number of **letters were** received.
> The majority of **nurses are** women.

But after *The number of ...*, we use a singular verb.

> The **number** of letters we receive **is** increasing.

Amount agrees with the verb.

> A large **amount** of money **was** collected.
> Large **amounts** of money **were** collected.

After a fraction or percentage, the verb agrees with the noun.

> Three quarters (of a **potato**) **is** water.
> Almost half (the **plants**) **were** killed.
> Sixty per cent of the **country was** held by the rebels.

C We use a singular verb after a subject with *every* or *each*.

> **Every pupil has** to take the test.
> **Each day was** the same as the one before.

We also use a singular verb after compounds with *every*, *some*, *any*, and *no*.

> **Everyone has** to take the test.
> **Someone was** waiting at the door.
> **Nothing** ever **happens** in this place.

But *all* and *some* with a plural noun take a plural verb.

> **All (the) pupils have** to take the test.
> **Some people were** waiting at the door.

NOTE

When *each* follows a plural subject, the verb is plural.

> **The pupils each have** to take the test.

D We use a singular verb after *who* or *what* as subject.

> ***Who wants** coffee?* ~ *We all do, please.*
> ***What's** happened?* ~ *Several things have happened.*

After *what/which* + noun, the verb agrees with the noun.

> *What/Which **day is** convenient?*
> *What/Which **days are** convenient?*

When there is no noun after *which*, the verb can be singular or plural.

> ***Which** of you **is** willing to take part?* (Which **one**?)
> ***Which** of you **are** willing to take part?* (Which **ones**?)

E Look at these sentences.

> ***None** (of the pupils) **has/have** failed the test.*
> ***Neither** of us **was/were** very impressed by the place.*
> *I don't know if **either** (of these batteries) **is/are** any good.*
> *If **any** of you **gets/get** into difficulty, just call for help.*

After a subject with *none, neither, either,* or *any* and a plural noun phrase, we can use either a singular or a plural verb. Both are used in writing, but a plural verb is more common in speech.

After *no*, the verb agrees with the noun.

> *No **pupil has** failed.*
> *No **pupils have** failed.*

F After *there*, the verb agrees with its complement.

> *There **was a party** at the office.*
> *There **were parties** all over town.*

NOTE

In informal speech you may hear *there's* before a plural.

> *There's **some friends** of yours outside.*

147 Nouns with a plural form

A Plural noun and plural verb

Some nouns are always plural.

> *The **goods were** found to be defective.*
> (NOT *The good was found to be defective.*)
> *My **belongings have** been destroyed in a fire.*
> (NOT *My belonging has been destroyed in a fire.*)

Some nouns of this kind are: *belongings, clothes, congratulations, earnings, goods, odds* (= probability), *outskirts* (= outer parts of a town), *particulars* (= details), *premises* (= building), *remains* (= what is left), *surroundings* (= what is around you), *thanks,* and *troops* (= soldiers).

Some nouns have a plural-only form which has a different meaning from the singular or uncountable form.

191

	Plural only
*my **arm(s)** and **leg(s)*** (parts of the body)	*to carry **arms*** (= weapons)
*the **content** of the message* (= what it says)	*the **contents** of the briefcase* (= what is inside it)
*an old **custom*** (= traditional activity)	*go through **customs** at the airport* (where goods are checked)
*did some **damage** to the car* (e.g. in an accident)	*pay **damages** of £10,000* (= compensation)
*he gave me a **look*** (= he looked at me)	*his good **looks*** (= appearance)
*have a high **regard** for her* (= a good opinion)	***regards** to your parents* (= good wishes)
*a **saving** of £10 on the normal price* (paying less than usual)	*robbed of his life **savings*** (= money saved, e.g. in a bank)

B Plural noun form but singular verb

There are some nouns ending in *-s* which normally take a singular verb.
> *The **news isn't** very good, I'm afraid.*
> ***Gymnastics looks** difficult, and it is difficult.*
> ***Maths was** my best subject at school.*
> ***Draughts is** a board game.*

Nouns of this kind include *news*; some words for sports and games, e.g. *athletics, billiards, bowls, darts, draughts, gymnastics*; some subjects of study, e.g. *economics, maths, physics, politics, statistics*; and some illnesses, e.g. *measles, diabetes.*

Some of these nouns can take a plural verb when they have a more concrete or specific meaning.
> *These **darts are** quite heavy.* (the objects, not the game)
> *His **politics are** very left-wing.* (= his political views)
> *The **statistics are** available on the Internet.* (some specific figures)

C Nouns ending in -s in both singular and plural

There are a few words which end in *-s* and can be either singular or plural.
> *The new comedy **series has** been a flop with viewers.*
> *Bird **species are** numerous in the area.*

Some nouns of this kind are *barracks* (= a building where soldiers live), *crossroads, headquarters, means, series, species,* and *works* (= a factory).

Barracks, headquarters, and *works* can take a plural verb even when they refer to a single building or a single group of buildings.
> *The company's **headquarters was/were** easy to find.*

148 Pair nouns

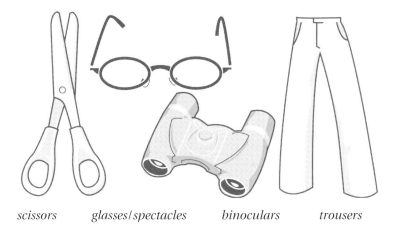

scissors   glasses/spectacles   binoculars   trousers

A We use a pair noun for certain things consisting of two similar parts. Most pair nouns refer to tools or other devices (e.g. *scissors, glasses*) or to clothes that cover your legs (e.g. *trousers, jeans*).

B A pair noun is plural and takes a plural verb.
> ***These trousers need** cleaning.*
> *I'm looking for my **glasses**. I've put **them** down somewhere.*
> *There **are some scissors** in the drawer.*

We cannot use *a* or numbers.
> NOT *a ~~trouser~~* and NOT *~~two trousers~~*

NOTE
Some pair nouns have no *-s* when they come before another noun.
> *I've spilt some coffee down my **trouser leg**.*

C We can use *pair of* or *pairs of.*
> *This **pair of trousers** needs cleaning.*
> *Have you got a **pair of binoculars**?*
> *Somehow I've managed to lose three **pairs of scissors**.*

We have to use *pair(s) of* if we want to say how many.

We can also use *pair* with two separate items, e.g. *socks, shoes, boots, trainers.*
> *I've packed six **pairs of** socks.*

But these nouns can be singular as well as plural.
> *I've lost **a sock**. It must be still in the washing-machine.*

D Some pair nouns are *binoculars, glasses, jeans, knickers, pants, pyjamas* (US *pajamas*), *scales* (for weighing), *scissors, shorts, spectacles* (= glasses), *tights,* and *trousers.*

Glass, scale, and *spectacle* can be singular with a different meaning.
*Can I have **a glass** of water, please?*
*The map has **a scale** of five kilometres to the centimetre.*
*The fireworks were **an** amazing **spectacle**.* (= sight)

149 Group nouns

A Group nouns refer to a group of people, e.g. *family, team, crowd.* They are sometimes called 'collective nouns'. After a singular group noun, the verb is usually singular, but it can be plural.
*The crowd **was**/**were** in a cheerful mood.*

NOTE
a   In the US a singular group noun is normally followed by a singular verb.

b   A group noun can be plural.
*The two **families get** on well together.*

> **TIP**
> The safest choice is the singular verb because this is much more common than the use of the plural.
> Say *The crowd was ...* rather than *The crowd were ....*

B We always use the singular to talk about the whole group. For example, we might refer to the group's size or make-up or how it compares with others.
*The **class consists** of twelve girls and fourteen boys.*
*The **union is** the biggest in the country.*

A plural verb is more likely when we see the group as individuals, especially when we talk about people's thoughts or feelings.
*The **class don't**/**doesn't** understand what the teacher is saying.*
*The **union are**/**is** delighted with the pay increase.*

C With a singular verb we normally use *it, its,* and *which/that.*
*The government **wants** to improve **its** image.*
*The crowd **which has** gathered here **is** in a cheerful mood.*
With a plural verb we normally use *they, their,* and *who/that.*
*The government **want** to improve **their** image.*
*The crowd **who have** gathered here **are** in a cheerful mood.*

D Group nouns include the following.

army	*community*	*government*	*(political) party*
association	*company*	*group*	*population*
audience	*council*	*jury*	*press*
band	*crew*	*majority*	*public*
board	*crowd*	*management*	*school*
choir	*enemy*	*military*	*society* (= club)
class	*family*	*minority*	*team*
club	*firm*	*navy*	*(trade) union*
college	*gang*	*orchestra*	*university*
committee			

NOTE
Military, *press* (= newspapers), and *public* do not have a plural form.
  The public has/have shown no interest.
  (NOT ~~The publics have shown no interest.~~)

E The names of institutions and companies are also group nouns.
  The United Nations is/are unable to act.
  Tesco sells/sell organic milk.

Sports teams can take a singular or plural verb.
  England is/are through to the World Cup finals.

F Some nouns have a plural meaning and take a plural verb, even though they do not end in -*s*.
  *Some **cattle have** got out into the road.*
  *The **police are** questioning a man.*

These words are *cattle* (= cows), *livestock* (= farm animals), *people*, *police*, and *staff* (= the people working in a business).

NOTE
For irregular noun plurals, e.g. *foot* → *feet*, *child* → *children*, > 282–284.

The articles: *a/an* and *the*

150 Introduction

Look at the articles in this paragraph.

> *The Royal Society for **the** Prevention of Accidents held **an** exhibition at Harrogate in **the** north of England. Some shelves were put up to display **the** exhibits. During **the** exhibition, **the** shelves fell down, injuring **a** visitor. It was **an** unfortunate incident.*

We use *a/an* only with a singular noun (*a visitor, an exhibition*) ; the plural or uncountable equivalent is *some* (***some** shelves*), or no article (*accidents*). We can use *the* with all types of noun.

A/an is the indefinite article, and *the* is the definite article. We use *the* when it is clear which one we mean. We say ***the** north of England* because there is only one north of England. We say ***an** exhibition* when we mention it for the first time, but after that we say ***the** exhibition*, meaning 'the exhibition already mentioned'. We also use *a/an* as complement when we are describing something: *It was **an** unfortunate incident.*

151 The form of the articles → Audio

A Before a consonant sound, the articles are *a* /ə/ and *the* /ðə/.
→ Audio

a shelf /ə/ + /ʃ/
a visitor /ə/ + /v/
a big exhibition /ə/ + /b/
the shelf /ðə/ + /ʃ/
the visitor /ðə/ + /v/
the big exhibition /ðə/ + /b/

Before a vowel sound the articles are *an* /ən/ and *the* /ði/.
→ Audio

an accident /ən/ + /æ/
an exhibition /ən/ + /e/
an interesting display /ən/ + /ɪ/
the accident /ði/ + /æ/
the exhibition /ði/ + /e/
the interesting display /ði/ + /ɪ/

B It is the pronunciation which matters, not the spelling of the word after the article. Note especially words beginning with *o*, *u*, or *h*, or abbreviations.
→ Audio

a one-day event /ə/ + /w/
a university/uniform/union /ə/ + /j/
a European country /ə/ + /j/
a holiday /ə/ + /h/
a U-turn /ə/ + /j/

an only child /ən/ + /əʊ/
an umbrella /ən/ + /ʌ/
an error /ən/ + /e/
an hour /ən/ + /aʊ/
an MI5 agent /ən/ + /e/

196

NOTE

a   Other words besides *hour* with a silent *h* are *heir*, *honour* and *honest*, e.g. **an honest person.**

b   With *hotel* we can pronounce *h* or leave it out.
      a *hotel* /ə/ +/h/   **an** *hotel* /ən/+ /əʊ/
     An hotel is rather formal and old-fashioned.
     There are also a few adjectives where we can use either *a* or *an*. They include *habitual*, *heroic*, and *historical*, e.g. **a/an historical** *fact*. If we use *an*, then the *h* is silent.

c   When *the* is stressed, it can mean 'the only' or 'the most important'.
      Notting Hill is THE /ðiː/ *place to be on carnival weekend.*
     For THE *Joan Collins*, > 162B.

152 The main uses of the articles

Look at how articles are used in this news report.

HOVERCRAFT STOWAWAY

A **hovercraft** *flying at 40 mph was halted in rough seas when* **a stowaway** *was discovered – on* **the outside**. *He was seen hiding behind* **a liferaft** *to avoid paying* **the £5 fare** *from Ryde, Isle of Wight to Southsea.* **The captain** *was tipped off by radio. He stopped* **the craft** *and* **a crewman** *brought* **the stowaway** *inside. A* **Hovertravel spokesman** *said: 'It was* **a very dangerous thing** *to do.* **The ride** *can be bumpy, and it would be easy to fall off.'*

(from *The Mail on Sunday*)

A First mention or mentioned before?

When something is first mentioned, the noun usually has *a/an*, e.g. **a** *hovercraft* and **a** *stowaway* in the first sentence of the report. When the same thing is mentioned again, the writer uses *the*.
     He stopped **the craft** *and a crewman brought* **the stowaway** *inside.*
It should be clear to the reader which craft and which stowaway is meant – the one we are already talking about.

Now look at this sentence from the report.
     The ride *can be bumpy, and it would be easy to fall off.*
Although the word *ride* has not been used before, the idea of a hovercraft ride from the Isle of Wight to Southsea is expressed in the first two sentences of the report. It is clear which ride is meant.

The relationship between *a/an* and *the* is like the relationship between *someone/something* and a personal pronoun (e.g. *he, it*).
     Police are questioning **a man/someone** *about the incident.* **The man/He** *was arrested when he arrived at Southsea.*
A man/someone is indefinite; *the man/he* is definite.

NOTE
We sometimes see a special use of *the* at the beginning of a story. This is the first sentence of a short story by Ruth Rendell.

> *A murderer had lived in the house, the estate agent told Norman.*
> This puts the reader in the middle of the action, as if we already know what house and what estate agent.

B *The* for something unique

When something is unique in the context, we use *the*.
> **The captain** *was tipped off by radio.*

We use *the* because in the context of the hovercraft ride, there is only one captain.

Now look at these examples.
> *A car stopped and* **the driver** *got out.* (A car has only one driver.)
> *Where's* **the volume** *on this radio?* (It has only one volume control.)
> *I'm just going to* **the post office**. (There is only one post office in the area.)
> *We were sitting on* **the patio**. (The garden has only one patio.)
> *We crossed* **the English Channel**? (There is only one English Channel.)
> **The Prime Minister** *is very popular.* (The country has only one PM.)
> **The sun** *was shining.* (There is only one sun in our solar system.)

C *The* with noun + phrase

We often use *the* when a phrase or clause comes after the noun and shows which one is meant.
> *Ours is* **the house on the corner**.
> *I'd like to get hold of* **the idiot who left this broken glass here**.

But if the phrase or clause does not give enough information to show which one is meant, we use *a/an*.
> *We live in* **a house overlooking the park**.

We cannot use *the* if there are other houses also overlooking the park.

We often use *the* when an of-phrase follows the noun.
> *We came to* **the edge of a lake**.
> **The roof of a house** *was blown off in the storm.*
> *They heard* **the sound of an aircraft** *overhead.*

But we can use *a/an* in an of-structure expressing quantity.
> *Would you like* **a piece of cake**?

D *The* with superlatives and with *last, next,* etc

We normally use *the* rather than *a/an* with superlative adjectives.
> *The Sears Tower is* **the tallest building** *in the US.*

The is also much more common than *a/an* in noun phrases with *first, last, next, only, right, same,* and *wrong.*
> *Is this* **the first time** *you've been to Britain?*
> *Let's stop at* **the next services**.
> *Who else can I talk to? You're* **the only friend** *I've got.*
> *I think you went* **the wrong way** *at the lights.*

NOTE

a   *An only child* is a child without brothers or sisters.

b   For *last week, next year,* etc without article, > 161H.

E *A/an*: specific or not?

A/an can mean either a specific one or any one.
> *I'm looking for **a pen**. It's a blue one. I was using it a few minutes ago.*
> (a specific pen)
> *I'm looking for **a pen**. I can't find one anywhere. Could you lend me one?*
> (any pen)

F *A/an* for describing

We can use a singular noun phrase as complement to describe something, especially a phrase with an adjective e.g. *big, beautiful.*
> *This is **a big house**, isn't it?*
> *Yesterday was **a beautiful day**.*
> *Riding on the outside of a hovercraft is **a very dangerous thing** to do.*
We use *a/an* before the noun, even though it is clear which one is meant.

We can sometimes do this in a phrase without an adjective.
> *Tim talks about nothing but football. He's **a fanatic**.*
> *The lack of a proper bus service is **a disgrace**.*

G *A/an* for classifying

We can use *a/an* in a noun phrase to classify something.
> *What kind of bird is that? ~ **A blackbird**, isn't it?*
> *Anglesey is **an island** off the north coast of Wales.*

Now look at these examples.
> *The gold medal winner was **an Irishman**.*
> *I'm proud to say that I'm **a socialist**.*
> *The victim, **a Catholic**, was taken to hospital.*
Here the phrases refer to someone's nationality or beliefs.

We use the same pattern to talk about a person's job.
> *My sister is **a doctor**.* (NOT *My sister is doctor.*)
> *I'd love to be **a racing driver**.* (NOT *I'd love to be racing driver.*)

153 The articles in generalizations

A This paragraph contains some generalizations about animals.

ANIMALS AND THEIR NOSES

*As with other parts of its equipment, **an animal** evolves the kind of nose it needs. **The hippo** has grown its ears and eyes on the top of its head, and its* *nostrils on top of its nose, for lying in water.* **Camels** *and* **seals** *can close their noses; they do it in the same way but for different reasons.* **The camel** *closes its nose against the blowing sand of the desert, and* **the seal** *against the water in which it spends most of its time.*

(from F.E. Newing and R. Bowood *Animals And How They Live*)

The paragraph is about hippos, camels, and seals in general and not about specific animals. For generalizations like this, we can use a plural or uncountable noun on its own, or a singular noun with *a*/*an* or *the*.

> **Camels** *can close their noses.* > B
> **A camel** *can close its nose.* > C
> **The camel** *can close its nose.* > D

But a sentence such as *The camels were carrying a heavy load* refers to a specific group of camels. We cannot use *the camels* for a generalization.

B The most common way of making a generalization is to use a plural or uncountable noun on its own without an article.

> **Blackbirds** *have a lovely song.*   **People** *should think twice.*
> *I hate waiting around at* **airports.**   **Time** *costs* **money,** *you know.*

In the first example, *blackbirds* means 'all blackbirds'.

C We can use *a*/*an* in a generalization.

> **A blackbird** *has a lovely song.*
> **A computer** *will only do what it's told to do.*

In the first example, *a blackbird* means 'any blackbird' or 'a typical blackbird'.

We normally use *a*/*an* when explaining the meaning of a singular word.

> **A refrigerator** *is where you put food to keep it cool.*
> **An oar** *is a thing you row a boat with.*

D We can sometimes use *the* with a singular noun to make a generalization. For example, we can do this with animals and plants.

> **The blackbird** *has a lovely song.*
> **The redwood tree** *grows to an enormous height.*

We use *the* with some kinds of people described in economic terms.

> **The customer** *is always right.*
> *It's* **the taxpayer** *who has to pay for all this.*

We also use *the* with inventions.

> *Nobody knows who invented* **the wheel.**

NOTE
For some groups of people (e.g. *the blind*), > 188.

154 The articles: some special uses

A We go *to the cinema/theatre* even if we do not mean a specific one.
We haven't been **to the cinema** *for ages.*

B If we are talking about television or radio in a general sense as a medium or a business, then we use the noun on its own.
Radio *leaves more to the imagination than* **television** *does.*
My friend has got a job in **television***.*

Compare these examples about watching and listening.
We **watch television** *in the evenings.*   *What's* **on TV?**
We sometimes **listen to the radio***.*   *What's* **on the radio?**
On the TV/on the television is also possible.

When we are talking about the physical objects, we use *a/an* or *the* in the usual way.
There was **a television/a radio** *on the shelf.*
Alice turned on **the television/the radio***.*

We say *the press* (= newspapers) and *the media* (= television, radio, and newspapers).
The media *love a nice scandal.*

C When we are talking about playing musical instruments, we use *the.*
Can you play **the piano?**
We normally mean a general ability to play any piano, not just a specific one.

But *the* is often left out in *play guitar.*
I **play guitar** *in a band.*

Sports and games are uncountable, so we use the noun on its own after *play* or *do.*
Do you **play tennis** *at school?*   *We* **do judo** *on Saturdays.*

D We use *the bus* and *the train* in a general sense as a means of transport.
I usually go to work **on the bus***.*
But we say *by bus* and *by train* without *the.* > 215E

When we talk about a specific vehicle, we use *a/an* or *the* in the usual way.
Our cat was run over by **a bus** *last month.*

E We say *the police.*
The police *arrived within five minutes.*

With *policeman, policewoman,* and *police officer,* we can use *a/an* or *the* in the usual way.
A **police officer** *arrived within five minutes.*

F Some words for kinds of surroundings usually have *the* when they have a general meaning. They are *town, country, countryside, sea,* and *seaside.*
> *Would you rather live in **the town** or **the country**?*
> *I'd love a day at **the seaside**.*

Here we do not mean a specific town, a specific country area, or a specific seaside place.

When we talk about a specific town, we use *a/an* or *the* in the usual way.
> *Below us in the valley lay **a small town**.*
> *Next morning we set off to view the sights of **the town**.*

But for *in town* and *to town,* > 160D

When we talk about a specific country area, we use *the* in the usual way.
> ***The countryside** around here is beautiful.*

155 *Twice a day, by the hour*, etc

A We can use *a/an* in expressions of frequency, price, and speed.
> *My brother shaves **twice a day**.*
> *These potatoes cost **one pound twenty a kilo**.*
> *The speed limit on motorways is **seventy miles an hour**.*

NOTE
We can also use *per* in expressions of price and speed, e.g. *seventy miles **per** hour / 70 mph.*

B We can say *by the* to say how something is measured.
> *Boats can be hired **by the hour** or **by the day**.*
> *Carpets are sold **by the square metre**.*

156 *A/an* or *one*?

A *A/an* and *one* both refer to a single thing, but *one* puts more emphasis on the number.
> *The family have **a** car.* (They can travel by road.)
> *The family have **one** car.* (They don't have two cars.)

B We use *one* when we mean a single one among a larger number. *One* often contrasts with *other*.
> ***One** shop was open, but the **others** were closed.*
> ***One** expert says **one** thing, and **another** says something different.*

In the of-structure, we use *one,* not *a/an.*
> ***One of** the shops was open.*

C We use *one* in phrases of time with nouns such as *morning*, *afternoon*, *evening*, *night*, *day*, and *weekend*.

> **One morning** *something very strange happened.*
> **One day** *my genius will be recognized.*

(At) one time usually means 'at a time in the past' or 'on one occasion in the past'.

> **At one time** / *Once I lived in a caravan.*
> **One time** / *Once we saw a strange light in the sky.*

At a/one time can mean 'at the same time'.

> *A team can have only six players on the court* **at a time/at one time**.

NOTE
For *a few*, *a little*, *a lot of*, and *a number of*, > 166.

157 *A/an*, *some*, and a noun on its own

A We use *a/an* only with a singular noun. *Some* with a plural or uncountable noun is equivalent to *a/an* with a singular noun.

> Singular: *There's* **a rat** *under the floorboards.*
> Plural: *There are* **some rats** *under the floorboards.*
> Uncountable: *There's* **some milk** *in the fridge.*

Here *a/an* and *some* express quantity. *A rat* means one rat, *some rats* means a number of rats, and *some milk* means an amount of milk.

We can sometimes use a plural or uncountable noun on its own, without *some*.

> *There are* **rats** *under the floorboards.*
> *There's* **milk** *in the fridge.*

Leaving out *some* here makes little difference to the meaning.

B Now look at these ways of classifying things, describing them, and generalizing about them.

		Classifying > 152G	Describing > 152F	Generalizing > 153
Singular:	*That's* **a rat**, *not a mouse.*	*It's* **a** *huge* **rat**.	**A rat** *will eat anything.*
Plural:	*Those are* **rats**, *not mice.*	*They're huge* **rats**.	**Rats** *will eat anything.*
Uncountable:	*Is this* **milk** *or cream?*	*It's fresh* **milk**.	**Milk** *is good for you.*

For these meanings we use *a/an* with a singular noun, or we use a plural or uncountable noun on its own. We do not use *some*.

158 *Sugar* or *the sugar*, *oil* or *the oil*, etc

A We can use an uncountable or plural noun on its own to make a generalization.

> ***Sugar*** *is bad for your teeth.* (= all sugar)
> *Adults have rights, so* ***children*** *should have them too.* (= all children)
> *Without* ***oil***, *modern life would come to a halt.* (= oil in general)
> ***Life*** *just isn't fair, is it?* (= life in general)

We use *the* when the meaning is more specific.

> *Could you pass* ***the sugar***, *please?* (the sugar on the table here)
> *My sister is looking after* ***the children*** *for us.* (our children)
> ***The oil*** *I got on my trousers won't wash out.* (a specific drop of oil)
> ***The life*** *of a Victorian factory worker wasn't easy.* (a specific kind of life)

We often use *the* when there is a phrase after the noun which makes the meaning more specific. We say *Life ...* (in general) but *The life of ...* (a specific person or group of people).

B Compare these two patterns, which have the same meaning.

> *I'm not an expert on* ***Irish history***.
> *I'm not an expert on* ***the history of Ireland***.

Here we can use an adjective + noun without *the*, or we use *the* + noun with an of-phrase.

Here are some more examples.

> *European architecture*   *the architecture of Europe*
> *American literature*   *the literature of America*

The same thing happens with a noun modifier or a possessive form.

> *town planning*   *the planning of towns*
> *Mozart's music*   *the music of Mozart*

C When an of-phrase follows a noun, we usually put *the* before the first noun.

> ***The safety of passengers*** *should be a priority.*

But when a phrase with a different preposition follows the noun, we use it without *the* if the meaning is fairly general.

> ***Safety on the railways*** *should be a priority.*
> ***Life in those days*** *wasn't easy.*
> ***Silk from Japan*** *was used to make the wedding dress.*

159 A singular noun on its own

Before a singular noun we normally put a word like *a*, *the*, *my*, *this*, *every*, etc. But there are some exceptions. We can use a singular noun on its own in the following cases.

A Before some nouns for institutions. > 160

> *How are you getting on at* ***college***?

B In some phrases of time. > 161
  *The concert is on **Thursday**.*

C In some fixed expressions where the noun is repeated or there is a contrast
  between the two nouns.
  *I lie awake **night** after **night**.*   *It was a fiasco from **start** to **finish**.*

D In a phrase with *by* expressing means. > 215E
  *It would be quicker by **train**.*

E In many idiomatic phrases, especially after a preposition. > 216
  *for **example**   in **fact**   on **holiday**   at **risk***

  But there are also idiomatic phrases with an article.
  *for **a change**   in **a hurry**   at **the moment**   on **the whole***

F We do not normally use *the* in these examples.
  *The President's cousin was appointed **Minister of Information**.*
  *Tony Blair was elected **party leader**.*

  Minister of Information and *party leader* both express a unique role. (There is
  only one.) We can use this pattern with verbs such as *appoint, elect, make,*
  and *proclaim*.

  We can also leave out *the* when the unique role follows *be* or *become*.
  *Tony Blair became **(the) party leader**.*

  We can do the same when the unique role follows *as*.
  *As **(the)** chairman, I have to keep order in the meeting.*
  But when the role is not unique, we use *a/an*.
  *As **a member** of this club, I have a right to come in.*

G Names of people and most place names have no article. > 162
  *for **Mr Mackintosh**   in **New York***

H We can sometimes leave out an article to avoid repeating it.
  *Put the knife and **fork** on the tray.*
  We can do this when two things are seen as closely linked, like a knife and
  fork. But when there is no link between them, we repeat the article.
  *I bought a sweater and **a book**.*

I We can leave out articles in some special styles such as news headlines and
  written instructions. > 30
  *Insert **plug** in **hole** in **side panel**.*

160 Articles with *school*, *prison*, etc

A There are some nouns that we can use without *the* when we are talking about the normal purpose of an institution.

> **School** *starts at nine o'clock.*   *The guilty men were sent to* **prison**.

Here *school* means 'school activities', and people are *sent to prison* for committing a crime.

But when we talk about a specific building, we use *the*.

> **The school** *is in the centre of the village.*
> *Mail is delivered to* **the prison** *every morning.*

Here *the school* means 'the school building', and *the prison* means 'the prison building'.

B Apart from words for institutions, there are a number of other nouns used in a similar way.

> *I'm usually in* **bed** *by eleven.*   **The bed** *felt very uncomfortable.*

In bed means 'sleeping/resting in a bed', but *the bed* means a specific bed.

C We use an article if there is a word or phrase modifying the noun.

> *The guilty men were sent to* **a high-security prison**.
> *I'm doing a course at* **the new college**.

When the noun is part of a name, there is usually no article. > 163

> *The guilty men were sent to* **Parkhurst Prison**.

D Here are some expressions with nouns of this type.

	Without article	With article
bed	*stay in bed, go to bed* (to sleep), *put a child to bed, get out of bed*	*lie on the bed, sit by the bed/ next to the bed*
church	*be in/at church, go to church* (to a service)	*visit the church, the Church of England, the Catholic Church* Compare: *at the mosque/the temple*
class	*be in class* (= in a lesson)	*stand at the front of the class, a/the class* (of pupils) Compare: *talk in the lesson/ leave the classroom*
college	*be at/in college* (as a student), *go to college, leave college, drop out of college*	
court	*appear in court, go to court, take someone to court*	*tell the court what happened*

	Without article	With article
home	*stay at home* As an adverb: *go/come/drive/ walk home*	*the home of a famous film star, a/the home for old people* Compare: *stay in the house*
hospital	*in hospital* (as a patient), *taken to hospital, go into hospital, leave hospital*	*in the hospital* (as a visitor), *work at the hospital* In US English: *in the hospital* (as a patient), *taken to the hospital*, etc.
jail	*be in jail* (as a prisoner), *go to jail, come out of jail*	*go to the jail* (as a visitor)
prison	*be in prison* (as a prisoner), *go to prison, come out of prison*	*go to the prison* (as a visitor)
school	*be in/at school* (as a pupil), *go to school, start/leave school, ready for school*	*go to the school* (as a visitor), *work at the school*
sea	*be at sea* (sailing), *go to sea* (as a sailor), *go/travel by sea*	*the fish in the sea, sail on the sea, under the sea, by/near the sea.* Compare: *at the seaside*
town	*meet in town, go to town*	*visit the town, in the town centre* Compare: *in the village, in the city*
university	*be at university* (as a student), *go to university*	Also possible in GB and normal in US English: *be at the university, go to the university*
work	*be at work, go to work, stop work, your place of work, out of work, looking for work*	Compare: *go to the office / go to the factory*

161 Articles in phrases of time

A Introduction

In a phrase of time we often use a singular noun without an article *in winter* *on Monday*	But we put *a/an* or *the* before an adjective + noun. ***a** very cold winter* We also use an article if there is a phrase or clause after the noun. ***the** Monday before the holiday* ***the** winter when we had all that snow*

In B–H there are some examples with various kinds of time phrase.

B Years

*The company was formed in **1981**.* *in **the year** 1981*
*The war lasted from **1812** to **1815**.*

C Seasons and months

*If **winter** comes, can **spring** be far behind?*   ***the winter** of 2002*
*It's nice here in **(the) summer**.*   ***a** marvellous **summer***
***June** is my favourite month.*
*The elections are in **March**.*

D Special times of the year

*I don't enjoy **Christmas** much.* *It was **a Christmas** I'll never forget.*
*Americans eat turkey at **Thanksgiving**.*

E Days of the week

*I must finish this report by **Monday**.* *I'm leaving on **the Wednesday** before*
(Monday of next week)   *Easter. That's **the** second **Wednesday** in April.*

*Our visitors are coming on **Friday**.* *This happened on **a Friday** in July.*
(Friday of this week)

*We usually go out **on Saturday** / on Saturdays.* (= every Saturday)	*We usually go out on **a Saturday**. Friday 12 May would be OK, but I'm busy on **the Thursday**.* (= the Thursday of that week)
	*I'll see you at **the weekend**.*

F Parts of the day and night

*At **midday** it was very hot.*	
*They reached the camp at **sunset**.*	*It was **a** wonderful **sunset**.*
*We'll be home before **dark**.*	*I couldn't see in **the dark**.*
*at **night**, by **day/night***	*in/during **the day/the night/ the morning/the afternoon/the evening***

In phrases of time we normally use these nouns on their own: *dawn, daybreak, sunrise; midday, noon; dusk, sunset, twilight; dark, nightfall; midnight*. But we use *a/an* or *the* when we talk about the physical aspect, e.g. not being able to see *in the dark*, rather than about the time.

G Meals

***Breakfast** is from seven o'clock.*	***The breakfast** we had at the hotel wasn't very nice.*
*I had a sandwich for **lunch**.*	*They all had **a** delicious **lunch**. **The meal** was perfect.*

H Phrases with *last* and *next*

*These flats were built **last year**.*	*The flats had been built **the previous year/the year before**.*
*We're having a party **next Saturday**.*	*They were having a party **the following Saturday**.*

Compare these phrases.

Seen from the present	Seen from the past
*I'm leaving **tomorrow**.*	*I was leaving **(the) next day**.*
*The match is **next week**.*	*The match was **the following week**.*

162 Names

A Most names of people and places are without *the*.
    Daniel   *Mrs Parsons*   *Texas*   *South Australia*

Some place names have *the*, especially names consisting of more than one word, but there are others which do not have *the*. For example, we say **the Black Sea** but *Lake Superior*. Two things affect whether a name has *the* or not. They are the kind of place it is (e.g. a sea or a lake), and the grammatical structure of the name. We often use *the* in these structures.

Of-phrase:	**the** Duke **of** Edinburgh	**the** Isle **of** Wight
Adjective:	**the American** School	**the Royal** Opera House
Plural form:	**the Johnsons**/the Johnson family	**the** West **Indies**

We do not usually use *the* before a possessive.
Possessive: **Cleopatra's** *Needle*

For more details about place names and *the*, > 163.

NOTE
A noun such as *doctor*, *professor*, or *president* can be part of a person's name.
    *I saw **Doctor Fry**.*
But when the noun is not part of a name, we use an article in the usual way.
    *I saw **the doctor**.*

B We can sometimes use an article with a person's name.
    *There's **a Laura** who works in our office.* (= a person called Laura)
    ***A Mr Wilson** called to see you.* (= someone called Mr Wilson)
    ***The Laura** I know has dark hair.* (= the person called Laura)
    *That's **a Hockney**, isn't it?* (= a picture by Hockney)

Here are some examples of *a*/*an* and *the* with place names which normally have no article.
    *There's **a Plymouth** in the US.* (= a place called Plymouth)
    ***The Plymouth** of today is very different from **the Plymouth** I once knew.*
    (Plymouth at different times)
    *Amsterdam is **the Venice** of the north.* (= the place like Venice)

Stressed *the* /ðiː/ before a name can mean 'the famous …'.
    I know a Joan Collins, but she isn't THE *Joan Collins.*
We can also stress *a* /eɪ/ to contrast with *the*.
    I know A *Joan Collins, but she isn't* THE *Joan Collins.*

163 Place names and *the*

For some general points about place names and *the*, > 162A. Here the different types of place name are dealt with in more detail.

A Continents, countries, and states

Most continents, islands, countries, states, and counties are without *the*.

a trip to Europe
on Bermuda
a holiday in France
through Ohio
in Hampshire
New South Wales

Exceptions are names ending with *republic* or *kingdom*.

the Dominican Republic
the UK

Plural names also have *the*.

the Netherlands
the US

B Regions

When the name of a continent or country (e.g. *America*) is modified by another word (e.g. *Central*), we do not use *the*.

Most other regions have *the*.

Central America *to North Wales*	*the South* *the Mid-West*
South-East Asia *in New England*	*the Midlands* *the Riviera*

C Mountains

Most mountains and hills are without *the*.

climbing (Mount) Kilimanjaro
up (Mount) Everest

A very few mountains have *the*.

the Matterhorn   *the Eiger*
Mountain ranges and hill ranges have *the*.
across the Alps
in the Cotswolds

D Lakes, rivers, and seas

Lakes are without *the*.

beside Lake Ontario

Rivers, canals, and seas have *the*.

on the (River) Avon
the Missouri (River)
building the Panama Canal
the North Sea
in the Pacific (Ocean)

E Cities and towns

Most cities, towns, suburbs, and villages are without *the*.	Exceptions are *The Hague* and *The Bronx*.
in Sydney *Kingswood, a suburb of Bristol* *at Nether Wallop*	

F Roads and streets

Most roads, streets, and parks are without *the*.	Some names with adjectives have *the*.

off Station Road
in Baker Street
Madison Avenue
along Broadway
in Central Park
Kew Gardens
	the *High Street*
	the *Botanical Gardens*
	We use *the* in this structure.
	   the *Bath Road* (= the road to Bath)
	
	We can also use *the* with some main roads in cities.
	   along **the** *Edgware Road*
	
	We use *the* with by-passes and motorways.
	   the *York by-pass*
	   the *M6 (motorway)*
	
	Other exceptions to the general rule are *The Avenue*, *The Mall*, and *The Strand*.

G Bridges

Some bridges are without *the*.	But there are also bridges with *the*.

across Magdalen Bridge
   Westminster Bridge
   near Tower Bridge
This includes the major London bridges.
	the *Sydney Harbour Bridge*
	the *Humber Bridge* (= the bridge over the Humber)
	The is used in American English.
	   the *Queensboro Bridge*

H Stations, churches, schools, etc

Most transport facilities, churches, schools, and other important buildings, as well as palaces and houses are without *the*.	We use *the* when there is an of-phrase.

to Euston (Station)	**the** Church of the Holy Trinity
Heathrow (Airport)	**the** University of Essex
St Paul's (Cathedral)	We generally use *the* when
Rugby (School)	there is an adjective or noun
at Essex (University)	modifier.
in Slough General Hospital	**the** Royal High School
Leeds Town Hall	**the** Old Town Hall
behind Buckingham Palace	**the** White House
at Clarence House	

I Theatres, hotels, etc

With theatres, cinemas, hotels, museums, galleries, and centres, we usually use *the* except with a possessive form.	Normally we use *the*.

St Martin's (Theatre)	**the** Prince Edward (Theatre)
Claridge's (Hotel)	I saw it at **the** Odeon (Cinema)
When the first word of the phrase is a	**the** Dorset (Hotel)
place name (e.g. *York*), we can	**the** Science Museum
sometimes use the phrase without	**the** National Gallery
the.	shopping in **the** Metro Centre
in York Museum	We use *the* with *building*.
	the Chrysler Building
Some US names with *center* are	
without *the*.	
near Rockefeller Center	

J Shops and restaurants

Most shops are without *the*.	We use *the* with shops and restaurants when there is an adjective or noun modifier.

shopping at Harrod's	**the** Kitchen Shop
in Next	at **the** Old Bakehouse (Restaurant)
A restaurant can be without *the* if it	Most pub names have *the*.
has a possessive form.	at **the** Red Lion (Inn)
at Charley's (Restaurant)	

Possessives and demonstratives

164 Possessives

A Introduction

In this conversation four people are discussing a date for a meeting.

Emma: *What about Friday?*
Luke: *I'll just look in **my** diary.*
Emma: *Have you got **your** diary, Tina?*
Tina: *I think so.*
Jason: *I haven't got **mine** with me.*
Luke: *I can't come on Friday. We're giving a party for one of **our** neighbours. It's **her** birthday.*

We use possessives to express a connection, often the fact that someone has something or that something belongs to someone. *My diary* is the diary that belongs to me. The possessive form of a noun has the same meaning. > 132B

> ***Luke's** diary   **our neighbour's** birthday*

There are possessive determiners (*my, your*, etc) and possessive pronouns (*mine, yours*, etc). Possessive determiners come before a noun.

> ***our** neighbour   **her** birthday   some of **your** friends*
> ***my** diary* (NOT ~~the diary of me~~ OR ~~the my diary~~)

Possessive determiners are sometimes called 'possessive adjectives'.

We leave out the noun when it is clear from the context what we mean, for example when the noun has just been mentioned. We use a possessive pronoun (e.g. *mine*) instead of a possessive determiner + noun (e.g. *my diary*).

> *I'll just look in my diary. ~ I haven't got **mine** with me.*
> *I took Lisa in my car because **hers** had broken down.*
> *I've got my opinion, and I'm sure you've got **yours**.*

A possessive pronoun can be a complement.

> *Is this diary **yours**? ~ No, I think it's Luke's.*
> (NOT ~~Is this diary to you?~~ OR ~~Is this diary of you?~~)

NOTE
For *my one, your one*, etc, > 179C Note.

B Form

	Determiners Singular	Plural	Pronouns Singular	Plural
First person	*my* pen	*our* house	*mine*	*ours*
Second person	*your* number	*your* coats	*yours*	*yours*
Third person	*his* father	*their* attitude	*his*	*theirs*
	her decision		*hers*	
	its location			

His is male, and *her* is female.
> *Luke's father* → **his** *father*
> *Emma's father* → **her** *father*

Its refers to something not human or to a place or an organization.
> *the roof of the car* → **its** *roof*
> *the country's exports* → **its** *exports*

Their is the plural of *his*, *her*, and *its*.
> *Luke and Emma's father* → **their** *father*
> *the interests of the two countries* → **their** *interests*

His can be either a determiner or a pronoun.
> *Has James got* **his** *mobile?*
> *I've got my mobile, but James hasn't got* **his**.

Its is a determiner but not a pronoun.
> *The restaurant is famous for* **its** *good food.*

We avoid using *its* without a following noun.
> *The east-coast route has its advantages, and the west-coast route has* **its**
> **advantages** *too.* (NOT *the west-coast route has its too.*)

We do not use an apostrophe with a possessive. (NOT *your's*).

Note that *it's* is a short form of *it is* or *it has*, > 290C.

C Possessives with parts of the body

We normally use a possessive with people's heads, arms, legs, etc, and their clothes, even if it is clear whose we mean.
> *What's the matter? ~ I've hurt* **my** *back.* (NOT *I've hurt the back.*)
> *We all got out of the car to stretch* **our** *legs.*
> *He just stood there with* **his** *hands in* **his** *pockets.*

But we usually use *the* in this pattern where a person is the object.

	Verb	Person	Prepositional phrase
The stone	*hit*	*the policeman*	**on the head.**
Someone	*pushed*	*me*	**in the back.**
Tom	*took*	*Karen*	**by the arm.**

215

We use *the* in the equivalent passive sentences.
> *A policeman was hit* **on the head**.

Compare these examples.
> *The stone hit him on* **the** *head.*
> *He had a bandage round* **his** *head.*
A person is the object (*him*) only in the first example.

D *A friend of mine*

My friend means a definite person, **the** person I am friends with. To talk about **a** person I am friends with, we say *one of my friends* or *a friend of mine*.

	Definite	Indefinite
Singular	*my friend*	*one of my friends* / *a friend of mine*
Plural	*my friends*	*some of my friends* / *some friends of mine*

Here are some examples of this of-structure.
> *I like The Strokes. I'm* **a fan of theirs**.
> *My brother has just seen* **an old girlfriend of his**.
> *Didn't you borrow* **some CDs of mine**?
> *I don't think my private life is* **any business of yours**.

We can also use the possessive form of names and other nouns in the of-structure.
> *We met* **a cousin of Nicola's**.
> *These are just* **some papers of my flatmate's**.

NOTE
In informal speech we can use *this, that, these,* or *those.*
> *I've been thinking about* **that suggestion of yours**.

E *Own*

We can use *own* after a possessive determiner.
> *I'd love to have* **my own** *flat.*
> *Students are expected to contribute* **their own** *ideas.*
My own means 'belonging to me and not to anyone else'.

There is also a structure with *of*.
> *I'd love a flat* **of my own**.
> (NOT ~~an own flat~~)

Sometimes *own* expresses the idea of doing something yourself without help.
> *You'll have to make* **your own** *bed.*
> (= You'll have to make your bed yourself.)

We can miss out the noun if the meaning is clear without it.
> *The ideas should be* **your own**.

On your own and *by yourself* mean 'alone'.
> *I don't want to walk home* **on my own**/*by myself.*

NOTE
Very own is more emphatic.
  *I never expected a little village to have **its very own** zoo.*
  *Hannah's dream was to have a pony of **her very own.***

165 Demonstratives

A In this conversation Debbie is choosing a birthday gift for her mother.
  Debbie: *I just want to look at **these** jugs. I might buy one for my mother.*
  Lauren: ***Those** glass ones are nice.*
  Debbie: *Yes, **this** one looks the sort of thing she might like.*
  Lauren: *What about **this**?*
  Debbie: *I don't like **that** so much.*

We use demonstratives to 'point to' something in the situation. *This* and *these* refer to something near the speaker. *That* and *those* refer to things further away. *This* and *that* are singular. *These* and *those* are plural.

	Near	Further away
Singular	*this* colour	*that* car
Plural	*these* flowers	*those* hills

We also use *this* and *that* with uncountable nouns as well as singular ones.
  ***this** coffee*   ***that** music*
For uncountable nouns, > 137.

We leave out the noun when it is clear from the context what we mean. When we do this we use a pronoun.

Determiner:	*What about **this** jug?*	*I like **those** pictures.*
Pronoun:	*What about **this**?*	*I like **those**.*

We can use *one* or *ones* instead of the noun.
> *What about **this one**?*
> ***These ones** are nice.*

B The basic meanings of 'near the speaker' and 'further away from the speaker' apply to both place and time.

	Place	Time
Near:	***this** book (**here**)* *these papers (**here**)*	*at **this** moment (= now)* ***these** days (= now)*
Further away:	***that** shop (**there**)* ***those** people (**there**)*	*at **that** time (= then)* *in **those** days (= then)*

When we are in a place or situation or at an event, we use *this* (not *that*) to refer to it.
> ***This town** has absolutely no night life.*
> *How long is **this weather** going to last?*
> ***This** is a great party, isn't it?*

We can use *that/those* with something already seen or talked about but no longer present in the situation.
> ***That dress** Tanya was wearing looked very smart.*
> ***Those things** I bought in the market were really cheap.*

This usage is rather informal.

We use *this* when we are talking about something that is about to happen.
> *I'm going to enjoy **this meal**.*

We use *that* for something that is over.
> ***That** was delicious.*

We use *this* or *these* for the present time.
> *My mother is staying with us **this week**.*
> *Things are different **these days**.*

We use *that* or *those* for the past.
> *I remember **that** terrible **storm**. My mother was staying with us **that week**.*
> *Things were different in **those days**. We didn't even have computers then.*

NOTE
In informal English, *this* (instead of *a/an*) can introduce the topic of a story or joke.
> ***This** girl knocked on our door one day and ...*

The scene is more immediate, as if we can see the girl in front of us.

C Look at these examples.
> ***This** is a great party, isn't **it**? I'm really enjoying **it**.*
> ***These** shoes are wet. I left **them** outside in the rain.*

When we mention something a second time, we use *it* or *they/them*. We do not usually use a demonstrative again.

D We can use a demonstrative with words for people.
   that waiter (over there)   *these people* (in here)
   We can also use the pronouns *this* and *that* when we identify someone.
   Mum, **this** *is my friend Leanne.* ~ *Hello, Leanne.*
   That *was Simon at the door.* ~ *Oh? What did he want?*

   On the phone we use *this* when we identify ourselves.
   Hello. **This** *is Steve. Is Claire there, please?*
   We usually use *that* when we ask who the other person is.
   Is **that** *you, Mark?*
   Who is **that**? / *Who is* **this**? (US: *Who is this?*)
   But we do not use these expressions when speaking face to face.

   NOTE
   We sometimes leave out *people* after *those*.
   Those *(people) who ordered lunch should go to the dining-room.*

E We can use *that* to refer to a statement or idea mentioned before.
   I haven't got an appointment. ~ *Oh,* **that** *doesn't matter.*
   Here *that* means 'the fact that I haven't got an appointment'.

   Here are two more examples from real conversations.
   The rooms are so big. **That's** *why it's cold.*
   Well, if you haven't got television, you can't watch it. ~ **That's** *true.*

   Sometimes we can use *this*, although *that* is more usual.
   I simply haven't got the money. **This is** / **That's** *the problem.*

   We use *this* and *that* in a number of idiomatic statements to express
   agreement or to say that someone has made a relevant point.
   That's *right.*   **That's** *the thing.*   **That's** *(just) it.*   **This is** *it.*
   In these expressions we stress the word at the end (*right, thing, it*).

   When we refer forward to what we are going to say, we use *this*.
   What I'd like to say is **this**. *The government has done a great deal to* ...

F We can use *that* or *those* in this pattern.
   She recognized the handwriting as **that** *of her husband.*
   (= the handwriting of her husband/her husband's handwriting)
   The best advice I've ever had is **that** *which my old teacher gave me.*
   (= the advice which my old teacher gave me)
   Some leaves are poisonous, especially **those** *of evergreen shrubs.*
   (= the leaves of evergreen shrubs)
   There's a big difference between studies which are scientific and **those**
   which are not.
   (= studies which are not)
   This use of *that* and *those* is rather formal.

Quantifiers

166 Large and small quantities

A What is a quantifier?

A quantifier is a word like *many, no,* or *some.* It usually comes before a noun.
  many *times*   **no** *tickets*   **some** *water*
A quantifier says how many or how much. For example, *many* expresses a large quantity, and *no* expresses zero quantity. Which quantifier we use can also depend on whether a noun is countable or uncountable. For example, we say **many** *bills* but **much** *money.* For details about the possible combinations, > 137B.

A quantifier can consist of more than one word, e.g. *lots of, a few.*
  lots of *fun*   **a few** *people*

We can also use a phrase with *number* or *amount.*
  a number of *problems*   **no amount of** *effort*

We often use an adjective with *number* or *amount,* e.g. *small, enormous.*
  a small number of *cases*   **an enormous amount of** *work*

Sometimes we can use an adverb of degree (e.g. *too, quite*) with a quantifier.
  too many *e-mails*   **quite a lot of** *money*
For the possible combinations, > 196F.

We can use a quantifier without a noun when the meaning is clear from the context. > 174
  *I expected to see lots of people, but there were only **a few**.*

In B–E there are some examples of how to express large and small quantities. Some of these forms are dealt with in more detail in 167–174.

B A large quantity

With either a plural or an uncountable noun.
  *There are **a lot of/lots of letters** for you.* > 167A,B
  *There's **masses/heaps/loads of time**.* (informal)

Only with a plural noun.
  Many questions *remain unanswered.* > 167A,B
  *A **large/considerable number of languages** have died out completely.*
  Numerous difficulties *were put in my way.*

Only with an uncountable noun.
  *We haven't had **much rain** lately.* > 167A,B
  *A dishwasher uses **a great deal of electricity**.*
  *A **large/considerable amount of data** has been gathered.*

Adjectives we can use before *number* or *amount* include *considerable, enormous, fair, large, substantial,* and *tremendous.*

NOTE
The verb agrees with the noun. > 146B
*A large number of **languages have** died out.*

C A quantity

With either a plural or an uncountable noun.
*I need to earn **some money**. > 172A*

Only with a plural noun
***A number of problems** have arisen.*

Only with an uncountable noun
*The machine makes **a certain amount of noise**.*

D A small quantity

Only with a plural noun
*I'm having **a few days** off work. > 176C–D*
***A small number of houses** will be built.*
*The group has only **a handful of** members.*
***Several people** were injured in the incident.* (perhaps four or five people)

Only with an uncountable noun
*I'll just have **a little water/a bit of water**. > 167C–D*
*A computer uses only **a small amount of electricity**.*

E Zero quantity

*There's **no milk** in the fridge. > 172C*
*I haven't sent **any e-mails** today. > 172A*

167 *A lot of, many, much, a few, a little*, and *a bit of*

A *A lot of, lots of, many*, and *much*

These words express a large quantity. We use *a lot of* and *lots of* with both plural and uncountable nouns.

Plural: *The town gets **a lot of visitors/lots of visitors** in summer.*
Uncountable: *You'll have **a lot of fun/lots of fun** at our Holiday Centre.*

Many goes before a plural noun and *much* before an uncountable noun.

Plural: *There aren't **many trains** on a Sunday.*
Uncountable: *There isn't **much traffic** on a Sunday.*

We can use *quite* and *rather* before *a lot of* (but not before *lots of, many,* or *much*).

*We get **quite a lot of** visitors.*

B *A lot of, lots of, many*, and *much* in statements and questions

As a very general rule, we use *a lot of/ lots of* in positive statements and *many* or *much* in negatives and questions.

> Positive: *We get **a lot of** visitors/**lots of** visitors.*
> Negative: *We don't get **many** visitors.*
> Question: *Do you get **many** visitors? How **many** visitors do you get?*

However, there are exceptions to this general rule. In positive statements we use *many* or *much* (but not *a lot of/ lots of*) after *very, so, too, as,* and *how.*

> ***Very many** crimes go unreported.*
> *I've got **so many** books there's no room for any more.*
> *There's **too much** concrete around here and not enough grass.*
> *I haven't taken **as many** photos this year.*
> *I know **how much** work you've put into the project.*

A lot of and *lots of* are rather more informal than *many/ much*. In informal English we can use *a lot of* in negatives and questions as well as in positive statements.

> *We don't get **a lot of** visitors / **many** visitors.*
> *Have you done **a lot of** work / **much** work on the project?*

Mainly in more formal English, we can use *many* and *much* in positive statements as well as in negatives and questions.

> ***Many** voices spoke out in protest.*
> *There has been **much** criticism of the government's policy.*

NOTE
We can use *not many / not much / not a lot of* + noun as subject or after a preposition. > 10C
> ***Not many** shops were open.*   *We arrived with **not a lot of** time to spare.*

C *A few, a little*, and *a bit of*

These words mean a small quantity. We use them mainly in positive statements. *A few* goes before a plural noun; *a little* and *a bit of* go before an uncountable noun.

> Plural: *I took **a few photos** of the animals.*
> Uncountable: *I've still got **a little money/a bit of money** left, fortunately.*

We often use *a few* in expressions of time.
> *I saw Lucy **a few days** ago.*

A (little) bit of means the same as *a little* but is more informal.
> *I'm just going to add **a (little) bit of** salt.*

We can use *quite* before *a few* and *a bit of.*
> *I took **quite a few** photos.*   *We've had **quite a bit of** rain.*
> This means a fairly large quantity, similar to *quite a lot of photos/rain*.

Only emphasizes the smallness of the number.
> *I **only** took **a few** photos.*
> This means a smaller number than we might expect.

NOTE
Little can also be an adjective meaning 'small in size', e.g. *a **little** flat / a small flat.*

D *Few* and *little*

Few and *little* without *a* have a negative meaning. Compare these examples.
  *Do people come here on holiday? ~ Yes, there are **a few** tourists.*
  (= some tourists/a small number of tourists)
  *Do people come here on holiday? ~ No, there are **few** tourists.*
  (= not many tourists)
  *Even at three in the morning there was **a little** traffic.*
  (= some traffic/a small amount of traffic)
  *It was three in the morning, so there was **little** traffic.*
  (= not much traffic)
Few and *little* used alone without *a* are rather formal. In conversation *not many* and *not much* are more usual.

We can use *very* before *few* or *little*.
  *There are **very few** tourists here.*
  (= a very small number of tourists)

E Special patterns with *many, few,* and *little*

Many, few, and *little* sometimes come after a determiner, e.g. *his, the, these.*
  *Tim introduced us to one of **his many** girlfriends.*
  ***The few** hotels in the area are always full.*
  *Only **these few** survivors are left to tell the story.*
  *I didn't want to waste **the little** money I had left.*

A great many is a little formal.
  ***A great many** crimes go unreported.*

NOTE
a   This pattern with *many a* is rather literary.
      ***Many a** ship has come to grief off the coast here.*
      ***Many a** time I have dreamed of starting a new life.*
    In informal speech *many times* or *lots of times* would be more usual.

b   *Many* and *few* can be a complement.
        *The disadvantages of the scheme are **many**.*
    This is rather literary. *Many* before the noun would be more usual.
        *The scheme has **many** disadvantages.*

168 Whole and part quantities

A Introduction

To talk about whole and part quantities, we can use words like *all* and *most*.
  *The story is in **all (of) the** newspapers.* (the whole group)
  *The bed takes up **most of the** space in here.* (the greater part)
We often use *of* with whole and part quantities.

Some quantifiers can express either large/small quantities or whole/part quantities. They include *a lot of, much, many, a few,* and *a little*.

223

Large/small > 166–167	Whole/part > B–H
*I found **a lot of** information on the Internet.* (a large amount)	*But **a lot of the** information I found wasn't very helpful.* (a large part)
*We didn't see **many** protesters on the streets.* (a large number)	***Many of the** protesters were wearing masks.* (a large part of the group)
*The artist sold **a few** paintings.* (a small number)	*The artist sold **a few of his** paintings.* (a small part of the total)
***Some** pages were missing.* (a number)	***Some of the** pages were missing.* (a part of the total)
	***Some of the** book was missing.* (a part)
We can use an uncountable noun (*information*) or a plural noun (*protesters, paintings, pages*) when expressing large or small quantities.	We often use *of* + determiner (*the, his*) + noun. As well as an uncountable or a plural noun, we can also use a singular noun (*book*).

In B–H there are some examples of how to express whole and part quantities. Some of these forms are dealt with in more detail in 169–174.

B The whole

***All (of) the** tickets have been sold.* > 169B
***The whole (of the)** show will be televised live.* > 169D
***Every** seat will be occupied.* > 171

C The greater part

*I slept through **most of the** film.* > 169A–B

D A large part

***A lot of the** passengers on the plane were backpackers.*
***Many of the** spectators left before the end.*
*I spend **much of my** time playing golf.*

E A part

*I answered **some of the** exam questions.* > 172D
*I did **part of the** exam.* > 172C

F Numbers

*About **a hundred of the** spectators left before the end.*
*I answered **six of the** exam questions.*
***Two of the** apples have gone bad.*

G A small part

> *A **few of the** apples have gone bad.*
> *Can you eat **a little of this** cake?*
> *We'll only miss **a bit of our** holiday.*
> ***Not many of the** motorists were carrying passengers.*
> *You haven't read **much of that** book yet.*

H No part

> ***None of my** friends went to the party.* > 169B
> *I **don't** like **any of these** colours.*

169 *All, most, half, none,* and *whole*

A We can use *all/most* before a plural or uncountable noun to make a generalization.

> ***All rabbits** love green food.*
> ***Most banks** have cash machines.*
> ***Most pollution** could be avoided.*

These sentences are about rabbits, banks, and pollution in general.

Compare these examples.

> ***Most people** just want a quiet life.* (people in general)
> ***Most of the people** here are strangers to me.* (a specific group of people)

As well as *most*, we can also use *a/the majority of* and *more than half*.

> ***A/The majority of banks** have cash machines.*
> ***More than half (of) the pollution** in the world could be avoided.*

The opposite is *a minority of* or *less than half*.

> ***A minority of banks** have no cash machine.*

NOTE

a   *All* + noun is sometimes used on written instructions about what people have to do.
    ***All tickets** must be shown.*   ***All visitors** report to Reception.*

b   For a generalization with a plural noun on its own, e.g. *Rabbits love green food*, > 153.

B When we are talking about something more specific, we use:
all/most/half/none + *of* + determiner + noun.

> ***All (of) our rabbits** died from some disease.*
> ***Most of the pubs** around here serve food.* (NOT ~~the most of the pubs~~)
> *I got the photocopying done at **half (of) the normal price**.*
> ***None of these jackets** fit me any more.*

In this pattern we cannot leave out *of* after *most* or *none*.

We can leave out *of* after *all* and *half*. But before a pronoun such as *it* or *them*, we always use *of*.

> *We had some rabbits, but **all of them** died.*
> *I read the book, but I couldn't understand **half of it**.*

We can use *a / an* with *half*.
> *We waited **half an hour**.   I ate **half a slice** of toast.*
Some nouns can follow *a half*, e.g. *a half hour, a half day*.
> *I work **a half day** on Thursdays.*
But this pattern has a more limited use than *half an hour* or *half a day*.

We can use *all* after an object pronoun.
> *The rabbits died. We lost **them all** / all of them.*
It can also come in mid position or after the subject.
> *These pictures are **all** quite valuable.*
> *The rabbits **all** died. / They **all** died.*

We cannot use *most* in mid position, but we can use *mostly*.
> *The pubs around here **mostly** serve food.*
> (= Most of the pubs around here serve food.)

NOTE
For *all* without a noun or pronoun, > 174B.

C   *None* means 'not any of the group'. We use it with the of-structure.
> ***None of the rabbits** survived. I'm afraid they all died.*
> (NOT *All of the rabbits didn't survive.*)

Not all means 'fewer/less than all'.
> ***Not all (of)** the rabbits died. Some of them survived.*

NOTE
For *no* and *none*, > 174C.

D   We can use *whole* as an adjective before a singular noun.
> *Did you listen to **the whole tape**? (NOT the all tape)*
> ***This whole idea** is completely crazy. (NOT this all idea)*
> *You didn't eat **a whole chicken**!*

We can also use *whole* as a noun.
> *Did you listen to **the whole of the tape**?*

Compare these examples.
> *We spent **all** day / the **whole** day on the beach.*
> (We were there from morning till evening.)
> *We spent **every** day on the beach. (every day of our holiday)*

170 *Both, either*, and *neither*

A   We use these words for two things.
> *The police set up barriers at **both ends** of the street. (the one **and** the other)*
> *If you're ambidextrous, you can write with **either hand**.*
> (the one **or** the other)
> ***Neither of the twins** is an especially attractive child.*
> (**not** the one **and not** the other)

B Compare the meaning of *both/neither* and *all/none*.

	Positive	Negative
Two:	**Both** *prisoners escaped.*	**Neither** *of the prisoners escaped.*
Three or more:	**All** *the prisoners escaped.*	**None** *of the prisoners escaped.*

C We use *both* before a plural noun.
> **Both houses** *are for sale.*

We can also use it before a determiner or with the of-structure.
> **Both (of) the houses** *are for sale.*
> **Both (of) these letters** *have been incorrectly addressed.*
> **Both (of) her parents** *are alcoholics.*

But we do NOT say ~~the both houses~~.

We can use *both* after an object pronoun.
> *Two prisoners escaped, but the police caught* **them both** / *both of them.*

It can also come in mid position or after the subject.
> *The teams are* **both** *confident of victory.*
> *The girls* **both** *enjoyed themselves./They* **both** *enjoyed themselves.*

NOTE
For the pattern *both her mother and her father,* > 233E.

D We use *either* and *neither* before a singular noun.
> **Either way** *is as good as the other.*
> **Neither car** *is very economical to run.*

We can also use them in the of-structure with a plural noun.
> *Is/Are* **either of your sisters** *married?*
> **Neither of our cars** *is/are very economical to run.*

In positions other than the subject, we usually use *either* rather than *neither*.
> *I don't like* **either** *of those pictures.*

This is more usual than *I like neither of those pictures.* But we use *neither* in the subject of a negative sentence.
> **Neither** *of those pictures appeals to me.*
> (NOT ~~Either/Both of those pictures don't appeal to me.~~)

171 *Every* and *each*

A We use *every* and *each* before a singular noun to mean all the members of a group.
> *There were flags flying from* **every/each building**.
> *Mike grew more nervous with* **every/each minute** *that passed.*

A subject with *every* and *each* has a singular verb.
> **Every/Each customer** *is greeted at the door.*

B In many contexts either *every* or *each* is possible, but there is a difference in meaning. *Every customer* means 'all the customers' and implies a large number. *Each customer is greeted at the door* means all the customers seen as individuals, as if we are thinking of greeting them one by one.

The following examples show the difference in meaning between *every* and *each*, although either word is possible in these contexts.
> *On the tape I could hear **every word** clearly.*
> (all the words, everything that was said)
> *The student had to look up **each word** in a dictionary.*
> (all the words one by one)
> ***Every child** is conditioned by its environment.*
> (all children in general)
> ***Each child** was given a medal with his or her name on.*
> (all the children individually)

Every usually suggests a larger number than *each*. *Each* refers to two or more things, but *every* refers to three or more.
> *United scored a goal in **each half/both halves**.*
> *Missiles were being thrown from **every direction/all directions**.*

We often use *every* to talk about things happening at regular intervals.
> *The noise wakes me up **every morning**.*
> *I go to the gym **every Thursday**.*
Each is possible here but less usual.

In these examples expressing frequency, we use *every* but not *each*.
> *The meetings are **every four weeks**.* (= at intervals of four weeks)
> *We visit my mother **every other weekend**.* (= every second weekend/on alternate weekends)

C We can use *almost* or *nearly* with *every* but not with *each*.
> *There were flags flying from **almost every building**.*

Every single means 'every one without exception'.
> *No one was left out. **Every single child** was given a medal.*

D We can use *each* (but not *every*) in these patterns.
> ***Each of the students** has a personal tutor.*
> *Before the visitors left, we gave **them each/each of them** a souvenir.*
> *The winners **each** received a prize.*

But we can use *every one of* + noun phrase. This emphasizes the fact that there are no exceptions.
> ***Every one of the students** has a personal tutor.*
> *We gave **every one of them** a souvenir.*
For the difference between *every one* (two words) and *everyone* (one word), > 180B Note a.

Each as an adverb can come after a noun.
> *The tickets are £10 **each**.*

228

E We cannot use a negative verb after *every* or *each*. Instead we use *none* and a positive verb.

> ***None of the doors*** *was/were locked.* (NOT ~~Every/Each door wasn't locked.~~)

But *not every* means 'fewer than all'.

> ***Not every door*** *was locked. Some of them were open.*
> (NOT ~~Not each door was locked.~~)

172 *Some, any,* and *no*

A *Some/any* expressing a quantity

Some with a plural or uncountable noun is equivalent to *a/an* with a singular noun. > 157

> *You'll need* ***some*** *wood,* ***a*** *hammer, and* ***some*** *nails.*

Here *some* is usually pronounced /səm/ or /sm/.

Some expresses a positive quantity. *Some nails* means 'a number of nails'. But *any* does not have this positive meaning. We use *any* mainly in negatives and questions.

> Positive: *I've got* ***some*** *nails.*
> Negative: *I haven't got* ***any*** *nails.*
> Question: *Have you got* ***any/some*** *nails?*

In a negative sentence we use *any* rather than *some*. This includes sentences with negative words like *never* and *hardly*.

> *I* ***never*** *seem to have* ***any*** *spare time.*
> *We've won* ***hardly any*** *games this season.*

Any is more usual in questions.

> *Have you got* ***any*** *nails? ~ Yes. / No. / I don't know.*
> *Did you catch* ***any*** *fish? ~ Yes, lots. / Yes, a few. / No, we didn't.*

But we use *some* to give the question a more positive tone, especially when making an offer or request. It may suggest that we expect the answer *yes*.

> *Did you catch* ***some*** *fish?* (= I expect you caught some fish.)
> *Would you like* ***some*** *cornflakes?* (= Have some cornflakes.)
> *Could you lend me* ***some*** *money?* (= Please lend me some money.)

In an if-clause we can use either *some* or *any*.

> *If you need* ***some/any*** *help, please let me know.*

We can use *any* in a main clause to express a condition.

> ***Any*** *problems will be dealt with by our agent.*
> (= If there are any problems, they will be dealt with by our agent.)

NOTE

In a negative sentence or a question we can sometimes use *any* with a singular noun.

> *I wrote to the company, but I didn't get* ***a*** *reply /* ***any*** *reply.*
> *Do you have* ***a*** *view/* ***any*** *view on the matter?*

Any is rather more emphatic than *a* here. In the first example we can use *any* to emphasize the fact that there was no reply. But in general *a/an* is more usual. We say *I haven't got a mobile* rather than *I haven't got any mobile*. For *any* with a singular noun meaning 'it doesn't matter which', > E.

B *Someone* or *anyone*, *something* or *anything*, etc

We choose between *someone/anyone*, etc in the same way as we choose between *some* and *any*.

Someone has been trying to kill me.
Polite complaints weren't getting me anywhere.
Have you got anything/something suitable to wear?
Could you do something for me?

For more details about *someone* etc, > 180.

C *No*

No is a negative word. We can use it with singular, plural, and uncountable nouns.

I'm afraid there is simply no alternative.
There are no rivers in Saudi Arabia.
We had no coffee, so we drank tea.

A sentence like *There is no alternative* is more emphatic than *There isn't an alternative* or *There isn't any alternative*. (For *any* + singular noun, > A Note .)

Compare these two sentences.

No warning was given.   *A warning was not given.*

We cannot use a subject with *any* to express this idea.
(NOT *Any warning was not given.*)

NOTE
For *no* and *none*, > 174C.

D *Some* expressing part of a quantity

Compare these two meanings of *some*.

Quantity: *There were some people in the studio.*
          /sm/ 'a number of people'
Part: *Some people enjoy quiz shows.*
          /sʌm/ 'some but not all'

Here are some more examples where *some* means 'some but not all'.

Some trains have a restaurant car.
Some fish can change their sex.
Some of the trains from this station go direct to Edinburgh.
Some of the fish in the tank were a beautiful blue colour.

Here *some fish* has a general meaning, and *some of the fish* has a more specific meaning.

When *some* means 'some but not all', we can use it in a negative sentence.

Some people don't enjoy quiz shows.

As well as a plural noun, we can also use *some* with a singular or an uncountable noun.

*I only watched **some of the programme**.*
*I like **some jazz** but not all of it.*

We can use *part of* instead of *some of* but only with a singular noun.

*I only watched **part of the programme**. (= a part of the programme).*
(BUT NOT *Part of the trains go to Edinburgh*)

We can also use *any of*.

*I was out, so I didn't see **any of the programme**.*

E *Any* meaning 'it doesn't matter which'

When *any* has this meaning, we can use it in positive sentences.

*You can choose **any colour** you like.*
*You can call on me **any time**. I'm always here.*
***Any passer-by** will be able to direct you to the town hall.*

All passers-by know where the town hall is, so it doesn't matter which one you ask. They are all a possible source of information.

At any minute/moment means 'very soon'.

*The bus should be here **at any minute**.*

Compare the meaning of *either* and *any*.

Two: *There are two colours. You can have **either** of them.*
Three or more: *There are several colours. You can have **any** of them.*

We can use compounds of *any* in the same way.

*The door isn't locked. **Anyone** could just walk in.*
*What would you like for lunch? ~ Oh, **anything**. I don't mind.*

F Other uses of *some*

Some with a singular noun can mean a person or thing whose identity is unknown.

***Some idiot** dropped a bottle.*
*The flight was delayed for **some reason** (or other).*

This suggests that it is not especially important who the idiot was or what the reason was.

Some day/time means an indefinite time in the future.

*I'll be famous **some day**/one day, you'll see.*
*You must come and see me **some time**.*

NOTE

a *Some* before a number means 'about'.
   ***Some twenty people** attended the meeting.*

b Stressed *some* /sʌm/ can express a strong and positive feeling about something.
   *That was **SOME** parade, wasn't it?*
   This means that the parade was an especially impressive one.

173 *Enough, plenty of, too many/much, another, some more,* and *other*

A *Enough*

We can use *enough* with a plural or an uncountable noun.
> *We had **enough chances** to win the game.*
> *Is there **enough room** for three people on the back seat?*
> *There aren't **enough bricks** here to build a wall.*

We can also use the of-structure for a part quantity.
> *I saw **enough of the film** to know I wasn't going to like it.*

NOTE
For *enough* as an adverb, > 196G.

B *Plenty of* and *too many / too much*

Plenty of means 'enough' or 'more than enough'. We use it with a plural or an uncountable noun.
> *There are **plenty of jobs** for qualified people.*
> *There's no need to hurry. We've got **plenty of time**.*

To express 'more than enough' when this is a bad thing, we use *too many* or *too much*.
> *I always take **too many clothes** on holiday. I really don't need so many.*
> *I spend **too much time** on my work. I never have time for anything else.*

C *Another* and *some more*

These express an extra quantity. We use *another* with a singular noun and *some more* with a plural or uncountable noun.
> Singular: *Would you like **another sausage**? ~ No, thank you. I've had enough.*
> Plural: *Have **some more beans**. ~ Thank you.*
> Uncountable: *Have we got **some more orange juice**? We've finished this carton.*

We always write *another* as one word.

Another can mean either 'an extra one' or 'a different one'.
> *We really need **another computer**. I hate sharing one.* (an extra one)
> *I think I'll buy **another computer** and scrap this one.* (a different one)

In some contexts we use *any more* rather than *some more*.
> *There isn't **any more** orange juice, I'm afraid.*
For the choice of *some* and *any*, > 172A.

Before *more* we can also use *a lot, lots, many, much, a few, a little,* and *a bit.*
> *I'll need **a few more** lessons before I can ski properly.*
> *Since the economic reforms there has been **a lot more** food in the shops.*
> *Can't you put **a little more** effort into it?*

D Other

Other is an adjective meaning 'different' or 'not the one just mentioned'.
> *We crossed to the **other** side of the road.*
> *Sarah was at the dinner, but I didn't know any of the **other** guests.*

Compare the use of *another*. > C

We can use *other* without a noun to refer to a thing or a person.
> *You take one bag and I'll take the **other** (one).*
> *One of the twins is fairer than the **other** (one).*

We can use *others* without a noun to refer to more than one.
> *Some pubs serve food, but **others** don't.*
> *I came on ahead. The **others** will be here soon.* (= the other people)

NOTE
The other day/week means 'recently'.
> *I saw that friend of yours **the other day**.*

E *Another* and *other* with numbers

We can use *another* before a plural number.
> *We were having such a good time we decided to stay on for **another three days**/for three more days.* (= an additional three days / an extra period of three days)

We can use *other* after a number.
> *This is the main bedroom, and there are **two other bedrooms** / two more bedrooms / another two bedrooms on the next floor.*

174 Quantifiers without a noun

A We can use a quantifier without a noun.

> *There are several large stores in London where you can buy practically anything; others are more specialized but still offer a wide choice of goods. **Most** have coffee shops and restaurants serving good, reasonably priced lunches and teas; **many** also have hairdressing salons.*

(from R. Nicholson *The London Guide*)

It is clear from the context that *most* means 'most large stores' and *many* means 'many large stores'. Here are some more examples that we might use in the same context.
> ***Some** sell food.*
> ***Two** have car parks.*
> ***A few** do not open until ten o'clock.*
> ***None** close for lunch.*

Here a word that we normally use as a quantifier is used on its own, like a pronoun.

We can also use the of-structure.

***Many of them** also have hairdressing salons.*
***None of them** close for lunch.*

Some quantifiers usually occur with *of*, e.g. *a bit of, a great deal of, a lot of, a number of, plenty of.* When we use *a lot, plenty*, etc without a noun, we drop the *of.*

*Not all the stores have late-night shopping, but **a lot** do.*
*If you want to climb a mountain there are **plenty** to choose from.*
*The area has millions of visitors, **a large number** arriving by car.*
Of must have a noun phrase or *it/them* after it.

*A lot **(of the stores/of them)** have late-night shopping.*

After some quantifiers we can use *one* instead of a singular noun. > 179B

*I tried three doors, and **each (one)** was locked.*
*The first bus was full, but **another (one)** soon arrived.*

B   *All* on its own has a limited use. These patterns are more usual.

*There are a number of large stores, and **all of them** open on Saturday.*
*There are a number of large stores, and they **all** open on Saturday.*
We do not usually say *All open on Saturday.*

But we can use *all* before a clause meaning 'everything' or 'the only thing'.

*I'm not hiding anything from you. I've told you **all (that) I know.***
***All you need** is love.*

C   We can use *each* on its own but not *every*.

*The states are represented in the Senate. **Each** (of them) sends two representatives.* (NOT *Every sends two representatives.*)

We cannot use *no* on its own. We use *none* instead.

*There are several routes up the mountain, but **none** (of them) are easy.*
(NOT *..., but no are easy.*)

Pronouns

175 Personal pronouns

A Introduction

Personal pronouns are words like *I, me, you*, or *he*. There are some examples in this real conversation. Avril and Lucy are talking about Lucy's brother.

WHAT DOES MATTHEW LOOK LIKE?

Avril: *If **we** said to **you** now, 'What does Matthew look like?' **you** probably wouldn't be able to give as good a description as **we** could.*

Lucy: *Oh yes, **I** could.*

Avril: *All right then. What does **he** look like?*

Lucy: *No, **you** describe **him** to **me** and **I**'ll tell **you** if **you**'re right.*

Avril: *Well, **he**'s quite tall, over six foot. And **he**'s thin.*

Lucy: *Well, yes, **I** suppose so.*

Avril: *Well, in proportion with his height, and **he**'s got fairly short black hair.*

Lucy: *Not very short.*

Avril: *Well, perhaps **it**'s grown since **I** saw him.*

Lucy: ***It**'s short as opposed to long.*

Avril: *I couldn't tell **you** what colour his eyes were.*

'Personal pronouns' do not always refer to people, although they often do. 'Personal' means first person (*I, me, we, us*), second person (*you*), and third person (*he, him, she, her, it, they, them*).

We cannot normally leave out a pronoun.

*Well, **he**'s quite tall.* (NOT ~~Well, is quite tall.~~)

*You describe **him** to me.* (NOT ~~You describe to me.~~)

But we can leave out some subject pronouns in informal speech. > 26A

(I) suppose so.

NOTE

a   Pronouns often have a weak spoken form, > 289.

b   We can leave out a pronoun to avoid repeating it.

   *Matthew has got short black hair **and is** quite tall / and he's quite tall.*

B Subject and object forms

These are the forms of the personal pronouns.

	Singular		Plural	
	Subject	Object	Subject	Object
First person	*I*	*me*	*we*	*us*
Second person	*you*	*you*	*you*	*you*
Third person	*he*	*him*	*they*	*them*
	she	*her*		
	it	*it*		

We use the subject form when the pronoun is the subject of a finite clause.
> *I couldn't tell you.*
> *Well, **he**'s quite tall.*

We use the object form when the pronoun is the object of a verb or preposition.
> *If you know what Matthew looks like, describe **him** to **me**.*
> *Avril isn't on holiday. I saw **her** yesterday.*

We also use the object form when the pronoun is on its own. Compare these two answers.
> *Who invited Matthew? ~ **Me**.*
> *Who invited Matthew? ~ **I** did.*

After *be* we normally use the object form.
> *The young man looked rather like Matthew, but it wasn't **him**.*
> *It wasn't **us** who caused all the trouble.*

NOTE
The subject pronoun is sometimes used after *be*.
> *The young man looked rather like Matthew, but it wasn't **he**.*

The subject pronoun here (*he*) is old-fashioned and formal. The object pronoun (*him*) is more usual.

> **TIP**
> Say *It's me* and not *It is I*.

C *And* or *or* with pronouns

We can use *and* or *or* to combine a pronoun with a noun phrase or with another pronoun. We do this especially with *I/me* and *you*.
> ***Matthew and I** are good friends.*
> *Lucy didn't know whether to ring **you or me**.*
> *Would **you and your sisters** like to come with us?*
> *It's a present from **Matthew and me**.*

We normally put *I/me* after *and* rather than before it.
> (NOT *~~I and Matthew are good friends.~~*)

NOTE

Pronoun usage with *and* or *or* is complicated. In informal English *me* is sometimes used in subject position, although it is not generally regarded as good English.

> *Matthew and me are good friends.*
> *You or him can have a turn now.*

There is a feeling among some English speakers that *I* is more correct than *me* in these patterns. So *and I* is sometimes used in positions where we would expect *and me*.

> *It's a present from Matthew and I.*

TIP

After *and*, choose the pronoun form as if it was on its own.

On its own	After *and*
I'm going out.	*Lucy and I are going out.*
Tom was with me.	*Tom was with Lucy and me.*

D Nouns and pronouns

We do not usually use a pronoun together with a noun.

> *Matthew is quite tall.*
> (NOT ~~Matthew he's quite tall.~~)
> *The two girls were talking about Matthew.*
> (NOT ~~The two girls they were talking about Matthew.~~)

But in informal speech we sometimes mention the topic of a sentence and then use a pronoun to refer to it.

> *Matthew, he's quite tall.*
> *Those new people, I saw them yesterday.*

We make clear what the topic is before we continue with the message.

In informal speech we can also use the following pattern to emphasize a topic.

> *He's quite tall, Matthew.*
> *I saw them yesterday, those new people.*

When the topic is the subject of the sentence, we can use an auxiliary verb.

> *He's quite tall, is Matthew.*
> *He's quite tall, Matthew is.*
> *It looks awful, does that colour.*
> *It looks awful, that colour does.*

NOTE

We sometimes use a phrase after a pronoun to make it clear who we mean.

> *We left-handed people should stick together.*
> *You kids had better go inside.*
> *Look at her over there.*

E Noun or pronoun?

We use a third-person pronoun instead of a full noun phrase when it is clear what we mean. In the conversation in A, Matthew is mentioned only once.
*What does **Matthew** look like?*
After that Avril and Lucy refer to him using pronouns because they know who they are talking about.
*What does **he** look like?*
*You describe **him**.*
*Well, **he**'s quite tall.*

But we sometimes need to use a noun rather than a pronoun, even for someone who has been mentioned before. Look at this paragraph from a novel.

> *When I first saw Tilly, **she** was twelve and fat. I was seven. **She** was tall even then, nearly as tall as Mum, and putting on too much weight. **Mum** used to encourage **her** to eat all the wrong things, chocolate bars and chips, crisps and cakes. Most days there'd be a dairy-cream sponge or a black forest cake defrosting on the kitchen counter. I believe **Mum** encouraged **Tilly** to eat because **she** wanted **her** to get fat and be unattractive to men. Women get like that with teenage girls, they can't face the competition. By the time **Tilly** was a teenager **she** was huge, all of fourteen stone.*
>
> (from B. Vine *Gallowglass*)

Because the paragraph is about two females, it is sometimes necessary to specify *Mum* or *Tilly*.
***Mum** used to encourage **her** to eat all the wrong things.*
The writer says *Mum* here to make it clear which person is meant. But *her* is possible later in the same sentence because it is clear from the context that *her* is Tilly.

For more examples of repeated nouns, > 22B.

NOTE
A third-person pronoun usually refers back to something already mentioned, but it can sometimes refer forwards.
*When **he** got home, Matthew rang to thank us.*

F *He, she, it,* and *they*

He/him, she/her, and *it* are singular. *He* means a male person, *she* means a female person, and *it* means something not human such as a thing, an action or an idea.
*Let's invite Mark. **He**'s great fun. I like **him**.*
*Let's invite Anna. **She**'s great fun. I like **her**.*
*Let's play that game. **It**'s great fun. I like **it**.*

Here are some contexts where we use *it*.

A thing: *I've lost my wallet. I can't find **it** anywhere.*
A substance: *Look at this water. **It**'s a funny colour.*
An animal: *What's that? Is **it** a beetle?* > Note a

An action: *I've been working out in the gym. **It** was exhausting.*
A situation: *We were left without any money. **It** was awful.*
A feeling: *Love makes the world go round, doesn't **it**?*
A statement or idea: *Everyone knows we cheated. **It** was obvious.*
As an empty subject: *It's raining.* > 36
To give emphasis: *It was Matthew the girls were talking about.* > 38D

We also use *it* to mean 'the unknown person' when we are talking about someone's identity.

> *There's someone at the door. **It's** probably the postman.*

Compare these sentences.

> *Don't you remember Celia? **She** was a great friend of mine.*
> *Don't you remember who first introduced us? **It** was Celia.*

They/them is plural and can refer to both people and things.

> *I like your cousins. **They're** great fun.*
> *I like these pictures. **They're** great.*

NOTE

a   We can use *he* or *she* for an animal if we know the animal's sex and we feel sympathy or interest. Compare these sentences.
> *He's a lovely little dog.*
> *It's a really vicious dog.*

b   We sometimes use *it* for a human baby of unknown sex.
> *Look at that baby. **It's** been sick.*

c   We do not normally stress *it*, but we can stress *this/that*.
> *Good heavens! Half past ten! Is THAT the right time?*
> (NOT ~~Is it the right time?~~)

G Referring to a person of unknown sex

There is a problem in English when we want to talk about a single person whose sex is not known. Here are three possible ways.

1   *When the millionth visitor arrives, **he** will be given a free ticket. **His** photo will be taken by a press photographer.*
2   *When the millionth visitor arrives, **he or she** will be given a free ticket. **His or her** photo will be taken by a press photographer.*
3   *When the millionth visitor arrives, **they** will be given a free ticket. **Their** photo will be taken by a press photographer.*

The use of *he* in (1) is widely seen as sexist and is less common than it used to be. But (2) can be clumsy and is often avoided, especially in speech. In (3) *they* is used with a singular meaning. Some people see this as incorrect, but it is very common, especially in informal English.

The problem disappears if we can use a plural noun. Compare these sentences.

> *A **student** may resit the exam if **he or she** fails at the first attempt.*
> ***Students** may resit the exam if **they** fail at the first attempt.*

> **TIP**
> When you're talking about a person and you don't know if it's a man or a woman, ...
> say *They'll win a million pounds*
> but write *He or she will win a million pounds.*

H *We/us*

We/us means the speaker and one or more other people. It can include or exclude the person spoken to.

We're late. ~ Yes, we'd better hurry, hadn't we? (*we* = you and I)
We're late. ~ You'd better hurry then, hadn't you? (*we* = he/she and I)

176 *You, one, we,* and *they* referring to people in general

A *You* and *one*

We can use *you* to mean 'people in general'.

You can wear anything you like to the theatre these days.
How do you train a police dog?
You don't like to complain, do you?

We can also use the third-person pronoun *one* with the same meaning.

One can wear anything one likes to the theatre these days.
How does one train a police dog?
One doesn't like to complain, does one?

One is more formal than *you* in these sentences. It is much less common than the equivalent pronoun in some other languages.

One can be an object.

Ice-cream is full of calories. It makes one hotter, not cooler.

It also has a possessive form *one's* and a reflexive/emphatic form *oneself.*

One should look after one's health.
One should look after oneself.

> **TIP**
> Avoid using *one* as a third-person pronoun
> Say *I hope so*, not ~~One hopes so.~~

NOTE
In Britain *one* is typical of upper-class speech, especially *one* used instead of *I*.
I hope/One hopes things will improve.
The pronoun *one* is not often used in American English.

B *We/us*

We can also mean 'people in general', 'all of us', especially when we talk about shared knowledge and behaviour.

We know that nuclear power has its dangers.
Language enables us to communicate.
We are 93 million miles from the sun.

C *They*

We can use *they* to mean 'other people in general', for example when we are talking about general beliefs.

They say / People say you can book cheaper flights on the Internet.
They say / Experts say the earth is getting warmer.

We can also use *they* to mean the relevant authorities.

They're going to increase taxes.
They should put a speed limit on this road.
They always show old films on TV on holiday weekends.

We cannot use *one* in these contexts.

NOT *One says the earth is getting warmer.*
NOT *One is going to increase taxes.*

For a comparison with the passive, e.g. *Taxes are going to be increased*, > 88D.

177 Reflexive pronouns, emphatic pronouns, and *each other*

A Form

We form reflexive and emphatic pronouns with *self/selves*.

	Singular	Plural
First person	*myself*	*ourselves*
Second person	*yourself*	*yourselves*
Third person	*himself, herself, itself*	*themselves*

For *oneself*, > 176A.

B The use of reflexive pronouns

We use a reflexive pronoun as an object when it refers to the same thing as the subject.

*I fell over and hurt **myself**.*
*You'd better prepare **yourself** for a shock.*

*The country declared **itself** independent.*
*If we're attacked, **we** will defend **ourselves**.*
*The company's directors have given **themselves** a big pay rise.*

Compare the reflexive pronoun and the personal pronoun.
*Luke is going to Italy, so **he's** teaching **himself** Italian.*
*Luke is going to Italy, so **I'm** teaching **him** Italian.*
*Debbie found **herself** a seat at the back and sat down.*
*Nicola arrived late, but **Debbie** found **her** a seat at the back.*

NOTE
We can use a reflexive pronoun in a sub-clause.
*We saw a man fall and hurt **himself**.*
*Giving **themselves** a pay rise wasn't very diplomatic of the directors.*

C Preposition + pronoun

After a preposition we sometimes use a personal pronoun (*me, you*, etc) to refer back to the subject, and we sometimes use a reflexive pronoun (*myself, yourself*, etc).

We use a personal pronoun after a preposition of place when it is clear that the pronoun must refer to the subject.
*I didn't have my driving licence with **me**.*
*My mother likes to have the family all around **her**.*

We sometimes use a reflexive pronoun to make the meaning clear or to emphasize it.
*Tom read an article about **himself** in the newspaper.*
(The article was about Tom and not about someone else.)
*I bought these chocolates for **myself**.*
(The chocolates are for me and not for anyone else.)

We use a reflexive pronoun to refer to the subject after combinations such as verb + preposition, adjective + preposition, or noun + preposition.
*The man next to me kept **talking to himself**.*
*I was **annoyed with myself** for making a mistake.*
*If you're going to succeed, you must have **confidence in yourself**.*

NOTE
When a reflexive pronoun comes after a preposition, it can refer back to the object rather than the subject.
*I showed **Tom** the article about **himself** in the newspaper.*

D Idioms with reflexive pronouns

There are some idiomatic uses of a verb + reflexive pronoun.
*I hope you **enjoy yourself**.* (= have a good time)
*Did the children **behave (themselves)**?* (= behave well)
*Can we just **help ourselves**?* (= take e.g. food)
In the idiom with *help*, we stress *self/selves*.

By yourself means 'alone'.
*Lauren was sitting in the corner **by herself** / on her own.*

Some verbs taking a reflexive pronoun in other languages do not do so in English.

*We'll have to **get up** early.*

*Won't you **sit down**?*

*I **feel** so helpless.*

*Can you **remember** what the man looked like?*

These verbs include: *afford, approach, complain, concentrate, feel* + adjective, *get up, hurry (up), lie down, relax, remember, rest, sit down, stand up, wake up, wonder, worry.*

These verbs do not usually take a reflexive pronoun: *bath, change* (your clothes), *dress, shave, undress, wash.*

*Tom **dressed** quickly and went down to breakfast.*

We can also say *Tom got dressed quickly.* > 90B

But we can use a reflexive pronoun with an action needing skill or effort.

*The old man was unable to **dress himself**.*

Dry in this context always has an object.

*Tom **dried himself/dried his hair** on a large yellow bath towel.*

NOTE

We can use a reflexive pronoun after *be, feel, look,* or *seem*.

*Claire didn't look **herself**/her usual self yesterday.*

(Perhaps she looked unwell.)

E Emphatic pronouns

The emphatic pronouns (*myself, yourself*, etc) have the same form as reflexive pronouns. (> A) We use an emphatic pronoun to emphasize a noun phrase. *Self/selves* is stressed.

*Walt Disney **himself** was the voice of Mickey Mouse.*

(Walt Disney and not someone else)

*The town **itself** is very ordinary, but it is set in lovely countryside.*

(the town and not its surroundings)

An emphatic pronoun can also mean 'without help'.

*We built the garage **ourselves**.*

*Did you do all this electrical wiring **yourself**?*

In this meaning, the pronoun usually comes at the end of the sentence.

By + reflexive pronoun has a similar meaning. > D

*Did you do all this electrical wiring **by yourself**/on your own?*

F A special use of *myself* and *yourself*

Myself and *yourself* are sometimes used instead of *I/me* and *you* even when there is no reflexive or emphatic meaning. This can happen after *and* or *or*.

*The Sales Manager **and myself** will be attending the meeting.*

*Enquiries should be answered either by Alice **or yourself**.*

This usage is rather formal.

Myself sometimes means 'as for me', 'as far as I am concerned'.
> *You can deal with the matter.* **Myself,** *I'll be on holiday.*
> *I can't stand football,* **myself.**
When used in this way, *myself* is usually separated off by a comma.

G *Each other / one another*

Look at this example.
> *Jane and Amy mailed* **each other.**
> *Jane and Amy mailed* **one another.**
These sentences both mean that Jane mailed Amy and Amy mailed Jane. The mail went in both directions.

Here are some more examples.
> *The students help* **each other/one another** *with their homework.*
> *We pass* **each other/one another** *in the corridor sometimes.*
> *Nigel and Chloe had their arms around* **each other/one another.**
> *The drivers blamed* **each other/one another** *for the accident.*

There is a possessive form *each other's/one another's*.
> *Nigel and Chloe were looking into* **each other's/one another's** *eyes.*

Compare *each other* and the reflexive pronoun.

They're looking at **each other.**   *They're looking at* **themselves.**

NOTE
There is also a pattern with *Each ... the other*.
> **Each** *driver blamed* **the other** *for the accident.*
> **Each** *of them was looking into* **the other's** *eyes.*
Compare *one ... the other*, where the action goes one way but is not returned.
> *An airline once employed two psychiatrists to watch the passengers and arrest anyone they thought might be a terrorist. On their first flight* **one** *of the psychiatrists arrested* **the other.**

178 Overview: personal pronouns, possessives, and reflexives

	Personal pronouns > 175		Possessives > 164		Reflexive pronouns > 177
	Subject	Object	Det	Pron	
Singular					
First person	*I*	*me*	*my*	*mine*	*myself*
Second person	*you*	*you*	*your*	*yours*	*yourself*
Third person	*he*	*him*	*his*	*his*	*himself*
	she	*her*	*her*	*hers*	*herself*
	it	*it*	*its*		*itself*
Plural					
First person	*we*	*us*	*our*	*ours*	*ourselves*
Second person	*you*	*you*	*your*	*yours*	*yourselves*
Third person	*they*	*them*	*their*	*theirs*	*themselves*

179 *One* and *ones*

A We sometimes use *one* or *ones* instead of a noun. Here are some examples from real conversations.

> *I felt I could afford a bigger car, and the **one** I'd got was on its last legs, really.* (*the one* = the car)
> *Now I will think everywhere I go on an aeroplane, 'Is this **one** going to come down?'* (*this one* = this aeroplane)
> *And what other stamps do you like besides Polish **ones**? ~ English **ones**. We've got a lot of those.* (*English ones* = English stamps)

One is singular and *ones* is plural. We use *one/ones* to avoid repeating a noun when it is clear from the context what we mean.

We cannot replace an uncountable noun with *one/ones*, but we can leave out the noun.

> *Do you prefer pop music or **classical**?*

B There are some patterns where we can either replace the noun with *one/ones* or simply leave out the noun.

After a demonstrative
> *These rings are expensive. **This (one)** costs £5,000.*

After *each, any, another, either* and *neither*
> *The houses all look the same, but **each (one)** is slightly different.*
> *Don't lose that key because I haven't got **another (one)**.*

245

After *which*
> *I couldn't answer some of the questions.*
> *~ **Which (ones)** did you find difficult?*
After a superlative
> *These photos are the **nicest (ones)**.*

C Sometimes when we leave out the noun, we have to use *one/ones* in its place. We cannot leave out *one/ones* in these structures.

After an adjective
> *I had an accident but not a **serious one**.*
> *We've still got a few games to play, but there aren't any **easy ones**.*
After *the*
> *This car is much better than **the one** we had before.*
> *These sweets are **the ones** I like.*
After *every*
> *We've been on lots of day trips, and **every one** was enjoyable.*

There are some exceptions to the rule that we must use *one/ones* after an adjective. We can sometimes leave it out when we use two adjectives.
> *Is this the **old** price or the **new (one)**?*
> *We've got **French** books and **German (ones)**.*

We can also leave out *one/ones* after *the* + adjective of colour.
> *My toothbrush is the **blue (one)**.*

NOTE
In informal speech you may hear *my one* instead of *mine*, *your one* instead of *yours*, etc.
> *This is your room key, but where's **mine**?/where's **my one**?* (BUT NOT ~~Where's my?~~)
For *mine*, *yours*, etc > 164A,B.

D We can replace *a/an* + noun with *one*.
> *I've got a map here if you need **one**.* (= a map)
> *I'm not used to weddings. I haven't been to **one** for ages.* (= a wedding)

Compare *one/some* and *it/they*.
> *I haven't got a backpack. I'll have to buy **one**.* (= a backpack)
> *I haven't got any boots. I'll have to buy **some**.* (= some boots)
> *I've got a backpack. You can borrow **it**.* (= the backpack)
> *I've got some boots, but **they** might not fit you.* (= the boots)
One and *some* are indefinite, like *a*. *It* and *they* are definite, like *the*.

180 *Everyone, something,* etc

A *Every, some, any,* and *no* form compounds ending in *-one/-body* and *-thing.* They also form compound adverbs ending in *-where.*

	every-	*some-*	*any-*	*no-*
-one	*everyone*	*someone*	*anyone*	*no one*
-body	*everybody*	*somebody*	*anybody*	*nobody*
-thing	*everything*	*something*	*anything*	*nothing*
-where	*everywhere*	*somewhere*	*anywhere*	*nowhere*

B *Everyone/everybody* means 'all the people'.
    Everyone *knows that red means danger.*
Someone/somebody means 'a person'.
    Someone *in the next street is having a party.*
No one/nobody means 'no people'.
    Nobody *will believe such a ridiculous story.*

Here *-one* and *-body* have the same meaning.

NOTE
a   *Every one* (two words) has a different meaning from *everyone* (one word).
    The comedian told several jokes. ***Everyone*** *laughed loudly.*
    (*everyone* = all the people; the stress is on *every-*.)
    The comedian told several jokes. ***Every one*** *of them I had heard before.*
    (*every one* = every joke; the stress is on *one*.)

b   *All* and *none* do not normally mean 'everyone' and 'nobody'. But we can say *all of / none of the people.*

c   Compare *someone* and *one*.
    Someone *knows what happened.* (= a person)
    One *knows what happened.* (= people in general > 176A)

C We use *-thing* for things, actions, messages, etc.
    I've got ***everything*** *I need, thank you.*
    Something *was happening at last.*
    It's best to keep quiet and say ***nothing****.*

NOTE
In speech *or something* can be used to show that the speaker is being vague.
    I can grab a sandwich ***or something*** *for lunch.* (= or something similar)

D *Everywhere* means '(in) all places'.
    I've been looking ***everywhere*** *for you.*
Somewhere means '(in) a place'.
    Have you put my bag ***somewhere****?*
Nowhere means '(in) no places'.
    There's ***nowhere*** *to sit down, I'm afraid.*

NOTE

in informal American English, *everyplace, someplace, anyplace, noplace* are also used.

E The difference between *some-* and *any-* in compounds is like the difference between *some* and *any* on their own. > 172

*There's **someone** at the door.*
*I'm not expecting **anyone**.*
*Park **somewhere** along here. **Anywhere** will do.*

F Pronouns in *-one/-body* have a possessive form.

*The guide collected **everyone's** passports.*
*I can get a lift in **somebody's** car.*

G We can use an adjective after *everyone,* etc.

*I heard **something interesting** today.*
*Let's go out **somewhere nice**.*
*Have you got **anything cheaper**?*

We can also use a phrase or clause.

***Nobody in our group** is interested in sightseeing.*
*I've told you **everything I know**.*

Before *every-, any-,* and *no-,* we can use adverbs such as *absolutely, almost, hardly, nearly,* and *practically.*

*I've done **absolutely nothing** with my life!*
*This plant will grow **almost anywhere**.*

We can use *else* after *everyone,* etc.

*Is there **anything else** you want?* (= any other thing)
*I don't like it here. Let's go **somewhere else**.* (= to another place)

NOTE

a   A phrase with *-one/-body* + *else* can be possessive.
   *But everyone **else's parents** let them stay out late.*

b   We cannot use *than* after *else.* We say *other than.*
   *How do you get kids to eat **something other than** fast food?*

H *Everyone, something,* etc take a singular verb.

***Is everything** all right?*   ***Someone has** left a message.*

After *-one/-body* we normally use *they/their,* even though the verb is singular.

***Everyone** was asked what **they** thought.*
***Somebody** has left **their** mobile here. ~ I think it's Paul's.*

NOTE

Someone and *something* usually have a singular meaning.

***Someone** was injured in the accident.* (= one person)
***Some people** were injured in the accident.* (= more than one person)
***Something** was stolen.* (= one thing)
***Some things** were stolen.* (= more than one thing)

Adjectives

181 Introduction

A This paragraph contains a number of adjectives.

> *Paradise Apartments are an **excellent** choice for an **independent** summer holiday. These **large**, **comfortable** apartments are along an **inland** waterway in a **quiet residential** area. The **friendly** resort of Gulftown with its **beautiful white sandy** beach is only a **short** walk away. The situation is **perfect**, and our charges are very **reasonable**.*

An adjective modifies a noun. The adjectives here express physical qualities (*large, sandy*) or an opinion (*excellent, beautiful*), or they classify something (*residential* so not *industrial* or *rural*).

B An adjective always has the same form. There are no endings for number or gender.

> *an **old** man   an **old** woman   **old** people*

But some adjectives can have comparative and superlative endings. > 203

> *My wife is **older** than I am.   This is the **oldest** building in the town.*

Most adjectives have no special form to show that they are adjectives. But there are some endings that we use when we form adjectives from other words.

> *a beauti**ful** view   a sand**y** beach   a resident**ial** area*

Some adjectives have the same form as adverbs, e.g. *fast, hard.* > 192C

C We can use two or more adjectives together.

> *a **large**, **comfortable** apartment*
> *a **beautiful white sandy** beach*

For details about the order of adjectives, > 185.
For the use of a comma between adjectives, > 185E.

We can put an adverb of degree (e.g. *very, really*) in front of most adjectives.

> *a **very large** apartment*
> *a **really beautiful** beach*

But we do not normally use an adverb of degree with a classifying adjective such as *residential* or *inland*.

> (NOT *a very inland waterway*)

182 The position of adjectives

A There are two main positions where an adjective can go. It can go before a noun, or it can go after a linking verb such as *be*.

The position before a noun is called 'attributive'.
*It is a **large** apartment.*
*Canterbury is a **lovely** city.*
*A **noisy** party kept us awake.*
*We face a **difficult** problem.*

The position after a linking verb such as *be* is called 'predicative'.
*The apartment is **large**.*
*Canterbury is **lovely**.*
*The party seemed very **noisy**.*
*Things are getting **difficult**.*

We can also sometimes put an adjective after a noun. > 184
*I've got a friend **keen** on fishing.*

NOTE

a   An adjective can also be an object complement.
*Why must you make things **difficult**?*
*A noisy party kept us **awake**.*

b   We can use some adjectives in a one-word reply or in an exclamation.
*I've got enough money. ~ Oh, **good**.*
*How **cold** your hands are!*

B We can use some adjectives after *as* or *than*.
*Could you let me know as soon **as possible**, please?*
*Everything was the same **as usual**.*
*Customers don't want to spend any more money **than necessary**.*
*I went to bed later **than usual**.*

C We can sometimes use an adjective immediately after a conjunction.
*Pick the fruit **when ripe**.* (= when **it is** ripe)
*Roast the potatoes **until crisp**.* (= until **they are** crisp)
__If possible__, I'd like some time to think it over. (= if **it is** possible)
__Although confident__ of victory, we knew it would not be easy. (= although
we were confident)
This pattern is used mainly in written English and especially in instructions
telling you how to do something.

D In literary English, an adjective can go before or after a noun phrase,
separated from it by a comma.
__Uncertain__, the woman hesitated and looked around.
*The weather, **bright and sunny**, had brought everyone out of doors.*

183 Adjectives used in one position only

A Attributive only

Some adjectives can go in attributive position (before a noun) but not in
predicative position.

*The house is right on a **main** road.* (BUT NOT ~~The road is main.~~)
*I woke in **utter** darkness.*
*The **outer** door is only locked at night.*

These adjectives are attributive only: *chief, elder* (= older), *eldest* (= oldest), *eventual, former* (= earlier), *indoor, inner, lone, main, mere* (*a mere child* = only a child), *only, outdoor, outer, own, premier, principal* (= main), *sheer* (= complete), *sole* (= only), *upper, utter* (= complete).

NOTE
a   *Same* cannot be predicative except with *the*.
 Yes, I had the same experience.
 *Yes, my experience was **the same**.*

b   In general, a noun as modifier is attributive.
 *a **water** pipe* *a **tennis** club* ***afternoon** tea*
 But a noun saying what something is made of can go in either position.
 *It's a **plastic** pipe. / The pipe is **plastic**.*

B Predicative only

Some adjectives can go in predicative position (after a linking verb such as *be*) but not in attributive position.
 *The children were soon **asleep**.* (BUT NOT ~~the asleep children~~)
 *I was **pleased** to see my friends again.*
 *One person was **ill** and couldn't come.*

These groups of words are predicative only.
Some words with the prefix *a-*: *afraid, alike, alive, alone, asleep, awake*
Some words expressing feelings: *ashamed, content, glad, pleased, upset*
Some words to do with health: *fine, ill, unwell, well,* > Note.

There is sometimes another word of similar meaning that we can use before a noun.
 *a **sleeping** child* or *being **asleep*** (BUT NOT ~~an asleep child~~)
 *a **living** person* or *being **alive*** (BUT NOT ~~an alive person~~)
 *the **frightened** dog* or *being **frightened/afraid*** (BUT NOT ~~the afraid dog~~)
 *a **satisfied** customer* or *feeling **satisfied/pleased*** (BUT NOT ~~a pleased customer~~)
 *a **lonely** feeling* or *feeling **lonely/alone*** (BUT NOT ~~an alone feeling~~)

Ashamed, glad, pleased, and *upset* can come before a noun when they do not refer directly to a person.
 *an **ashamed** look* *the **glad** news* *a **pleased** expression* *an **upset** stomach*

NOTE
Ill and *well* referring to health can sometimes come before a noun. *Ill* can do this when it is modified by an adverb.
 *The doctor had been called out to a **severely ill** patient.*
Well can come before a noun in a negative sentence.
 *My father is not a **well** man.*
For more about *good* and *well*, > 192G.

184 Adjectives after nouns and pronouns

A Some adjectives can have a prepositional phrase after them.
*People were **anxious for news**.*
*The suitcase was **full of old clothes**.*
For more examples of adjectives with a preposition, > 225.

The adjective + prepositional phrase can go directly after the noun.
***People anxious for news** kept ringing the emergency number.*
*I found **a suitcase full of old clothes**.*
But we cannot put it before the noun.
NOT *A ~~full of old clothes suitcase was found~~.*

NOTE

a   When an adjective is the object complement, it follows a noun or pronoun.
*The uncertainty was making **people anxious**.*

b   The adjective *available* can come before or after a noun
*None of the **available dates** are convenient.*
*None of the **dates available** (for travel) are convenient.*
Possible and *imaginable* can come after the noun when we use *every, all,* or a superlative adjective.
*We took the shortest **possible route**/the shortest **route possible**.*
*There were designs in every **imaginable colour**/every **colour imaginable**.*

c   The adjective also comes after the noun in a few titles and idiomatic phrases.
*the **Director General**   the **Princess Royal**   the **sum total***

B Sometimes the position of the adjective depends on the meaning.
*The amount of money **involved** is quite small.* (= relevant)
*It's a rather **involved** story.* (= complicated)
*The person **concerned** is out today, I'm afraid.* (= relevant)
*A number of **concerned** people have joined the protest.* (= worried)
*There were twenty people **present** at the meeting.* (= there)
*The **present** situation is extremely dangerous.* (= now)
*What would be the **responsible** course of action?* (= sensible)
*The person **responsible** for the mistake has been fired.* (= whose fault it is)

C Adjectives come after a compound with *every-, some-, any-,* and *no-.*
*Let's find **somewhere quiet**.   You mustn't do **anything silly**.*

185 The order of adjectives

A When two or more adjectives come before a noun, there is often a fixed order.
*a **beautiful sandy** beach* (NOT *a ~~sandy beautiful beach~~*)
*a **nice long blue** skirt* (NOT *a ~~blue long nice skirt~~*)
*a **new electronic** device* (NOT *an ~~electronic new device~~*)
The order of adjectives and noun modifiers depends mainly on the kind of meaning they express. Words like *beautiful* or *nice*, which express the

speaker's opinion, come first. Words expressing purpose or type, such as *electronic*, come later.

B We sometimes use two nouns together.
> *the **town wall***   *the **Finance Minister***   *winter evenings*

Here we use the nouns *town* and *finance* like adjectives, to modify *wall* and *minister*. When we use both adjective and noun modifiers, then the adjectives come first.
> *the **old town** wall*   *the **former Finance** Minister*   ***dark winter** evenings*

C The different kinds of modifier usually go in the following order. An adjective in Group 1 comes first, and a word from Group 11 goes closest to the noun.

1	Opinion:	*beautiful, nice, wonderful, excellent, awful, etc*
2	Size:	*long, large, small, short, tall, etc*
3	Most other qualities:	*clear, busy, famous, friendly, soft, quiet, etc*
4	Age:	*new, old*
5	Shape:	*round, square, fat, thin, wide, narrow, etc*
6	Colour:	*blue, red, white, black, etc*
7	Participle forms:	*running, missing, covered, broken, etc*
8	Origin:	*British, Italian, American, Chinese, etc*
9	Material:	*sandy, wooden, brick, paper, plastic, etc*
10	Type:	*electronic, human, chemical, domestic, urban, money (problems), etc*
11	Purpose:	*alarm (clock), tennis (court), walking (boots), etc*

Here are some examples.
> *an **old cardboard** box* (age + material)
> *a **German industrial** company* (origin + type)
> *a **large black pocket** handkerchief* (size + colour + type)
> ***plastic packaging** materials* (material + purpose)
> *a **small square** room* (size + shape)
> *a **new improved** formula* (age + participle form)
> *a **nice, friendly** person* (opinion + quality)
> *two **excellent public tennis** courts* (opinion + type + purpose)

In general, the modifier closest to the noun has the closest association with the noun. For example, in the phrase *two excellent public tennis courts*, the word *tennis* is closely associated with *courts*, whereas *excellent* does not have such a clear connection with *courts*.

The rules are not absolute, and the order can sometimes be different. For example, we sometimes prefer to put a short adjective before a long one.
> *a **big horrible** building*

NOTE
Old and *young* referring to people often come next to the noun.
> *a dignified **old** lady*   *a pale **young** man*

Here *old* and *young* are not strongly stressed.

D A modifier can consist of a two-word compound.
   *a powerful **high-speed** electric drill*
   *an **18-carat** gold chain*
   *an old **pale blue** football shirt*

E Sometimes we use two adjectives of similar meaning, for example two from Group 3 in C. When this happens, the shorter one often comes first.
   *a **bright, cheerful** smile   a **soft, comfortable** chair*

Sometimes two different orders are both possible.
   *a **peaceful, happy** place / a **happy, peaceful** place*

We often put a comma (or a short pause in speech) between two adjectives of similar meaning.

F We sometimes put *and* between two attributive adjectives.
   *a **soft, comfortable** chair / a **soft and comfortable** chair*
We can do this when the adjectives have a similar meaning. But we do not normally use *and* between adjectives with different kinds of meanings.
   *a **beautiful sandy** beach* (opinion + material)

We use *and* when the adjectives refer to different parts of something.
   *a **black and white** sweater* (partly black and partly white)

We use *but* when the adjectives refer to two qualities in contrast.
   *a **cheap but effective** solution*

G The order of predicative adjectives is less fixed than the order before a noun. We normally use *and* before the last adjective.
   *The chair was soft **and** comfortable.*
   *We were all cold, wet, **and** hungry.*

An adjective expressing an opinion often comes last.
   *The city is old and **beautiful**.*

We can use *but* when the two qualities are in contrast.
   *The solution is cheap **but** effective / cheap and effective.*

NOTE
In informal English we can use *nice and/lovely and* before an adjective expressing a desirable quality.
   *The room was **nice and warm**.* (= nicely warm)

186 Gradable and ungradable adjectives

Most adjectives are gradable – they express qualities which can exist in different grades or degrees. For example, we can talk about different degrees of warmth, difficulty, or tiredness.

> *It's **very/extremely warm** today.*
> *I thought the test questions were **fairly difficult**.*
> *I feel **a bit tired** now.*

Some adjectives are ungradable. Many of them express qualities such as magnificence or perfection, which cannot exist in different degrees. We do not normally use words like *very*, *extremely*, *fairly*, or *a bit* with an ungradable adjective, but we can use *absolutely*.

> *It's **absolutely boiling** today.   I feel **absolutely exhausted** now.*

With some ungradable adjectives we can also use *completely* or *totally*.

> *You're asking something that's **completely impossible**, I'm afraid.*
> *It's a **totally incredible** story.*

Here are some examples of ungradable adjectives.

absurd	*delicious*	*exhausting*	*ideal*	*stunning*
amazed	*delighted*	*extraordinary*	*impossible*	*terrible*
amazing	*determined*	*false*	*incomprehensible*	*terrific*
appalled	*devastated*	*fascinated*	*incredible*	*terrified*
appalling	*devastating*	*fascinating*	*ludicrous*	*terrifying*
awful	*dreadful*	*ghastly*	*magnificent*	*thrilled*
brilliant	*enormous*	*gorgeous*	*marvellous*	*thrilling*
certain	*essential*	*horrible*	*perfect*	*useless*
complete	*exhausted*	*huge*	*ridiculous*	*vast*

We can use *really* and *so* with both gradable and ungradable adjectives.

> *The food was **really good/so good**.*
> *The food was **really delicious/so delicious**.*

TIP

Don't use *very* with an ungradable adjective like *freezing* or *excellent*.

Say *It's freezing* or *It's very cold* but NOT ~~It's very freezing~~.

Say *It's excellent* or *It's very good* but NOT ~~It's very excellent~~.

NOTE

a   Sometimes in informal speech, *rather, fairly,* or *pretty* is used with an ungradable adjective.
> *The task is **fairly impossible**.   I feel **pretty exhausted** now.*

b   For the meaning of *quite* with a gradable/ungradable adjective, > 197.

187 *Amusing* and *amused*, *interesting* and *interested*

Compare the adjectives ending in *-ing* and *-ed*.

*The film made us laugh a lot. It was very **amusing**.*	*The audience laughed a lot. They were very **amused**.*
*I talked to an **interesting** man.*	*I was **interested** in what he was telling me.*
*I find these statistics **confusing**.*	*I'm **confused** by these statistics.*
*This weather is **depressing**, isn't it?*	*Don't you feel **depressed** when it rains so much?*
Adjectives ending in *-ing* express the idea that something affects us. A film is *amusing* because it makes us laugh. It can also be *interesting*, *exciting*, or *boring*.	Adjectives ending in *-ed* express the feelings we have about something. We are *amused* when we see something funny. We can also be *interested*, *excited*, or *bored*.

Some pairs of adjectives like this are:

alarming, amazing, amusing, annoying, boring, confusing, depressing, disappointing, exciting, exhausting, fascinating, frightening, interesting, pleasing, puzzling, relaxing, shocking, surprising, thrilling, tiring, worrying	*alarmed, amazed, amused, annoyed, bored, confused, depressed, disappointed, excited, exhausted, fascinated, frightened, interested, pleased, puzzled, relaxed, shocked, surprised, thrilled, tired, worried*

188 *The* + adjective

A *The poor, the disabled,* etc

We can use *the* + adjective to refer to some groups of people in society.
> *In those days **the poor** had a miserable time.*
> (= poor people in general)
> *There are more churchgoers among **the old** than among **the young**.*
> (= old/young people in general)

We can also say *poor people, old people*, etc with the same general meaning.
> *In those days **poor people** had a miserable time.*

When we want to talk about a specific person or group of people, we use *a young man, the old people*, etc.
> *A young man has been arrested.* (NOT ~~A young has~~ ...)
> *The old people have gone on a coach trip.* (NOT ~~The old have gone~~ ...)

The + adjective takes a plural verb.
> *The old are more frequently ill than the rest of the population.*
But we do not add an *-s* to the adjective. (NOT ~~the olds~~)

Some adjectives and participle forms used in this way are: *blind, dead, deaf, disabled, disadvantaged, elderly, handicapped, homeless, hungry, living, middle-aged, old, poor, privileged, rich, sick, sighted, strong, underprivileged, unemployed, weak, young.*

The adjective can have an adverb in front of it.
   *the **very** rich   the **severely** disabled   the **partially** sighted*
Some adjectives normally have an adverb.
   *the **more/less** fortunate   the **mentally** ill*

NOTE

a   In a few contexts, *the* + participle can mean a specific group of people rather than people in general.
   The injured *were taken to hospital.*
   It can also mean one specific person.
   The accused *was found not guilty.*

b   There are a few words that can come after *a/an* referring to a specific person.
   *Now a superstar, she was **an unknown** only two years ago.*

c   There are a few adjectives that we can use as nouns, such as colour words. They can form a plural with *-s*.
   *a **black*** (= a black person)   *the **Greens*** (= supporters of the green movement)

d   Some adjectives of nationality can be used with *the* to mean a whole people, e.g. *the French, the Swiss.*

B *The supernatural, the absurd,* etc

There are some adjectives and participle forms that we can use after *the* to refer to things in general which have a particular quality.
   *Lots of people believe in **the supernatural**.*
   *It was a journey into **the unknown**.*
The supernatural means 'supernatural happenings in general'.

Here *the* + adjective/participle takes a singular verb.
   *The new **takes** over from the old.*

Some words used in this way are *absurd, mysterious, new, old, ordinary, supernatural, unexplained, unknown.*

C *The unexpected, the good thing,* etc

There are a few words that we can use after *the* with a more specific meaning.
   *And then, suddenly, **the unexpected** happened.* (= something that was unexpected)
   *Have you heard **the latest**?* (= the latest news)
   *We fear **the worst**, but we must hope for **the best**.*
   *At this time of year I leave home in **the dark**.*
   *I'm sorry, but you're asking **the impossible**.*

We use *the* + adjective/participle + *thing* to talk about a particular aspect of a situation. This pattern is rather informal.
   The good thing *about friends is that you can choose them, unlike relatives.*
   The annoying thing *(about it) was that there were empty seats in the stadium, but they still wouldn't let us in.*
We cannot leave out *thing* here.

In this pattern with *thing* we can use many different words. Some of these are: *amazing, annoying, awful, best, funny, good, great, interesting, nice, odd, remarkable, sad, strange, worst.*

Adverbials

189 Introduction

A Each of these sentences contains one or more adverbials.
> *Slowly we were moving forwards.*
> *The queue stretched **around the block**.*
> *We have **now** been waiting **forty minutes**.*
> ***Eventually** we reached the entrance.*

Very often an adverbial is an extra element which could be left out. For example, we could say *We reached the entrance* without an adverbial. Putting in an adverbial adds something to the meaning. It tells us how, when, or where something happened.

B An adverbial can be a single word or a phrase. A common kind of adverbial is a prepositional phrase.
> *The queue stretched **around the block**.*   *I wish I'd stayed **at home**.*

An adverbial can also be a simple adverb, e.g. *forwards, patiently*. There can be an adverb of degree (e.g. *very*) in front of the adverb.
> *The queue was moving **forwards**.*   *Everyone waited **very patiently**.*

An adverbial can also be a noun phrase, although this is less frequent.
> *We have been waiting **forty minutes**.*   *I heard the news **last week**.*

> **TIP**
> Try not to confuse the words *adverb* and *adverbial*.
> An **adverb** is a word class, like a noun or adjective. An adverb is a word like *softly, carefully, now, today, there, certainly*.
> An **adverbial** is a sentence element, like a subject or object. It can be a single-word adverb, or it can be a phrase. Examples are *badly, maybe, in a strange way, at the moment, outside the college, this morning*.

C Sometimes an adverbial is necessary to complete a sentence. > 4
> *The queue stretched **around the block**.*
> *The first performance is **tomorrow**.*
> *I put the tickets **in my wallet**.*

Here the sentence would not make sense without the adverbial.

D Some adverbials can also be used to modify other parts of the sentence. For example, an adverbial can come after a noun. > 143
> *The performance **yesterday** was brilliant.*
> *The car **in front of us** was going very slowly.*
> *The announcement **last week** came as a shock to all of us.*

An adverb of degree can modify an adjective or an adverb. > 196
*The performance was **quite** good.*
*Everyone waited **very** patiently.*

190 The position of adverbials

A Introduction

The position of adverbials is a complicated area of grammar. There is usually more than one possible place in a sentence where an adverbial can go. Basically, it can go at the beginning, in the middle, or at the end of a sentence.

Front position: ***Naturally**, we were hoping for good news.*
Mid position: *We were **naturally** hoping for good news.*
End position: *We were hoping for good news, **naturally**.*

For more details about each of these positions, > B–F.

Where we put an adverbial depends on a number of factors, such as what type of adverbial it is – manner, or time, or frequency, and so on. For details about the position of the different types of adverbial, > 193–202.

The best position may also depend on how long the adverbial is – whether it is a single word or a longer phrase. The choice is often a matter of style: for example, a long phrase goes better at the beginning or end of a sentence rather than in the middle.

*I can't answer that question **in a satisfactory way**.*
(NOT ~~I can't in a satisfactory way answer that question.~~)

Another factor is the information structure of the sentence. We sometimes choose to put an adverbial in front position to link with the previous sentence or to give greater emphasis to the adverbial. > 34A

*The man was taken to a police station. **There** he was searched and found to be carrying a quantity of heroin.*
*I had a long wait. **In the end** I got to see a doctor.*

Sometimes the choice of position can affect the meaning of a sentence.

***Clearly**, he didn't explain things.* (= It is clear that he didn't explain things.)
*He didn't explain things **clearly**.* (= He didn't explain things in a clear way.)

NOTE
We sometimes use commas with adverbials. Commas are more likely with longer phrases and with certain types of adverbial, such as a truth adverbial.

B Front position

Front position is at the beginning of a clause.

***Sure enough**, there was an enormous queue.*
***Just** wait a moment, could you?*
***After a while** I got used to the noise of the traffic.*
Most types of adverbial can go here.

If there is a conjunction (e.g. *but, because*), it comes before the adverbial in front position.

> *The noise of the traffic was terrible. But **after a while** I got used to it.*
> *We invest in shares because **in the long run** their value will increase.*

We often put an adverbial in front position when it relates to what has gone before.

> *We stopped to get some petrol. And **then** the car wouldn't start.*
> *I've got a busy week. **On Tuesday** I have to go to London.*

For more examples, > 34A.

C Mid position

Mid position is close to the verb. If there is an auxiliary verb, the adverbial usually comes immediately after it.

> *Those kids are **always** hanging around the streets.*

The adverbial also comes immediately after the ordinary verb *be*.

> *This camera is **definitely** faulty.*

If there is a simple-tense verb, the adverbial comes before it.

> *We **usually** deal with the mail first.*

Here are some more examples of adverbials in mid position.

Subject	(Auxiliary) (Ordinary verb *be*)	Adverbial	(Verb)	
It	*doesn't*	***often***	*rain*	*in the Sahara.*
I	*'ve*	***just***	*had*	*a chat with Jill.*
Things	*will*	***very soon***	*start*	*to improve.*
The story	*is*	***probably***		*untrue.*
Someone		***probably***	*made*	*the story up.*
You		***always***	*look*	*smart.*

If there are two auxiliaries, then mid position is usually after the first one.

> *I've **just been** chatting to Jill.*
> *Things **will soon be** looking up.*

But adverbs of manner and some adverbs of degree go after the second auxiliary in mid position.

> *We've **been patiently** queuing for tickets.*
> *You **could have completely** spoiled everything.*

NOTE

In a question there is inversion of subject and auxiliary before an adverbial in mid position.

> *Have you **just** had a chat with Jill?*
> *How does Matthew **always** look so smart?*

Here the adverbial follows the subject.

D Phrases in mid position

Most types of adverbial can go in mid position. Adverbials in mid position are usually single-word adverbs, but a short phrase with an adverb of degree such as *very*, *quite*, or *hardly* is also possible.

*I would **very much** like to visit your country.*
*We **hardly ever** go out in the evenings.*

Most other kinds of phrase cannot go in mid position. Compare these sentences.

*You **always** look smart.* (adverb in mid position)
*You look smart **all the time**.* (phrase in end position)
(NOT *You all the time look smart.*)

But phrases which are truth adverbials, comment adverbials, or linking adverbials can sometimes go in mid position.

*The experiment has **on the whole** proved unsuccessful.*
This pattern is rather formal.

E Mid position before an auxiliary

When there is an auxiliary verb, a mid-position adverb usually comes after the auxiliary. > C

*I've **always** liked the Beatles.*
*You're **obviously** dying to make a start.*

But we sometimes put an adverb after the subject and before an auxiliary or before the ordinary verb *be*.

*I **always** did like the Beatles.*
*You **obviously** ARE in a bit of trouble.*
This happens with emphatic *do*, or when the verb is stressed (*obviously* ARE).

Some adverbs such as truth adverbs usually come before a negative auxiliary.

*You **obviously** haven't been listening to me.*
*It **probably** doesn't matter very much.*

Some adverbs can come before or after the negative auxiliary. Look at these examples with *really* and *deliberately*.

*I **really** don't know the answer.* (I don't know at all.)
*I don't **really** know the answer.* (I am unsure.)
*I **deliberately** didn't leave the computer on.* (I left it off on purpose.)
*I didn't **deliberately** leave the computer on.* (I left it on by mistake.)

Look at these examples where words are left out after the auxiliary (*will*, *do*).

*Will you be going to the party? ~ Yes, I **probably** will.*
*My husband usually gets up early, but I **never** do.*
Here the adverb comes after the subject and before the auxiliary.

An adverb also goes before *have to*, *used to*, and *ought to*.

*I **never** have to wait long for a bus.*
*There **definitely** used to be a footpath through the woods.*

NOTE
With *used to* we can put the adverb after *used*, but this is rather formal.
*There used **definitely** to be a footpath through the woods.*

F End position

Sometimes an adverbial comes at the end of a clause.

*It doesn't often rain **in the Sahara**.*
*Everyone waited **very patiently**.*
*I wish I'd stayed **at home**.*

Almost all types of adverbial can go in end position. For details about more than one adverbial in end position, > 191.

If there is an object, then the adverbial usually goes after it.

*I wrapped the parcel **carefully**.* (NOT *I wrapped carefully the parcel.*)
*We'll finish the job **next week**.* (NOT *We'll finish next week the job.*)

But a short adverbial can go before a long object.

*I wrapped **carefully** all the glasses and ornaments.*

Here the adverb of manner can also go in mid position.

*I **carefully** wrapped all the glasses and ornaments.*

When there are two clauses, the position of the adverbial can affect the meaning.

*They agreed **immediately** that the goods would be replaced.*
(an immediate agreement)
*They agreed that the goods would be replaced **immediately**.*
(an immediate replacement)

TIP

Don't put an adverb in front of a short object.
Say *We finished the job quickly*, NOT *We finished quickly the job*.

---

191 Order of adverbials in end position

A Sometimes there is more than one adverbial in end position. Usually a shorter adverbial goes before a longer one.

*Sam waited **impatiently outside the post office**.*
*We sat **indoors most of the afternoon**.*
*A policeman inspected the car **thoroughly in a very officious manner**.*

B When there is a close link in meaning between a verb and an adverbial, then the adverbial goes directly after the verb. For example, we usually put an adverbial of place next to *go, come*, etc.

*I don't want to go **to school** today.*
*Why did you come **home** late?*

C Phrases of time and place can go in either order.

*There was an accident **last night on the by-pass**.*
*There was an accident **on the by-pass last night**.*

D Manner, time, and place usually come before frequency.
   *Sarah gets up **early occasionally**.*
   *I can find my way around **quite easily, usually**.*
The adverb of frequency can also go in front or mid position.
   ***Usually** I can find my way around quite easily.*
   *I can **usually** find my way around quite easily.*

E When certain types of adverbial come in end position, we usually put them last, as a kind of afterthought.
   *Simon has been delayed by the traffic, **perhaps**.* (truth adverbial)
   *Someone handed the money in at the police station, **incredibly**.* (comment adverbial)
   *I've got a bicycle. I don't ride it very often, **however**.* (linking adverbial)
This happens more often in speech than in writing.

192 Adverb forms

A Look at these two examples.
   *I'm going on holiday **soon**.*
   *I'm going on holiday **shortly**.*

Some adverbs, like *soon*, have a form which is unrelated to other words. Adverbs of this kind include *always, just, often, never, perhaps, quite, rather, seldom, soon, very*.

Many adverbs are formed from an adjective and *-ly*, like *shortly*, which is related to the adjective *short*.

> **There are some spelling rules for adverbs ending in *-ly*.**
> After a consonant, final *y* changes to *i*, e.g. *easy → easily*. > 280A
> With a consonant + *le*, *le* changes to *-ly*, e.g. *probable → probably*. > 278D
> The ending *-ic* changes to *ically*, e.g. *magic → magically*. > 278D
> After *ll* we add *-y*, e.g. *full → fully*. > 279B Note

B There are some adjectives which end in *-ly*, e.g. *friendly*. We cannot add another *-ly* to such an adjective. Instead we can use a phrase with *manner, way*, or *fashion*.
   Adjective: *We received a **friendly** greeting.*
   Adverbial: *They greeted us **in a friendly manner**.* (NOT *friendlily*)

Sometimes we can use another adverb formed from an adjective of similar meaning.
   Adjective: *That's not very **likely**.*
   Adverbial: *That **probably** won't happen.*

Some adjectives ending in *-ly* are *costly, cowardly, friendly, likely, lively, lonely, lovely, silly*, and *ugly*.

Participle forms such as *annoying* and *surprising* form adverbs in *-ly*.
> *It was **surprisingly** cold for the time of year.*

But we cannot usually form adverbs from participles ending in *-ed*.
> *Everyone stared **in astonishment**.*
> (NOT *Everyone stared ~~astonishedly~~.*)

The only exceptions are a few participles ending in *-ted*,
e.g. *excited, exhausted.*
> *The crowd shouted **excitedly**.*

C Some adverbs have the same form as adjectives.

Adjective	Adverb
*Louise caught the **fast** train.*	*The train was going quite **fast**.*
*We didn't have a **long** wait.*	*We didn't have to wait **long**.*
*I had an **early** night.*	*I went to bed **early**.*

Here are some more adverbs of the same kind.
> *The man pointed the gun **straight** at me.*
> *Can't you sit **still** just for a minute?*
> *The aircraft flew **low** over the town.*
> *He threw the ball **high** in the air.*
> *We were all trying **hard** not to laugh.*

For pairs of adverbs such as *hard* and *hardly*, > E.

D Sometimes the adverb can be with or without *-ly*. In these examples there is no difference in meaning, but it is more informal to leave out *-ly*.
> *If you buy goods in bulk, you can sell them **cheap**/**cheaply**.*
> *Do you have to talk so **loud**/**loudly**?*
> *Get there as **quick**/**quickly** as you can.*
> *Go **slow**/**slowly** round this corner.*

Others are *direct(ly)*, *fair(ly)*, and *tight(ly)*.

We use the form without *-ly* only in frequent combinations like *talk loud, go slow, fly direct,* or *play fair*. With longer or less common expressions, we use *-ly*.
> *The chairman cleared his throat rather **loudly**.*
> *We need to act **quickly**.*

NOTE
a   *Right* and *wrong* are both adjectives and adverbs of manner.
> *I'll try to do it **right** this time.*

Rightly and *wrongly* express a comment.
> *The caretaker decided **rightly** to call the police.*

b   *First* and *last* are both adjectives and adverbs.
> *Karen took **first** place/came **first** in the race.*

Firstly and *lastly* are linking adverbs.
> ***First**/**Firstly**, I'd like to thank you all for coming.*

E There are some pairs such as *hard* and *hardly* which are both adverbs but which have different meanings.

*You deserve a rest because you've worked **hard**.*
*It'll take **hardly any** time at all. (hardly any* = almost no)
*I often see my parents. They live quite **near**.*
*Beckham **nearly** scored, but his shot went just wide.* (= almost)
*I had to stay up **late** to finish my homework.*
*I used to see a lot of Donna, but she hasn't been around **lately**.* (= recently)
*The men raised their hands **high** in the air.*
*The theory is **highly** controversial.* (= very)
*How **deep** can a submarine go?*
*The new tax is **deeply** unpopular.* (= very, intensely)
*Employees of the airline travel **free**.*
*The prisoners can move around **freely**.* (= without being controlled)
*The thing that annoys me **most** is that no one has apologized to me.*
*There may be a few showers, but it will be **mostly** dry.* (= mainly)

For *hardly* expressing time, e.g. *we had hardly arrived when ...* , > 238D.

F *Hourly, daily, weekly,* and *monthly* are formed from *hour, day,* etc. They can be either adjectives or adverbs.

Adjective: *The company publishes a **monthly** newsletter.*
Adverb: *The newsletter is published **monthly**.*

G *Good* is an adjective.

*I think it's a **good** design.*

Well is the equivalent adverb.

*I think the design works **well**.*

Well can also be an adjective meaning 'in good health'.

*Unfortunately my sister wasn't **well** enough to travel.*
How are you? ~ *Very **well**, thank you./Fine, thank you.*

We often use *well* with a participle.

*The event was **well organized**.*
*A **well-built** man in his thirties came into the room.*

Other examples are: *well-behaved, well-dressed, well-established, well-fed, well-informed, well-meaning, well-preserved, well-timed.*

Sometimes we use *good* with a participle.

*Andrew is basically a **good-natured** person.* (He has a good nature.)

We do this with participles formed from nouns, e.g. *good-hearted, good-humoured, good-tempered.* Note also *good-looking.*

NOTE
The phrase *all being well / if all goes well* means 'if everything is all right'.
*We should arrive at about five o'clock, **all being well**.*

193 Adverbials of manner

A Adjectives and adverbs

Look at these examples.

Adjective	Adverb
*We're looking for a **quick** solution to the problem.*	*We want to solve the problem **quickly**.*
*Kate is **fluent** in Russian.*	*She speaks Russian **fluently**.*
*Try to make a **sensible** choice.*	*Try to choose **sensibly**.*
An adjective comes before a noun (e.g. *solution*), or it is a complement of *be* (*is fluent*).	An adverb of manner comes after a verb (e.g. *choose*) or after a verb + object (e.g. *solve the problem*). Most adverbs of manner are formed from an adjective + *-ly*.

Compare these different types of verb.

Linking verb + adjective	Action verb + adverb
*The official **was** very **polite**.*	*He **listened politely**.* (NOT *He listened polite.*)
A linking verb is a verb like *be, seem, become, feel, look*.	An action verb is a verb like *listen, drive, work, argue, meet*. > 51

Some verbs can be either a linking verb or an action verb.

Linking verb + adjective	Action verb + adverb
*The speaker **looked nervous**.* (*looked* = seemed/appeared)	*He **looked nervously** around.* (*looked* = directed his eyes)
*The atmosphere **grew tense**.* (*grew* = became)	*The plants **grew rapidly**.* (*grew* = increased in size)
*The milk **smelled funny**.* (*smelled funny* = had a funny smell)	*Steve **smelled** the milk **suspiciously**.* (*smelled* = sniffed, used his nose)

B Prepositional phrases of manner

We can often use a prepositional phrase to express manner.
*I had to choose my words carefully / **with care**.*
*The policeman inspected the car officiously / **in an officious manner**.*
*Can't we discuss this sensibly / **in a sensible way**?*
*The winning numbers are randomly chosen/are chosen **at random**.*

We can often use an adjective or adverb to intensify the meaning.

*I had to choose my words with **great**/**considerable** care.*
*The policeman inspected the car in a **very**/an **extremely** officious manner.*

C Position of adverbials of manner

We put an adverbial of manner mostly in end position. Here are some real examples from stories.

*'I didn't know whether to tell you or not,' she said **anxiously**.*
*The sun still shone **brightly** on the quiet street.*
*We continued our labours **in silence**.*

A one-word adverb can sometimes come in mid position.

*I **quickly** ran and got my coat.*

The adverbial can sometimes come in front position for emphasis.

***Gently** fry the banana pieces.*

This is more common in writing than in speech. The last two examples are from a novel and a cookbook.

194 Adverbials of place and time

A Position

Adverbials of place and time often go in end position.

*There has been another shooting incident **at a US high school**.*
*It's my brother's birthday **tomorrow**.*
*A ferry was being repaired **last night** after running aground **in the Thames**.*
*The office is closed **for two weeks**.*

For more than one adverbial in end position, > 191.

Adverbials of place and time can also go in front position. > 34A

*We've got friends staying till Friday. And **on Saturday** my parents arrive.*

Here *Saturday* contrasts with *Friday*.

Some short adverbials of time can go in mid position.

*I've **just** remembered something.*   *We'll **soon** be home.*

These include: *already, at once, finally, immediately, just* (= a short time ago), *no longer, now, recently, since, soon, still, then, yesterday*.

Phrases of time and place can also come after a noun.

*The tennis courts **in the park** aren't used very much.*
*Exports **last year** broke all records.*

B *Yet*

We use *yet* to talk about something that is expected.

*Have you found a job **yet**? ~ No, not **yet**.*
*I got up late. I haven't had breakfast **yet**.*

Yet comes at the end of a question or negative statement.

We can use *yet* in mid position, but it is a little formal.
> *We have not **yet** reached a decision on the matter.*

NOTE
For *yet* meaning 'but', > 235A.

C *Still*

We use *still* to talk about something going on longer than expected.
> *I got up late. I'm **still** having breakfast.*
> *Is your grandfather **still** working?*

In positive statements and questions, *still* goes in mid position.

In negative statements, *still* goes before the auxiliary.
> *The child **still** hasn't learned to read.*

This is more emphatic than *The child hasn't learned to read **yet**.*

NOTE
a   *Still* can go after a negative auxiliary when we express surprise.
> *You don't **still** use this old software, do you?*
This pattern is often followed by a question tag.

b   We can use *still* in front or end position to give it extra emphasis.
> *You mean he's 84 and **still** he hasn't retired!*
> *You mean he's 84 and he's working **still**!*

D *Already*

We use *already* to talk about something happening sooner than expected.
> *I got up early. I've **already** had breakfast.*
> *Have you **already** replied to the letter? ~ Yes, I answered it straight away.*

We use *already* mainly in mid position in positive statements and questions.

Already in front or end position has more emphasis.
> ***Already** our new boss has made big changes.*
> *Is it lunch time **already**? How time flies.*

Already can also go before a stressed auxiliary.
> *When are you going to reply to the letter? ~ I **already** HAVE replied to it.*

E *No longer, any more,* and *any longer*

We use *no longer* to talk about something coming to an end. It goes in mid position.
> *I'm afraid the person concerned **no longer** works here.*
> *These products are **no longer** manufactured.*

No longer is a little formal.

We can also use a negative sentence with *any more* or *any longer* in end position.
> *They don't make these products **any more**.*
> *I'm not going to wait here **any longer**.*

F *Long* and *far*

We normally use the adverbs *long* and *far* only in questions and negative statements.

> *Have you been waiting **long**?*
> *It's not **far** from here to the motorway.*

In positive statements we use *a long time/a long way*.

> *I had to wait **a long time**. / I had to wait ages.*
> *It's **a long way** from here to Vladivostock.*

But we use *long* and *far* after *too*, *so*, and *as*, and before *enough*.

> *The speech went on **too long**.*
> *I'm annoyed because I've had to wait **so long**/wait such a long time.*
> *I don't live **as far** from the office as you do.*
> *Let's go back now. We've walked **far enough**.*

NOTE

We can also use the comparative and superlative forms of *long* and *far* in positive statements.

> *The journey takes **longer** in the rush hour.*
> *I live **furthest** from the office. You all live nearer than I do.*

G *After* and *afterwards*

We do not often use *after* as an adverb. We use *afterwards* or *after that*.

> *I'll video the talk, so we can play it back **afterwards**.*
> *It's extra time now, and **after that** it'll be penalties.*

But we can say *the day after* and *the week after*.

> *I ordered a CD, and it arrived **the day after** / the next day / a day later.*
> *I'm on holiday next week, so I'll see you **the week after**.*

Soon after and *soon afterwards* are both possible.

> *The man was taken to hospital and died **soon after** / **soon afterwards**.*

195 Adverbials of frequency

A An adverbial of frequency says how often something happens.

> *I **sometimes** go out and get a take-away meal.*
> *The computer crashes **occasionally**.*
> ***Generally** there'll be a party somewhere on a Saturday.*

Here are some common adverbs of frequency.

Full frequency:	*always*
Almost full frequency:	*normally, usually, generally*
High frequency:	*often, frequently*
Medium frequency:	*sometimes, occasionally*
Low frequency:	*seldom, rarely, not ... often*
Zero frequency:	*never, not ... ever*

Seldom and *rarely* are a little formal.
> *We **seldom/rarely** travel abroad.*
Often with the negative is neutral in style.
> *We **don't often** travel abroad.*

B An adverb of frequency usually goes in mid position.
> *The bus doesn't **usually** stop here.*
> *I can **never** open these packets.*
> *It's **always** busy on a Friday.*
> *I **often** wonder who buys these things.*

C In a negative sentence, *sometimes, occasionally,* and *frequently* go before the auxiliary in mid position.
> *It's often crowded in here. You **sometimes can't** get a table.*

Always and *ever* go after the negative auxiliary.
> *I **haven't always** done this for a living, you know.*

As a general rule, *often, normally, usually,* and *generally* go after the negative auxiliary.
> *I **don't often** ride my bike to college.*

NOTE
Often, normally, usually, and *generally* can sometimes come before the negative auxiliary. There is little difference in meaning between these two examples.
> *The photocopier **isn't often** working.* (= The photocopier is seldom working.)
> *The photocopier **often isn't** working.* (= The photocopier is often out of order.)

D Some adverbs of frequency can go in front or end position.
> ***Normally** I tip taxi drivers.*
> *We all make mistakes **sometimes**.*
These adverbs are *normally, usually, generally, frequently, sometimes,* and *occasionally*.

Often can go in end position.
> *Doctors get called out at night quite **often**.*
This happens especially with *very* or *quite*.

A lot meaning 'often' goes in end position (and not mid position).
> *I missed half my schooling. I was ill **a lot**.*

The adverbs *daily, weekly,* etc go in end position.
> *Are you paid **weekly** or **monthly**?*

In instructions, *always* and *never* go in front position.
> ***Never** try to adjust the machine while it is switched on.*

NOTE
For *never, seldom,* and *rarely* in front position with inversion of subject and auxiliary, > 10F.
> ***Never** have I felt better.*

E *Never* is a negative word meaning 'not ever'.
> *I would **never** do a thing like that.* (= I **wouldn't ever** do it.)
> *We **never** ask for your password.* (= We **don't ever** ask for your password.)

We use *ever* mainly in questions.
> *Have you **ever** done any ballroom dancing?* ~ *No, never.*

But we can also use *ever* with negative words such as *not* or *hardly*.
> *I would**n't ever** do a thing like that.*
> *You **hardly ever** buy me flowers.*

We do not normally use *ever* in positive statements.
> *I **always** buy a lottery ticket.* (NOT ~~I ever buy a lottery ticket.~~)

Ever can add emphasis to a negative.
> ***No one ever** said that to me before.*
> ***Nothing ever** happens in this place.*
> *I **never ever** want to see that awful man again.*

We can also use *ever* in a condition or a comparison.
> ***If** you **ever** feel like a chat, just drop in.*
> *The river was higher **than** I'd **ever** seen it.*

NOTE
If ever can go before the subject.
> ***If ever** you feel like a chat, just drop in.*

F We can also use a phrase with *every*, *most*, or *some* to express frequency.
> ***Every summer** we all go sailing together.*
> *The postman calls **most days**.*
> ***Some evenings** we don't have the television on at all.*

These phrases can go in front or end position.

We can also use *once*, *twice*, *three times*, etc.
> *The committee meets **once a month**.*
> *Two tablets to be taken **three times a day**.*
> *The car has already been repaired **several times**.*

These phrases usually go in end position, but they can go in front position for emphasis.
> ***Seven days a week** we get lorries thundering past the building.*

NOTE
Other phrases expressing frequency include *as a rule* (= normally), *from time to time* (= occasionally), and *now and then* (= occasionally).
> ***As a rule**, Monday isn't a very busy day.*
> *Interest rates may be changed **from time to time**.*

196 Adverbs of degree

A Modifying an adjective or adverb

We can use an adverb of degree before an adjective.
> *It's a **very** simple idea.*
> *I get **so** bored with nothing to do.*
> *I think so, but I'm not **absolutely** certain.*
> *It's getting **a bit** hot in here.*

For the use of these adverbs with gradable and ungradable adjectives, > 186.

We can also use an adverb of degree before another adverb.

*You could improve your performance **quite** easily.*
*I'll have to decide **fairly** soon.*
*I **hardly** ever see Kate nowadays.*

Here are some adverbs of degree.

Full degree: *absolutely, completely, entirely, quite* (= completely > 197),
                    totally
High degree: *awfully* (informal), *extremely, real* (informal), *really,*
                    terribly (informal), *too, very*
Medium degree: *fairly, pretty* (informal), *quite* (= fairly > 197), *rather,*
                    somewhat
Low degree: *a bit* (informal), *a little, slightly*
Very low degree: *hardly, scarcely*
Zero degree: *not ... at all*
Comparison: *as, less, least, more, most, so*

We can use a fraction or percentage.

*I still feel **half** asleep.*
*The forecast was **ninety per cent** accurate.*

B More details about adverbs of degree

After a phrase with *very*, we can add *indeed* for emphasis.

*The customer was red in the face. He was very angry **indeed**.*

Awfully can go with desirable qualities as well as undesirable ones.

*Thank you very much. That's **awfully** kind of you.*
*You must think me **awfully** stupid.*

Somewhat, a little, a bit, and *slightly* do not usually go with desirable
qualities. We tend to use them to refer to undesirable aspects.

*These diagrams are **a bit confusing**.*
(BUT NOT *These diagrams are a bit clear.*)
*The journey was **somewhat stressful**.*
(BUT NOT *The journey was somewhat enjoyable.*)

But we can use an adjective expressing something desirable if it is in the
comparative form.

*The rest of the journey was **somewhat more enjoyable**.*

We can also use *not ... very* to express a low degree.

*These diagrams aren't **very** clear.*
*The journey wasn't **very** enjoyable.*

We often use *not very* in a negative judgement.

*The photos aren't **very** good.*

This is more usual than *The photos aren't good.* or *The photos are bad.*

At all can go in end position, or it can go before the word it modifies.
> *I didn't feel nervous **at all**. / I didn't feel **at all** nervous.*

NOTE
a   *Real* can be used instead of *really*, especially in informal American English.
> *It felt **real** good to have a shower.*

b   In informal English we can use *that* instead of *so* when we are making a comparison.
> *Maybe the idea isn't so silly / **that** silly after all.* (= not as silly as I thought)

C Modifying a comparative or a superlative

Some adverbs of degree can come before a comparative adjective or adverb.
> *This gadget makes the job **much** easier.*
> *We'll have to move **a bit** quicker if we're going to get there on time.*
> *Our pay rise is so small that we're **no** better off/we aren't **any** better off.*

We can use *a bit, a little, a lot, any, much, no, rather, slightly, somewhat,* and *very much.*

With a superlative we can use *easily* or *by far.*
> *This is **easily** the most popular style.*
> *We offer **by far** the best value.*

By far can go in end position.
> *We offer the best value **by far**.*

NOTE
Before *as* we can use *twice, three times, four times,* etc.
> *The winner got **twice as** many votes as the runner-up.*
> *The new mall will be **five times as** big as the old one.*

We can also use *three times, four times,* etc before a comparative.
> *The new mall will be **five times bigger** than the old one.*

D Modifying a verb

We can use an adverb of degree to modify a verb.
> *Do you **really** want to be successful in life?*
> *We were **rather** hoping to have a look around.*
> *The doorman **absolutely** refused to let us in.*
> *The suitcase was so heavy I could **hardly** lift it.*

In mid position we can use *absolutely, almost, completely, hardly, just, nearly, quite, rather, really, scarcely, slightly,* and *totally.*

We often use an adverb of degree before a passive participle.
> *The car was **badly damaged** in the accident.*
> *Our schedule has been **completely disrupted** by the delays.*

Almost, just, and *nearly* go before a negative auxiliary.
> *I **just** don't see what the problem is.*

Really can also go here. >190E

Absolutely, completely, rather, and *totally* can go in either end position or mid position.
> *I **absolutely** agree. / I agree **absolutely**.*
> *I **completely** forgot the time. / I forgot the time **completely**.*

Some adverbs go only in end position.

*First impressions matter **a lot**.*

*I miss you **terribly**.*

These are *a bit, a little, a lot, awfully, more, (the) most, somewhat,* and *terribly.*

We can use *much* or *very much* in a negative sentence or a question.

*I didn't enjoy the meal **much** / **very much**.*

But in a positive sentence we use *very much* and not *much* on its own.

*I enjoyed the meal **very much**.*

(NOT ~~I enjoyed the meal much.~~)

NOTE

a   *Very much* usually goes in end position. In rather formal English it can go in mid position.

   *I would **very much** like to accept your offer.*

b   Before a passive participle we can use either *much* or *very much*.

   *Politicians are generally **(very) much** distrusted by the public.*

E Modifying a preposition

Some adverbs of degree can modify a preposition.

*The offices are **right in** the centre of town.*

*The way Polly was behaving seemed **very out of** character.*

*I walked **straight into** a lamp-post.*

For more examples, > 208D.

F Modifying a quantifier

We can use these combinations of adverb and quantifier.

very/so/too + many/much/few/little

   ***Very few** people have legs exactly the same length.*

   *There are **so many** different products on the market.*

   *I've got **too much** work to do.*

such/rather/quite + a lot (of)

   *I've made **such a lot of** mistakes.*

   *There are **rather a lot of** dishes to wash up.*

quite + a few/a bit (of)

   *There are **quite a few** dishes to wash up.*

   *I lost **quite a bit of** money.*

almost/nearly + all/every

   ***Almost all** the chairs were occupied.*

   *There seems to be a plane crash **nearly every** week.*

hardly any

   *There's **hardly any** difference between the two designs.*

a lot/much/a bit/a little/any/no + more/less
> *You'd get **a lot less** money without a qualification.*
> *There's sun, sand and sea and **much more** besides.*
> *I'd like **a bit more** time to decide.*

G *Too* and *enough*

Too comes before an adjective or adverb.
> *The water is **too cold** to swim in.*
> *Hang on. You're going **too fast**.*

Much, far, or *rather* can come before *too*.
> *This coat is **much too** big for me.*
> *A game of chess would take **far too** long.*

Enough comes after an adjective or adverb.
> *Are you **old enough** to drive a car?*
> *I didn't react **quickly enough**.*

Compare *too* and *enough*.
> *The water is **too cold**.*
> *The water isn't **warm enough**.*

NOTE
For *enough* as a quantifier, > 173A.
> *There isn't **enough time**.*

H Adverbs of degree and *a/an*

We can use most adverbs of degree between *a/an* and an adjective.
> *a **very** warm welcome   a **fairly** important meeting   a **rather** nice restaurant*

But not all adverbs of degree can go in phrases like these. We do not normally use *so* in this position.
> *We received **such a warm** welcome.* (NOT ~~a so warm welcome~~)
> *It was **such a good** opportunity.* (NOT ~~a so good opportunity~~)

We use the same pattern with *quite*.
> *I had **quite an important** meeting.*
> *It was **quite a painful** blow to the head.*

This is more usual than *a quite important meeting* or *a quite painful blow*, although *a quite ...* is also possible.

With *rather*, both patterns are possible.
> *I had **rather an important** meeting.*
> *I had **a rather important** meeting.*

Too or *as* + adjective go before *a/an*.
> *You've cut **too short a piece**.* (NOT ~~a too short piece~~)
> *You don't get **as nice a view** on this side.* (NOT ~~an as nice view~~)

We can also use *so* and an adjective before *a/an*, although the pattern with *such* is more usual.
> *You don't get **so nice a view**/**such a nice view**.*

We can use *such, quite,* and *rather + a/an +* noun without an adjective.
> *Why are you making **such a fuss**?*
> *We had to wait **quite a while**.*
> *It's **rather a pity** we can't go out.*

We can also use *a bit of.*
> *Sorry. The flat's in **a bit of a mess**.*

We sometimes use *quite* in this pattern to express a positive feeling about something impressive.
> *That was **quite a party**.*

The meaning is similar to *That was **some** party.* > 172F Note b

197 More details about *quite* and *rather*

A In British English, *quite* has two meanings.

Medium degree: 'fairly'	Full degree: 'completely'
*The task is **quite difficult**.* *The film was **quite good**.* *I feel **quite tired**.*	*The task is **quite impossible**.* *The film was **quite brilliant**.* *I feel **quite exhausted**.*
Quite means 'fairly' when it comes before a gradable adjective.	*Quite* means 'completely' when the adjective is ungradable.
Quite + like/enjoy *I **quite enjoyed** the film. It was quite good.* (***quite** = to some extent*)	*Quite + agree/understand* *I **quite agree**.* *You're quite right.* (***quite** = completely*)
This expresses a positive opinion but not as positive as *I **really** enjoyed the film* or *It was **very** good.*	*Not quite* means 'not completely'. *What you said is **not quite true**.* *Can I correct just one thing?*

B *Quite* is not usually stressed before an adjective or adverb.
> *It's quite* WARM *today.* (focus on the warmth)
> *We were home quite* LATE. (focus on the lateness)

Sometimes we can stress *quite* before a gradable adjective. We do this to limit the force of the adjective or adverb.
> *It's* QUITE *warm, but not as warm as it was.* (focus on the medium degree)
> *We were home* QUITE *late but not very late.* (focus on the medium degree)

C *Quite* and *rather* have a similar meaning, but there are some differences in use. When we make a favourable comment about something, we usually prefer *quite* to *rather*.

> *It's **quite nice** here.*
> *It was **quite** a **good** party, wasn't it?*

If we are being positive, then *quite* is unstressed.

In unfavourable comments, we usually prefer *rather*.

> *It's **rather depressing**/quite depressing here.*
> *It was **rather** a **dull** party/quite a dull party, wasn't it?*
> *The new timetable is **rather confusing**/quite confusing.*

Rather in a favourable comment often means 'to a surprising or unusual degree'.

> *I expected the party to be dull, but actually it was **rather** good.*
> *The test paper is usually difficult, but this one was **rather** easy.*

198 *Only* and *even*

A We use *only* and *even* to focus on a particular word or phrase. To make clear what we are focusing on, we put *only* before the relevant word or phrase.

> *Most of the guests were strangers to me. I knew **only one** other person there.*
> *I speak **only a little** French, I'm afraid.*

Only can also be in mid position.

> *Most of the guests were strangers to me. I **only** knew **one** other person there.*
> *I **only** speak **a little** French, I'm afraid.*

We stress the word we want to focus on, e.g. *one, little*.

In official written English, e.g. on notices, *only* comes after the word or phrase it is focusing on.

> *Waiting limited to **30 minutes only**.*

Even goes in mid position or before the word or phrase we are focusing on.

> *Emma has been everywhere. She's **even** been to **the North Pole**.*
> *My brother always wears shorts, **even in winter**.*

Both these examples express surprise.

NOTE
Compare *even* and *also*.
> *Everyone laughed, **even** the teacher.*
> (It is surprising that the teacher laughed.)
> *We've invited the whole class, and **also** the teacher.*
> (We have added the teacher to the invitation list.)

B When we focus on the subject, we put *only* or *even* before it.

> ***Only you** would do a silly thing like that.*
> ***Even the experts** don't know the answer.*

C There are a number of other uses of *only*. For example, we can use it when we talk about something happening a surprisingly short time ago.

> *I tidied this room up **only yesterday**, and now it's in a mess again.*

Only just can mean 'a very short time ago'.

> *I'm new here. I've **only just** moved to the area.*

It can also mean 'with little to spare'.

> *I **only just** caught the train. It left as soon as I got on.*

NOTE

a   For inversion after a phrase with *only*, > 10F.
> ***Only** at weekends **do we** get a chance to meet.*

b   *Only* can also be an adjective.
> *The **only** thing in the fridge was a small piece of cheese.*

D We can use *even* in negative sentences.

> *I'm not interested in politics. I **don't even** know who the Prime Minister is.*
> *I know nothing about cricket. I've **never even** seen a game.*

Here *even* goes in mid position.

We can also use *even* before a comparative adjective.

> *It was pretty warm yesterday, but it's **even warmer** today.*

199 Viewpoint adverbials

These express the idea that we are looking at a situation from a particular aspect or point of view.

> ***Financially**, we've had a difficult year.*
> *Can you manage **transport-wise**, or do you need a lift?*
> *The building is magnificent **from an architectural point of view**, but it's hell to work in.*
> ***As far as insurance is concerned**, we can fix that up for you.*
> *The scheme is **economically** beneficial but **environmentally** disastrous.*

These adverbials usually go in front or end position, or they can modify an adjective (***economically** beneficial*).

200 Truth adverbials

A A truth adverbial expresses what the speaker knows about the truth of a statement: how likely it is to be true, or to what degree it is true. Here are some examples with adverbs.

> ***Perhaps/Maybe** there's a problem with the software.*
> *We've **certainly/definitely/undoubtedly** made a good start.*
> ***Basically**, I just want a car that will get me from A to B.*
> *The website hasn't been updated, **presumably**.*
> ***Clearly**, the matter is extremely urgent.*
> *A businessman **allegedly** had two of his rivals killed.*

Most of these adverbs can go in front, mid or end position. *Certainly,* *definitely,* and *probably* usually go in mid position. But we put a truth adverb before a negative auxiliary.

> You **certainly** *haven't wasted any time.*
> *The website* **presumably** *hasn't been updated.*

B We can also use a prepositional phrase.

> *It's a great idea* **in my opinion.**
> *I'm not sure.* **In fact** *I've no idea.*
> *The results are pretty good* **on the whole.**

A phrase usually goes in front or end position. Mid position is rather formal.

> *I will* **of course** *keep you informed.*

C We can also use *I think, I expect,* etc, with the same kind of meaning as a truth adverbial.

> **I think** *it's a great idea.* (= In my opinion it's a great idea.)
> *There's been a power cut,* **I expect.** (= There's **probably** been a power cut.)
> **I'm sure** *we've gone wrong.* (= We've **definitely** gone wrong.)

201 Comment adverbials

A We can use an adverb to make a comment on the message expressed in the rest of the sentence.

> **Luckily** *no one was killed.*
> (= It was lucky that no one was killed.)
> *The newspapers weren't interested in the story,* **surprisingly.**
> **Unfortunately,** *we didn't win anything.*

These adverbs usually go in front or end position.

We can also use *I'm afraid, I'm surprised,* etc, with the same kind of meaning.

> **I'm surprised** *the newspapers weren't interested in the story.*
> **I'm afraid** *we didn't win anything.*

B We can also use an adverb to comment on someone's behaviour.

> **Wisely** *the cashier didn't argue with the gunman.*

As well as in front position, the adverb can go in mid position, or in end position as an afterthought.

> *The cashier* **wisely** *didn't argue with the gunman.*
> *The cashier didn't argue with the gunman,* **wisely.**

Compare the adverbs of comment and manner.

> *I* **stupidly** *left the car unlocked.*
> (= It was stupid of me to leave the car unlocked.)
> *The man stared* **stupidly** *at us.*
> (= The man stared at us in a stupid manner.)

C We can use a phrase with *to* for someone's feelings about something.
   To my surprise, the newspaper wasn't interested in the story.
   Chloe was invited to the show to her great delight.

D We can point out that we are being honest.
   Frankly, I'm not very interested in old cars.
   I don't see what else we can do, to be honest.
For more examples with a to-infinitive, > 100C.

E Most comment adverbials usually go in front or end position, especially a phrase or clause. A phrase or clause can sometimes go in mid position, but this is rather formal.
   The spectators, to their horror, saw the whole tragedy unfolding.
   I am, to be perfectly frank, feeling rather annoyed with you.

202 Linking adverbials

A A linking adverb relates to the previous clause or sentence. Here are some real examples.

   *When Beethoven was fourteen, he was forced to give lessons to support his parents. **However**, he still found time to take a few violin lessons, and he went on composing.*

   *If you pay the bill in full within 25 days, you won't be charged interest. **Otherwise** you are charged interest on any balance outstanding.*

   *But the baby does not just grow bigger and heavier. Its shape and body proportions **also** change as it grows up.*

   *In an emergency, medical treatment is available at the big hospitals. If you have travel insurance, you may need to contact the company's emergency number **as well**.*

A linking adverbial most often goes in front position, but it can go in mid or end position.

B Here are some ways of relating one clause or sentence to another.

Adding something:	*Ministers have to run the government, and **in addition**, they have to look after their constituents.* > 233C
Expressing a contrast:	*I know you don't believe these stories. **Nevertheless**, they're all perfectly true.* > 235B
Contradicting:	*I expect you're tired now. ~ **On the contrary**, I feel fighting fit.*
Correcting:	*I'll see you tomorrow then. **Or rather** on Monday.*
Rephrasing:	*The matter is under consideration. **In other words**, they're thinking about it.*

Expressing a result:	*It will take a long time for the changes to become effective, and the old system will **consequently** continue for some time.* > 236B
Comparing:	*The government sold the telephone service to private investors. Gas and electricity were privatized **in the same way**.*
Ordering:	*Of course the man is guilty. **Firstly**, he had a motive, and **secondly**, his fingerprints were on the gun.*
Summing up:	***In conclusion**, I'd like to say a few words about future prospects.*
Giving examples:	*Colours are associated with feelings. Blues and greens, **for example**, are considered to be cool and restful.*
Picking up a topic:	*I think I'll have the sausages. ~ **Talking** of sausages, did you know there's a barbecue on Saturday?*
Changing the subject:	*It would be nice if you could tell me something about your background. And this conversation is being recorded, **by the way**.*
Supporting a statement:	*I think I'd better be going. It's past midnight, **after all**.*
Dismissing something:	*I don't know whether we did the right thing. **Anyway**, it doesn't matter now.*

Comparison

203 The comparison of adjectives

A Introduction

These sentences make comparisons between different things.

Comparative: *It's **warmer** in here than outside.*
*Driving is **more convenient** than taking a bus.*

Superlative: *This is the **oldest** building in the town.*
*She's the **most irritating** person I've ever met.*

For the two ways of forming the comparative and superlative (*warmer,
warmest* or *more/most convenient*), > B.
For irregular forms, e.g. *good → better, best,* > F.

We often use *than* after a comparative (*more convenient **than** ...*). For more
details about patterns with the comparative and superlative, > 206.

NOTE
Some people believe that we should use a comparative for two items and the superlative for
more than two. But in informal English the superlative is often used to refer to one of only
two items.
    *Which of these two photos is better/**best**?*

B Regular comparison

These are the regular forms.

		Comparative	Superlative
Short adjective:	*warm*	*warmer*	*warmest*
Long adjective:	*convenient*	***more** convenient*	***most** convenient*

Short adjectives end in *-er* and *-est*. Long adjectives have *more* and *most*. For
more details, > C–E.

> **There are some spelling rules for *-er/-est*.**
> There is no doubling of *e*: *fine → finer* > 278A
> There is doubling of some consonants: *hot → hottest* > 279
> *y* changes to *i*: *heavy → heavier* > 280.

Adjectives ending in *-ng* are pronounced with /g/ before *-er/-est*,
e.g. *younger* /ˈjʌŋgə/, *longest* /ˈlɒŋgɪst/

NOTE
In formal English *a most …* can mean 'a very …'. Compare these sentences.
> Superlative: *The train is **the most convenient way** to get from here to London.*
> High degree: *The train is **a most convenient** means of transport.*
> (= a very convenient means of transport)

C One-syllable adjectives (e.g. *nice, sure*)

Most of these end in *-er/-est*.
> *This coat is the **nicest**.*

Some one-syllable adjectives can either have *-er/-est* or *more/most*.
> *I wish I felt **surer/more sure** about what I'm doing.*
Such adjectives include: *clear, fair, free, keen, proud, rude, safe, sure, true, wise*. But we do not normally use *more* with adjectives of concrete meaning such as *big, cold, fast,* or *short*.
> (NOT ~~Our new flat is more big.~~)

We use *more/most* (and not *-er/-est*) with *real* and with adjectives ending in *ed*, e.g. *bored, pleased*.
> *The film made the story seem **more real**.*
> *Those **most pleased** by the decision were the local residents.*
Note also *more right* and *more wrong*.
> *The theory is nonsense. It just couldn't be **more wrong**.*

D Two-syllable adjectives (e.g *useful, stupid*)

Many of these have *more/most*.
> *Can't you do something **more useful**?*

These adjectives have *more/most*.
Ending in *ful*:	*careful, helpful, hopeful, peaceful, useful*, etc
Ending in *less*:	*helpless, useless*, etc
Ending in *ing*:	*boring, pleasing, tiring, willing*, etc
Ending in *ed*:	*amused, annoyed, ashamed, confused, surprised*, etc
Some others:	*afraid, cautious, central, certain, complex, correct, eager, exact, famous, foolish, formal, frequent, mature, modern, normal, recent.*

Some two-syllable adjectives can either have *-er/-est* or *more/most*.
> *That's the **stupidest/the most stupid** idea I've ever heard.*
Such adjectives include: *able, clever, common, cruel, feeble, gentle, handsome, likely, narrow, pleasant, polite, quiet, secure, simple, sincere, stupid, tired.*

Most two-syllable adjectives ending in *y* have *-er/-est*, although *more/most* is also possible.
> *Life would be **easier** if I had a job.*
Such adjectives include: *angry, busy, crazy, dirty, easy, empty, friendly, funny, happy, healthy, heavy, hungry, lively, lonely, lovely, lucky, nasty, pretty, silly, thirsty, tidy, ugly, wealthy.*

E Three-syllable adjectives (e.g. *difficult*)

Adjectives of three or more syllables have *more/most*.
   *Skiing is **more difficult** than it looks.*
   *Making money isn't the **most important** thing in the world.*

But we can use *un-* before certain two-syllable adjectives with *-er/-est* added
to them, e.g. *unhappier, untidiest, unpleasantest*.

F Irregular comparison

There are a few irregular forms.
   *There must be a **better** way of doing this.*
   *That's the **best** game I've ever seen.*
   *The weather is getting **worse**.*
   *What's the **worst** thing that could happen?*

Adjective	Comparative	Superlative
good	*better*	*best*
bad	*worse*	*worst*
far	*farther/further*	*farthest/furthest* > G

NOTE
a   The adjectives *well* (= in good health) and *ill* have the same irregular forms as
   good and *bad*.
      *I feel **better** now.*   *She looks **worse** today.*

b   For *elder*, > G.

G Some special forms

Farther/further and *farthest/furthest* express distance. We use them as
adjectives and adverbs.
   *The **farthest/furthest** moon is 13 million kilometres from Saturn.*
   *I can't walk any **farther/further**.*

Further (but not *farther*) can mean 'more' or 'additional'.
   *Let's hope there are no **further** problems.*

Elder and *eldest* mean the same as *older* and *oldest*. We use them mainly to
talk about ages in a family.
   *Have you got an older/**elder** brother?*
   *The oldest/**eldest** daughter married a pop singer.*
Elder and *eldest* go before the noun.
   (NOT *My brother is elder than me.*)

Latest and *last* mean different things. *Latest* means 'furthest ahead in time' or 'newest'.

> *What's the **latest** time we can leave and still get there on time?*
> *This jacket is the **latest** fashion.*
> (NOT *This jacket is the last fashion.*)

Last means 'previous' or 'final'.

> *I had my hair cut **last** week.* (= the week before this one)
> *The **last** bus goes at midnight.* (= the final bus of the day)

Nearest and *next* mean different things. *Nearest* means the shortest distance away.

> *Where's the **nearest** phone box?* (= closest, least far)

Next means 'following in a series'.

> *I'm having my hair cut **next** week.* (= the week after this one)
> *We have to get out at the **next** stop.* (= the stop after this one)
> *There's a newsagent's in the **next** street.* (= the street beside this one)

204 The comparative and superlative of adverbs

A Some adverbs have the same form as adjectives, e.g. *hard, straight, early*. > 192C. They have *-er/-est* in the comparative and superlative.

> *You'll have to work **harder** if you want to pass the exam.*
> *Let's see who can shoot the **straightest**.*
> *Tim got to work a few minutes **earlier** than usual.*

B There are a few irregular forms.

> *I find these pills work **best**. They're really good.*
> *My tooth was aching **worse** than ever.*
> *How much **farther/further** is it?*

Adverb	Comparative	Superlative
well	*better*	*best*
badly	*worse*	*worst*
far	*farther/further*	*farthest/furthest* > 203G

C Adverbs with *-ly* have *more/most*.

> *You'll have to draw the graph **more accurately** than that.*
> *The first speaker presented his case the **most convincingly**.*

But *early* is an exception. > A

Adverbs not formed from adjectives (e.g. *often*) also have *more/most*.

> *I wish we could meet **more often**. I hardly ever see you.*

But *soon* is an exception.

> *If we all help, we'll get the job finished **sooner**.*

D Some adverbs can be with or without *-ly*. > 192D

> *I got the bike fairly* **cheap/cheaply**.

These adverbs have two different comparative and superlative forms. The forms with *-er/-est* are more informal.

> *You could get one* **cheaper/more cheaply** *secondhand.*
> *It's the newcomers who protest the* **loudest**/*the* **most loudly** *against new building here.*

205 *More, most, less, least, fewer,* and *fewest*

We can use these words to compare quantities.

Plural	Uncountable
more (= a larger number) *There are* **more** *cars in Los Angeles than people.*	*more* (= a larger amount) *You've got* **more** *money than I have.*
most (= the largest number) *Of all the countries in the world, Britain has the* **most** *ghosts.*	*most* (= the largest amount) *Claire is always studying. She does the* **most** *work.*
fewer/less (= a smaller number) *I buy* **fewer/less** *CDs these days than I used to.*	*less* (= a smaller amount) *If you want to be healthy, you should eat* **less** *fat.*
fewest/least (= the smallest number) *We're bottom of the league. We've got the* **fewest/least** *points.*	*least* (= the smallest amount) *I'm the busiest person here. I have the* **least** *spare time.*

TIP

Use *fewer* or *fewest* with plural nouns, e.g. *fewer* accidents, *the* **fewest** cars. Some people think that *less accidents* and the *least cars* are incorrect, although they are commonly used.

206 Patterns expressing a comparison

A *Than*

After a comparative we often use *than* with a phrase or clause.
> *Glasgow is bigger **than Edinburgh**.*
> *Going out alone is more difficult for women **than for men**.*
> *The hotel was more expensive **than I had expected**.*
> *Flying is a lot quicker **than going by train**.*
> *There were a lot more people in town **than usual**.*

For *than* + pronoun, > D.

B *Less* and *least*

Less and *least* are the opposites of *more* and *most*.
> *The theory is **less** complex/**more** simple than you might think.*
> *It's the **least** complex/the **most** simple explanation of the facts.*

We use *less* with both long and short adjectives.
> *It's cheaper.*   *It's **less expensive**.*
> *It's more expensive.*   *It's **less cheap**.*

Here are some more examples with *less* and *least*.
> *My back hurts **less** if I lie down.*
> *I see Vicky **less** often now that we don't work together.*
> *The subway is the **least** expensive way to get around New York.*

C *As* and *so*

We use a positive statement with *as ... as ...* to say that things are equal.
> *Many motels are **as** comfortable **as** hotels.*
> *My sister is **as** tall **as** you.*

We can use *as ... as ...* in idiomatic phrases like these.
> *as hard as iron* (= very hard)   *as light as a feather* (= very light)

In a negative statement we can use either *as ... as ...* or *so ... as ...*.
> *I don't drink **as/so** much coffee **as** you do.*
> (= I drink less coffee than you do.)
> *These new chairs aren't **as/so** comfortable **as** the old ones.*
> (= They are less comfortable than the old ones.)

We use *as* (not *so*) with the second part of the comparison. After *as* we can use a phrase or clause.
> *The film isn't as good **as the book**.*
> *I'll do the job as quickly **as (is) humanly possible**.*
> *The profits weren't as great **as we had hoped**.*

NOTE
a   We can use the pattern *as* + adjective + *a/an* + noun. > 196H
>   *This isn't **as interesting an article** as the last one I read.*
>   (= This article isn't as interesting as the last one I read.)
>   (BUT NOT ~~This isn't an as interesting article as the last one I read.~~)

287

We can also use this pattern with *such*.
> *This isn't **such an interesting article** as the last one I read.*

b Note this use with numbers and measurements.
> *The temperature is often **as** high **as** 40 degrees.*
> (= The temperature is often 40 degrees, which is very high.)

D Pronouns after *as* and *than*

A pronoun directly after *as* or *than* has the object form.
> *Phil is very tall. I'm not as tall as **him**.*
> *The other team played better than **us**.*

But if there is a verb after the pronoun, then the pronoun has the subject form.
> *Phil is very tall. I'm not as tall as **he is**.*
> *The other team played better than **we did**.*

NOTE
You may hear a sentence like *I'm not as tall as he* with a subject pronoun at the end. This is formal and old-fashioned. It is more usual to say *I'm not as tall as **him**/as **he is**.*

E Leaving out *as* or *than*

We can leave out *as* or *than* and the following phrase or clause if the meaning is clear without it.
> *I liked the old chairs. These new ones aren't as/so comfortable.*
> *The film is OK, but the book is much better.*
> *It's more difficult to find your way in the dark.*

F Patterns with the superlative

After a superlative we often use a phrase of time or place, an of-phrase, or a relative clause.
> *It's going to be the most exciting pop festival **ever**.*
> *Which is the oldest city **in the world**?*
> *The Trans-Siberian railway is the longest journey **of all**.*
> *It's the most marvellous film **I've ever seen**.*
> *Peter is the least aggressive person **I know**.*

We sometimes use a pattern with *one of/some of*.
> *The elephant is **one of** the largest animals in the world.*
> *This area has **some of** the worst housing in the country.*

G *Much bigger, easily the biggest*, etc

We can use an adverb of degree before a comparative or before *as*.
> *France is **much** bigger than Switzerland.*
> *Yes, I think I understand. I'm feeling **a little** less confused now.*
> *I'll need **a lot** more paper.*
> *The simulation is **just** as exciting as the real thing.*
> *I've got **nowhere near** as much time as I need for the job.*

We can use *even* before a comparative.

> *The new stadium will be **even** bigger than the present one, which holds 75,000 spectators.*

We can use *easily* and *by far* before a superlative.

> *This is **easily** the nicest place in town.*
> *I'm using **by far** the most effective method.*

The stays next to the superlative (e.g. *the nicest*).

For more examples of adverbs of degree modifying a comparative or superlative, > 196C.

NOTE
a   For e.g. *ever more confused*, > 207A Note.

b   For e.g. ***twice** as quick*, ***ten times** better*, >196C Note.

H *Same, like*, etc

We can also make comparisons with *same, like, similar*, and *different*.

> *You look **the same as** ever.*
> *I've got a computer **like** yours.*
> *The system here is **similar to** how we do it in Italy.*
> *Volleyball is quite **different from** basketball.*

207 Special patterns with the comparative

A Comparatives with *and*

We use this pattern with *and* to express a continuing change.

> *The plant grew **taller and taller**.*
> *The problem is becoming **worse and worse**.*
> *The air is getting **more and more polluted**.*
> *The roads are very congested. There's **more and more** traffic all the time.*

With *more*, we do not repeat the adjective.

> (NOT *The air is getting more polluted and more polluted.*)

We can also use *less*.

> *I was feeling **less and less enthusiastic** about the whole plan.*

NOTE
The pattern *ever* + comparative also expresses a continuing change.

> *The plant grew **ever taller**.*   *The air is getting **ever more polluted**.*

B Comparatives with *the ... the ...*

We use this pattern with *the ... the ...* to say that a change in one thing is linked to a change in another.

> ***The longer** the journey (is), **the more expensive** the ticket (is).*
> ***The further** you travel, **the more** you pay.*
> ***The older** you get, **the harder** it becomes to find a job.*
> ***The less** care you take, **the more** mistakes you'll make.*

Prepositions

208 Introduction

A A preposition is a word like *in*, *to*, or *for*. It can also be more than one word: *out of, in front of*. A preposition usually comes before a noun phrase.

into the building   *at* two o'clock   *without* a coat

Some prepositions can also come before an adverb.

until tomorrow   *through* there

B A phrase like *on my desk* or *at the office* is called a prepositional phrase. A prepositional phrase often functions as an adverbial. > 189B

*Everything was quiet **at the office**.*

A prepositional phrase can sometimes come after a noun. > 143

*The panic **at the office** meant that I got home late.*

There are many idiomatic combinations where a particular preposition follows a verb, adjective, or noun. > 222–226

***wait for** a bus   **afraid of** the dark   an **interest in** music*

C We can use certain prepositions before a gerund. > 114–117

*We succeeded **in reaching** an agreement.*

But an infinitive cannot be the object of a preposition.

NOT *We succeeded in to reach an agreement.*

We cannot use a preposition before a that-clause.

NOT *We're hoping for that it stays fine.*

We use one of these patterns.

*We're hoping **for fine weather**.   We're hoping (that) it stays fine.*

But we can use a preposition before a wh-clause. > 255

*I'd better make a list **of what** we need.*

D We can modify a preposition.

***almost at** the end   **right in front of** me   **halfway up** the hill*
***all over** the floor   **just off** the motorway   **directly after** your lesson*

E Some words can be either a preposition or an adverb.

Preposition: *I waited for my friend **outside** the bank.*
    *We haven't seen Julia **since** last summer.*
    *There was no lift, so we had to walk **up** the stairs.*
Adverb: *My friend went into the bank, and I waited **outside**.*
    *We saw Julia last summer, but we haven't seen her **since**.*
    *There was no lift, so we had to walk **up**.*

Some words can be either a preposition of time or a conjunction. > 238A

Preposition: *We must have everything ready **before** their arrival.*
Conjunction: *We must have everything ready **before** they arrive.*

F In some patterns a preposition goes at the end of a clause.

Wh-question: *Who did you go to the party **with**?* > 15D
Infinitive clause: *I've got a CD for you to listen **to**.* > 98D
Passive: *War reporters sometimes get shot **at**.* > 87D
Relative clause: *That's the shop I was telling you **about**.* > 268D

209 Prepositions of place

A Basic meanings

*There are some people **in**/**inside** the café. The man is waiting **outside** the café.*

*There's a TV **on** the table. There's a photo **on top of** the TV. There's a dog **under(neath)** the table.*

*There's a picture **over**/**above** the fireplace.*

*She's going **up** the steps, and he's coming **down** the steps.*

*The road goes **through** a tunnel. The car is going **in**/**into** the tunnel. The lorry is coming **out of** the tunnel.*

*She's taking the food **off** the trolley and putting it **on**/**onto** the shelves.*

The bus is **at** the bus stop. It is **alongside** the kerb. It is going **from** the city centre **to** the university.

The lorry is going **away from** York and travelling **towards** Hull.

The man is sitting **next to/by/beside** the woman. Their table is **close to/near** the door.

The bus is **in front of/ahead of** the car. The lorry is **behind** the car. The car is **between** the bus and the lorry.

The woman is walking **along** the pavement **past** the supermarket.

The man is on the pavement **opposite** the bank. The bank is **across** the road.

There are security guards **among** the crowds. They are present **throughout** the area.
(= in all parts of the area)

They're running **around/round** the track.

Your foot must stay **within/inside** the circle.

The man is leaning **against** the wall.

The submarine is 500 metres **below/beneath** the surface.

Would they find the promised land **beyond** the mountains?
(= on the other side of the mountains)

NOTE
We use *of* with some prepositions of place: *ahead of, in front of, on top of, out of*.
Outside of is also possible.
> *You should have a life **outside (of)** work.*
You may also hear *inside of, off of*, or *alongside of*, especially in American English, but they are regarded as non-standard in British English.
Americans sometimes use *out* without *of*.
> *I was looking **out** the window.*

B Position and movement

Most prepositions of place can say where something is or where it is going.

| Position: | *There was a barrier **across** the road.* |
| Movement: | *A dog ran **across** the road in front of us.* |

At usually expresses position, and *to* expresses movement.

| Position: | *Everyone was **at** the café.* |
| Movement: | *Everyone went **to** the café.* |

As a general rule, *in* and *on* express position, and *into* and *onto* express movement.

Position:	*We were sitting **in** the café.*
	*She stood **on** the balcony.*
Movement:	*We went **into** the café.*
	*She walked **onto** the balcony.*

But we also use *in* and *on* for movement, especially in informal English.
> *We went **in** the café.*
> *Someone pushed me **in** the swimming-pool.*
> *Babies often throw things **on** the floor.*

After *lay, place*, and *put* we usually use *in* or *on* rather than *into* or *onto*.
> *They laid the body **on** a blanket.*
> *A number of advertisements were placed **in** the newspapers.*
> *I put a clean sheet **on** the bed.*

After *sit* we use *in* or *on*.

> *Tom sat down **in** the armchair.*   *We could go and sit **on** that seat.*

NOTE
Compare these examples.
> *We walked **on** the beach (for half an hour).*
> *We walked (from the car park) **onto** the beach.*

C Other meanings

Prepositions of place can also have more abstract meanings.
> *No one is **above**/**beyond** criticism.* (= too good to be criticized)
> *Our next game is **against** Arsenal.* (The opposing team is Arsenal.)
> *The band is **among** the most successful ever.* (= one of the most successful)
> *The party is right **behind** its leader.* (= supporting its leader)
> *She's really **into** yoga and that kind of thing.* (= interested in yoga)
> *I went to a lecture **on** Einstein.* (= about Einstein)
> *We are working **towards** a common goal.* (= working to bring closer)

For more prepositions with abstract meanings, > 215.
For prepositions of time, > 211.

Prepositions are often used in idiomatic combinations.
> ***Above all**, we must keep our nerve.* > 216
> *The police are **looking into** the matter.* > 222

210 *At, on,* and *in* expressing place

A We use *at* to give the position where something is.

> *The car was waiting **at** the lights.*   *There's someone **at** the door.*

Here we see *the lights* and *the door* as a point in space. Compare *There's someone in the phone box* (> C), where we see the phone box as all around the person.

We use *at* with a building or institution when we mean the normal purpose the building is used for.
> *My friends are **at** the theatre.* (= watching a play)
> *My sister is fifteen. She's still **at** school.* (= attending school)

We use *at* for someone's home.
> *I had a cup of coffee **at** Alice's (house/flat).*

We also use *at* with a social event.
> *We met **at** Adam's party, didn't we?*   *Jo spent the afternoon **at** the races.*

B *On* is two-dimensional. We use it for a surface.

> *Don't leave your glass **on** the floor.*
> *There were lots of pictures **on** the walls.*

We use *on* for position on a line such as a river, road, or frontier.
> *Paris is **on** the Seine.*
> *The house is right **on** the main road, so it's a bit noisy.*

For ***in** Bond Street/**on** Fifth Avenue,* > E.

NOTE
We use *on* to say that we are carrying something with us.
> *I'm afraid I haven't got any money **on**/with me.*

C *In* is three-dimensional.
> *I had five pounds **in** my pocket.*
> *Who's that girl **in** the green dress?*
> *There were three people **in** the waiting room.*

Compare *in* and *at* with buildings.
> *It was cold **in** the library.* (= inside the building)
> *We were **at** the library.* (= using the library)

D In general we use *in* for a country or town.
> *Tom is **in** Canada at the moment.*   *My sister works **in** Birmingham.*

With a small place we can use *at* or *in*.
> *We used to live **at**/**in** a place called Menston.*

We can use *at* with a town or city if we see it as a point on a journey.
> *I had to change trains **at** Birmingham.*

We use *on* with a small island and *in* with a large island.
> *We spent a week **on** Corfu.*   *The company has a factory **in** Ireland.*

E Compare the use of *at, on,* and *in* in these phrases.

at	*on*	*in*
		in Spain/Bristol
at 52 Grove Road	*on* 42nd Street (US)	*in* Grove Road
at your house	*on* the third floor	
at the station	*on* the platform	
at home/work/school		*in* the room/lesson
	on the page	*in* a book/newspaper
	on the screen	*in* the photo/picture
	on the island	*in* the country
at the seaside	*on* the beach/coast	
	on the right/left	*in* the middle
		in the distance
	on the back of an envelope	*in* the back of the car
at the back/end/front of the queue		*in* a queue/line/row

211 More details about prepositions of place

A *Above, over, below,* and *under*

Above and *over* have similar meanings.
> *There was a clock **above**/**over** the entrance.*
> *My bedroom is **above**/**over** the kitchen, so I get all the cooking smells.*

When something covers an area, we prefer *over*.
> *Thick black smoke hangs **over** the town.*

When the two things are in contact, we use *over* and not *above*.
> *Someone had spread a sheet **over** the body.*

We also use *over* for movement to the other side.
> *The horse jumped **over** the wall.*
> *Did the ball go **over** the goal line?*
> *Somehow we had to get **over**/across the river.*

We prefer *over* before a number.
> *There are well **over** fifty thousand people in the stadium.*

But we use *above* for a measurement that we think of as vertical.
> *Temperatures will rise **above** thirty degrees.*
> *The land here is only a couple of metres **above** sea level.*

Below is the opposite of *above*.
> *The treasure was buried two metres **below** ground.*
> *Temperatures will fall **below** freezing.*

The opposite of *over* is *under*.
> *Come **under** the umbrella, or you'll get wet.*
> *The town lies **under** a thick black cloud of smoke.*

We use *under* rather than *below* with ages and with sums of money.
> *You have to be **under** 15 to buy a half-price ticket.*
> *The winner will collect just **under** £2 million.*

With most other kinds of measurement, either *below* or *under* is possible.
> *The party's support has fallen to **below**/**under** 20 per cent.*

B *Top* and *bottom*

On top of is a preposition.
> *There's a monument **on top of** the hill.*

We can also use *top* and *bottom* in patterns like these.
> *When you get **to the top** of the hill, you turn left.*
> *Sign your name **at the bottom** of the page.*

C *Through, across,* and *along*

through *the gate*   **across** *the road*   **along** *the path*

When you go through, you go in at one end and out at the other. We talk about going *through* a gate, a tunnel, a forest, a hole, and so on.
  *The water is pumped **through** pipes.*
  *The burglar got in **through** the window.*

When you go across, you go from one side to the other. We talk about going *across* a road, a river, a bridge, a frontier, and so on.
  *You can get **across** the Channel by ferry.*

We use *along* when we follow something that goes in a line. We talk about going *along* a path, a road, a coast, a corridor, and so on.
  *We were walking **along** the line of the old Iron Curtain.*

Compare *along* and *across* in these examples.
  *We cruised **along** the canal for a few miles.*
  *We walked **across** the canal by a footbridge.*

D *To, towards,* and *up to*

We use *to* for a destination and *towards* for a direction.
  *We're going **to** Oxford. We're going to look around the colleges.*
  *We're going **towards** Oxford. I think we're going the wrong way.*

Up to means moving to a position right in front of someone or something.
  *A man came **up to** me in the street and asked for money.*
  *Lisa walked boldly **up to** the front door and rang the bell.*

It can also mean movement to a higher level.
  *I filled the bottle **up to** the top.*

NOTE
We also use *up to* to talk about a maximum number.
  ***Up to** thirty people are believed to have been killed in the explosion.*

E *Near, close, by,* and *next to*

Near, near to, and *close to* mean 'not far from'.
> *Motherwell is **near** Glasgow.*
> *There's a taxi rank quite **near (to)** the hotel.*
> *You shouldn't put a heater **close to** curtains.*
Here *close* is pronounced /kləʊs/.

Near (to) and *close to* have comparative and superlative forms.
> *We were gradually getting **nearer (to)** our destination.*
> *I was sitting **closest to** the door.*

Nearby and *close by* mean 'not far away'.
> *We don't serve dinner, but there is an excellent restaurant **nearby / close by**.*

By means 'at the side of' or 'very near'.
> *We live right **by** the hospital.*
> *Come and sit **by** me.*

Next to means 'directly at the side of'.
> *The woman sitting **next to** me was smoking the whole time.*
> *There's a newsagent's **next to** the post office.*

NOTE
Nowhere near means 'a long way from'.
> *Birmingham is **nowhere near** Glasgow.*

F *In front of, before, behind, after,* and *opposite*

When we are talking about position, we prefer *in front of* to *before*.
> *There's a statue **in front of** the museum.*
> *Tina spends hours **in front of** the mirror.*

We prefer *behind* to *after*.
> *The car **behind** us ran into the back of us.*

Before usually means 'earlier in time', and *after* means 'later in time'. But we also use *before* and *after* to talk about what order things come in.
> *J comes **before K**.*
> *K comes **after J**.*

Opposite means 'on the other side from'. Compare *in front of* and *opposite*.
> *Simon was sitting **in front of** me in the cinema.*
> *Simon was sitting **opposite** me at lunch.*

G *Between* and *among*

We use *between* with a small number of things, especially with two things.
> *The bungalow is **between** two houses.*
> (= There is a house on both sides of the bungalow.)
> *The ball went **between** the player's legs.*
> *It's an area of countryside **between** three quite large towns.*
For expressions such as *a conflict between* and *a link between*, > 226D.

Among suggests a larger number.
*I thought I caught sight of someone **among** the trees.*

H (A)round and about

Around or *round* means movement in a circle > 209A. We can also use it to
mean 'in different directions' or 'in different places'.
*We just like driving **around/round** the country visiting different places.*
*There were piles of old magazines lying **around/round** the flat.*
Americans use *around* rather than *round*.

We can use *about* in the same way.
*Everyone was rushing **around/about** the place in a panic.*

212 *At, on*, and *in* expressing time

A We use *at* with a particular time such as a clock time or a meal time.
*The performance starts **at** eight o'clock.*
*I'll see you **at** breakfast.*
***At** that time there were no mobile phones.*
*We're very busy **at** the moment.*

We also use *at* with short holiday periods.
*The family is always together **at** Christmas/**at** Thanksgiving.*
*Are you doing anything **at** the weekend?* (US: **on** *the weekend*)

We also use *at* with ages.
*A sporting career can be over **at** thirty.*

B We use *on* with a day.
*The meeting is **on** Tuesday/**on** 7 August.*
*I have to go to an interview **on** that day.*
*Do they play football games **on** Christmas Day/**on** Easter Sunday?*

On can mean 'immediately after'.
***On** his arrival, the President held a press conference.*

C We use *in* with longer periods.
*I'll have to make my mind up **in** the next few days.*
*We'll have lots of time **in** the summer holidays.*
*The term starts **in** September.*
*The company was set up **in** 1997.*
***In** the 16th century only about 5 million people spoke English.*

We also use *in* with a part of a day.
*Why don't you come over **in** the afternoon?*
*I always work better **in** the mornings.*

But we use *on* if we say which day.

*Why don't you come over **on** Friday afternoon?*
*The incident occurred **on** the evening of 12 May.*

NOTE

We say *in the night* but *at night* without *the*.
   *I heard a noise **in the** night.* (= in the middle of the night)
   *The windows are shut **at** night.* (= when it is night)

D We can use *in* to say how long something takes.

*Have you read 'Around the World **in** Eighty Days'?*
*Lots of athletes can run a mile **in** four minutes.*

We can also use *in* for a time in the future measured from the present.

*We take our exams **in** three weeks.*
(= three weeks from now/in three weeks' time)

Compare these examples.

*You can walk there **in** half an hour.* (It takes half an hour.)
*I'm going out **in** half an hour.* (= half an hour from now)

E Sometimes we can use an expression of time without a preposition.

*I received the letter **last Thursday**.*
*I'm starting a new course **next year**.*
*We've got visitors **this week**.*
*The same thing happens **every time**.*
*You aren't going to lie in bed **all day**, are you?*
*Don't be late **tomorrow morning**.*
*A **week later** I got a reply.*

We do not normally use *at, on,* or *in* with *last, next,* or *this,* with *every* or *all,* with *yesterday* or *tomorrow,* or with the adverb *later.*

In some contexts we can either use the preposition or leave it out.

*Something unusual happened **(on) that day**.*
*Profits were £50 million, compared with £35 million **(in) the previous year**.*
*They agreed to play the match **(on) the following Sunday**.*

In informal English, and especially in American English, we can sometimes leave out *on* before a day.

*I'll see you **(on) Monday**.*

NOTE

a   We can use other prepositions with *last, every,* etc.
       ***After this week**, I'll need a holiday.*   *I feel nervous **during every flight**.*

b   We do not use a preposition with *these days* (= nowadays).
       *It's all done by computers **these days**.*

213 *For, since,* and *ago*

A We use *for* with a period of time to say how long something continues.
> *The kids play computer games **for** hours on end.*
> *I once stayed at that hotel **for** a week.*
> *I just want to sit down **for** five minutes.*

We do not use *for* before a phrase with *all.*
> *It rained **all day**.* (NOT ~~It rained for all day.~~)

And we do not usually use *for* before a phrase with *whole.*
> *It rained the whole day.*

This is more usual than *It rained for the whole day.*

B We often use *for* and *since* with the perfect.

for	since
*Rachel has worked for the company **for** five years now.*	*Rachel has worked for the company **since** 1999.*
*We haven't been to the theatre **for** months.*	*We haven't been to the theatre **since** April.*
*I've been waiting here **for** twenty minutes.*	*I've been waiting here **since** twelve o'clock.*

We use *for* + length of time.
   for *two years*   **for** *a week*
   for *four days*   **for** *a few minutes*
	We use *since* + time when.
	   since *2003* **since** *last week*
	   since *Monday* **since** *half past two*

We can sometimes leave out *for* in informal English.
   I've been waiting twenty minutes.
	We sometimes also use *since* with an event.
	   *I haven't been anywhere **since** the concert.*

NOTE
For more examples with *for* and *since,* > 46D.
We can also use *since* as a conjunction. > 238A
For the pattern *It's months **since** we last went to the theatre,* > 46E.

C We use the adverb *ago* for something that happened in the past at a time measured from the present.
> *Rachel joined the company five years **ago**.* (= five years before now)
> *We last went to the theatre months **ago**.* (= months before now)
> *An hour **ago** I was still in bed.* (= an hour before now)

Ago comes after the length of time (*five years, months, an hour*).

When we look back from the past to an even earlier time, we usually use the adverb *before.*
> *Rachel left the company last year. She'd joined them five years **before**.*
> (= five years before last year)

This is more usual than *She'd joined them five years ago.*

D Compare these examples referring to the past and the future.

Looking into the past	Looking into the future
I've been here (for) ten minutes.	*I'll stay (for) ten minutes.*
I've been here since twenty to four.	*I'll stay until four o'clock.* > 214C
I arrived ten minutes ago.	*I'm leaving in ten minutes.*

214 More prepositions of time

A Place and time

Some prepositions of place can also be used as a preposition of time.
I'll be with you between three and half past.
It must have been close to ten when I finally got home.
Lots of people work from nine o'clock to five. > D
You can do the journey inside an hour.
I had a stream of visitors throughout the day.
Towards midnight people were starting to leave.
We can park here up to six o'clock. > C
At, on, and *in* can also express either place (> 210) or time (> 212).

B *During* and *over*

Look at these examples.
Nobody does any work during the festival.
The office will be closed during August.
We use *during* with an event (*the festival*) or a specific period (*August*).
It means the whole period.

We cannot use *during* + length of time.
The office will be closed for a month. (NOT *during a month*)
The festival went on for five days. (NOT *during five days*)

But we can use *during* with a specific period of time.
No one does any work during the five days of the festival.
I've been extremely busy during the last few weeks.

We can also use *during* for a period in which a shorter action takes place.
The e-mail arrived during the meeting.
I have to make several trips abroad during the next few weeks.

During is a preposition; *while* is a conjunction.
My phone rang during lunch.
My phone rang while I was having lunch.

We can also use *over* for a whole period of time.

> **Over/During** *the past year, 25,000 refugees have entered the country.*
> *Free meals will be served to the poor* **over/during** *the Christmas period.*

NOTE

a   When something continues for a complete period, we can also use *throughout*
    or *all through*.
    > *The population grew rapidly during/***throughout** *the 19th century.*
    > *The man at the end of the table kept staring at me during/***all through** *lunch.*

b   The adverb *over* can mean 'finished'.
    > *The meeting was soon* **over***.*

C *Till/until* and *by*

We use *till/until* to say when something comes to an end.

> *We sat there* **till/until** *the end of the show.*
> *I'll be working here* **till/until** *next April.*

Till is more informal than *until*.

We can also use *up to*.

> *I'll be working here* **up to** *next April.*

Not ... till/until means that something happens later than expected.

> *We did***n't** *get home* **till/until** *half past two in the morning*
> *On Sundays I sometimes* **don't** *get up* **till/until** *lunchtime.*
> *The new law will* **not** *come into force* **until** *next year.*

By means 'not later than'.

> *I have to be at work* **by** *nine.* (= at nine or earlier)
> *They should have replied to my letter* **by** *now.* (= now or earlier)
> *Debbie is going to pay me back* **by** *Friday.* (= on Friday or earlier)

Compare the use of *before*.

> *Debbie is going to pay me back* **before** *Friday.* (= earlier than Friday)

NOTE

a   *Till/until* does not express place.
    > *We walked* **to** *the bridge /* **as far as** *the bridge.* (NOT ~~till/until the bridge~~)

b   We can use *till/until* as a conjunction.
    > *We walked on* **till/until** *we got to the bridge.*
    We cannot use *by* on its own as a conjunction, but we can use *by the time*.
    > *It was raining* **by the time** *we got to the bridge.*

D *From ... to/till/until*

We use *from* for the time when something starts.

> *Tickets will be on sale* **from** *next Wednesday.*
> **From** *seven in the morning there's constant traffic noise.*

We can use *from ... to* or *from ... till/until* for the times when something
starts and finishes.

> *The cricket season lasts* **from** *April* **to** *September.*
> *The road will be closed* **from** *Friday evening* **till/until** *Monday morning.*

Americans use *through*, e.g. *from Friday* **through** *Monday.*

E *Before* and *after*

Look at these examples.

*I usually go jogging **before** breakfast.*
*Everyone will need to study the proposals **prior to** our discussions.*
*People felt nervous **after** the attack on the World Trade Center.*
***Following** a change of sponsor, the competition now has a new name.*

Prior to (formal) means 'before'. *Following* means 'after' or 'as a result of'.

215 Prepositions: other meanings

A

Prepositions can have meanings other than place or time. Here are some examples.

*We were arguing **about** politics.*
***According to** the opinion polls, the government is very popular.*
*The resort was very crowded. And **as for** the accommodation, it was awful.*
*We need some advice **as to** what we should do next.*
*I'm reading a book **by** Thomas Keneally.*
***Contrary to** popular belief, prisons are not holiday camps.*
*The couple want to stay together **for the sake of** the children.*
*The product should be assembled **in accordance with** the instructions.*
*Who's **in charge of** this department?*
*Almost all the voters were **in favour of** independence.*
*Profits have fallen ten per cent, **in line with** forecasts.*
*The furniture has to be the right size **in relation to** the size of the room.*
*Can I use a pencil **instead of** a pen?*
*How effective are speed cameras **in terms of** road safety?*
***On behalf of** the company, I would like to express my thanks.*
*No action has been taken **regarding** / **with regard to** my complaint.*
*The book is better **than** the film. > 206A*
*Brazil won the game **thanks to** a late goal from Ronaldo.*
*It's **up to** you what you do next. You decide.*
*This train goes to Birmingham **via** Oxford.*

B

For has a number of different meanings. Here are some of them.

*Could you do something **for** me, please?* (= to help me)
*I've called in **for** a chat.* (purpose, > 240C)
*She's a very clever child **for** her age.* (= considering her age)
*Are people **for** the scheme or against it?* (= in favour of/supporting)

When *for* means 'in favour of', it is normally stressed.

C

With has these meanings.

*I went to the concert **with** a friend.* (We were together.)
*Matthew is the man **with** long hair.* (He has long hair.)
*I cut the wood **with** an electric saw.* (I used an electric saw. > D)
*We all set to work **with** enthusiasm.* (= enthusiastically)
***With** people watching I felt embarrassed.*
(= Because people were watching, ... > 128B)

Without is the opposite of *with*.
> *Who's the man **without** any shoes on?*
> *We all set to work, but **without** enthusiasm.*

NOTE
We can use *with* + noun to form an adverbial expressing manner or feeling.
> *I listened to the discussion **with interest**.*
With certain nouns we use *in*.
> *The losers sank to the ground **in despair**.*
For *to* in a comment adverbial such as *to my horror*, > 201C.

D We use *with* and *by* to express means. We use *with* to talk about an
instrument, something we use to help us do something.
> *The thieves broke the door down **with** a hammer.*
> *Just stir this **with** a wooden spoon, could you?*

We can also use *by means of* to explain how something is done.
> *The site was made secure **by means of** a sophisticated alarm system.*

We use *by* before an ing-form.
> *The thieves got in **by breaking** the door down.*
> ***By stirring** the mixture, you stop it sticking to the pan.*

In a passive sentence we use *by* before the agent. > 89A
> *The door was broken down **by** the thieves/**with** a hammer.*
> *The motor is powered **by** electricity.*

NOTE
Sometimes we can use either *with* or *by*.
> *I paid **with** a credit card/**by** credit card.*
After *by* expressing means we do not use *a/an* or *the*.

E We use *by* + noun for a means of transport.
> *I usually prefer to travel **by** train.*
We do not use *a/an* or *the*.
> (NOT *I usually prefer to travel by a train.*)

Such phrases with *by* include: *by aeroplane, by air, by bicycle, by bike, by boat,
by bus, by car, by coach, by ferry, by hovercraft, by hydrofoil, by plane, by rail,
by road, by sea, by ship, by taxi, by train, by tube, by underground.*

We do not normally use *by* to mean a specific bicycle, car, etc.
> *I'll go **on** my bike.* (NOT *I'll go by my bike.*)
We can use phrases like *in the/my car, in a taxi, on the/our boat, on the bus/
coach/ferry/train*, etc.

We say *on foot* and *on horseback*.
> *I came here **on foot**.* (= I walked here.)
On foot is more usual than *by foot*.

We can also use *by* for means of communication, e.g. *by e-mail, by fax,
by letter, by phone, by post, by radio.*
> *I sent the information **by** post.*
> *I spoke to Tim **by** phone / on the phone.*

We can use other prepositions with *bike, car,* etc. These examples express movement.
*The passengers got **into/out of** the car/taxi.*
*Emma got **on/off** her bike/the bus/the train.*
*We went **on board** the ship.*

F *Of* has a number of different meanings.

*a tin **of** soup* > 138A   *some **of** my friends* > 168
*the end **of** the game* > 133C   *our first sight **of** land* > 257

We can also use *of* in this pattern.
*These souvenirs are **of** no value.* (They have no value.)
*She's an actress **of** great ability.* (She has great ability.)

G We can use *as* to express a role or function.
*Maria has come along **as** our guide.* (She is our guide.)
*I'm having to use the sofa **as** a bed.* (It is a bed.)
After *as* we normally use a determiner (e.g. *our, a*), but for a phrase like
as Queen without *the,* > 159F.

We use *like* to make a comparison.
*A hang-glider can soar through the air **like** a bird.*
*I think Louise looks a bit **like** Kylie Minogue.*
***Like** everyone else, I have to pay my taxes.*

Compare *as* and *like*.
*He speaks **as** an expert. He is after all a professor.*
*He talks **like** an expert, but really he knows very little.*

NOTE
a   We can use *anything* or *nothing* to modify *like*.
*Of course it isn't my coat. It's **nothing like** mine, is it?*

b   *Unlike* is the opposite of *like*.
*It's **unlike** Sarah to be late. She's usually very punctual.*

H We use *except (for), apart from, with the exception of,* and *but (for)* to talk
about an exception.
*Everyone was there **except (for)/but (for)/apart from** James, who was ill.*
*Everyone was there **with the exception of** James.*
*I hate fish. I can eat anything **except/but** fish.*
*I swear to tell the truth, the whole truth, and nothing **but** the truth.*

I Some prepositions have a similar meaning to a conjunction.
*I studied physics **as well as** chemistry.* (= and I studied chemistry)
*The barbecue was cancelled **due to** the weather.*
(= because the weather was bad)

Such prepositions include the following:
as well as, besides, in addition to, along with, together with > 233D
in spite of, despite > 235D
as a result of > 236B
because of, due to, owing to, in view of, on account of, considering > 239C

216 Idiomatic phrases with prepositions

A There are many idiomatic phrases beginning with a preposition. Most of them are without *a/an or the*. Here are some examples.

__Above all__ we don't want any accidents.
__At first__ I couldn't see a thing, but then my eyes adjusted to the dark.
I've managed to finish this crossword __at last__.
Of course I know you. I recognized you __at once__.
I'd like to buy this picture if it's __for sale__.
Try to see it __from__ my __point of view__.
You have to pay half the cost of the holiday __in advance__.
Yes, I am thinking of leaving. __In fact__ I've resigned.
__Of course__ you can't trust the weather in Britain.
I drive about ten thousand miles a year __on average__.
I'll be __on holiday__ next week.
I heard the news either __on television__ or __on the radio__.
There are so many different computers __on the market__.
There were one or two problems, but __on the whole__ things went smoothly.
I've been __out of work__, but I'm starting a new job soon.
The government is __under pressure__ to do something about the problem.

B *In time (for/to)* means 'early enough', but *on time* means 'punctual(ly)'.
Oh, good. You're back __in time__ for tea.
The train left __on time__ at 11.23.

Note also *in good time* and *just in time*.
We got back __in good time__ for tea. (= with plenty of time to spare)
We got back __just in time__ for tea. (= with little time to spare)

C *In the beginning* means 'at first', and *at the beginning of* + noun phrase refers to the time when something starts.
__In the beginning__ / At first the company struggled to survive, but now it is very successful.
The students return to Oxford __at the beginning of__ the academic year.

In the end means 'finally', and *at the end of* + noun phrase refers to the time when something finishes.
There were arguments, but __in the end__ / finally we managed to reach an agreement.
Most students have jobs to go to __at the end of__ the course.

D *In the way* means 'blocking the way', and *on the way* means 'on a journey'.
Don't leave your bike there. It'll be __in the way__.
It's a long journey. We can stop for a meal __on the way__.

Phrasal verbs and prepositional idioms

217 Verbs with adverbs and prepositions → Audio

A Verb + adverb

A verb + adverb is called a 'phrasal verb'.
> ***Come in** and **sit down**.*
> *What time did you **get up**?*
> *You'd better **take off** your shoes.*
> *I **threw away** my old briefcase.*

The adverbs (e.g. *in, down, up*) are sometimes called 'adverb particles'. They combine with verbs to form phrasal verbs (e.g. *come in, take off*).

B Verb + preposition

A verb + preposition is called a 'prepositional verb'.
> *I was **looking at** the photo.*
> *We didn't **go into** all the details.*
> *What did you **think of** the film?*

Prepositions (e.g. *at, into, of*) combine with verbs to form prepositional verbs (e.g. *look at, go into, think of*). The preposition has an object (e.g. *the photo, all the details, the film*). For more examples of prepositional verbs, > 222.

NOTE
Not everyone agrees about what to call these verbs. Sometimes 'phrasal verb' is used to mean both verb + adverb and verb + preposition. It is of course more important to use the words correctly than to worry about what to call them. But remember that there are differences between the use of adverbs and the use of prepositions. > 219

218 The grammar of phrasal verbs

A Word order

Some phrasal verbs are intransitive, but others have an object.

Intransitive:	*Suddenly the lights **went out**.*
	*A chair had **fallen over**.*
Transitive:	*Someone **turned out** the lights.*
	*Someone had **knocked over** a chair.*

When a phrasal verb has an object, the adverb can usually go either before or after the object.

Before the object:	*I **threw away** my old briefcase.*
	*We **woke up** the neighbours.*
After the object:	*I **threw** my old briefcase **away**.*
	*We **woke** the neighbours **up**.*

When the object is a pronoun, the adverb goes after it.

*My old briefcase was falling to pieces, so I **threw it away**.*
*The neighbours weren't very pleased. We **woke them up**.*
*Paul borrowed some money from Sarah and never **paid her back**.*

When the object is a long phrase, the adverb usually goes before it.

*I **threw away** that rather battered old briefcase.*
*We **woke up** just about everyone in the street.*
*Paul never **paid back** all that money he borrowed.*

B Adverb in front position

To give the adverb extra emphasis, we can sometimes put it in front position, especially when it expresses movement.

*The door opened, and **out** ran the children.*
*Five minutes later, **along** came another bus.*

There is usually inversion of subject and verb: in the first example *ran* comes before *the children*. But when the subject is a pronoun, there is no inversion.

*The door opened, and out **they ran**.*

C Nouns formed from phrasal verbs

Some verb + adverb combinations can be used as a noun.

a **walkout** by key workers	information on the **handout**
a **hold-up** at the bank	a **take-away** meal
a **takeover** bid for the company	a **stand-in** for the leading actor
an hour before **take-off**	a car **breakdown**

The stress is usually on the first syllable: '*take-off*.

NOTE

a   Some nouns have the adverb before the verb.
    *an **outbreak** of rioting   the amused **onlookers***

b   We can also sometimes use a passive participle + adverb before a noun.
    *a **rolled-up** newspaper   a **broken-down** car*

219 Differences between phrasal and prepositional verbs

A Adverbs and prepositions

A phrasal verb is a verb + adverb, e.g. *give away* > 218. Adverbs include *away*, *back*, and *out*.

A prepositional verb is a verb + preposition, e.g. *pay for* > 222. Prepositions include *at*, *for*, *from*, *into*, *of*, and *with*.

Some words can be either an adverb or a preposition. They include *about*, *along*, *around*, *down*, *in*, *off*, *on*, *over*, *round*, *through*, and *up*.

*When I heard the voice, I looked **round**. (adverb)*
*We were looking **round** the museum. (preposition)*

B Word order with an object

Look at the difference between the possible word orders with the adverb *away* and the preposition *for*.

Phrasal verb	Prepositional verb
*Lisa **gave away** her jewellery.* *Lisa **gave** her jewellery **away**.* The adverb can go before or after the object.	*Lisa **paid for** the meal.* (NOT *Lisa paid the meal for.*) The preposition goes before its object.
A pronoun always goes before the adverb. *She gave **it away**.*	A pronoun goes after the preposition. *She paid **for it**.*
	But the preposition comes at the end in some patterns. > 208F *What did Lisa **pay for**?*

C Stress

With a phrasal verb, the stress usually falls on the adverb, especially when it comes at the end of a clause. → Audio *Lisa gave her jewellery a'way.* *Let's go. Come 'on.*	With a prepositional verb, the stress usually falls on the verb and not the preposition. → Audio *Lisa 'paid for the meal.* *It de'pends on the weather.*

D The passive

Many phrasal and prepositional verbs can be passive.

Phrasal verb	Prepositional verb
*The alarm has been **switched off**.* *The building was **pulled down** last year.* We usually stress the adverb: *pulled 'down.*	*The matter will be **dealt with**.* *The children are being **looked after** by a neighbour.* We do not usually stress the preposition: *'looked after.*

E Word order with adverbials

Phrasal verb	Prepositional verb
An adverbial usually goes after the phrasal verb. *The plane took off **on time**.* *The candidate stood up **nervously**.*	An adverbial can often go between the verb and preposition. *I can't concentrate **properly** on my work.* *I looked **carefully** at the photo.*
It does not go between the verb and its adverb. NOT *He stood nervously up.*	It does not go between the preposition and its object. NOT *I looked at carefully the photo.*

F Verb + clause

A phrasal verb can sometimes be followed by a gerund clause, a wh-clause, or a that-clause.

*I've given up **skiing**.*
*Read through **what** you've written.*
*We found out **(that)** the story was untrue.*

A prepositional verb can sometimes be followed by a gerund clause or a wh-clause.

*I don't believe in **paying** taxes.* > 115
*The answer you get depends on **who** you ask.* > 255
We cannot use a that-clause after a prepositional verb.

NOT *I don't believe in that I should pay taxes.*

220 Phrasal verb meanings

A Some phrasal verbs are easy to understand if you know the meaning of each word.

*You'll have to **turn round** here and **go back**.*
*The man stopped and **put down** his suitcase.*
These verbs express movement.

But often the phrasal verb has an idiomatic meaning.

*I've **given up** smoking.* (= stopped)
*The idea has **caught on** in a big way.* (= become popular)

B Sometimes there is a one-word verb with the same meaning as the phrasal verb. The phrasal verb is usually more informal.

*Are you going to **carry on**/**continue** your studies?*
*Experts are trying to **find out**/**discover** the cause of the accident.*
*We must **fix up**/**arrange** a meeting.*

The problem won't just **go away/disappear.**
You have failed to **keep up/maintain** *your monthly payments.*
You've **left out/omitted** *two names from the list.*
I'd like to **put off/postpone** *a decision as long as possible.*
They've **put up/raised** *prices by 20 per cent.*
I got someone to **take away/remove** *all the rubbish.*

C Some verbs combine with a number of different adverbs.
The child took two steps and **fell down.**
Enthusiasm for the sport has **fallen off.** (= become less)
Simon and Chloe have **fallen out.** (= quarrelled)
I'm afraid the deal **fell through.** (= didn't happen)

And the most common adverbs can combine with many different verbs.
The cat got up a tree and couldn't **climb down.**
These trousers are so tight I can't **bend down.**
A pedestrian was **knocked down** *by a car.*
Interest rates may **come down** *soon.*

D A phrasal verb can have more than one meaning.
There was a parked car blocking the lane, and we couldn't **get by.** (= pass it)
Tom has very little income, but he **gets by.** (= manages to live)

E We can use an adverb with the verb *be.*
We'll be **away** *on holiday next week.* (= in another place)
Will you be **in** *tomorrow?* (= at home/work)
Long skirts are **in** *at the moment.* (= in fashion)
The barbecue is **off** *because of the weather.* (= not taking place)
Is there anything **on** *at the cinema?* (= showing, happening)
I rang but you were **out.** (= not at home/work)
The party's **over.** *It's time to go.* (= at an end)
What's **up?** (= What's the matter?/What's happening?)

221 Some common adverbs in phrasal verbs

TIP
Many phrasal verbs have idiomatic meanings, but the verbs do not
necessarily have to be learned separately. For example, if you learn that
calling someone back means returning a phone call, then you can guess
that *phone back* and *ring back* mean the same thing. It may help to make
lists of phrasal verbs that you come across. Where possible, try to group
them according to the meaning of the adverb.

Here are some adverbs often used in phrasal verbs.

down = to the ground
 knocked down/pulled down *the old hospital,* **burn down**, **cut down** *a tree*
down = on paper
 write down *the number,* **copy down, note down, take down**
down = becoming less
 turn down *the volume,* **slow down**, *a fire* **dying down**
down = stopping completely
 a car that **broke down**, *a factory* **closing down**
off = away
 set off *on a journey, a plane* **taking off**, **see** *someone* **off** *at the airport,*
 take *a day* **off**, **sell** *goods* **off** *cheaply*
off = disconnected
 turn off/switch off *the television,* **cut off** *the electricity,* **ring off**
off = succeeding
 the plan didn't **come off**, *we managed to* **pull** *it* **off**
on = wearing
 had *a jumper* **on**, **put** *my shoes* **on**, **trying** *a coat* **on**
on = connected
 turn on/switch on *the light,* **leave** *the radio* **on**
on = continuing
 carry on/go on *a bit longer,* **keep on** *doing something,* **work on** *late,*
 hang on / hold on *(= wait)*
out = away, disappearing
 put out *a fire,* **blow out** *a candle,* **wipe out** *all the data,* **cross out** *the word*
out = completely, to an end
 clean out *a cupboard,* **fill out** *a form,* **work out** *the answer,* **write out**
 in full, **wear out** *the motor,* **sort out** *the mess, it* **turned out** *OK in the end*
out = to different people
 give out/hand out *copies of the worksheet,* **share out** *the food between us*
out = aloud
 read out *all the names,* **shout out, cry out, speak out** *(= say sth publicly)*
out = clearly seen
 can't **make out** *the words,* **point out** *a mistake,* **pick out** *the best*
over = from start to finish
 read over/check over *what I've written,* **think over / talk over** *a problem,*
 go over *the details*
up = growing, increasing
 step up *production,* **turn up** *the volume,* **blow up / pump up** *a tyre*
up = completely
 eat/drink *it all* **up**, **use up** *all the paper,* **clear up/tidy up** *the mess,*
 pack up *my things,* **lock up** *before leaving,* **cut up** *into pieces,* **sum up**
 (= summarize)

222 Prepositional verbs

A A prepositional verb is a verb + preposition.
> *I don't **believe in** eating meat.*
> *Who does this bag **belong to**?*
> *I can't **concentrate on** this book.*
> *The flat **consists of** four rooms.*
> *The fare **depends on** when you travel.*
> *I was **listening to** the weather forecast.*
> *An idea has just **occurred to** me.*
> *What does this number **refer to**?*
> *We'll have to **wait for** a taxi.*

Which preposition goes after the verb is mainly a matter of idiom.

NOTE
For more examples with verb + preposition + gerund (e.g. *believe in eating*), > 115A.

B Some verbs can take a number of different prepositions. Each combination has a different meaning. Here are some examples with *look*.
> *I had to stay at home and **look after** my little brother.*
> *Come and **look at** the view.*
> *Can you help me **look for** my mobile?*
> *The police are **looking into** the incident.*
> *People **look on** this neighbourhood as very desirable.*
> *We spent a couple of hours **looking round** the shops.*

Here are some other verbs which combine with different prepositions.
> *The doctor will be **calling on** a number of patients.* (= visiting)
> *I'll **call for** you at about seven.*
> (I'll come to your home so that we can go somewhere together.)
> *The United Nations has **called for** a cease-fire.* (= demanded)
> *I don't **care about** the exam.* (I am not worried about or interested in it.)
> *My parents don't **care for** modern art.* (They don't like it.)
> *Someone has to **care for** the sick.* (= look after)
> *I will **deal with** the matter immediately.* (= do something about)
> *The company **deals in** commercial properties.* (= buys and sells)
> *People are **dying of** hunger.* (They are dying because they are hungry.)
> *I was **dying for** some fresh air.* (= wanting very much)

Compare these two examples.
> *Poor management **resulted in** huge losses.*
> *The huge losses **resulted from** poor management.*

C We can use *about* after many different verbs expressing speech or thought.
> *We were **talking about** renting a flat.*
> *Our neighbours **complained about** the noise.*
> *We'll have to **decide about** our holiday.*

Compare *ask about* and *ask for*.

*We **asked about** cheap tickets.* ('Please tell us about cheap tickets.')
*We **asked for** cheap tickets.* ('Please give us cheap tickets.')
For more about patterns with *ask,* > 264D.

We can sometimes use *of* meaning 'about', but it is rather formal.
*The Prime Minister spoke **of**/**about** his vision of the country's future.*

With some verbs, *about* and *of* have different meanings.
*I was **thinking about** my work.* (= turning over in my mind)
*I couldn't **think of** the man's name.* (It wouldn't come into my mind.)
*What did you **think of** the hotel?* (What was your opinion?)
*We're **thinking of**/**about** starting our own business.* (= deciding about)
*I **heard about** your recent success.* (Someone told me about it.)
*I've never **heard of** Bagley. Where is it?* (The name is unfamiliar to me.)
*Last night I **dreamed about** something that happened years ago.*
(= imagined in my sleep)
*I used to **dream about**/**of** making a number one hit.*
(= think how much I would like)
*I wouldn't **dream of** criticizing you.* (It wouldn't enter my mind.)

D We usually use *to* before the person our words are directed at.
*We were **talking to**/with our friends.*
*They **complained to** their neighbours about the noise.*

But we say *laugh at, smile at,* and *argue with.*
*Everyone **laughed at** the clown.*   *Are you **arguing with** me?*

Shout at can suggest anger.
*The farmer **shouted at** us to keep out.*
*Matthew **shouted to** his friends across the street.*

We *communicate with someone.*
*The government even made it an offence to **communicate with** foreigners.*
But we *communicate something to someone.* > 223C

When we use the telephone, we *ring, (tele)phone,* or *call* a person.
We do not use *to.*
*I had to **phone** my boss.*

E Some verbs have a similar meaning to a prepositional verb, but they take a direct object and not a preposition.
*The troops have **entered** the city.* (NOT ~~The troops have entered into the city.~~)
*We were **discussing** politics.* (NOT ~~We were discussing about politics.~~)
*We **reached** our destination.* (NOT ~~We reached to our destination.~~)
Such verbs include: *accompany, answer* (> Note), *approach, control, demand, desire, discuss, enter* (> Note), *expect, influence, lack, marry, obey, reach, remember, request, resemble, seek, suit.*

The equivalent noun takes a preposition.
*their **entry into** the city   a **discussion about** politics*
*our **demand for** justice*

315

Some verbs can take either a direct object or a preposition, depending on the meaning.

*I **paid** the taxi-driver / **paid** the bill.*
*I **paid for** the taxi / **paid for** the meal.*
*The police **searched** the whole house.*
*They were **searching for** drugs / **looking for** drugs.*
*The committee **approved** the plans.* (= accepted, allowed)
*I don't **approve of** cruelty to animals.* (I don't think it is right.)
*The train **leaves** Exeter at ten fifteen.* (= goes from Exeter)
*The train **leaves for** Exeter at ten fifteen.* (= leaves on its journey to Exeter)

NOTE

a   We use *answer to* and *enter into* only with special meanings.
   *Don't forget the company has to **answer to** its shareholders.* (= explain its actions to)
   *The two sides have **entered into** negotiations.* (= begun)

b   *Meet* and *visit* often take a direct object, but you may hear *meet with* and *visit with*, especially in American English.

223 Verb + object + preposition

A Some prepositional verbs have an object between the verb and preposition.

	Verb	Object	Preposition	
We have to	***translate***	*the article*	***into***	*English.*
You can	***insure***	*your belongings*	***against***	*theft.*
The company	***spends***	*a lot of money*	***on***	*advertising.*

In the passive, the preposition comes directly after the verb.

*The article has to be **translated into** English.*
*Your belongings can be **insured against** theft.*
*A lot of money is **spent on** advertising.*

Here are some more examples of this type of prepositional verb.

*Just **compare** these figures **with** those for last year.*
*I'd like to **congratulate** you **on** your success.*
*The press **criticized** the government **for** doing nothing.*
*Most people **prefer** the new system **to** the old one.*
*The old cinema has been **turned into** a night club.*
*Did you **thank** Daniel **for** helping us?*

NOTE

For more examples with verb + object + preposition + gerund
(e.g. *thank Daniel for helping*), > 115B.

B Compare these pairs of sentences.

*You can't **blame** the government **for** everything.*
*You can't **blame** everything **on** the government.*
*The artist **presented** the President **with** a portrait of the White House.*

*The artist **presented** a portrait of the White House **to** the President.*
*The company **provides** its customers **with** a first-class service.*
*The company **provides** a first-class service **to/for** its customers.*

C We can use *about* after *tell/ask* + object.
*Has anyone **told** you **about** the new timetable?*
*I've been **asking** people **about** their plans for next year.*
We can also *ask someone for something.*
*We **asked** our friends **for** some help.*
This means that we asked them to give us some help.

After *inform* and *warn* we can use *about* or *of*.
*We will **inform** customers **about/of** any changes to the arrangements.*
*I should **warn** you **about/of** the difficulties you may face.*
When warning someone not to do something, we can use *against*.
*My friends **warned** me **against** deciding in a hurry.*

After *communicate, describe, explain,* and *write,* we use *to* before the person receiving the message.
*Paul was eager to **communicate** the news **to** his neighbours.*
*Can you **describe** the man **to** me?*
*I **explained** our problem **to** the tour guide.*
*Lots of people **write** letters **to** the Queen.*
For more details about this pattern with *communicate, describe,* etc, > 6F.

D Sometimes the verb + object + preposition has an idiomatic meaning.
*It's the nurse's job to **take care of** the patients.* (= look after)
*We ought to **make the most of** this lovely weather.*
(= get the maximum benefit from)
*The speaker **took no notice of** the interruption.* (= ignored)
*Perhaps I should **put my faith in** alternative medicine.* (= fully believe in)

Sometimes the verb and prepositional phrase have an idiomatic meaning.
*We have to **take** a number of factors **into consideration**.* (= consider)
*The latest crisis has **thrown** everyone **into a panic**.* (= made everyone panic)
*The constant noise **drives** me **to distraction**.* (= makes me very annoyed)
*He has been **put out of action** by a back injury.* (= stopped from working)

224 Verb + adverb + preposition

A A verb can have both an adverb and a preposition after it.

	Verb	Adverb	Preposition	
My sister	*fell*	*down*	*on*	*the ice.*
The room	*looked*	*out*	*over*	*farmland.*
The astronomer	*gazed*	*up*	*at*	*the stars.*

Combinations like these are called 'phrasal-prepositional verbs'.

Sometimes the meaning is idiomatic. Here are some examples.

> *The others left half an hour ago. I'll never **catch up with** them now.*
> (= go faster and reach)
> *I'm trying to **cut down on** my calorie intake.* (= reduce)
> *You've got to **face up to** the situation.* (= not avoid)
> *I don't have that information right now. Can I **get back to** you?*
> (= answer at a later time)
> *I'll **get round to** filling that form in some time.* (= find time)
> *My cousin has decided to **go in for** teaching.* (= begin a career)
> *Are you **looking forward to** your holiday?*
> (= thinking with pleasure about a future event)
> *Why should we have to **put up with** poor service?* (= tolerate)

B   There can be an object between the verb and adverb.

	Verb	Object	Adverb	Preposition	
Are we going to	**let**	*anyone else*	**in**	**on**	*the secret?*
Laura has	**taken**	*us*	**up**	**on**	*our invitation.*
Each enquiry	**brought**	*the police*	**up**	**against**	*a blank wall.*

225 Adjective + preposition

A   Some adjectives can be followed by a preposition.

> *The place was **crowded with** tourists.*
> *The town is **famous for** its huge market.*
> *The man was found **guilty of** burglary.*
> *You'll be **late for** work.*
> *We're **ready for** action.*
> *We're rather **short of** time.*
> *The job is **similar to** the one I did before.*
> *That kind of remark is **typical of** a man.*

Many of these adjectives express feelings.

> ***afraid of** the dark*   ***confident of** victory*   ***crazy about** country music*
> ***eager for** news*   ***fed up with** housework*   ***fond of** seafood*
> ***impressed by/with** your performance*   ***interested in** ballet*
> ***jealous of** other people's success*   ***keen on** fishing*
> ***pleased with/about** my exam results*   ***proud of** her achievements*
> ***satisfied with** my score*   ***surprised at/by** what happened*
> ***thrilled at/by** the prospect*   ***tired of** walking*
> ***worried about/by** this setback*

NOTE
For adjective + preposition + gerund, > 116.

B Some adjectives can take different prepositions, depending on the meaning.

We are *angry with someone about something.*
> *The tourists were **angry about** the mix-up over tickets.*
> *Why are you **angry with** me? It's not my fault.*

We are *anxious about* a problem.
> *Everyone was **anxious about** terrorist attacks.*
Anxious for means 'wanting'.
> *The whole family were **anxious for** news about the missing boy.*

We are *concerned about* or *concerned at* a problem.
> *The government is **concerned about/at** the rise in crime.*

Concerned for means 'wanting'.
> *We are **concerned for** the child's welfare.*

Concerned with means 'about' or 'involved in'.
> *My research is **concerned with** social trends.*

We can be *sorry about something* or *sorry for doing something.*
> *I've kept you waiting. **Sorry about** that.*
> *I'm **sorry for** keeping/to keep you waiting.*

We also feel *sorry for* people.
> *I feel **sorry for** Kate living in that awful place.*

C We use *good at, bad at,* etc to talk about ability.
> *Mike is **good at** skating.* (He can skate well.)
> *I was always **bad at** any kind of sport.* (I couldn't do sport very well.)
> *You're **brilliant at** maths, you know.* (*brilliant* = very good)
> *They say the English are **hopeless at** learning foreign languages.*
> (*hopeless* = very bad)

We use *at* with an activity and *with* to talk about other things.
> *I'm no good **at** budgeting.*
> *I'm no good **with** money.*

We use *good for* and *bad for* to say if something benefits you or not.
> *Regular exercise is **good for** you.*
> *Eating too much fatty food is **bad for** anyone.*

To say how we behave towards someone, we can use *good to, rude to,* etc.
> *Thank you. You've been very **good to** me/**kind to** me.*
> *I thought you were a bit **rude to** your teacher.*
> *The waiter was barely **polite to** us.*

226 Noun + preposition

A Some nouns can combine with a preposition.

*I think there's a good **chance of** fine weather.*
*Here's an **example of** what I mean.*
*This is the **key to** the whole problem.*
*My main problem is a **lack of** money.*
*What's the **reason for** this sudden change of mind?*
*There's plenty of **room for** all our luggage.*
*They put a **tax on** tobacco.*
*I'm having **trouble with** the computer.*
*I've found a **way of/method of** getting round the problem.*

Some nouns can take different prepositions.

*I was listening to a **discussion of/about/on** the political situation.*
*The Beatles had a great **influence on/over** their generation.*
*The staff have a rather aggressive **attitude to/towards** customers.*

B Look at these examples.

Verb/Adjective + preposition	Noun + preposition
*I used to be **afraid of** flying.*	*I conquered my **fear of** flying.*
*He's **interested in** art.*	*He talked about his **interest in** art.*
*We were **invited to** the party.*	*We had an **invitation to** the party.*
*No one **objected to** the idea.*	*There was no **objection to** the idea.*
*It **protects** you **from/against** the wind.*	*It gives **protection from/against** the wind.*
*I'm **researching into** GM food.*	*I'm doing **research into** GM food.*

Here we use the same preposition after the noun as we do after a related verb or adjective.

Now compare these examples.

Adjective + preposition	Noun + preposition
*The athlete was **proud of** his performance.*	*His **pride in** his performance was obvious.*
*You're very **fond of** chocolate, aren't you?*	*We've noticed your **fondness for** chocolate.*

Here we use a different preposition after the noun.

Sometimes the verb has a direct object, but the noun takes a preposition.

Verb	Noun + preposition
*I can't **answer** the question.*	*What's the **answer to** the question?*
*They **attacked** the government.*	*Their **attack on** the government made headlines.*
*I've **damaged** my car.*	*There's some **damage to** my car.*

Verb	Noun + preposition
*The opposition parties **demanded** an inquiry.*	*Their **demands for** an inquiry were ignored.*
*We should **respect** our environment.*	*We should have **respect for** our environment.*

C A number of nouns to do with needs and desires are followed by *for*.
　　*There is a great **need for** low-cost housing.*
　　*World leaders expressed their **desire for** a lasting peace.*
Such nouns include: *appetite, application, demand, desire, need, preference, request, taste, wish.*

D Compare the use of *with* and *between* in these examples.
　　*Police say there is a **link with**/**connection with** another murder.*
　　*Police say there is a **link between**/**connection between** the two murders.*

　　*The psychiatrist's **relationship with** the patient is very important.*
　　*The **relationship between** the psychiatrist and the patient is very important.*

　　*There is a sharp **contrast with** the other side of town.*
　　*There is a sharp **contrast between** the two sides of town.*

Note also these combinations.
　　*What's the **difference between** American football and soccer?*
　　*This treatment is an **alternative to** conventional medicine.*
　　*The material can be used as a **substitute for** wood.*

Compare the use of *in* and *of* in these examples.
　　*There has been a **rise of** 20 points **in** the Financial Times Share Index.*
　　*Figures show a **reduction of** three per cent **in** the price of raw materials.*

Sentences with more than one clause

227 Types of clause

Here is a paragraph from a book of strange but true stories.

ATTEMPTED SUICIDE

A New York painter decided to end it all by throwing himself off the Empire State Building. He took the lift up to the 86th floor, found a convenient window and jumped. A gust of wind caught him as he fell and blew him into the studios of NBC Television on the 83rd floor. There was a live show going out, so the interviewer decided to ask the would-be suicide a few questions. He admitted that he'd changed his mind as soon as he'd jumped.

(from J. Reid *It Can't Be True!*)

A Main clauses

A main clause is one that could stand alone as a sentence.
> *He took the lift up to the 86th floor.*   *A gust of wind caught him.*
For the structure of a main clause, > 4.

We can use *and, or, but,* and *so* to join two or more main clauses.
> *He took the lift up to the 86th floor, **and** he jumped.*
> *He could go through with it, **or** he could go back down again*
> *He jumped from the 86th floor, **but** he survived.*
> *It was a live show, **so** the host invited him on.*
Two main clauses linked together like this are called 'co-ordinate clauses'.

When the subject of the two clauses is the same, we can often leave it out, especially after *and* and *or*.
> *He took the lift up to the 86th floor **and** (he) jumped.*
We can also leave out the auxiliary verb to avoid repeating it.
> *He could go through with it **or** (he could) go back down again.*

We can link more than two clauses. Usually *and* comes only before the last one.
> *He took the lift ..., found a convenient window and jumped.*

NOTE
We can begin a sentence with *and, or, but,* or *so* to link to the previous sentence.
> *A gust of wind caught him as he fell and blew him into the studios of NBC Television on the 83rd floor. **And** it happened that there was a live show going out at the time.*
At one time some people believed that it was incorrect to begin a sentence with *and, or, but,* or *so*. This attitude is now less common, and you will often see such sentences.

B Sub-clauses

A sub-clause cannot stand alone as a complete sentence.

A gust of wind caught him **as he fell**.
He admitted **that he'd changed his mind**.

Here *as he fell* and *that he'd changed his mind* are 'subordinate clauses' or sub-clauses. In a sub-clause we often use a linking-word like *as, that, when, if,* or *because*. And sometimes we use a relative pronoun such as *who* or *which*. > 266.

A man **who jumped off the Empire State Building** *was miraculously saved.*

The word order in a sub-clause is the same as in a main clause.

He admitted that **he'd changed his mind**.
(NOT ~~He admitted that he his mind had changed.~~)

NOTE
When we leave out *that*, the sub-clause has the same form as a main clause.
He admitted **he'd changed his mind**.
The clause is a sub-clause and not a main clause because it is the object of *admitted* and does not stand alone.

C Finite and non-finite clauses

A non-finite clause has an infinitive, a gerund, or a participle.

The interviewer decided **to ask** *him a few questions.*
He regrets now **having jumped**.
Finding *a convenient window, he threw himself out of it.*

These non-finite verb forms often have no subject, but they can sometimes have one.

The show having ended, *the man left the studio.*

Some patterns with participles (*Finding ..., The show having ended, ...*) can be formal or literary in style. > 127–128

Compare the verbs in these finite clauses.

The interviewer **decided** *that he* **would ask** *him a few questions.*
He **regrets** *now that he* **jumped**.
When he **found** *a convenient window, he* **threw** *himself out of it.*

A finite clause can be a main clause or a sub-clause. A finite verb has a subject, e.g. (**he** *found*, **he** *threw*), although it is sometimes left out after *and* and *or*. > A

228 What comes after the verb?

When we add a sub-clause to a main clause, the type of sub-clause we can use often depends on the verb in the main clause. For example, after the verb *accept* we can use a that-clause but not a to-infinitive.

The company **accepted that** *they would pay damages.*
(NOT ~~The company accepted to pay damages.~~)

But with *agree* we can use either a that-clause or a to-infinitive.
*The company **agreed that** they would pay damages.*
*The company **agreed to** pay damages.*

Here are some possible patterns that come after a verb.

Pattern after a verb	Example
That-clause > 253A	*I know **(that)** you're busy.*
Object + that-clause > 253B	*He promised **me (that)** he would be here.*
Wh-clause > 253A	*I wonder **what's happened**.*
Object + wh-clause > 253B	*Remind **me what** the password is.*
Question word + to-infinitive > 108	*Have you decided **where to go**?*
Object + question word + to-infinitive > 108B	*No one has ever taught **me how to cook** properly.*
To-infinitive > 101	*We're aiming **to be** back by five.*
Object + to-infinitive > 105	*We persuaded **Sarah to come** with us.*
For + object + to-infinitive > 109	*I've arranged **for my mail to be** sent on.*
Object + infinitive without *to* > 110C	*This show always makes **me laugh**.*
Gerund > 101	*I suggested **waiting** a bit longer.*
Object + gerund > 113E	*They've stopped **us using** the pool.*
Preposition + gerund > 115A	*I used to dream **of going** on the stage.*
Object + preposition + gerund > 115B	*I must warn **you against wearing** expensive jewellery.*

Here are some details of verbs and the patterns that come after them. With some verbs there is more than one possibility. The most common uses are shown here, but for more details, see the sections referred to above.

Verb	Common patterns with a sub-clause
accept	*accept **(that)** something is so*
accuse	*accuse someone **of doing** something*
admit	*admit **(that)** you did something, admit **doing** something*
advise	*advise someone **to do** something, advise (someone) **what to do**, advise (someone) **against doing** something*
agree	*agree **(that)** something is so, agree **to do** something*
aim	*aim **to do** something*
allow	*allow someone **to do** something*
apologize	*apologize (to someone) **for doing** something*
arrange	*arrange **that** something will happen, arrange **to do** something, arrange **for** someone **to do** something*
assume	*assume **(that)** something is so*
avoid	*avoid **doing** something*

Verb	Common patterns with a sub-clause
believe	*believe (**that**) something is so, believe **in doing** something*
cause	*cause something **to happen***
choose	*choose **to do** something*
consider	*consider (**that**) something is so, consider **what** is happening, consider something **to be** so, consider **doing** something*
decide	*decide (**that**) something should happen, decide **what** you're going to do, decide **to do** something, decide **what to do***
demand	*demand (**that**) someone does something, demand **to do** something*
deny	*deny (**that**) something is so, deny **doing** something, deny **having done** something*
doubt	*doubt (**that**) something is so, doubt **if/whether** something is so*
dream	*dream (**that**) something will happen, dream **of doing** something*
expect	*expect (**that**) something will happen, expect **to do** something, expect someone **to do** something*
explain	*explain (**that**) it was a mistake, explain **what** happened*
force	*force someone **to do** something*
help	*help (**to**) do something, help someone (**to**) do something*
hope	*hope (**that**) something will happen, hope **to do** something*
insist	*insist (**that**) something should happen, insist **on doing** something*
intend	*intend **to do** something, intend **doing** something*
invite	*invite someone **to do** something*
involve	*involve **doing** something*
know	*know (**that**) something is so, know **what** is happening*
learn	*learn **to do** something, learn **how to do** something*
let	*let someone **do** something*
like	*like **doing** something, like **to do** something, like someone **doing** something, like someone **to do** something, like **it when** something happens*
make	*make something **do** something*
mind	*don't mind **what** happens, don't mind **doing** something, don't mind someone **doing** something, don't mind **if** I do something*
need	*need **to do** something*
object	*object (**that**) something is so, object **to doing** something, object **to** someone **doing** something*
offer	*offer **to do** something*
permit	*permit someone **to do** something*
persuade	*persuade someone **to do** something*
predict	*predict (**that**) something will happen, predict **what** will happen*
prefer	*prefer **to do** something*
pretend	*pretend (**that**) something is so, pretend **to do** something*
prevent	*prevent someone (**from**) **doing** something*
promise	*promise (**that**) something will happen, promise someone (**that**) something will happen, promise **to do** something*

Verb	Common patterns with a sub-clause
propose	*propose (**that**) something should happen, propose **doing** something, propose **to do** something*
refuse	*refuse **to do** something*
remind	*remind someone (**that**) something is so, remind someone **what** is happening, remind someone **to do** something*
require	*require someone **to do** something*
show	*show someone (**that**) something is so, show (**that**) something is so, show (someone) **what** happens, show something **to be** so*
stop	*stop **doing** something, stop someone (**from**) **doing** something*
succeed	*succeed **in doing** something*
suggest	*suggest (**that**) something should happen, suggest **doing** something*
suppose	*suppose (**that**) something is true, suppose something **to be** true*
teach	*teach someone **to do** something, teach someone **how to do** something*
understand	*understand (**that**) something is so, understand **what** is happening*
want	*want **to do** something, want someone **to do** something*
warn	*warn (**that**) something might happen, warn someone (**that**) something might happen, warn someone not **to do** something, warn someone **against doing** something*
wish	*wish (**that**) something would happen, wish **to do** something*
wonder	*wonder **why** something is so, wonder **if/whether** something will happen*

But remember that these verbs are not always followed by a sub-clause. Many of them can also be followed simply by a noun phrase as object or by a prepositional phrase.

> *The teacher accepted our apology.*
> *They've agreed to the proposal.*

229 Clause combinations

We can link a number of clauses together. In speech you sometimes hear a number of main clauses linked by *and*.

> *So I went to bed and I had to get up and get dressed and go and pick him up.*

For more about linking main clauses, > 233–236.

But speech does not consist only of main clauses. Sub-clauses are also used. Look at the structure of these sentences spoken in conversation.

Main clause – Adverbial clause – Main clause – Adverbial clause

> *I became a policeman when I was twenty-nine, and I've enjoyed it because every day is interesting.*

Main clause – To-infinitive clause – Main clause – To-infinitive clause – Adverbial clause

It takes me an hour and a quarter to get to Bangor, and it takes Jane about an hour and a half to get to Stafford because they're such bad roads.

This sentence from a conversation contains a number of main clauses and sub-clauses.

Well, we hung about waiting for a representative to come and tell us what to do, and after an hour and a half nobody came, so we took a taxi and went into Basle, and because we'd missed the train we decided to stay the night there.

Here are some real examples of clause combinations in written English.

Adverbial clause – Main clause – Main clause

When I was about ten years old I used to go and watch Brighton and Hove Albion football club with my father and we would stand on the East Terrace at every home game.

Main clause – Adverbial clause – Gerund clause

Many cities have drive-in movies, where you can watch a film without leaving your car.

Main clause – To-infinitive clause – Gerund clause

Most Inuit people use refrigerators to stop their food from getting cold.

If-clause – That-clause – Main clause

If you've always thought that a swimming-pool would be far too expensive, then this is the one for you.

Main clause with a relative clause – To-infinitive clause – Adverbial clause – That-clause – To-infinitive clause

Japan, which has no fossil fuel reserves of its own, wants to stockpile plutonium because it believes that it can develop the technology to transform it into plentiful and cheap electricity.

230 The unreal present and past

A In some kinds of sub-clause, tenses are used differently from how they are used in a main clause. This happens after expressions like *as if, as though, if* (> 243), *imagine, suppose, supposing, it's time,* and *would rather* (> 81E).

Look at these clauses with a past-tense verb.

*Imagine you **wanted** to murder someone. How would you go about it?*
*Suppose we **won** the lottery. What would we do with the money?*

In the first example, the past tense expresses something unreal in the present, something that is not so. (You don't want to murder anyone.) In the second example it expresses a future event as a theoretical possibility. (It is unlikely that we will really win the lottery.)

NOTE
Some of the expressions above can be followed by the subjunctive *were.* > 231C

B We can also use the present tense with most of the expressions in A. This makes the situation sound less theoretical and more real.

*Imagine you **want** to murder someone.*
This wall looks as if it's about to fall down.
*Suppose we all **give** a few pounds and then **buy** one big present?*

We use the past tense in a clause after *it's time (that)* ...

*Your hair's getting rather long. It's time you **had** it cut.*
*It's late. It's time we **were** going.*

In the second example the meaning is the same as *It's time (for us) to go.* We cannot use the present tense here. (NOT ~~It's time we're going~~).

We generally use the past tense (rather than the present) in a sub-clause after *would rather.*

*I'd rather we **went** out somewhere. I'm fed up with staying in.*
But for *I'd rather go out somewhere, > 81E.*

C The following examples are about a past situation. There is a sub-clause with a past-perfect verb.

*The speaker ignored the interruption. He continued as if no one **had spoken.***
*You don't need insurance. I travelled round the world last year without any. ~ But supposing you'**d had** an accident. What then?*

An expression like *as if* or *supposing* with the past perfect expresses something unreal in the past, something that was not so. (Someone did speak. You didn't have an accident.)

231 The subjunctive

A The subjunctive is the base form of a verb. There is no *-s* in the third person singular.

*The committee recommended that the scheme **go** ahead.*
*The Opposition is insisting that the Minister **resign**.*
*It is important that an exact record **be** kept.*
*They agreed to our proposal that an advertisement **be** placed in the newspaper.*

We can use the subjunctive in a that-clause when expressing the idea that something is necessary. It comes after a clause with a word such as *advisable, anxious, ask, demand, essential, important, insist, necessary, proposal, propose, recommend, recommendation, request, suggest, suggestion,* or *vital.*

Only in the third person singular is the subjunctive different from the normal verb form. In the plural there is no difference except in the verb *be.*

*The committee recommended that both schemes **go** ahead.*
*The committee recommended that both schemes **be** approved.*

B The subjunctive is rather formal. It is used more in American English than in British English, where *should* or other forms of the verb are often used.

> *The committee recommended that the scheme **should go** ahead.*
> *The Opposition is insisting that the Minister **resigns**.*

C There is a past subjunctive form *were*, which we can use instead of *was* in the first and third person singular.

> *If I **was**/**were** a bit taller, I could reach.*
> *Suppose the story **was**/**were** true.*

We can use the subjunctive *were* after *as if, as though, if, suppose, supposing,* and *wish*.

The subjunctive *were* is a little formal, but it is often used in the idiom *if I were you* meaning 'in your place'.

> *It's a good offer. **If I were you**, I'd accept it.*

232 Verbs after *wish* and *if only*

A *Wish ... would*

This pattern expresses a wish for a future change in the situation.

> *I wish Simon **would reply** to my e-mails.* (I want him to reply to them.)
> *I wish people **wouldn't leave** litter.* (I want them to stop leaving litter.)

Wish ... would can express a rather abrupt request or a complaint.

> *I wish you **wouldn't smoke**. It makes the place smell awful.*

B *Wish ...* past tense / *could*

This pattern expresses a wish that the present situation should be different.

> *I wish I **had** more spare time.*
> *We all wish we **knew** the answers to these questions.*
> *I wish I **could help** you, but I'm afraid I can't.*

I wish I could help implies that I can't help.

We cannot use *would* here.

> (NOT *I wish I would have more spare time.*)

C *Wish ...* past perfect / *could* + perfect

This pattern expresses a wish about the past.

> *I wish I **had** never **bought** this car. It's been nothing but trouble.*
> *I wish you**'d told** me you had a spare ticket for the show.*
> *I bet your parents were surprised when you told them the news. I wish I **could have seen** their faces.*

We cannot use *would*.

> (NOT *I wish I would never have bought this car.*)

329

D *If only*

If only has a similar meaning to *I wish*, and we use it in the same patterns.
> *If only Simon **would reply** to my e-mails.* > A
> *If only I **had** more spare time.* > B
> *If only I **could have seen** their faces.* > C

If only is more emphatic than *wish*. It often expresses regret about the past.
> *If only you**'d told** me you had tickets for the show. I'd have loved to go.*

Only can sometimes be in mid position.
> *If I'd **only** stopped to think, I would never have done anything so stupid.*

And, or, but, so, etc

233 Words meaning 'and'

A We can use *and* to link two clauses.
> *I've seen the film, **and** I've read the book.*
> *Shakespeare wrote plays, **and** he was an actor.*

The adverbs *too* and *as well* are more emphatic than *and*.
> *I've seen the film. I've read the book **too**.*
> *Shakespeare wrote plays, and he was an actor **as well**.*
These adverbs usually come in end position.

Also goes in mid position.
> *The town is an important rail junction, and it **also** has an airport.*

Plus as a conjunction is informal.
> *I've had a terrible day at work, **plus** my train was cancelled.*

B In a negative sentence we use *either* rather than *too* or *as well*.
> *I haven't seen the film, and I haven't read the book **either**.*
> (NOT *I haven't read the book too.*)
For *or* with the negative, > 234B.
> *I haven't seen the film **or** read the book.*

C We can also use *besides* and *what's more* to link two clauses.
> *I'm too tired to go for a walk. **Besides**, it looks like rain.*
> *It's dangerous to ride a motor-bike without a helmet. **What's more**, it's against the law.*
We use these expressions to make an extra point, for example to back up our argument.

And then and *on top of (all) this/that* are informal.
> *I have to pay the rent. **And then** there's the electricity.*
> *We've got workmen in the house. **On top of that**, my sister is staying with us.*

Furthermore, moreover, and *in addition* are a little formal and more typical of written English.
> *Some people in rural areas have no car. **Furthermore**, there is little public transport, and so they find it difficult to get about.*
> *The country was hit hard by the oil crisis. **Moreover**, its economy was already extremely weak.*
> *Police have been making house-to-house inquiries, and **in addition** the murdered man's family have appealed to the public for information.*

D We can use the prepositions *as well as, in addition to*, and *besides* with a noun phrase or an ing-form.

> *Shakespeare was an actor **as well as** a writer.*
> ***In addition to** doing all my usual work, I have to write a report.*
> ***Besides** the rent, I have to pay for the electricity.*

We can also use *along with* and *together with*.

> *The city has several golf courses, **along with** swimming-pools and tennis courts.*
> ***Together with** a film crew, the team are walking towards the South Pole.*

These prepositions are usually followed by a noun phrase.

NOTE

In rather formal English we can also use the pattern *as + be* or auxiliary verb + subject. It expresses the idea that what is true of one thing is also true of another.

> *The children's motivation is excellent, **as is their concentration**.*
> *Shakespeare wrote plays, **as did Marlowe**.*

For *and so is their concentration*, > 27B.

E When talking about two things, we can use *both ... and ...* or *not only ... but (also) ...* to give extra emphasis.

> *Shakespeare was **both** a writer **and** an actor.*
> *It's **not only** dangerous to ride without a helmet, **but** it's **(also)** illegal.*

We can put *not only* in front position.

> ***Not only** is it dangerous to ride without a helmet, but it's (also) illegal.*

In this position, *not only* is followed by inversion. > 10F

234 Words meaning 'or'

A We use *or* to express an alternative.

> *I'd like to study at Oxford **or** Cambridge.*
> *We can take a bus, **or** we can walk.*

We can also use *alternatively*.

> *We can cancel the meeting. (Or) **alternatively**, we can find another venue.*

Either ... or is more emphatic than *or* on its own.

> *You'll have to go **either** right **or** left.*
> *I've **either** left my bag on the bus **or** at the office.*
> ***Either** we pay someone to do the job, **or** we do it ourselves.*

Or can mean 'if not'. We can also use *or else* or *otherwise*.

> *We'd better go now, **or (else)** we'll be late.*
> *Put the receipt somewhere safe, **otherwise** you'll lose it.*

B We often use *or* in a negative sentence.
> *We were stuck. We couldn't go forwards or backwards.*
> *I didn't know whether to laugh or cry.*

Neither … nor is more emphatic and can be a little more formal.
> *We were stuck. We could go neither forwards nor backwards.*
> *An illiterate person is someone who can neither read nor write.*
> *Neither the post office nor the bank was/were open.*

We use a positive verb form, e.g. *could go.*

235 Words meaning 'but'

A We use *but* to express a contrast.
> *Julie is twenty but (she) looks younger.*
> *Canberra is the capital of Australia, but it isn't the biggest city.*

We can also use the adverb *though*. In informal English it usually comes in end position.
> *Julie is twenty. She looks younger, though.*

In more formal English, *though* often comes after the first phrase of the sentence.
> *Mass tourism can bring economic benefits. On the whole though, its long-term impact is negative.*

We sometimes use *yet* at the beginning of a clause.
> *Many of Britain's royal 'traditions' seem centuries old, (and) yet they are in fact relatively new.*

NOTE
There is a special use of *may* in a clause followed by *but.*
> *These pens are cheap / These pens may be cheap, but they're useless.*

B The adverbs *however* and *nevertheless* are both a little formal.
> *The fire destroyed thousands of homes. However, only six people lost their lives.*
> *At first sight the figures appear random. Nevertheless, a pattern can be observed.*

These words can also go in other positions.
> *Only six people, however, lost their lives,.*
> *Only six people lost their lives, however.*
> *A pattern can nevertheless be observed.*
> *A pattern can be observed nevertheless.*

We can also use *even so* and *all the same*.
> *She had lots of friends. Even so, she often felt lonely.*
> *I didn't want a present, but all the same I was grateful / I was grateful all the same.*

NOTE

The adverb *still* can have the same meaning as *however* or *nevertheless*.
*I'm sleeping on a friend's sofa. **Still**, it won't be for long.*

C We can use a sub-clause with the conjunction *although*, which is sometimes shortened to *though*.
*I was furious, **though** I tried not to show it.*
***Although** Canberra is the capital of Australia, it isn't the biggest city.*
Compare the use of *but*.
*Canberra is the capital of Australia, **but** it isn't the biggest city.*

Even though is more emphatic than *although*.
*They allowed me to continue the course **even though** I failed the first-year exams.* (NOT ~~even although I failed~~)

In the following pattern with *though*, an adjective or adverb goes in front position.
***Important though** it is, this issue is not relevant to our discussion.*
***Well though** the team played, they never really looked like winning.*

NOTE

We can use *as* with an adjective or adverb in front position.
***Strange as** it may seem, I've never been to Paris.*

D We can use the prepositions *despite* and *in spite of* with a noun phrase or an ing-form.
*The parade went ahead **despite** the heavy rain.*
***In spite of** being the capital of Australia, Canberra isn't the biggest city.*

We cannot use *despite* or *in spite of* before a finite clause.
(NOT ~~In spite of it is the capital~~...)
But we sometimes use *despite the fact that* or *in spite of the fact that*, especially if the two clauses have different subjects.
*No new safety measures have been introduced, **despite the fact that** a serious accident happened three months ago.*
But *although* is usually neater.
*No new safety measures have been introduced, **although** a serious accident happened three months ago.*

E Sometimes we can use *whereas* meaning 'but'.
*Red is a warm colour, **but/whereas** blue is cold.*
We can use *whereas* when we are talking about a comparison rather than a conflict between two ideas.

We can use *while* with the same meaning.
*I'm right-handed **whereas/while** my brother is left-handed.*

We can also use *on the other hand* to link two sentences.
*Birmingham is a big city. Warwick, **on the other hand**, is quite small.*

NOTE
We use *on the contrary* when we mean that the opposite is true.
Warwick isn't a big city. **On the contrary,** *it's quite small.*

236 Words meaning 'so'

A We use *so* to express a result.
I was tired, **so** *I went to bed.*
It hasn't rained for ages, (and) **so** *the ground is very dry.*
So comes at the beginning of a clause.

We can sometimes use *so that* to express result.
I hope it stays fine **so that** *we can have a picnic.*
But *so that* is more commonly used to express purpose. > 240B

B We can also use *as a result* and *consequently*.
More women are needed in employment. **As a result,** *they are having fewer children.*
The computer was incorrectly programmed, and **consequently** *the rocket crashed.*

We can use the preposition *as a result of* before a noun phrase or ing-form.
The rocket crashed **as a result of** *a computer error.*
As a result of *lying in the sun too long, we got sunburnt.*

The adverb *therefore* is a little formal.
There has been no rainfall for some time. The ground is **therefore** *very dry.*
The scheme has been a failure. **Therefore** *it should be scrapped.*

Thus is also formal and used mainly in written English.
Passengers would be able to travel direct from Cardiff through the Channel Tunnel, **thus** *avoiding the need to cross London by tube.*

C This pattern with *so* or *such* and a that-clause expresses a result.
The ground is **so** *dry* **(that)** *the plants are dying.*
(= The plants are dying as a result of the ground being so dry.)
There was **so** *much steam* **(that)** *we couldn't see a thing.*
The place looked **such** *a mess* **(that)** *I couldn't invite anyone in.*

We cannot use *very* or *too* in these sentences.
(NOT ~~The ground is very dry that the plants are dying.~~)

NOTE
The following pattern with inversion is emphatic and rather formal.
So dry is the ground that *the plants are dying.*

Adverbial clauses

237 Introduction

A Compare these sentences.

Adverb:	*We could play cards **afterwards**.*
Prepositional phrase:	*We could play cards **after the meal**.*
Clause:	*We could play cards **after we've eaten**.*

An adverbial clause functions in the same way as an adverb or a prepositional phrase. It often begins with a conjunction such as *after, because,* or *so that.*

This chapter is mainly about clauses of time, reason, and purpose. Conditional clauses are dealt with in the next chapter (sections 243–251). For clauses with *although* and *despite,* > 235C–D.

B An adverbial clause usually goes in front position or end position.

__If you like__, we could play cards.
We could play cards __if you like__.

NOTE
It is sometimes possible for the adverbial clause to go in mid position, but this is less usual.
We could, __if you like__, play cards.

C An adverbial clause can be non-finite. For example, we can use a clause with a to-infinitive or a participle.

Just check it again __to make sure__.
I was sitting in the park __eating my sandwiches__.

We can also use a preposition + gerund or a conjunction + participle.

You can't work all day __without taking__ a break now and then.
I often listen to music __while driving__.

NOTE
After some conjunctions, we can leave out the subject and the verb *be* when the meaning is clear without them.
A car must be taxed __when__ (it is) __on the road__.
__Although__ (we were) __shocked__, we were also very relieved.
Leaving out the subject and verb here is more typical of written English. For more examples with a conjunction + adjective, > 182C.

238 Clauses of time

A Conjunctions of time

An adverbial clause of time often begins with a conjunction.

After *we'd finished work, we all went to the pub.*
Think carefully *before* *you make a decision.*
Once *you've done the basic course, you can go on to the more advanced one.*
A lot has happened *since* *I last saw you.*
I can't discuss the report *until* *I've read it.*
Mozart could write music *when* *he was only five.*

Conjunctions of time include: *after, as, as soon as, before, once, since, till/until, when, whenever, while.*

After, before, since, and *till/until* can also be prepositions.

After *work, we all went to the pub.*
A lot has happened *since* *last summer.*

B Non-finite clauses of time

A non-finite clause can have a gerund with *after, before, on,* and *since.*
> 114

I felt guilty *after eating* *all those chocolates.*

We can also use a participle after *once, until, when, whenever,* and *while.*
> 126

Take care *when crossing* *the road.*
Please wait *until told* *to proceed.*

We can also use a participle without a conjunction. > 127

Take care *crossing* *the road.*
Having glanced *at the letter, Jack pushed it aside.*

C *When, while,* and *as*

These conjunctions have similar uses but also some important differences. We use all three words to talk about more than one thing happening at the same time.

I almost fell *when/while/as I was coming down the stairs.*

While and *as* suggest something continuing for a period of time.

The model had to sit still *while* *we drew her.*
As we were cycling along, we saw a fox.

But to talk about a certain time in your life, use *when.*

I wonder what I'll be doing *when* *I'm thirty.*

When the clause of time refers to a short action 'interrupting' a longer one, we use *when* with the short action.

We were cycling along *when* *we saw a fox.*
When *I arrived, the party was in full swing.*

We can also use *when* to talk about two short actions which happen one after the other.

> **When** *I clicked on the icon, the screen went blank.*

For more examples of *when* with the past continuous and past simple, > 47C.

When can also mean 'every time'.

> *I cycle to work* **when** *it's fine.*
> **When** *something goes wrong, people look for someone to blame.*

Whenever and *every time/each time* are more emphatic.

> *I cycle to work* **whenever** *it's fine.*
> **Every time** *I see a record shop I just have to go in.*

For more about words ending in *-ever*, > 242A.

We can use *as* (but not *while*) to express the idea that a change in one thing goes with a change in another.

> *The mixture hardens* **as** *it cools.*
> **As** *we drove further north, the weather got worse.*

Compare **The** *further north we drove, ...,* > 207B.

Just as means 'at that exact moment'.

> **Just as** *we came out of the club, the rain started.*

D *As soon as, no sooner, hardly,* etc

We use *as soon as* to emphasize the idea of one thing coming immediately after another.

> **As soon as** *the gates were open, the crowds rushed in.*

We can also use *immediately* or *the moment*.

> **Immediately** *you hear any news, let me know.*
> **The moment** *you hear any news, let me know.*

But Americans do not use *immediately* as a conjunction.

We can also use these patterns with *no sooner* and *hardly*.

> *Jeremy was* **no sooner** *in bed* **than** *the doorbell rang.*
> *I had* **hardly** *started work* **when/before** *I felt a pain in my back.*

In both patterns we can use inversion.

> **No sooner** *was Jeremy in bed* **than** *the doorbell rang.*
> **Hardly** *had I started work* **when/before** *I felt a pain in my back.*

E *By, before,* and *until*

By is a preposition and not a conjunction.

> **By** *ten o'clock there were hundreds of people in the queue.*

We use *by the time* to introduce a clause.

> **By the time** *the ticket office opened, there were hundreds of people in the queue.* (NOT *By the ticket office opened, there were* ...)

We can use *by the time* or *before* to express the idea of something happening later than expected.

*It was midday **by the time** I got to the office.*
*It was midday **before** I got to the office.*

These patterns with *not ... till/until* and *not ... before* express the same idea.

*I did**n't** get to the office **until** midday / **until** it was almost lunch time.*
*I did**n't** get to the office **before** midday / **before** it was almost lunch time.*

We can also use *before* after a phrase expressing length of time.

*It was months **before** James dared to ask Laura out.*
(= It was months later that James dared to ask Laura out.)

239 Clauses of reason

A We form an adverbial clause of reason with a conjunction such as *because*.

*I made a mistake **because** I was tired.*
*People use cars **because** they're convenient.*
*Why don't you buy that coat? ~ (**Because**) it's too expensive.*

A clause with *because* usually comes after the main clause, but it can come first.

***Because** I was tired, I made a mistake.*

We can also use *as, since, seeing (that)*, and *now (that)*.

***As** the weather is usually warm, many of the homes have swimming-pools.*
***Since** the pay was so poor, I didn't apply for the job.*
***Seeing** (that) it's so late, why don't you stay the night?*
*I can get here much more easily **now** (that) I've got a car.*

These conjunctions can go before or after the main clause.

For meaning 'because' is rather literary.

*The cause of the accident is unclear, **for** there are many factors involved.*
For with this meaning always comes after the main clause.

NOTE
Compare these two negative sentences, both with *because*.
I didn't go to the exhibition because I was too busy. I'm sorry I missed it.
(= The reason why I didn't go to the exhibition is that I was too busy.)
I didn't go to the exhibition because I was interested. I went there to meet my friends.
(= It is not true that I went to the exhibition out of interest.)
The first example is an explanation of why you didn't go. The second corrects a mistaken belief about your reason for going.

B We can also use a participle clause to express reason. > 128

***Being** tired, I made a mistake.*
***Having spent** all my money, I couldn't pay the hotel bill.*
*With water **flooding** into the building, people were moving things upstairs.*

C We can also use the prepositions *because of, due to, in view of, on account of,* and *owing to.*

> The project was abandoned **because of** the cost.
> The singer's latest tour has been cancelled **due to** illness.
> I would advise you not to invest in the scheme **in view of** the risks involved.
> No one goes out at midday **on account of** the heat.
> **Owing to** circumstances beyond our control, the event has been cancelled.

We sometimes use *due to the fact that* or *in view of the fact that* as conjunctions.

> The applicant's failure to get the job was solely **due to the fact that** he lacked the necessary qualifications.

Out of can express a motive for an action.

> I had a look just **out of** curiosity.

240 Clauses of purpose

A We can use a to-infinitive to express purpose.

> I went out **to buy** a newspaper. > 100A

In order to and *so as to* are more emphatic. They are also a little formal.

> You need to know the length and width **in order to** calculate the area.
> Why not pay in instalments **so as to** spread the cost?

The negative is *in order not to* or *so as not to.*

> We should allow plenty of time **in order not to** be late.
> Young people like to wear what their friends do **so as not to** be different.

But we cannot use *not to* on its own.

> (NOT *We should allow plenty of time not to be late.*)

NOTE
We can use *for* + noun phrase + to-infinitive to express purpose. > 109B

> There was a book **for visitors to write** their comments in.

B We can also use a finite clause with *so that.*

> You should keep milk in a refrigerator **so that** it stays fresh.
> I wrote it in my diary **so that** I wouldn't forget.
> Students learn to analyse situations **so that** problems can be solved.

So that is often followed by the present simple or by *will, would, can,* or *could.*

We can sometimes use *to avoid* or *to prevent* instead of a negative clause with *so that.*

> I always use sunscreen **so that** I don't get burned.
> I always use sunscreen **to avoid** getting burned.

In informal English, and especially in American English, *so* can be used on its own without *that.*

> You should keep milk in a refrigerator **so** it stays fresh.

In order that is more formal and less common than *so that*.
*You will be given full details shortly **in order that** you may make
your arrangements.*

C We can use *for* with a noun phrase to express the purpose of an action.
*We went out **for** some fresh air.*
*Why not come over **for** a cup of coffee?*

To express the general purpose or use of something, we normally use *for* with
an ing-form.
*This paper is **for printing** photos on.*
*A saw is a tool **for cutting** wood.*

But we use a to-infinitive to talk about a specific need or a specific action.
*We must buy some paper **to print** those photos on.*
*I used an electric drill **to make** the holes.*
*I need a saw **to cut** this wood.* (NOT ~~I need a saw for cutting this wood.~~)

After *use* there can be either *for* + ing-form or a to-infinitive.
*We use a ruler **for measuring** / **to measure** things.*

241 *As* and *like*

A We can use *as* and *like* as conjunctions.
*I entered the data into the computer, **as/like** I'd been told to do.*
*My brother behaved **as/like** he usually does – badly.*
Like as a conjunction is informal. In more formal English, and especially in
British English, *as* is preferred to *like*.
*The event passed off peacefully, **as** it had done the previous year.*
*Doctors need time off, **as** everyone else does.*

But the equivalent preposition is *like* rather than *as*.
*Doctors need time off **like** everyone else.*
*Doctors, **like** everyone else, need time off.*

B We can use a clause with *as* to express the idea that what you are saying is
already known or expected.
As you know, I'm short of cash at the moment.
As the report shows, the problems are much worse than we thought.
*I was absolutely terrified, **as** you can imagine.*

We do not normally use *like* in this kind of clause, except informally with *say*.
As/Like I said, you're welcome to stay here.

C We can use *as if* and *as though* to say how something seems.
*It was **as if** / **as though** I was dreaming the whole thing.*
*Chloe looked **as if** / **as though** she was asleep.*
*I feel **as if** / **as though** everyone is laughing behind my back.*
*People are behaving **as if** / **as though** nothing had changed.*
The verbs *be*, *look*, *feel*, and *seem* are often used in this pattern. For verb tenses with *as if* / *as though*, > 230.

We can also use this pattern for what we can see is probably going to happen.
*It looks **as if** / **as though** it's going to be a nice day.*

We can use *like* instead of *as if* / *as though*.
*Chloe looked **like** she was asleep.*
*Now it seems **like** we're getting somewhere.*
*It looks **like** it's going to be a nice day.*
Like is informal here.

We can also use *like* + ing-form.
*It looks **like being** a nice day.*
*Do you feel **like going** to the cinema?*

242 *Whoever, whatever,* etc and *no matter*

A We can use *whoever, whatever, whichever, whenever, wherever,* and *however* with the meaning 'it doesn't matter who', 'it doesn't matter what', etc.
***Whoever** runs the country, we're always in a mess.*
*I won't change my mind, **whatever** you say.*
*The journey takes ages, **whichever** route you take.*
*I can't draw faces, **however** hard I try.*

We can also use *no matter*.
*I won't change my mind, **no matter what** you say.*
***No matter where** we go on holiday, you never enjoy it.*

NOTE
We can use *whoever, whatever,* etc in questions and in relative clauses.
***Whatever** are you going to do?* > 16G
***Whatever** you say won't change my mind.* > 273

B *Whether ... or ...* means 'it doesn't matter if ... or ...'.
***Whether** the Conservatives **or** Labour get in, it makes no difference.*
***Whether** you walk along the road **or** cut across the fields, it still takes twenty minutes.*
*You have to pay a month's rent in advance, **whether** you like it **or not**.*

Conditional sentences

243 Introduction

A Most conditional sentences have a sub-clause starting with the word *if*. We can use many different verb forms in conditional sentences. Here are some real examples.

*If you **haven't got** television, you **can't watch** it.*
*If you **go** to one of the agencies, they **have** a lot of temporary jobs.*
*If someone else **has requested** the book, you **would have to give** it back.*
*If you **lived** on the planet Mercury, you **would have** four birthdays in a single Earth year.*

In general we use verb forms in conditional sentences in the same way as in other kinds of sentences.

*If you**'ve finished** work for today, you **can go** home.*
Compare: *You**'ve finished** work for today, so you **can go** home.*

In an open condition (when something may or may not happen), we use the present tense: *if you **go** to one of the agencies*. When we talk about something unreal, we often use the past tense: *if you **lived** on the planet Mercury*. After an unreal condition, we use *would* in the main clause: *you **would** have four birthdays*.

B There are some verb forms which often go together. These patterns are usually called Types 1, 2, and 3.

Type 1: *If the company **fails**, we **will lose** our money.* > 245
Type 2: *If the company **failed**, we **would lose** our money.* > 246
Type 3: *If the company **had failed**, we **would have lost** our money.* > 247

There is another pattern which we can call Type 0.

Type 0: *If the company **fails**, we **lose** our money.* > 244

C The if-clause usually comes before the main clause, but it can come after it.

If you're in a hurry, you needn't wait for me.
You needn't wait for me if you're in a hurry.
A comma between the clauses is more likely when the if-clause comes first and less likely when it comes at the end.

D We can use conditional sentences in a number of different ways: not only to give information but also, for example, when we request, advise, criticize, and so on.

Use	Example
Requesting:	*If you're going into town, could you post this letter for me, please?*
Advising:	*If your headache persists, you should see a doctor.*
Criticizing:	*If you'd remembered your passport, we wouldn't be in such a rush.*
Suggesting:	*We can go for a walk if you like.*
Offering:	*If you'd like a sandwich, just help yourself.*
Warning:	*If you don't save the information to disk, you risk losing it.*
Threatening:	*If you don't leave immediately, I'll call the police.*

244 Type 0 conditionals

A The pattern is *if* ... + present ... + present.
*If the doorbell **rings**, the dog **barks**.*
*If you **add** twelve and fifteen, what **do** you **get**?*
*The batteries **take** over if the mains supply **fails**.*
This pattern means that one thing always follows automatically from another.

We can use *when* instead of *if* when the meaning is 'each time'.
***If/When** I reverse the car, it makes a funny noise.*
(= Each time I reverse the car, ...)
For more about *if* and *when*, > 249A.

B We can also use Type 0 for the automatic result of a possible future action.
*If the team **win** tomorrow, they **get** promotion to a higher league.*
We could also use a Type 1 conditional with *they will get*.

245 Type 1 conditionals

A This is a very common type. The basic pattern is *if* ... + present ... + *will*.
*If it **rains**, the reception **will take** place indoors.*
*If we **don't hurry**, we **won't get** there in time.*
*If we **want** to ask questions, **will** we **be** allowed to?*
*The milk **will go** off if you **leave** it by the radiator.*
The if-clause expresses an open condition. In the first example, *if it rains* leaves open the question of whether it will rain or not. The present simple (*rains*) expresses future time. For more examples of the present used in this way, e.g. *Let's wait until everyone arrives*, > 59.

We do not normally use *will* in the if-clause.
(NOT ~~If it will rain,~~ ...)
But we can use *will* in the if-clause to talk about something that is further in the future than the action of the main clause.
*If this medicine does me/**will do** me good, I'll take it.*
For *will* in the if-clause expressing willingness, > 245D.

NOTE
We can use *shall* instead of *will* after *I/we*. > 54A
*If we don't hurry, we **will/shall** miss the train.*

B As well as the present simple, we can use the present continuous or perfect.
*If we're **having** a party, we'll have to invite the neighbours.*
*If I've **finished** my work by ten, I'll probably watch a film on TV.*

As well as *will*, we can use other modal verbs and similar expressions in the main clause.
*If someone sees me, how **can** I **explain** what I'm doing?*
*If you change the time of your flight, you **may** be **charged** a fee.*
*I'm **going to look** silly if I can't answer any of the questions.*

We can also use the imperative in the main clause.
*If you've got a problem, **ring** our Helpline.*
*If you make a mistake, **don't panic**.*

C A present tense in the if-clause can refer to the present.
*If you **think** modelling is glamorous, think again.*
*If it's **raining** already, I'm definitely not going out.*

D We can use *will* in the if-clause for willingness and *won't* for a refusal.
*If all of you **will lend** a hand, we'll soon get the job done.*
*If the car **won't start**, I'll have to ring the garage.*
For more about this meaning of *will* and *won't*, > 54D.

We can use *will* in the if-clause for a request.
*If you'll **take** a seat, someone will be with you in a moment.*
*If you'll just **sign** here, please. Thank you.*

E Instead of a Type 1 conditional with *If you* + simple present, we can use this pattern with *and* and *or* in informal speech.
*Touch me **and** I'll scream.*
(= If you touch me, I'll scream.)
*Go away **or** I'll scream.*
(= If you don't go away, I'll scream.)

246 Type 2 conditionals

A The basic pattern is *if* ... + past ... + *would*.
> *If I **had** lots of money, I **would travel** round the world.*
> *I'd **tell** you the answer if I **knew** what it was.*
> *If we **didn't think** the plane was safe, we **wouldn't fly** it.*

Here the past tense expresses an unreal condition. In the first example, *if I had lots of money* means that really I haven't got lots of money; I am only imagining a situation where I have. For more examples of the past used in this way, > 230.

We do not normally use *would* in the if-clause.
> (NOT *If I would have lots of money, ...*)

NOTE

a   We can use *should* instead of *would* after *I/we*.
> *If I had lots of money, I **would/should** travel round the world.*
Would is more usual. *Should* is rather literary here.

b   In informal American speech *would* is sometimes used to express an unreal condition.
> *If those people **would get** a nuclear bomb, it would be a great threat to us.*
But this is not acceptable in writing, so you should avoid it.

c   We sometimes use *were* instead of *was* in an if-clause. > 231C
> *If I **was/were** a billionaire, I would travel round the world.*

B We also use the Type 2 pattern for a theoretical possibility in the future.
> *If we **caught** the early train tomorrow, we'**d be** in York by lunch time.*
> *If you **lost** the video, you **would have to pay** for a new one.*

Here the past tense refers to a possible future action such as catching the early train tomorrow.

Compare Types 1 and 2.
> Type 1: *If we **stay** in a hotel, it **will** be expensive.*
> Type 2: *If we **stayed** in a hotel, it **would** be expensive.*

Type 1 expresses the action as an open possibility – we may or may not stay in a hotel. Type 2 expresses the action as a theoretical possibility only, something more distant from reality.

Sometimes it can be more polite to use Type 2 rather than Type 1, for example when making a request.
> ***Would** it **be** all right if I **brought** a friend?* ~ *Yes, of course.*

Here Type 1 would be more direct and less tentative.

C You might occasionally see a mixture of Types 1 and 2.
> *If England **win** against Germany tonight, it would be a miracle.*

However, this is unusual. Normally we do not mix Types 1 and 2.
> (NOT *If I've got lots of money, I would travel round the world.*)

TIP
Do not mix Types 1 and 2.
Say *If you break it, you will have to pay for it.*
OR *If you broke it, you would have to pay for it.*
NOT ~~*If you break it, you would have to pay for it.*~~
and NOT ~~*If you broke it, you will have to pay for it.*~~

NOTE
a   We can use a mixture of the past tense and *will* when we combine a past condition with
     a future result.
          *If they **posted** the parcel yesterday, it **won't get** here before Friday.*

b   A Type 2 pattern can be the past of a Type 1, for example in reported speech.
          Type 1: *Don't go. If you **accept** the invitation, you **will regret** it.*
          Type 2: *I told you that if you **accepted** the invitation, you **would regret** it.*

D As well as the past simple, we can use the past continuous or *could* in the
     if-clause.
          *If the sun **was shining**, everything would be perfect.*
          *If I **could have** my child looked after, I would go out to work.*

As well as *would*, we can use other modal verbs such as *could* or *might* in the
main clause.
          *If I had a light, I **could** see what I'm doing.*
          *If we could re-start the computer, that **might** solve the problem.*
We can also use continuous forms.
          *If Shakespeare was alive today, he **would be writing** for television.*

E We can use *would* in the if-clause for a request.
          *If you **wouldn't mind** holding the line, I'll try to put you through.*
          *If you'd just **sign** here. please. Thank you.*

We can also use *would like*.
          *If you'd **like** to see the exhibition, it would be nice to go together.*

247 Type 3 conditionals

A The basic pattern is *if* … + past perfect … + *would* + perfect.
          *If you **had taken** a taxi, you **would have got** here in time.*
          *I **would have bought** that guitar yesterday if I'd **had** enough money.*
          *My brother **would have been promoted** if he'd **stayed** in his job.*
          *We'd **have gone** to the talk if we'd **known** about it.*
          (= We would have gone if we had known.)

Here the verb forms refer to something unreal, to an imaginary past action.
In the first example, *if you had taken a taxi* means that really you didn't take
a taxi; I am only imagining a situation where you did. For more examples of
the past perfect used in this way, > 230C.

We cannot use the past simple or the past perfect in the main clause.
(NOT ~~If you had taken a taxi, you had got here in time.~~)

And we do not normally use *would* in the if-clause.
(NOT ~~If you would have taken a taxi, you would have got here in time.~~)

NOTE
You may occasionally hear a form such as *would have taken* (OR *had have taken*) in an if-clause in informal speech. But many people regard it as incorrect, and it is not acceptable in writing, so you should avoid it.

B We can use *could* + perfect in the if-clause.
*If I **could have warned** you in time, I would have done.*

As well as *would*, we can use other modal verbs such as *could* or *might* in the main clause.
*If I'd written the address down, I **could have saved** myself some trouble.*
*The plan **might not have worked** if we hadn't had a piece of luck.*
We can also use continuous forms.
*If he hadn't been evicted by his landlord, he **wouldn't have been sleeping** on the streets.*

C We can mix Types 2 and 3.
*If Tom **was** ambitious, he **would have found** himself a better job years ago.*
*If you **hadn't woken** me up in the night, I **wouldn't feel** so tired now.*

We can also use a Type 1 condition with a Type 3 main clause.
*If you **know** London so well, you **shouldn't have got** so hopelessly lost.*

248 *Should, were, had,* and inversion

The following types of clause are rather formal.

A We can use *should* in an if-clause to talk about something that might possibly happen.
*If you **should** fall ill, the company will pay your hospital expenses.*
*If I **should** be chosen as your representative, I would do my best for you.*
More neutral would be *If you fall ill, ...* and *If I was chosen ... .*

We can also use *happen to.*
*If you (should) **happen to** fall ill, the company will pay your hospital expenses.*

B Sometimes we use *were* instead of *was.* > 231C
*If the picture was/**were** genuine, it would be worth a million pounds.*

We can also use *were to* for a theoretical possibility.
*If the decision **were to** go against us, we would appeal.*

C In a condition with *should* or *were*, we can invert the subject and verb and leave out *if*.

> ***Should*** *you fall ill, the company will pay your hospital expenses.*
> ***Should*** *we not succeed, the consequences would be disastrous.*
> ***Were*** *the picture genuine, it would be worth a million pounds.*
> ***Were*** *the decision to go against us, we would appeal.*

We cannot do this with *was*.

> *If the picture **was** genuine, it would be worth a million pounds.*
> (NOT ~~Was the picture genuine, it would be worth a million pounds.~~)

We can also use inversion with the past perfect (Type 3, > 247).

> ***Had*** *you taken a taxi, you would have got here on time.*
> ***Had*** *I not carried out the order, I would have been sacked.*

But an if-clause (*If you had taken a taxi*) is more common, especially in informal English.

D Look at these examples with *if ... not for*.

> *You saved my life.* ***If it hadn't been for*** *you, I'd have drowned.*
> (= **Without** you, I'd have drowned.)
> *I'd give up teaching **if it wasn't/weren't for** the holidays.*

We can also use *but for*. > 251B

> ***But for*** *you, I'd have drowned.*

249 More details about *if*

A *When* and *if*

When we talk about the future, we use *when* for something that will happen and *if* for something that might happen.

> ***When*** *the doctor comes, can you let her in?* (The doctor **will** come.)
> ***If*** *the doctor comes, can you let her in?* (The doctor **might** come.)

We use *if* (not *when*) for an unreal condition.

> ***If*** *I had a credit card, I would spend even more money.*
> (I **don't** have a credit card.)

In some contexts either *when* or *if* is possible. > 244A

> *I always feel guilty **when/if** I use my credit card.*

B *Then*

After an if-clause we can use *then* in the main clause.

> *If the figures don't add up, **then** you must have made a mistake.*
> *If no one else has requested the book, **then** you can keep it for another three weeks.*

Here *then* is not an adverb of time. It emphasizes the link between the condition (e.g. *no one else has requested the book*) and the result of the condition being met (e.g. *you can keep it*). We cannot use *so* in this way.
(NOT ~~If the figures don't add up, so you must have made a mistake.~~)

C Short clauses

We can sometimes use a short clause with *if* leaving out the subject and the verb.
*I'd like a room with a view of the sea **if** (that is) **possible**.*
***If** (you are) **in difficulty**, ring this number.*
We can do this when the meaning is still clear without the missing words.

For *if so* and *if not,* > 28D.

D *What if*

We can use *what if* to ask someone to imagine a situation.
***What if** the tickets don't arrive in time?*
***What if** you'd had an accident?*

We can also use it to make a suggestion.
***What if** we all meet in London at the weekend?*

Suppose and *supposing* are used in the same way as *what if.* > 230
***Supposing** the tickets don't arrive in time?*

E *Even if*

We use *even if* to express both a condition and a contrast.
*I'm going to finish this report **even if** it takes all night.*
(This report may or may not take all night, but I'm going to finish it.)

We cannot use *even* on its own as a conjunction.
NOT ~~I'm going to finish this report even it takes all night.~~

Compare *even if* and *even though*.
***Even if** the rumour is untrue, people will still believe it.*
(The rumour may or may not be untrue.)
***Even though** the rumour is untrue, people will still believe it.*
(The rumour is untrue.)

250 *Unless*

A *Unless* with a positive verb is equivalent to *if* with a negative verb.
　　*The club will go bankrupt **unless** it finds a new backer soon.*
　　(= ... **if** it doesn't find a new backer soon.)
　　***Unless** I get up when I wake, I feel tired all day.*
　　(= **If** I don't get up when I wake, ...)
　　*We're going to have a picnic – **unless** it rains, of course.*
　　(= **if** it doesn't rain, of course.)

In these examples, the main clause is negative.
　　*You can't get your money back **unless** you've got a receipt.*
　　(= You can get your money back **only if** you've got a receipt.)
　　*Won't you join us? ~ Not **unless** you apologize first.*
　　(= I'll join you **only if** you apologize first.)

B We do not normally use *unless* meaning *if ... not* to express an unreal condition.
　　***If** you didn't talk so much, you'd get more work done.*
　　***If** the horse hadn't fallen, it would have won the race.*
　　(NOT *Unless the horse had fallen, it would have won the race.*)

We do not use *unless* to talk about a feeling which would result from something not happening.
　　*Laura will be upset **if** you **don't** come to her party.*
　　*I'll be very surprised **if** you **don't** get the job.*
　　(NOT *I'll be very surprised unless you get the job.*)

251 Other ways of expressing a condition

A As long as, provided, etc

As well as *if*, we can use *as long as* or *so long as* to express a condition.
　　*You can smoke **as long as** you do it outside the building.*
　　*I don't care what a car looks like **so long as** it gets me from A to B.*

We can also use *provided (that)*, *providing (that)*, and *on condition that*.
　　*The machine will go on working for years **provided (that)** it is looked after properly.*
　　*We are willing to accept your offer **providing (that)** payment is made within seven days.*
　　*The country was given aid **on condition that** it signed a trade agreement.*
These conjunctions are more formal.

B *In case of, with,* etc

We can use the prepositions *in case of* and *in the event of*.
> ***In case of*** *fire, break glass.* (on a sign)
> (= **If** there is a fire, ...)
> ***In the event of*** *a major emergency, local hospitals would be alerted.*
> (= **If** there was a major emergency, ...)

The prepositions *with*, *without*, and *but for* can also express a condition.
> ***With*** *a bit more time, we could do a proper job.*
> (= **If** we had a bit more time, ...)
> ***Without*** *my mobile, I would have been in big trouble.*
> (= **If** I hadn't had my mobile, ...)
> ***But for*** *the climate, Edinburgh would be a perfect place to live.*
> (= **If** it wasn't for the climate, ...)

In that case means 'if that is so'.
> *I've lost my ticket.* ~ ***In that case*** *you'll have to buy another one.*

We can also use *otherwise* to express a condition. It means 'if that is not so'.
> *I'd better write the address down,* ***otherwise*** *I'll forget it.*

C *In case*

Compare *if* and *in case*.
> *I'll get some money from the cashpoint* ***if*** *I need some.*
> (I'll wait until I need some and then get it.)
> *I'll get some money from the cashpoint* ***in case*** *I need some.*
> (I'll get it now because I might need it later.)

Here are some more examples with *in case*.
> *You should insure your belongings* ***in case*** *they get stolen.*
> (= ... because they might get stolen.)
> *I left a glass of water by my bed* ***in case*** *I woke up thirsty in the night.*
> (= ... because I might wake up thirsty in the night.)

We can also use *should* or *might* in a clause with *in case*.
> *I'll take my mobile* ***in case*** *you* ***should/might*** *need to contact me.*

We can use *in case* as an adverbial.
> *I'll get some money from the cashpoint (just)* ***in case***.

But for *in case of,* > B.

NOTE
In American English *in case* can mean the same as *if*.
> *If you need /* ***In case*** *you need any help, let me know.*

Noun clauses

252 Introduction

A A noun clause begins with *that*, a question word, or *if/whether*.
*I expected **that** there would be difficulties.*
*The price depends on **where** you want to sit.*
*We'll have to decide **if/whether** we can afford it.*

A that-clause relates to a statement.
There would be difficulties. → ... ***that** there would be difficulties*
A wh-clause relates to a wh-question.
Where do you want to sit? → ... ***where** you want to sit*
A clause with *if* or *whether* relates to a yes/no question.
Can we afford it? → ... ***if/whether** we can afford it*

B In informal English we can often leave out *that*.
*I knew (**that**) you weren't listening to me.*

In a clause relating to a question, we normally use the same word order as in a statement.
*We'll have to decide if/whether **we can** afford it.*
(NOT ~~We'll have to decide if/whether can we afford it.~~)

We can sometimes use a to-infinitive with a question word or *whether*.
> 108
*The problem was **where to plug** in all the electrical equipment.*

C We use the term 'noun clause' because these clauses generally function in the same way as noun phrases: they can be the subject, the object, or the complement, or they can come after a preposition.

As subject:	***That he could be mistaken** wasn't possible.*
	> 254A
As object:	*I noticed **that the door was open**.* > 253
As complement:	*The result is **that no one knows what to do**.*
	> 254C
After a preposition:	*We had a talk about **who should be invited**.* > 255

We can also use noun clauses in other patterns.

With it:	*It wasn't possible **that he could be mistaken**.* > 254B.
After an adjective:	*I'm **disappointed that I didn't get the job**.* > 256A
After a noun:	*I heard a **rumour that the professor has been kidnapped**.* > 256B

Noun clauses are used in indirect speech after verbs like *say* and *ask*. > 259
*You **said** you wanted to come with us.*
*Someone **asked** what the matter was.*

253 Noun clause as object

A A noun clause can be the object of a verb.

> *We regret **that you did not find our product satisfactory.***
> *I can't believe **anyone would be so stupid.***
> *The figures show **how much the population has increased.***
> *I wonder **whether that's a good idea.***

There are many different verbs that we can use before a noun clause. Here are some of the most common ones.

agree	*consider*	*mean*	*see*	*suspect*
ask	*feel*	*point out*	*show*	*think*
assume	*find*	*realize*	*suggest*	*understand*
believe	*know*	*say*	*suppose*	*wonder*

NOTE

Sometimes we put *not* in the main clause when you might expect it in the noun clause.

> *I **don't think** we've got time.*   *I **don't expect** it'll take very long.*

This is more usual than *I think we haven't got time* or *I expect it won't take very long.*
We prefer to put *not* in the main clause with *believe, expect, imagine, suppose,* and *think.*

B Sometimes there is an indirect object.

> *We told **the driver** we were in a hurry.*
> *I persuaded **Laura** that she ought to give up smoking.*
> *The woman asked **the policeman** what was happening.*

The indirect object is usually a person. > 6A

The verbs we can use in this pattern include the following.

advise	*convince*	*persuade*	*remind*	*tell*
ask	*inform*	*promise*	*show*	*warn*
assure	*notify*	*reassure*	*teach*	*write* > Note
bet				

With some of these verbs we cannot leave out the indirect object. > 259C

NOTE

An indirect object with *write* in this pattern is used mainly in American English.

> *He **wrote me that** he couldn't come.*

In British English *wrote to me* is more usual.

C With certain verbs we can use a phrase with *to.*

> *We explained **to the driver** that we were in a hurry.*
> *I mentioned **to Karen** that you would be here.*

The verbs that we can use in this pattern include the following.

admit	*declare*	*mention*	*recommend*	*say*
announce	*explain*	*point out*	*remark*	*suggest*
complain	*indicate*	*propose*	*report*	*write*

We can always leave out the phrase with *to.*

D We can use a noun clause after a passive verb.

*It **was assumed that** the stock market would continue to rise.*

For more details, > 92A.

254 Noun clause as subject and as complement

A We sometimes use a noun clause as the subject of a sentence.

***That you want to be independent** is only natural.*

***How they're going to enforce the law** isn't clear.*

But it is more usual to put the noun clause later in the sentence. > B

We cannot leave out *that* when the clause is the subject.

(NOT ~~You want to be independent is only natural.~~)

We can use *whether* (but not *if*) when the clause is the subject.

***Whether I'll be able to come** depends on a number of things.*

B We often use *it* and put the noun clause at the end of the sentence.

*It's only natural **that you want to be independent**.*

*It isn't clear **how they're going to enforce the law**.*

*It's hard to say **if/whether it's going to rain or not**.*

*It was easy to see **how it could have happened**.*

We do this because the clause is long and comes more naturally at the end.

NOTE

a For *it* with *seem, happen* etc, > 36C.

*It **seems** that I've made a mistake.*

b For *it* with a passive verb, > 92A.

*It **is feared** that many lives have been lost in the earthquake.*

c We can use the following pattern with *it* as the object. > 36B

*They haven't made **it** clear how they're going to enforce the law.*

C A noun clause can be a complement of *be*.

*The truth is **that I don't get on with my flat-mate**.*

*The advantage of DVD is **that it gives you much better picture quality**.*

Before *be* we often use nouns like these: *advantage, answer, effect, explanation, fear, idea, point, problem, reason, result, situation, truth.*

255 Noun clause after a preposition

A A wh-clause or *whether* can come after a preposition.

*The government is looking **into what needs to be done**.*

*Then there's the question **of who pays for all this**.*

*The singer made no comment **on whether he had sold his story to a newspaper**.*

We cannot use *if* in this pattern.

We cannot use a that-clause after a preposition. Compare these examples.
*No one told me **that** Nicola **was** ill.*
*No one told me **about** Nicola's **illness**.*
*No one told me **about** Nicola **being** ill.* > 115B.
(BUT NOT ~~No one told me about Nicola was ill~~)

B Many verbs, nouns, and adjectives can be followed by a particular
preposition: *wonder **about**, an effect **on**, surprised **at**, interested **in***. Some
combinations of this kind can be followed by a wh-clause or *whether*.
> *The elections will have an **effect on whether** the President can push ahead
> with reforms.*
> *I'm **interested in how** business decisions are made.*

Sometimes we can leave out the preposition.
> *I was **wondering (about) who**'s going to be in this band.*
> *We were all **surprised (at) how** cold it was.*

Here are some expressions with verbs and adjectives where we can leave out
the preposition.

to agree (about/as to/on)	*certain (about/as to/of)*	*surprised (at)*
to ask (about)	*to decide (about/on)*	*to think (about/of)*
aware (of)	*to report (about/on)*	*to wonder (about)*
to care (about)	*sure (about/as to/of)*	*to worry (about)*

But in these expressions we do not leave out the preposition.

anxious about	*an effect on*
a belief about/as to	*an inquiry about/as to/into*
confused about/as to	*interested in*
a difficulty about/as to/over	*a report about/on*
a discussion about/of/on	*some research into/on*

256 Noun clause after an adjective or noun

A We can use a that-clause after some adjectives.
> *It's **essential that you fit smoke alarms.***
> *I'm **hopeful we can reach an agreement.***
> *The girl was **sure she would be able to recognize her attacker.***
> *I was as **certain** as I could be **that my calculations were correct.***

The adjectives that we can use in this pattern include the following.

afraid	*certain*	*convinced*	*hopeful*	*sorry*
amazed	*clear*	*disappointed*	*nice*	*sure*
annoyed	*concerned*	*glad*	*pleased*	*surprised*
aware	*confident*	*grateful*	*satisfied*	*worried*

We can also use a wh-clause after some adjectives.

*I wasn't **sure what the time was.***

*Are you **aware who is causing all this trouble?***

For details about the use of a preposition before the wh-clause, > 255B.

B We can use a that-clause after some nouns.

*The **news that the plane had crashed** came as a terrible shock.*

*You can't get around the **fact that his fingerprints were on the gun.***

*Whatever gave you the **idea that I can sing?***

*There's a **rumour** going round **that the exam papers have been stolen.***

We do not normally leave out *that* except occasionally in informal speech.

The nouns that we can use in this pattern are mainly to do with thoughts or speech. They include the following.

assumption	*concern*	*fact*	*news*	*statement*
belief	*danger*	*hope*	*report*	*suggestion*
claim	*evidence*	*idea*	*rumour*	*view*

257 Nominalization

A Compare these three examples.

Main clause: ***The campaign succeeded,*** *and this meant that lives were saved.*

Noun clause: *The fact **that the campaign succeeded** meant that lives were saved.*

Noun phrase: ***The success of the campaign*** *meant that lives were saved.*

A statement like *The campaign succeeded* can be a main clause, or we can turn it into a that-clause and use it as part of a larger sentence. Sometimes we can also turn a clause into a noun phrase such as *the success of the campaign.* Here this involves changing a verb (*succeeded*) into a noun (*success*). Using a noun phrase rather than a clause is called 'nominalization'. Especially in written English, it is often neater to use a phrase.

Here are some more examples.

Clause	Phrase
The residents protested.	***The residents' protests*** *were ignored.*
The document was published.	***The publication of the document*** *was delayed.*
The landscape is beautiful.	*We were attracted by **the beauty of the landscape.***

The last example involves changing an adjective (*beautiful*) into a noun (*beauty*).

B When we change a clause into a noun phrase, the subject of a clause either has the possessive form or comes in an of-phrase.

Clause	Phrase
I was happy.	*Nothing could spoil **my happiness.***
Our visitor departed.	***Our visitor's departure** / **The departure of our visitor** was a great relief.*
The film ended.	*I missed **the end of the film.***

With people we use a possessive form, and sometimes we can use the of-structure. With things we use *of*. For more details about the choice of the possessive form or *of*, > 133.

C A verb + object becomes a noun + preposition + object.

Clause	Phrase
They will open the new skateboard park.	*The opening **of** the new skateboard park is eagerly awaited.*
Someone attacked the army post.	*The attack **on** the army post took place yesterday.*
They've changed the law.	*There's been a change **in** the law.*
I've requested a transfer.	*I've made several requests **for** a transfer.*

The most common preposition after a noun is *of*. For more details, > 226.

D An adverb in a clause is equivalent to an adjective in a noun phrase.

Adverb	Adjective
*The residents protested **angrily.***	*The residents' **angry** protests were ignored.*
*The landscape is **amazingly** beautiful.*	*Discover the **amazing** beauty of the landscape.*

Indirect speech

258 Introduction

A We use direct speech when we report someone's words by quoting them.

> *'I'll go and heat some milk,' said Agnes.* (from a story)
>
> *Gould was the first to admit, 'We were simply beaten by a better side.'* (from a newspaper report)
>
> *'Made me laugh more than any comedy I have seen in the West End this year' – Evening Standard* (from an advertisement for a play)

B Instead of quoting the exact words we can report the meaning in our own words and from our own point of view. This is called 'indirect speech' or 'reported speech'.

> *Agnes said **she would go and heat some milk**.*
>
> *Gould admitted **that his team were beaten by a better side**.*
>
> *One of the critics claims **it's the funniest play in the West End**.*

Here the indirect speech is the object of *said*, *admitted*, or *claims*. These are verbs of reporting. > 259

NOTE

a   When we use indirect speech, we normally express the meaning of what was said rather than the exact words that were spoken.

> *'I had a really great time.'* ➔ *She said she had enjoyed herself.*

b   We can report thoughts as well as speech or writing.

> *I **thought** I had plenty of time, but in fact I only just made it.*

The speaker thought 'I've got plenty of time', but the thoughts were not necessarily expressed in speech.

Often *think* is used to report expressions of opinion.

> *My careers advisor **thinks** I should do business studies.*

In the context of a discussion between the careers advisor and the student, it is clear that the opinion was expressed in speech.

C We often use *that* in indirect speech, but in informal English we can leave it out, especially after a common verb like *say*.

> *Tom says **(that)** he'll only be five minutes.*

We can sometimes use a gerund clause or a to-infinitive clause.

> *Gould admitted **having lost** to a better side.* > 265E
>
> *I warned you **to take** care.* > 265D

NOTE

a   Sometimes the indirect speech comes first (in a finite clause), and the information about who said it comes at the end, as a kind of afterthought.

> *His team were beaten by a better side, Gould admitted.*
>
> *There will be no trains on New Year's Day, the rail companies announced yesterday.*

We do not begin with *That* ... when the indirect speech comes first.

b   We can use a phrase with *according to* to show who said something.

> ***According to** Gould, his team were beaten by a better side.*

D With direct speech, we can sometimes invert the verb of reporting and the subject. This happens mainly in literary English, for example in stories.

'I'll see you later,' **said Sam**.
'But that's not true,' **replied the man**.

We can do this with most verbs of reporting, but not with a verb like *tell* which has an indirect object.

We do not usually put a personal pronoun after the verb.

'Nice to meet you,' **he said**.

E You may see a mixture of direct and indirect speech. This is from a newspaper report about a man staying at home to look after his children.

But Brian believes watching the kids grow up and learn new things is the biggest joy a dad can experience. 'Some people think it's a woman's job, but I don't think that's relevant any more.'

F When someone says something that goes on for more than a single sentence, we do not need to use a verb of reporting in every sentence. This is from a newspaper report about a court case.

Prosecutor David Andrews **said** *Wilson had stolen a gold wedding ring and credit card and had used the card to attempt to withdraw money from a bank. In the second offence Wilson had burgled premises and taken a briefcase containing takings from a shop. Police had later recovered the bank notes from his home.*

It is clear that the whole paragraph is reporting what the prosecutor said. It is not necessary to say, for example, that ***Mr Andrews added that*** *police had later recovered the bank notes from his home.*

259 Verbs of reporting

A We can use a verb of reporting with a that-clause or a wh-clause.

Polly **says** *(that) she isn't feeling very well.*
He **wondered** *why everyone was smiling.*

Most verbs of reporting can also be used with direct speech.

Polly **says**, *'I'm not feeling very well.'*
'Why is everyone smiling?' he **wondered**.

We also use verbs of reporting with other patterns such as a to-infinitive clause or a gerund clause. > 265

We **asked** *the waiter to bring another bottle.*
I've **apologized** *for keeping everyone waiting.*

NOTE
Some verbs express how a sentence is spoken.
'Oh, not again,' she **groaned**.
Such verbs include *groan, laugh, murmur, mutter, scream, shout, sigh, sob,* and *whisper*.
They are typically used with direct speech in stories and novels.

B There are many different verbs of reporting. Here are some that we can use before a that-clause or a wh-clause.

admit	*ask*	*hear*	*point out*	*suppose*
agree	*believe*	*inquire*	*read*	*think*
announce	*consider*	*insist*	*say*	*understand*
argue	*feel*	*know*	*suggest*	*wonder*

With many of these verbs we can use a passive pattern with *it*. > 92A
> *At that time it **was** already **known** that the earth orbited the sun.*

NOTE
In informal speech *be like* is sometimes used, especially by younger speakers, when quoting someone's words.
> *We were making a bit of a noise, and my dad **was like**, 'What's going on here?'*

C Sometimes there is an indirect object after the verb of reporting.
> *No one **told me** you were leaving.*
> *The police have **warned the public** that the man is dangerous.*

The verbs we can use in this pattern include the following.

advise	*inform*	*promise*	*remind*	*warn*
assure	*notify*	*reassure*	*tell*	

With some of these verbs we cannot leave out the indirect object.
> *We **informed everyone** that the time had been changed.*
> (NOT ~~We informed that the time had been changed.~~)
These verbs are *assure, inform, notify, reassure, remind,* and *tell* (> 260).

We can use the verb of reporting in the passive.
> *Everyone **was informed** that the time had been changed.*

NOTE
For *write* with an indirect object, > 253B Note.

D Sometimes we use a phrase with *to* after a verb of reporting.
> *Can someone **explain to me** what's happening?*
> *I **suggested to the others** that we should meet them here.*

The verbs that we can use in this pattern include the following.

admit	*declare*	*mention*	*recommend*	*say*
announce	*explain*	*point out*	*remark*	*suggest*
complain	*indicate*	*propose*	*report*	*write*

We can always leave out the phrase with *to*.

E As well as verbs of reporting, we can also use an adjective such as *sure* or *certain*.

I'm sure someone's been looking through my papers.

260 *Tell, say,* and *ask*

A We normally use an indirect object after *tell*.

You told me you didn't like Chinese food.
Simon told us he was going to Australia.
(NOT *Simon told he was going to Australia.*)

But after *say* we do not use an indirect object.

You said you didn't like Chinese food.
Simon said he was going to Australia.
(NOT *Simon said us he was going to Australia.*)

B We can use either a that-clause or a wh-clause after *say* or *tell*.

Kate told me (that) she's fed up.
Kate said (that) she's fed up.
Kate told me what the matter was.

Say + wh-clause is used in a negative statement or a question where the information is not actually reported.

Kate didn't say what the matter was.
Did your brother say how long he would be?

Say + wh-clause is less usual in a positive statement.

NOTE
We can use *tell* + indirect object + *about*.
Kate told us about the fight she had with her boyfriend.
We use *say* with *about* only if the information is not actually reported.
What did Kate say about her boyfriend?
The company won't say anything about its plans.

C There are a few expressions where we can use *tell* without an indirect object.

I'm not very good at telling stories.
Paul told a very funny joke.
You mustn't tell lies. You should always tell the truth.
The pupils have learned to tell the time.
Can you tell the difference between tap water and bottled water?
(= distinguish)

NOTE
You may sometimes see *tell* without an indirect object before *how* or *of*.
The couple told how they had been held hostage.
I remember crying when the radio told of the death of the King.

D After *say* we can use a phrase with *to*.

I said to him, 'I've been mugged.'

But this is less usual in indirect speech.

*I **said** I'd been mugged.*
*I **told him** I'd been mugged.*

We prefer either of these to *I said to him I'd been mugged.*

But we can use a phrase with *to* if the information is not reported.

*The mayor will **say** a few words **to** the guests.*
*What did the boss **say to** you?*

E We use *talk* and *speak* to say who was speaking, to whom, for how long, or what about.

*Daniel was **talking** to a very attractive young woman.*
*The President **spoke** for an hour.*
*We don't **talk** about politics.*

We do not use them as verbs of reporting.

*The announcer **said** that he had a surprise for us.*
(NOT *~~The announcer talked/spoke that he had a surprise for us.~~*)

F We can use *ask* with or without an indirect object.

*Kate looked a bit upset, so I **asked** (her) if there was anything wrong.*

For *tell* and *ask* in indirect orders and requests, > 264.

*We **told/asked** Kate to hurry up.*

Compare *ask* and *say* in direct and indirect speech.

Direct speech	Indirect speech
*'What time is it?' he **asked**/**said**.* →	*He **asked** what time it was.*
*'The time is …,' he **said**.* →	*He **said** what time it was.*

261 Changes in indirect speech

A People, place, and time

Imagine a situation where Andrew and Tina are at home one afternoon. Tina wants to go out in the car, but it refuses to start. She rings the garage and asks a mechanic if he can come and see to it. He is too busy to come right away, but he agrees to come the next morning.

Mechanic: *I'll be at your house at eight tomorrow morning.*

A moment later Tina reports this to Martin.

Tina: *The mechanic says **he'll** be **here** at eight tomorrow morning.*

Now a different speaker is giving the message, so where the mechanic said *I'll be …*, Tina says *he'll be …* . And the speaker is in a different place, so *at your house* for the mechanic becomes *here* for Tina.

Next day the mechanic has not arrived even by nine o'clock, so Tina rings him again.

Tina: *You said you would be here at eight this morning.*
Now the time has changed. It is a day later, so instead of *tomorrow morning,*
Tina says *this morning.* And the promise is now out of date, so *will* becomes
would. For changes to verb forms, > 262.

When we report something, we have to take account of changes in the
situation – a different speaker, a different place, or a different time.

B Pronouns and possessives

When you report what someone else has said, both pronouns and possessives
can change.
'I'm really enjoying myself.' → *Kate said **she** was enjoying **herself.***
'I like your new hairstyle.' → *Martin said **he** liked **my** new hairstyle.*

C Adverbials of time

Here are some typical changes from direct to indirect speech.

Direct speech	Indirect speech
now	*then/at that time/immediately*
today	*yesterday/that day/on Tuesday*, etc
yesterday	*the day before/the previous day/on Monday*, etc
tomorrow	*the next day/the following day/on Thursday*, etc
this week	*last week/that week*
last year	*the year before/the previous year/in 1990*, etc
next month	*the month after/the following month/in August*, etc
an hour ago	*an hour before/an hour earlier/at two o'clock*, etc

D Reporting *this* and *that*

When we are talking about things other than time, *this* or *that* usually
changes to *the* in indirect speech, or the phrase is replaced by *it.*

'This steak is nice.' → *Kirsty said **the** steak was nice.*
'I'd like to buy that guitar.' → *Tom saw a guitar. He said he wanted to buy **it.***

262 Verb tenses in indirect speech

A Verbs of reporting

A verb of reporting can be in a present tense.
*The forecast **says** it's going to rain.*
I've heard they might close this place down.
Here the present simple or present perfect tense suggests that the reported
statements were made not long ago and that they are still relevant. For
written statements such as *The article says fast food is bad for you,* > 42G.

After a present-tense verb of reporting, we do not change the tense in indirect speech.

'I'm hungry.' → *Robert says he's hungry.*

*'I **took** drugs when I was younger.'* → *The singer says he **took** drugs when he was younger.*

A verb of reporting is often in a past tense.

*The forecast **said** it was going to rain.*

*Robert **said** he's hungry.*

We can always use the past tense, even if the words were spoken a very short time ago. After a past-tense verb of reporting we often change the tense in indirect speech.

It's going to rain. → *The forecast said it **was** going to rain.*

For details > B–C.

NOTE

Continuous forms are sometimes used informally to report what was said, especially when summarizing the main point of a message.

*The authorities **are saying** that the school will have to close.*

*This politician on TV last night **was saying** there's hardly any rainforest left.*

B The tense change and when we use it

When the verb of reporting is in a past tense, we often change the tense in indirect speech from present to past. In general we are more likely to change the tense if we are unsure whether the statement is still true and still relevant.

When a statement is untrue or out of date, then we change the tense.

*Oh, they live in Bristol, do they? I thought they **lived** in Bath.*

(They don't live in Bath.)

*The forecast said it **was** going to rain and it did.*

(The forecast is now out of date.)

We also use the past tense when we are reporting in a neutral way and we do not want to suggest that the statement is necessarily true.

'Our policies are the right ones.' → *The Minister said that the party's policies **were** the right ones.*

This use of the past tense gives an objective tone to the reporting of people's views in the news media.

Sometimes we can use the same tense in reported speech as in direct speech. This happens when the statement is still relevant.

'I know the way.' → *Karen told me she **knows**/knew the way, so there's no need to take a map.*

'It's going to rain.' → *The forecast said it's going to rain / it was going to rain today.*

Using the present tense makes the speaker sound more confident that Karen really does know the way and that it really is going to rain. However, it is always possible to change the tense, even when the statement is still relevant.

> **TIP**
> After *said* and *told* it is safest to change the tense from present to past.
> *'I'm tired.'* → *She said she **was** tired.*

C The form of the tense change

The tense change in indirect speech is a change from present to past.
*'I **feel** awful.'* → *Louise said she **felt** awful.*
'You're crazy.' → *Simon thought I **was** crazy.*
*'I've **got** a headache.'* → *I told them I **had** a headache.*

If the verb phrase is more than one word, then the first word of the verb phrase changes from present to past.
*'We're **going** the wrong way.'* → *I knew we **were** going the wrong way.*
*'I **haven't** finished.'* → *Laura said she **hadn't** finished.*
*'The kids **have** been swimming.'* → *Steve said the kids **had** been swimming.*
*'The matter **is** being investigated.'* → *They told me the matter **was** being investigated.*

So the present continuous changes to the past continuous, the present perfect to the past perfect, and so on.

D Past and past perfect in indirect speech

If the verb in direct speech is past, then it usually changes to the past perfect.
'I passed my driving test yesterday.' → *Paul told me he**'d passed** his driving test.*
'We were sailing on the lake last weekend.' → *They told me they**'d been** sailing on the lake.*

The use of the past perfect makes it clear that the sailing is further in the past than when they told me about it. If we don't change the tense – *They told me they were sailing* – this could mean that the sailing holiday was not yet over.

Look at these examples.
*'I **feel** very stressed.'* → *Lucy said she **felt** very stressed. She certainly didn't look well.*
*'I **felt** very stressed.'* → *Lucy said she**'d felt** very stressed, but she seems to have got over it now.*

Here we have to use the past perfect in indirect speech to show that the feeling was in the past when it was reported.

But when it is clear that something happened long before it was reported, we do not need to use the past perfect.
*'I once **lived** in a palace.'* → *Joshua told me that he once **lived** in a palace.*
*'Rome **wasn't** built in a day, you know.'* → *The teacher reminded us that Rome **wasn't** built in a day.*

We do not change a past-tense verb when it refers to something unreal.
*'I wish I **had** a dog.'* → *My sister used to say she wished she **had** a dog.*
*'If I **knew**, I'd tell you.'* → *Amy said that if she **knew**, she would tell us.*

If the verb in direct speech is in the past perfect, then it does not change.
'I was annoyed because I'd left my coat on the train.' → *Jack said he'd been annoyed because he'd left his coat on the train.*

NOTE
The past perfect in indirect speech can relate to three different verb forms.
'I've seen the film.' → *She said she'd seen the film.*
'I saw the film last week.' → *She said she'd seen the film the week before.*
'I didn't watch it because I'd seen it before.' → *She said she'd seen it before.*

E Modal verbs in indirect speech

Some modal verbs change in indirect speech.
'You'll regret it.' → *I told them they'd regret it.*
'I can drive.' → *I said I could drive.*
'It may snow.' → *They thought it might snow.*
The changes are *will* → *would*, *can* → *could*, and *may* → *might*.

Other modal verbs do not change.
'A walk would be nice.' → *We thought a walk would be nice.*
'You should come back tomorrow.' → *They told me I should go back the next day.*
There is no change with *would, could, should, might, ought to, had better*, and *used to*.

Must can stay the same or change to *had to*.
'I must go now.' → *Sarah said she must go / she had to go.*
When it refers to the future, it can change to *would have to*.
'I must go soon.' → *Sarah said she must go / she had to go / she would have to go soon.*
But when *must* expresses certainty, it usually stays the same, but it can change to *had to*.
'There must be some mistake.' → *I thought there must be / there had to be some mistake.*

Mustn't and *needn't* can stay the same, or they can change.
'You mustn't lose the key.' → *I told Matthew he mustn't lose / he wasn't to lose the key.*
'You needn't wait for us.' → *We said they needn't wait / didn't need to wait / didn't have to wait for us.*

NOTE
a   *Shall* for the future changes to *would*.
     'I shall be making a complaint.' → *He said he would be making a complaint.*
     Shall meaning 'ought to' changes to *should*.
     'What shall I write about?' → *She wondered what she should write about.*
     For *She wondered what to write about*, > 108.

b   There are sometimes other ways we can report a sentence with a modal verb. > 265
     'Would you like to come for tea?' → *They invited me for tea.*

263 Reporting questions

A When we report a question, we use verbs such as *ask, enquire, want to know,* or *wonder.*

Here are some examples of how we report a wh-question.
> *'Where did you have lunch?'* → *I **asked** Elaine **where** she'd had lunch.*
> *'What time does the flight get in?'* → *I'll **enquire what** time the flight gets in.*
> *'Who have you invited?'* → *Peter is **wondering who** we've invited.*
> *'When is the lecture?'* → *Someone **wants to know when** the lecture is.*

When we report a yes/no question, we use *if* or *whether.*
> *'Is there a café in the museum?'* → *Tom was **asking if/whether** there was a café in the museum.*
> *'Has the drug been properly tested?'* → *People **want to know if/whether** the drug has been properly tested.*

NOTE
After *if/whether* we can use *or not* to stress the need for a yes/no answer.
> *They want to know **if/whether** it's safe **or not**.*
> *They want to know **whether or not** it's safe.*
> (BUT NOT *They want to know if or not it's safe.*)

B In an indirect question the word order is usually subject + verb, as in a statement
> *I asked Elaine where **she'd had** lunch.*
> Compare: ***She'd had** lunch in the canteen.*
> *I'll enquire what time **the flight gets** in.*
> Compare: ***The flight gets** in at three o'clock.*
> (NOT *I'll enquire what time does the flight get in.*)

NOTE
We use inversion in the indirect question in sentences like this.
> *Where **did Elaine have** lunch, I was wondering.*
Here the reporting verb comes at the end of the sentence, as a kind of afterthought.

C In an indirect question the tense can change from present to past in the same way as in a statement. > 262
> *'What **do you want**?'* → *The man asked what we **wanted**.*
> *'**Can** we take photos?'* → *Anna wondered if we **could** take photos.*

D We can use an indirect question form after *say, tell,* etc when we are talking about the answer to a question.
> *Did your friend **say when** she would be calling?*
> *I wish you'd **tell** me **whether** you agree.*
> *I haven't been **informed what** time the flight gets in.*

E We can use an indirect question to ask for information. > 17
> ***Could you tell me what** time it is, please?*

264 Reporting orders and requests

A To report an order or request, we usually use *tell/ask* + object + to-infinitive.
'*Please wait outside.*' → *The teacher* **told us to wait** *outside.*
'*I want you to relax.*' → *My therapist is always* **telling me to relax.**
'*Could you help us, please?*' → *We* **asked someone to help** *us.*
'*Would you mind not smoking?*' → *A nurse* **asked Tim not to smoke.**
As well as *tell* and *ask*, there are a number of other verbs we can use such as *command*, *request*, and *urge*. For more details about this pattern, > 105B.

B There are other ways of reporting orders and requests. We can also use *must*, *should*, *have to*, or *be to*.
My therapist is always telling me **I must** / **I should** *relax.*
The teacher said we **had to** *wait* / *we* **were to** *wait outside.*

Sometimes we can report the order or request in the form of an indirect statement or question.
My therapist is always telling me she wants me to relax.
A nurse asked Tim if he would mind not smoking.

C We can use the passive before the to-infinitive.
I'm always **being told** *to relax.*
We **were asked** *to form a queue.*

D We can use *ask* with or without an indirect object. Compare these examples.
'*May I sit down?*' → *Mark* **asked to sit** *down.*
'*Please sit down, Mark.*' → *The boss* **asked Mark to sit** *down.*

We use *ask for* with a noun phrase to report a request to have something.
'*Can I have a receipt, please?*' → *I* **asked** *(the assistant)* **for** *a receipt.*

We can also use the following pattern with *ask for* and a passive to-infinitive.
The villagers are **asking for** *a speed limit* **to be introduced.**

To report a request for permission, we use *ask if/whether*.
'*Do you mind if I smoke?*' → *Tim* **asked if/whether** *he could smoke.*

265 Reporting offers, warnings, apologies, etc

A Introduction

Besides statements, questions, and requests, there are many other kinds of sentence that we can report, such as an offer or an objection. We can often do this by reporting them in the form of an indirect statement or question.
'*I can lend you some money.*' → *Stella* **said** *she could lend me some money.*
'*Why should I have the smallest room?*' → *Emma* **wondered** *why she should have the smallest room.*

But it is often neater to use a verb like *offer* or *object* which makes clear the purpose of what was said.

> *'I can lend you some money.'* → *Stella **offered** to lend me some money.*
> *'Why should I have the smallest room?'* → *Emma **objected** to having the smallest room.*

Sometimes we can use a that-clause with verbs of this kind (> H–I). But after most of these verbs we use a different pattern. Here are some examples.

B A single clause

> *'I'm sorry.'* → *The man **apologized**.*
> *'Thank you very much.'* → *I **thanked** the driver.*
> *'We really must have a sea view.'* → *The guests **insisted** on a sea view.*
> *'Be careful. The path is slippery.'* → *He **warned** us about the path.*

C Verb + to-infinitive

> *'I'm not going to walk all that way.'* → *I **refused to walk**.*
> *'I'll see to the computer for you.'* → *Paul **promised to see** to the computer.*

Verbs we can use in this pattern include *agree, offer, promise, refuse, threaten,* and *volunteer*.

D Verb + object + to-infinitive

> *'You really ought to call in the experts.'* → *Jane **advised us to call** in the experts.*
> *'Would you like to stay at our house?'* → *Some friends have **invited me to stay**.*

Verbs we can use include *advise, invite, remind,* and *warn*.

E Verb + gerund

> *'I'm afraid I've lost the photo.'* → *Luke **admitted losing** the photo.*
> *'Let's move on to a night club.'* → *Someone **suggested moving** on to a club.*

Verbs we can use include *admit, deny,* and *suggest*.

F Verb + preposition + gerund

> *'I'm sorry I was in such a bad mood.'* → *Sarah **apologized for being** in such a bad mood.*
> *'Why do I have to tidy up after everyone?'* → *Lucy **was complaining about having** to tidy up after everyone.*

Prepositional verbs we can use in this pattern include *apologize for, complain about, confess to, insist on,* and *object to*.

G Verb + object + preposition + gerund

'Well done for speaking up like that.' → We **congratulated Chloe on speaking** up.
'Why didn't you take your opportunity?' → Carl's friend **criticized him for not taking** his opportunity.

Prepositional verbs we can use in this pattern include *accuse ... of, blame ...for, congratulate ... on, criticize ... for, praise ...for, thank ... for,* and *warn... about.*

NOTE
We can also use the phrasal verb *tell off.*
  'You really can't spend so much time phoning your friends.' → The boss **told me off for phoning** my friends.

H Verb + that-clause

'Club officials are to wear suits.' → The club **insists** (**that**) the officials wear suits.
'I'm afraid I've lost the photo.' → Luke **admitted** (**that**) he had lost the photo.

Verbs we can use include *admit, advise, agree, complain, confess, deny, forecast, insist, object, predict, promise, recommend, remind, suggest, threaten,* and *warn.*

I Verb + object + that-clause

'Be careful. The path is very slippery.' → He **warned us** (**that**) the path was very slippery.
'Don't worry. There'll be a seat for you.' → They **assured me** (**that**) I would get a seat.

Verbs we can use in this pattern include *assure, promise, reassure, remind,* and *warn.*

Relative clauses

266 Introduction

A This sentence is from a newspaper.

A body recovered from the River Severn at Tewkesbury at the weekend is thought to be a man who disappeared from the Midlands in January, police said yesterday.

The sentence contains a noun phrase (*a man*) + a relative clause (*who disappeared from the Midlands in January*). The relative clause begins with a pronoun (*who*). Compare the use of a personal pronoun and a relative pronoun.

*The body is that of a man. **He** disappeared in January.*
*The body is that of a man **who** disappeared in January.*

A relative clause can also follow a compound pronoun beginning *every-, some-, any-,* or *no-.*

*The body is that of **someone who** disappeared in January.*

These sentences also contain relative clauses.

*We can't ignore the difficulties **which lie ahead**.*
*The tension **that has gripped the city** began to ease yesterday.*
*There are a lot of pupils here **whose parents have divorced**.*

Here the relative clauses begin with *which, that,* and *whose*.

Sometimes we can use a clause without a relative pronoun. > 268E

*They've charged me for a phone call **I didn't make**.*
*The bus **we were waiting for** never came.*

We do not use the personal pronoun that we would need in a main clause.

a man who disappeared in January
(NOT *a man who he disappeared in January*)
the difficulties which lie ahead
(NOT *the difficulties which they lie ahead*)

The relative pronoun (*who, which*) replaces the personal pronoun (*he, they*) as the subject of the clause. The same thing happens when the relative pronoun is the object of the clause.

a body that they found in the river
(NOT *a body that they found it in the river*)

The relative pronoun (*that*) replaces the personal pronoun (*it*). But here we still need the personal pronoun *they* as subject. For more about relative pronouns as subject and object, > 268B.

NOTE
We sometimes use another clause inside a relative clause.
*It is the body of a man who **the police think** was murdered.*
*We can't ignore the difficulties which **we know** lie ahead.*
In the second example we put the clause *we know* inside the relative clause *which lie ahead*.

B Compare a relative clause with other ways of modifying a noun.

An adjective or noun:	*a **dead** body*
	*a **Midlands** man*
A phrase:	*a body **in the river***
	*a man **from the Midlands***
A participle clause:	*a body **recovered from the river*** > 274
	*a man **missing since January*** > 274
A full relative clause:	*a body **which police recovered from the river***
	*a man **who disappeared from the Midlands***

We usually choose a pattern that enables us to express all the relevant information in the shortest way. For example, *a Midlands man* or *a man from the Midlands* would be more usual than *a man who comes from the Midlands*.

C A relative clause usually comes directly after the noun it relates to, but it can come later in the sentence. These two examples are from real conversations.

*I can't think of any good **films** at the moment **that I'd like to see**.*
*The **train** was just pulling out of the station **that we were supposed to connect with**.*

But it is usually best to put the relative clause directly after the noun so that it is clear what the clause relates to.

*At the moment I can't think of any good **films that I'd like to see**.*
*The **train that we were supposed to connect with** was just pulling out of the station.*

D The use of commas with relative clauses

Relative clauses can be divided into those without commas and those which are separated off from the rest of the sentence by one or two commas. Whether we use commas or not (or whether we pause when speaking) makes a difference to the meaning. Look at these two paragraphs.

Without commas	With commas
*Two cars had to swerve to avoid each other. One car left the road and hit a tree, and the other ended up on its roof. The driver of the car **which hit a tree** was killed.*	*A car had to swerve to avoid a horse and left the road. The driver of the car, **which hit a tree**, was killed.*
In speech we do not pause before the clause without commas. The clause tells us which of the two cars is meant. The sentence would be incomplete without the relative clause.	In speech there is a short pause before the clause with commas. The clause adds extra information about the car. It does not identify the car because in this context there is only one. The sentence would still make sense without the relative clause.

Here is another example.

Without commas	With commas
*Cars **which cause pollution** should be banned.* (Some cars cause pollution and should be banned.)	*Cars, **which cause pollution**, should be banned.* (All cars cause pollution and should be banned.)
The clause without commas tells us what kind of cars are meant.	The clause with commas adds information about cars in general.

267 Types of relative clause

Some relative clauses are without commas, and some have commas. > 266D Both these basic kinds of clause have different uses, as shown below. There are three types of relative clause without commas (> A–C) and two types with commas (> D–E)

A Identifying clauses

A relative clause without commas can identify which one we mean.
*Who was that man **who said hello to you**?*
*I can't find the book **that I was reading**.*
The clause *that I was reading* identifies which book we are talking about.

An identifying clause often comes after a noun phrase with *the*.
*I like **the** course that I'm doing now.*
We do not normally use *my, your*, etc.
(NOT ~~I like my course that I'm doing now.~~)

Both *my* and the relative clause identify the course, but we do not need to use more than one of them. But we can use *this, that, these*, or *those*.
*Have you got **those** photos you took at the weekend?*

B Classifying clauses

A relative clause without commas can say what kind of thing we are talking about.
*We're looking for a pub **that serves food**.*
*I hate people **who laugh at their own jokes**.*
The clause *that serves food* describes the kind of pub we mean. A classifying clause often comes after a noun phrase with *a/an* (*a pub*) or a plural noun (*people*).

C Clauses used for emphasis

We can use a relative clause without commas in a pattern with *it + be*. > 38D
> *It's my husband **who** does the cooking, not me.*

Here the pattern emphasizes the phrase *my husband*.

D Adding clauses

We can use a relative clause with a comma to add more information about a noun. > 269
> *I'll be away on 10 June, **which is a Thursday**.*
> *Aristotle was taught by Plato, **who founded the Academy at Athens**.*

The clause *who founded the Academy at Athens* adds extra information about Plato. We can leave out the adding clause and the sentence still makes sense.

NOTE
After a phrase with *a/an*, the question of whether a comma should be used is less clear.
> *My brother had a teddy bear which he used to carry around everywhere.*

This could be written with or without a comma and spoken with or without a pause before *which*.

E Connective clauses

A relative clause with a comma can tell us what happened next.
> *I shouted to the man, **who ran off**.*
> *Jack put a match to the paper, **which instantly caught alight**.*

We use a connective clause to link two actions. In spoken English we often prefer to use two main clauses.
> *I shouted to the man, **and** he ran off.*

268 More details about relative clauses without commas

Here we look at *who, which, that,* and *whom* in relative clauses without commas. (For the use of commas, > 266D.) We also look at relative clauses without a pronoun.

A *Who, which,* and *that*

We use *who* for a person and *which* for something not human such as a thing, an action, or an idea.
> *The **hairdresser who** usually does my hair was ill.*
> *It was a **dream which** came true.*

The difference between *who* and *which* is like that between *he/she* and *it*. But *who* and *which* can go with a plural noun as well as a singular one.
> ***People who** haven't got cars can't shop at these out-of-town stores.*
> *Why import **things which** we could produce ourselves?*

We can use *that* with any noun.

> The **hairdresser that** *usually does my hair was ill.*
> *It was a* **dream that** *came true.*
> *Why import* **things that** *we could produce ourselves?*

With people, *who* is more usual than *that* in writing, but both are used in conversation. After other nouns, both *which* and *that* are possible, but *which* can be a little formal.

That is more usual than *which* after a quantifier or pronoun.

> *There was* **little that** *could be done to help the victims.*
> *I've thought of* **something that** *I'd like for my birthday.*

In this last example we can leave out *that*:

> *something I'd like for my birthday.* > E

> **TIP**
>
> As a general rule, in informal or neutral English use *who* with people and *that* with other nouns. Say *the man who phoned* but *the bus that came*.

B Relative pronoun as subject and object

The relative pronoun can be the subject or the object of the clause.

Subject	Object
Never buy from people **who sell** *out of suitcases.* (**They sell** out of suitcases.) *I've got a computer program* **that does** *the job for me.* (**It does** the job for me.)	*They're the same actors* **that** *we* **saw** *at the theatre.* (We **saw them** at the theatre.) *It's a job* **which** *you could* **do** *yourself quite easily.* (You could **do it**.)
	We often leave out an object relative pronoun. > E *They're the same actors we saw at the theatre.* *It's a job you could do yourself quite easily.*

C *Whom*

We mostly use *who* as a subject relative pronoun, but it can be an object.

> *I met an old friend* **who** *I hadn't seen for years.*

We can also use *whom* as an object pronoun.

> *I met an old friend* **whom** *I hadn't seen for years.*

But *whom* is formal and rather old-fashioned. In everyday speech we usually use *that*, or we leave out the pronoun.

> *I met an old friend* **that** *I hadn't seen for years.*
> *I met an old friend I hadn't seen for years.*

376

We can use *whom* as the object of a preposition (> D). It is also used in adding clauses (> 269).

D Prepositions in a relative clause without commas

Who, which, or *that* can be the object of a preposition.
*I'll introduce you to the man **who** I share a flat **with**.*
(I share a flat **with him**.)
*There are a number of factors **which** we have no control **over**.*
(We have no control **over them**.)
*That's the reality of the world **that** we live **in**.*
(We live **in it**.)
In informal English the preposition comes in the same place as in a main clause. In the first example, compare the relative clause *who I share a flat with* and the main clause *I share a flat with him*. In both clauses *with* follows *share* + object.

We can leave out the relative pronoun. > E
*I'll introduce you to the man **I share a flat with**.*
*There are a number of factors **we have no control over**.*

In more formal English, we can put the preposition before *whom* or *which*.
*The person **with whom** I share a flat seems to have disappeared.*
*Politics is a topic **in which** I have absolutely no interest.*
We cannot leave out *whom* or *which* here, and we cannot use *who* or *that*.

NOTE
For prepositions in a relative clause with commas, > 269C.

E Leaving out the relative pronoun

We can leave out the pronoun from a relative clause without commas when it is **not** the subject of the clause. This happens especially in informal English.
*I need to talk to someone **I can really trust**.*
*That man **you were sitting next to** never said a word.*
*This has been the wettest summer **anyone can remember**.*
*He certainly could not have committed the crime **he was accused of**.*
Here the relative clauses begin with the pronouns *I, you, anyone,* and *he*. But when the relative clause has a noun subject, it is more usual to use a relative pronoun such as *that*.
*Nearby was a rope ladder **that two girls** were climbing up.*

We do not leave out a subject relative pronoun.
*The architect **who** designed this building won an award.*
(NOT ~~The architect designed this building won an award.~~)

269 More details about relative clauses with commas

Here in A–E we look at adding clauses. These are relative clauses which add extra information. (For the use of commas, > 266D.)

A This news item contains a sentence with an adding clause.

*Darren Curry, **who studied at both Brooklands School and Walton College in Chedworthy**, has reason for double celebrations. He was recently awarded a degree in history at Nottingham University and has had his first book published.*

The clause adds information that the reader may not know, although the sentence still makes sense without the adding clause. This kind of clause is rather formal and typical of a written style.

B We separate the adding clause from the main clause, usually with commas.

*Einstein, **who failed his university entrance exam**, went on to discover relativity.*
*Police seized the drugs, **which have a street value of £20 million**.*

We can also use dashes or brackets.

*The new manager is nicer than the old one – **whom the staff disliked**.*
*The cat (**whose name was Molly**) was sitting on the window-sill.*

In an adding clause we use *who*, *whom*, *whose*, or *which* but we do not normally use *that*. And we cannot leave out the relative pronoun from an adding clause.

C A preposition can go before the relative pronoun, or it can stay in the same place as in a main clause.

*Tim's hobby is photography, **on which** he spends most of his spare cash.*
*Tim's hobby is photography, **which** he spends most of his spare cash **on**.*

It is more informal to leave the preposition at the end.

Here are some more examples.

*I lived in a flat in London, **which** I paid a high rent **for**.*
(I paid a high rent **for it**.)
*There was a bomb scare, **as a result of which** the area was evacuated.*
(**As a result of that** the area was evacuated.)

We can also begin an adding relative clause with a preposition + *which* + noun.

*We didn't get home until half past midnight, **by which time** everyone else had gone to bed.*
(**By that time** everyone else had gone to bed.)
*The company may be obliged to lay off staff, **in which case** the unions are sure to object.*
(**In that case** the unions are sure to object.)

Here we use *which* as a determiner before a noun (*which time, which case*).

NOTE
For prepositions in a relative clause without commas, > 268D.

D We can use a quantifier such as *all, one*, or *some* with *of whom/of which* to express a whole or part quantity.

> *The police received a number of bomb warnings, **all of which** turned out to be false alarms.*
> (**All of them** turned out to be false alarms.)
> *At the time of the accident there were two people in the chair lift, **one of whom** was slightly injured.*
> *There are hundreds of TV channels, **some of which** operate 24 hours a day.*

NOTE
In formal English the quantifier sometimes comes after *of whom* or *of which*.
*The company plans to open twelve new outlets, **of which five** will be in the UK.*

E *Which* can relate to a whole clause, not just to a noun.

> *The team has lost again, **which** doesn't surprise me.*
> (**The fact that** the team has lost again doesn't surprise me.)
> *Anna and Matthew spent the whole time arguing, **which** annoyed me.*
> *I get paid a bit more now, **which** means I can afford to run a car.*
> *The men helped carry the furniture indoors, **for which** I was very grateful.*

We cannot use *what* here.

> (NOT *The team has lost again, what doesn't surprise me.*)

For *what* as a relative pronoun, > 272.

F The patterns that we use in adding clauses can also be used in connective clauses to say what happened next.

> *Joshua presented the flowers to Susan, **who burst into tears**.*
> *I dropped a box of eggs, **all of which broke**.*

270 *Whose*

A *Whose* has a possessive meaning.

> *We stopped to help some people **whose car** had broken down.*
> (**Their** car had broken down.)

In a relative clause we use *whose* as a determiner before a noun (*whose car*).

> (NOT *some people whose the car had broken down*)

B *Whose* + noun can be the subject or object of the relative clause.

> *Doctors are people **whose work** is obviously useful.*
> *The prize goes to the contestant **whose performance** TV viewers like best.*

379

It can also be the object of a preposition.

> *I wish to thank all those people **without whose** help I would never have got this far.*
> *My best friend was Martin, **at whose** wedding I had first met my future wife.*
> *The neighbour **whose** dog I'm looking **after** is in Australia.*

We can use *whose* in a clause with commas.

> *The ball fell to Collins, **whose shot** hit the post.*

C *Whose* usually relates to a person: *some **people whose** car had broken down.* But it can relate to other nouns which do not refer directly to people, especially nouns which suggest human activity or organization.

> *It's the poorer **countries whose** exports are earning less money.*
> *I wouldn't fly with an **airline whose** safety record is so bad.*
> *She sang a beautiful **song, whose** sentiments moved the audience.*

Instead of *whose* relating to a thing, we can use the following pattern with *the* + noun + *of which*.

> *She sang a beautiful song, **the sentiments of which** moved the audience.*
> *We are introducing a new system, **the aim of which** is to cut costs.*
> *You should look up any word **the meaning of which** is unclear.*

NOTE
The + noun can sometimes come after *of which*.
> *You should look up any word **of which the meaning** is unclear.*

271 Relative adverbs

A There are relative adverbs *where*, *when*, and *why*.

> *The house **where** I used to live has been knocked down.*
> *Do you remember the time **when** we all went to a night club?*
> *The reason **why** we can sell so cheaply is because we buy in bulk.*

We use *where* after nouns like *place, area, country, house, situation*. We use *when* after nouns like *time, day, moment, period*. We use *why* after *reason*.

NOTE
We can use *where* and *when* without a noun.
> ***Where** I used to live has been knocked down.*
> (= **The place where** I used to live ...)
> *Do you remember **when** we all went to a nightclub?*
> (= ... **the time when** we all went to a nightclub?)

B Instead of a clause with *where*, we can use one of these patterns.

> *The house **in which** I used to live has been knocked down.*
> *The house **(that)** I used to live **in** has been knocked down.*

The pattern with *in which* is rather formal. In informal English *the house I used to live in* is more usual.

Instead of *when* or *why*, we can use this pattern.

> *Do you remember the time (**that**) we all went to a night club?*
> *The reason (**that**) we can sell so cheaply is because we buy in bulk.*

NOTE
After a pronoun ending in -*where*, we can drop the preposition from the end of the clause.
> *This place reminds me of **somewhere** I used to live.*
> *When you're famous, people follow you **everywhere** you go.*

C Clauses with *where* or *when* can be separated off by commas.
> *We walked up to the top of the hill, **where** we got a marvellous view.*
> *I'd rather go next week, **when** I won't be so busy.*

We cannot leave out *where* or *when* here, and we cannot use *that*.

D With the noun *way*, we can use these patterns.
> *I hate the **way in which** these adverts keep popping up on the screen.*
> *I hate the **way that** these adverts keep popping up on the screen.*
> *I hate the **way** these adverts keep popping up on the screen.*

The way in which is more formal.

NOTE
We can also use *how*.
> *I hate **how** these adverts keep popping up on the screen.*

272 The relative pronoun *what*

We can use *what* in this pattern.

> *We'd better write a list of **what** we need to pack.*

(= **the things that** we need to pack)

> *I was going to buy a coat, but I couldn't find **what** I wanted.*

(= **the thing that** I wanted)

But *what* cannot relate to a noun.

(NOT ~~the coat what I wanted~~)

NOTE
We can use *what* in indirect speech. > 263
> *You haven't told me **what** we need to pack.*
We can also use *what* to emphasize part of the sentence. > 38E
> ***What** I wanted was a coat.*

273 *Whoever, whatever,* etc

We can form relative clauses with *whoever, whatever, whichever, wherever,* and *whenever.*

> ***Whoever*** *painted this graffiti ought to clear it up.*
> (= **the person who** painted this graffiti – no matter who it is)
> *I'll spend my money on **whatever** I like.*
> (= **the thing that** I like – no matter what it is)
> ***Wherever*** *I choose for a picnic always turns out to be unsuitable.*
> (= **the place that** I choose - no matter where it is)

We cannot use *who* in this pattern.
> (NOT ~~Who designed this building ought to be shot.~~)

We have to use a noun before the relative pronoun *who.*
> ***The person who*** *designed this building ought to be shot.*

But we can use *what.* > 272
> *I'll spend my money on **what** I like.*

274 Participle relative clauses

A Active participles

We can use an active participle in a shortened relative clause.
> *Who are those people **taking** photos over there?*
> (= those people **who are taking** photos)
> *The official took no notice of the telephone **ringing** on his desk.*
> (= the telephone **that was ringing** on his desk)

The participle can refer to the present (*are taking*) or the past (*was ringing*).

The active participle can refer to a state as well as an action.
> *All the equipment **belonging** to the club was stolen.*
> (= all the equipment **that belongs** to the club)
> *Fans **wanting** to buy tickets started queuing early.*
> (= fans **who wanted** to buy tickets)

We can also use it to report a message.
> *We received a letter **telling** us about the arrangements.*
> *They've put up a sign **warning** of the danger.*

We can sometimes use the active participle for a repeated action.
> *People **travelling** into London every day are used to the hold-ups.*
> (= people **who travel** into London every day)

But we do not normally use the active participle for a single complete action.
> *The man **who escaped** from prison is said to be dangerous.*
> (NOT ~~The man escaping from prison is said to be dangerous.~~)

NOTE
We can use this kind of relative clause in a sentence with *there + be.* > 35F
> ***There were*** *some people **taking** photos.*

B Passive participles

We can use a passive participle in a shortened relative clause.
> *Applications **received** after the deadline cannot be considered.*
> (= applications **which are received** after the deadline)
> *The first British TV commercial, **broadcast** in 1955, was for toothpaste.*
> (= **which was broadcast** in 1955)
> *Police are trying to identify a body **recovered** from the river.*
> (= a body **which has been recovered** from the river)

We can use the passive participle for both single and repeated actions.

NOTE
We can also use a continuous form of the passive participle.
> *Transport policy is the subject **being discussed** in Parliament this afternoon.*

C Word order with participles

We can sometimes put a participle before a noun, like an adjective. > 123
> *We could hear the sound of **running** water.*

We can also put it after the noun in a shortened relative clause.
> *We could hear the sound of water **running** through the pipes.*

When the participle has a phrase of more than one word with it, then it cannot come before the noun.
> (NOT ~~We could hear the sound of through the pipes running water.~~)

275 Infinitive relative clauses

A

Look at this pattern with an adjective and a to-infinitive.
> *Which was the **first** country **to win** the Rugby World Cup?*
> (= the first country **that won** the Rugby World Cup)
> *The **last** person **to leave** will have to turn out the lights.*
> (= the last person **who leaves**)
> *You're the **only** student **to sign** up for the course.*
> (= the only student **who has signed** up for the course)
> *Ronald Reagan was the **oldest** man **to become** US President.*
> (= the oldest man **who became** US President)

We can use a to-infinitive after an ordinal number (*first, second*, etc); after *next* and *last*; after *only*; and after a superlative adjective (e.g. *oldest*).

We can use a passive to-infinitive.
> *The first British monarch **to be filmed** was Queen Victoria.*

B

We can use a to-infinitive in this pattern with a preposition + *which*.
> *This is an ideal location **from which to explore** the Lake District.*
> *I need a piano of my own **on which to practise**.*

This pattern is rather formal. In informal English we can leave out *which* and put the preposition at the end.
> *I need a piano of my own **to practise on**.*

Spelling and pronunciation of word endings

276 The -s/-es ending

A Spelling

To form the regular plural of a noun or the third-person singular of a simple-present verb, we usually add -s.

rooms   games   words   looks   opens

After a sibilant sound we add -es.

kisses   watches   bushes   taxes

But if the word ends in e, we just add -s.

places   supposes   prizes

A few nouns ending in o add -es.

potatoes   tomatoes   heroes   echoes

But most just add -s.

radios   pianos   photos   studios   discos   kilos   zoos

NOTE
Sometimes *y* changes to *i*, e.g. *carry* ➔ *carries*. > 280

B Pronunciation

The -s/-es ending is pronounced /s/ after a voiceless sound, /z/ after a voiced sound, and /ɪz/ or /əz/ after a sibilant.

Voiceless:	*hopes* /ps/, *fits* /ts/, *clocks* /ks/
Voiced:	*cabs* /bz/, *rides* /dz/, *days* /eɪz/, *throws* /əʊz/
Sibilant:	*loses* /zɪz/ or /zəz/, *bridges* /dʒɪz/ or /dʒəz/, *washes*, /ʃɪz/ or /ʃəz/

The possessive form of a noun is pronounced in the same way.

Mike's /ks/   *my teacher's* /əz/   *the boss's* /sɪz/ or /səz/

277 The *-ed/-d* ending

A Spelling

The ed-form of most regular verbs is simply verb + *-ed*.
   *play**ed**   walk**ed**   seem**ed**   offer**ed**   fill**ed***
If the verb ends in *e*, we just add *-d*.
   *mov**ed**   continu**ed**   pleas**ed**   smil**ed***

NOTE
Sometimes we double a consonant before *-ed*, e.g. *stop* ➔ *stopped*. > 279
Sometimes *y* changes to *i*, e.g. *carry* ➔ *carried*. > 280

B Pronunciation

The *-ed/-d* ending is pronounced /t/ after a voiceless sound, /d/ after a
voiced sound, and /ɪd/ after /t/ or /d/.

Voiceless:	*jumped* /pt/, *liked* /kt/, *wished* /ʃt/
Voiced:	*robbed* /bd/, *closed* /zd/, *enjoyed* /ɔɪd/, *allowed* /aʊd/
/t/ or /d/:	*waited* /tɪd/, *expected* /tɪd/, *landed* /dɪd/, *guided* /dɪd/

278 Leaving out *e*

A We often leave out *e* before an ending with another vowel. For example, we
normally leave it out before an ing-form.
   make ➔ *making*   *shine* ➔ *shining*   *use* ➔ *using*
But we keep a double *e* before *ing*.
   see ➔ *seeing*   *agree* ➔ *agreeing*

When we add *-ed*, *-er*, or *-est* to a word ending in *e*, we do not write a double *e*.
   type ➔ *typed*   *late* ➔ *later*   *nice* ➔ *nicest*

B We usually leave out *e* before other endings that start with a vowel,
e.g. *-able*, *-ize*, *-al*.
   advise ➔ *advisable*   *mobile* ➔ *mobilize*   *culture* ➔ *cultural*

But there are exceptions.
   notice ➔ *noticeable*   *courage* ➔ *courageous*
Some words ending in *ce* or *ge* keep the *e* before *a* or *o*.

Some words with *-able* can be spelled either with or without the *e*.
   like ➔ *likeable/likable*   *size* ➔ *sizeable/sizable*

C We do **not** usually leave out *e* before a consonant.
   move ➔ *moves*   *nice* ➔ *nicely*   *care* ➔ *careful*

Exceptions are words ending in *ue*.
   argue ➔ *argument*   *true* ➔ *truly*   *due* ➔ *duly*

NOTE

a   We can keep the *e* in *judgement/judgment* and *acknowledgement/acknowledgment*.

b   We leave out the *e* when we form the adverb from *whole* ➔ *wholly*.

D To form an adverb from an adjective, we normally add *-ly*,
e.g. *quick* ➔ *quickly*. But when an adjective ends in a consonant + *le*, we just
change the *e* to *y*.
>   *simple* ➔ *simply*   *possible* ➔ *possibly*

Note also that when an adjective ends in *-ic*, we add *-ally* to form the adverb.
-ically is pronounced /ɪkli/.
>   *dramatic* ➔ *dramatically*   *idiotic* ➔ *idiotically*
An exception is *public* ➔ *publicly*.

279 The doubling of consonants

A Doubling happens in a one-syllable word that ends with a single vowel and a
single consonant, such as *win, put, sad, plan.*
>   *win* ➔ *winner*   *put* ➔ *putting*   *sad* ➔ *saddest*   *plan* ➔ *planned*
We double the consonant letter before a vowel.

We also double the consonant before *-y*.
>   *fog* ➔ *foggy*   *Tom* ➔ *Tommy*

Compare these two verbs.
>   *tap* /tæp/ ➔ *tapping*
>   *tape* /teɪp/ ➔ *taping*

B We do not double *y, w,* or *x*.
>   *stay* ➔ *staying*   *slow* ➔ *slower*   *fix* ➔ *fixed*
We do not double when there are two consonants at the end of the word.
>   *work* ➔ *working*   *hard* ➔ *harder*
We do not double when there are two vowels.
>   *keep* ➔ *keeping*   *broad* ➔ *broadest*

NOTE

If an adjective ends in *ll*, we just add *y* to form the adverb. We do not add a third *l*.
>   *full* ➔ *fully*   *dull* ➔ *dully*   *shrill* ➔ *shrilly*

C When the word has more than one syllable, then we double the consonant
only if the last syllable is stressed.
>   *for'get* ➔ *for'getting*   *pre'fer* ➔ *pre'ferred*

We do not usually double a consonant in an unstressed syllable.
>   *'open* ➔ *'opening*   *'enter* ➔ *'entered*

But we double the letter *l* in an unstressed syllable.
  travel → *travelled   marvel* → *marvellous   jewel* → *jeweller*
We also double the letter *p* in some verbs.
  handicap → *handicapped   worship* → *worshipping*

NOTE
Americans usually write a single *l* in an unstressed syllable.
  traveled   marvelous   jeweler

280 Consonant + *y*

A When a word ends in a consonant + *y*, we cannot simply add *-s*.
  study → *studies   country* → *countries*
The *y* changes to *ie* before *s*.

Before most other endings, the *y* changes to *i*.
  study → *studied   silly* → *sillier   lucky* → *luckily   happy* → *happiness*

We do not change *y* after a vowel.
  day → *days   buy* → *buyer*
But *pay*, *lay*, and *say* have irregular forms *paid*, *laid*, and *said* /sed/. Note also
day → *daily*.

NOTE
a There are a few exceptions where *y* does not change after a consonant.
    shy → *shyly   sly* → *slyness   dry* → *dryer/drier*
  But *dry* → *dried*.

b We form the possessive in the usual way.
    Singular: *the lady's name*
    Plural: *the ladies' names*

c We do not change *y* when it is part of someone's name.
    Mr and Mrs Grundy → *the Grundys*

B We keep *y* before *i*.
  copy → *copying   hurry* → *hurrying   lobby* → *lobbyist*

We change *ie* to *y* before *-ing*.
  die → *dying   lie* → *lying*

Irregular noun plurals

281 Introduction

Most countable nouns have a regular plural in *-s*/*-es*.
> *hand* → *hands*   *date* → *dates*   *bus* → *buses*

For details of spelling and pronunciation, > 276.
For the plural of compound nouns, > 131B.
For the use of plural nouns, > 131C.

Some nouns have an irregular plural.
> *man* → *men*   *life* → *lives*   *stimulus* → *stimuli*

Irregular plurals are formed in a number of different ways, for example by changing a vowel or consonant sound or by adding an unusual ending.

282 Vowel and consonant changes

A Vowel changes

Some plurals are formed by changing the vowel sound.
> *foot* → *feet*   *goose* → *geese*   *man* → *men*   *mouse* → *mice*
> *tooth* → *teeth*   *woman*/'wʊmən/ → *women* /'wɪmɪn/

NOTE
We also use *men* and *women* in words like *Frenchmen* and *sportswomen*.

B The ending *-en*

There is an old plural form *-en* which has survived in these two nouns.
> *child* /tʃaɪld/ → *children* /'tʃɪldrən/   *ox* → *oxen*

C Consonant changes

With some nouns we change *f* to *v* and add *-s*/*-es*.
> *calf* → *calves*   *half* → *halves*   *knife* → *knives*   *leaf* → *leaves*
> *life* → *lives*   *loaf* → *loaves*   *shelf* → *shelves*   *thief* → *thieves*
> *wife* → *wives*   *wolf* → *wolves*

Some nouns ending in *f* or *fe* are regular, e.g. *beliefs, chiefs, cliffs, safes*. A few can have either form, e.g. *scarf* → *scarfs*/*scarves*.

D Voicing

Some nouns ending in *th* have a regular written plural, but there are two possible pronunciations.
> *path* /pɑ:θ/ → *paths* /pɑ:θs/ or /pɑ:ðz/

The last two sounds of *paths* are often voiced. Other examples are *baths, mouths, truths,* and *youths* (= young people).

Some plurals in *ths* are regular, e.g. *births, deaths, months.* These are pronounced with /θs/.

There is also voicing in the last syllable of *houses.*
    house /haʊs/ → *houses* /ˈhaʊzɪz/

E *Penny, pence,* and *pennies*

When we are talking about an amount of money, we use *pence* as the plural of *penny.*
    *Seventy-five **pence**, please.*

Pennies are individual penny coins.
    *I found an old tin with a lot of **pennies** in it.*

F *Person, persons,* and *people*

Person has two plurals: *persons* and *people.*
    *Authorized **persons** only may enter.*
    *There were lots of **people** on the streets.*
People is more usual and less formal.

A people is a large group such as a nation.
    *The Celts were a tall, fair-skinned **people**.*
    *One day the **peoples** of this world will live in peace.*

283 Nouns which do not change in the plural

Some nouns have the same form in the singular and the plural.
    Singular: *I heard **an aircraft** passing low overhead.*
    Plural: *I kept hearing **aircraft** passing low overhead.*

These nouns are *aircraft, hovercraft, spacecraft,* etc; some animals, e.g. *sheep, deer*; and some kinds of fish, e.g. *cod, salmon.*

For nouns ending in *-s* in both singular and plural, e.g. *one **means** / various **means** of transport,* > 147C.
Some nationality words ending in *-ese* can be singular or plural, e.g. *one **Chinese** / several **Chinese**.*

284 Irregular plural endings

There are a number of foreign words which have come into English, mainly from Latin and Greek, and these have plural endings which are less common in English.

-a /ə/	*criterion* → *criteria* *curriculum* → *curricula*
	medium → *media* *phenomenon* → *phenomena*
-ae /iː/	*formula* → *formulas/formulae*
-is → *-es* /iːz/	*analysis* → *analyses* *crisis* → *crises* *hypothesis* → *hypotheses*
	oasis → *oases* *synthesis* → *syntheses*
-us → *-i* /aɪ/	*cactus* → *cacti* *nucleus* → *nuclei* *stimulus* → *stimuli*
	The plural *cactuses* is also possible.

NOTE

a   Not every noun ending in *on*, *um*, or *us* has an irregular ending.
   electron → *electrons*   *museum* → *museums*   *bonus* → *bonuses*

b   In informal speech, words with the plural ending *-a* are sometimes used as if they were singular.
   *I don't believe what the **media is** telling us.*
   Many people would consider this to be incorrect.

c   The word *data* is the plural of *datum*, which is little used. *Data* is also often used as an uncountable noun.
   *Not enough data **is/are** available.*
   *Users can control how **much data is** sent over the network.*

Irregular verbs

285 Introduction

A

Regular verbs	Irregular verbs
A regular verb can have these endings: -s, -ing, and -ed.	An irregular verb can also have -s and -ing, but we do not simply add -ed.

Base form:	*look*	*play*	Base form:	*steal*	*find*
s-form:	*looks*	*plays*	s-form:	*steals*	*finds*
ing-form:	*looking*	*playing*	ing-form:	*stealing*	*finding*
Past tense:	*looked*	*played*	Past tense:	*stole*	*found*
Past participle:	*looked*	*played*	Past participle:	*stolen*	*found*

The past tense and the past/passive participle are irregular.

Past tense: *Someone* **stole** *the card.*

Past participle: *Who has* **stolen** *the card?*

B Look at these examples.

Regular verb:	*I've painted the wall.*	*I've* **repainted** *the wall.*
Irregular verb:	*I've written the report.*	*I've* **rewritten** *the report.*

A verb form such as *painted* (regular) or *written* (irregular) is not changed by a prefix such as *re-*, *fore-*, or *mis-*. For example, if *tell* is irregular, then so is *foretell*.

286 List of irregular verbs

The more common verbs are in **bold** type.

Base form	Past tense	Past/passive participle
A		
arise /əˈraɪz/	**arose** /əˈrəʊz/	**arisen** /ərˈɪzn/
awake /əˈweɪk/	**awoke** /əˈwəʊk/	**awoken** /əˈwəʊkən/
B		
be /biː/ > 65	**was** /wɒz/, **were** /wɜː(r)/	**been** /biːn/
bear /beə(r)/	**bore** /bɔː(r)/	**borne** /bɔːn/
beat /biːt/	**beat** /biːt/	**beaten** /ˈbiːtn/
become /bɪˈkʌm/	**became** /bɪˈkeɪm/	**become** /bɪˈkʌm/

begin /bɪ'gɪn/	**began** /bɪ'gæn/	**begun** /bɪ'gʌn/
bend /bend/	bent /bent/	bent /bent/
bet /bet/	bet /bet/	bet /bet/
bid /bɪd/ (= offer money)	**bid** /bɪd/	**bid** /bɪd/
bid (= order)/bɪd/	bade /beɪd/	bidden /'bɪdn/
bind /baɪnd/	bound /baʊnd/	bound /baʊnd/
bite /baɪt/	**bite** /baɪt/	**bitten** /'bɪtn/
bleed /bli:d/	bled /bled/	bled /bled/
blow /bləʊ/	**blew** /blu:/	**blown** /bləʊn/
break /breɪk/	**broke** /brəʊk/	**broken** /'brəʊkən/
breed /bri:d/	bred /bred/	bred /bred/
bring /brɪŋ/	**brought** /brɔ:t/	**brought**/brɔ:t/
broadcast /'brɔ:dkɑ:st/	broadcast /'brɔ:dkɑ:st/	broadcast /'brɔ:dkɑ:st/
build /bɪld/	**built** /bɪlt/	**built** /bɪlt/
burn /bɜ:n/	**burnt** /bɜ:nt/	**burnt** /bɜ:nt/
	burned /bɜ:nd/	burned /bɜ:nd/
burst /bɜ:st/	burst /bɜ:st/	burst /bɜ:st/
bust /bʌst/	bust /bʌst/	bust /bʌst/
	busted /'bʌstɪd/	busted /'bʌstɪd/
buy /baɪ/	**bought** /bɔ:t/	**bought**/bɔ:t/
C		
cast /kɑ:st/	**cast** /kɑ:st/	**cast** /kɑ:st/
catch /kætʃ/	**caught** /kɔ:t/	**caught** /kɔ:t/
choose /tʃu:z/	**chose** /tʃəʊz/	**chosen** /'tʃəʊzn/
cling /klɪŋ/	clung /klʌŋ/	clung /klʌŋ/
come /kʌm/	**came** /keɪm/	**come** /kʌm/
cost /kɒst/ > Note a	**cost** /kɒst/	**cost** /kɒst/
creep /kri:p/	crept /krept/	crept /krept/
cut /kʌt/	**cut** /kʌt/	**cut** /kʌt/
D		
deal /di:l/	**dealt** /delt/	**dealt** /delt/
dig /dɪg/	**dug** /dʌg/	**dug** /dʌg/
dive /daɪv/	dived /daɪvd/	dived /daɪvd/
	dove /dəʊv/	
do /du:/ > Note b	**did** /dɪd/	**done** /dʌn/
draw /drɔ:/	**drew** /dru:/	**drawn** /drɔ:n/
dream /dri:m/	**dreamt** /dremt/	**dreamt** /dremt/
	dreamed /dri:md/	**dreamed** /dri:md/
drink /drɪŋk/	**drank** /dræŋk/	**drunk** /drʌŋk/
drive /draɪv/	**drove** /drəʊv/	**driven** /'drɪvn/
dwell /dwel/	dwelt /dwelt/	dwelt /dwelt/
E		
eat /i:t/	**ate** /et/	**eaten** /'i:tn/
F		
fall /fɔ:l/	**fell** /fel/	**fallen** /'fɔ:lən/
feed /fi:d/	**fed** /fed/	**fed** /fed/
feel /fi:l/	**felt** /felt/	**felt** /felt/
fight /faɪt/	**fought** /fɔ:t/	**fought** /fɔ:t/

find /faɪnd/	**found** /faʊnd/	**found** /faʊnd/
fit /fɪt/ > Note c	**fitted** /ˈfɪtɪd/	**fitted** /ˈfɪtɪd/
	fit /fɪt/	**fit** /fɪt/
flee /fliː/	fled /fled/	fled /fled/
fling /flɪŋ/	flung /flʌŋ/	flung /flʌŋ/
fly /flaɪ/	**flew** /fluː/	**flown** /fləʊn/
forbid /fəˈbɪd/	forbade /fəˈbeɪd/	forbidden /fəˈbɪdn/
forecast /ˈfɔːkɑːst/	forecast /ˈfɔːkɑːst/	forecast /ˈfɔːkɑːst/
forget /fəˈget/	**forgot** /fəˈgɒt/	**forgotten** /fəˈgɒtn/
forgive /fəˈgɪv/	**forgave** /fəˈgeɪv/	**forgiven** /fəˈgɪvn/
forsake /fəˈseɪk/	forsook /fəˈsʊk/	forsaken /fəˈseɪkən/
freeze /friːz/	froze /frəʊz/	frozen /ˈfrəʊzn/
G		
get /get/	**got** /gɒt/	**got** /gɒt/
		gotten /ˈgɒtn/ > Note d
give /gɪv/	**gave** /geɪv/	**given** /ˈgɪvn/
go /gəʊ/ > Note e	**went** /went/	**gone** /gɒn/ > Note f
grind /graɪnd/	ground /graʊnd/	ground /graʊnd/
grow /grəʊ/	**grew** /gruː/	**grown** /grəʊn/
H		
hang /hæŋ/	**hung** /hʌŋ/	**hung** /hʌŋ/
	hanged /hæŋd/	**hanged** /hæŋd/ > Note g
have /hæv/ > Note h	**had** /hæd/	**had** /hæd/
hear /hiːə(r)/	**heard** /hɜːd/	**heard** /hɜːd/
hide /haɪd/	**hid** /hɪd/	**hidden** /ˈhɪdn/
hit /hɪt/	**hit** /hɪt/	**hit** /hɪt/
hold /həʊld/	**held** /held/	**held** /held/
hurt /hɜːt/	**hurt** /hɜːt/	**hurt** /hɜːt/
K		
keep /kiːp/	**kept** /kept/	**kept** /kept/
kneel /niːl/	knelt /nelt/	knelt /nelt/
	kneeled /niːld/	kneeled /niːld/
knit /nɪt/	knit /nɪt/	knit /nɪt/
	knitted /ˈnɪtɪd/	knitted /ˈnɪtɪd/
know /nəʊ/	**knew** /njuː/	**known** /nəʊn/
L		
lay /leɪ/ > Note i	**laid** /leɪd/	**laid** /leɪd/
lead /liːd/	**led** /led/	**led** /led/
lean /liːn/	leant /lent/	leant /lent/
	leaned /liːnd/	leaned /liːnd/
leap /liːp/	leapt /lept/	leapt /lept/
	leaped /lept/	leaped /lept/
learn /lɜːn/	**learnt** /lɜːnt/	**learnt** /lɜːnt/
	learned /lɜːnd/	**learned** /lɜːnd/
leave /liːv/	**left** /left/	**left** /left/
lend /lend/	**lent** /lent/	**lent** /lent/
let /let/	**let** /let/	**let** /let/
lie /laɪ/ > Note i	**lay** /leɪ/	**lain** /leɪn/

Irregular verbs

light /laɪt/   lit /lɪt/   lit /lɪt/
     lighted /'laɪtɪd/   lighted /'laɪtɪd/

lose /lu:z/   lost /lɒst/   lost /lɒst/

M

make /meɪk/   made /meɪd/   made /meɪd/

mean /mi:n/   meant /ment/   meant /ment/

meet /mi:t/   met /met/   met /met/

mistake /mɪs'teɪk/   mistook /mɪs'tʊk/   mistaken /mɪs'teɪkən/

mow /məʊ/   mowed /məʊd/   mown /məʊn/
     mowed /məʊd/

P

pay /peɪ/   paid /peɪd/   paid /peɪd/

put /pʊt/   put /pʊt/   put /pʊt/

Q

quit /kwɪt/   quit /kwɪt/   quit /kwɪt/
     quitted /'kwɪtɪd/   quitted /'kwɪtɪd/

R

read /ri:d/   read /red/   read /red/

rid /rɪd/   rid /rɪd/   rid /rɪd/

ride /raɪd/   rode /rəʊd/   ridden /'rɪdn/

ring /rɪŋ/   rang /ræŋ/   rung /rʌŋ/

rise /raɪz/   rose /rəʊz/   risen /'rɪzn/

run /rʌn/   ran /ræn/   run /rʌn/

S

saw /sɔ:/   sawed /sɔ:d/   sawn /sɔ:n/
     sawed /sɔ:d/

say /seɪ/ > Note j   said /sed/   said /sed/

see /si:/   saw /sɔ:/   seen /si:n/

seek /si:k/   sought /sɔ:t/   sought /sɔ:t/

sell /sel/   sold /səʊld/   sold /səʊld/

send /send/   sent /sent/   sent /sent/

set /set/   set /set/   set /set/

sew /səʊ/   sewed /səʊd/   sewn /səʊn/
     sewed /səʊd/

shake /ʃeɪk/   shook /ʃʊk/   shaken /'ʃeɪkən/

shed /ʃed/   shed /ʃed/   shed /ʃed/

shine /ʃaɪn/   shone /ʃɒn/   shone /ʃɒn/
     shined /ʃaɪnd/   shined /ʃaɪnd/ > Note k

shoot /ʃu:t/   shot /ʃɒt/   shot /ʃɒt/

show /ʃəʊ/   showed /ʃəʊd/   shown /ʃəʊn/
     showed /ʃəʊd/

shrink /ʃrɪŋk/   shrank /ʃræŋk/   shrunk /ʃrʌŋk/
     shrunk /ʃrʌŋk/

shut /ʃʌt/   shut /ʃʌt/   shut /ʃʌt/

sing /sɪŋ/   sang /sæŋ/   sung /sʌŋ/

sink /sɪŋk/   sank /sæŋk/   sunk /sʌŋk/

sit /sɪt/   sat /sæt/   sat /sæt/

slay /sleɪ/   slew /slu:/   slain /sleɪn/

sleep /sli:p/ · slept /slept/ · slept /slept/
slide /slaɪd/ · slid /slɪd/ · slid /slɪd/
sling /slɪŋ/ · slung /slʌŋ/ · slung /slʌŋ/
slink /slɪŋk/ · slunk /slʌŋk/ · slunk /slʌŋk/
slit /slɪt/ · slit /slɪt/ · slit /slɪt/
smell /smel/ · smelt /smelt/ · smelt /smelt/
· smelled /smeld/ · smelled /smeld/
sow /səʊ/ · sowed /səʊd/ · sown /səʊn/
· · sowed /səʊd/

speak /spi:k/ · **spoke** /spəʊk/ · **spoken** /'spəʊkən/
speed /spi:d/ > Note l · sped /sped/ · sped /sped/
· speeded /'spi:dɪd/ · speeded /'spi:dɪd/
spell /spel/ · spelt /spelt/ · spelt /spelt/
· spelled /speld/ · spelled /speld/
spend /spend/ · **spent** /spent/ · **spent** /spent/
spill /spɪl/ · spilt /spɪlt/ · spilt /spɪlt/
· spilled /spɪld/ · spilled /spɪld/
spin /spɪn/ · spun /spʌn/ · spun /spʌn/
spit /spɪt/ · spat /spæt/ · spat /spæt/
split /splɪt/ · **split** /splɪt/ · **split** /splɪt/
spoil /spɔɪl/ · spoilt /spɔɪlt/ · spoilt /spɔɪlt/
· spoiled /spɔɪld/ · spoiled /spɔɪld/

spread /spred/ · **spread** /spred/ · **spread** /spred/
spring /sprɪŋ/ · sprang /spræŋ/ · sprung /sprʌŋ/
stand /stænd/ · **stood** /stʊd/ · **stood** /stʊd/
steal /sti:l/ · **stole** /stəʊl/ · **stolen** /'stəʊlən/
stick /stɪk/ · **stuck** /stʌk/ · **stuck** /stʌk/
sting /stɪŋ/ · stung /stʌŋ/ · stung /stʌŋ/
stink /stɪŋk/ · stank /stæŋk/ · stunk /stʌŋk/
stride /straɪd/ · strode /strəʊd/ · stridden /'strɪdn/
strike /straɪk/ · **struck** /strʌk/ · **struck** /strʌk/
string /strɪŋ/ · strung /strʌŋ/ · strung /strʌŋ/
strive /straɪv/ · strove /strəʊv/ · striven /'strɪvən/
swear /sweə(r)/ · **swore** /swɔ:(r)/ · **sworn** /swɔ:n/
sweep /swi:p/ · swept /swept/ · swept /swept/
swell /swel/ · swelled /sweld/ · swelled /sweld/
· · swollen /'swəʊlən/
swim /swɪm/ · swam /swæm/ · swum /swʌm/
swing /swɪŋ/ · swung /swʌŋ/ · swung /swʌŋ/

T
take /teɪk/ · **took** /tʊk/ · **taken** /'teɪkən/
teach /ti:tʃ/ · **taught** /tɔ:t/ · **taught** /tɔ:t/
tear /teə(r)/ · **tore** /tɔ:(r)/ · **torn** /tɔ:n/
tell /tel/ · **told** /təʊld/ · **told** /təʊld/
think /θɪŋk/ · **thought** /θɔ:t/ · **thought** /θɔ:t/
thrive /θraɪv/ · thrived /θraɪvd/ · thrived /θraɪvd/
· throve /θrəʊv/ · thriven /'θrɪvn/
throw /θrəʊ/ · **threw** /θru:/ · **thrown** /θrəʊn/

Irregular verbs

thrust /θrʌst/	thrust /θrʌst/	thrust /θrʌst/
tread /tred/	trod /trɒd/	trodden /'trɒdn/
U		
understand /ʌndə'stænd/	**understood** /ʌndə'stʊd/	**understood** /ʌndə'stʊd/
upset /ʌp'set/	upset /ʌp'set/	upset /ʌp'set/
W		
wake /weɪk/	woke /wəʊk/	woken /'wəʊkən/
wear /weə:(r)/	**wore** /wɔ:(r)/	**worn** /wɔ:n/
weave /wi:v/	wove /wəʊv/	woven /'wəʊvn/
weep /wi:p/	wept /wept/	wept /wept/
wet /wet/	wet /wet/	wet /wet/
	wetted /'wetɪd/	wetted /'wetɪd/
win /wɪn/	**won** /wʌn/	**won** /wʌn/
wind /waɪnd/	**wound** /waʊnd/	**wound** /waʊnd/
withdraw /wɪð'drɔ:/	**withdrew** /wɪð'dru:/	**withdrawn** /wɪð'drɔ:n/
wring /rɪŋ/	wrung /rʌŋ/	wrung /rʌŋ/
write /raɪt/	**wrote** /rəʊt/	**written** /'rɪtn/

NOTE

a *Cost* is regular when it means 'estimate the cost'.
> *We've **costed** the project.*

b The third person singular of the simple present of *do* is *does* /dʌz/.

c *Fit* is usually regular in Britain but irregular in the US.

d *Gotten* is used in some contexts in American English. *Have gotten* means 'have become'.
> *The pain's gotten a lot worse.*

e The third person singular of the simple present of *go* is *goes* /gəʊz/.

f For *gone to* and *been to*, > 65D.

g We use *hanged* only to talk about hanging a person.

h The third person singular of the present tense of *have* is *has* /hæz/.

i *Lay* (past tense *laid*) means 'put something somewhere'.
> *They **laid** the plans on the dining-room table.*
> *Lie* (past tense *lay*) means 'be horizontal' or 'be in a certain place'.
> *They **lay** in bed half the morning.*
> *Lie* meaning 'tell an untruth' is regular.
> *He **lied** to the police about his movements.*

j The third person singular of the present tense of *say* is *says* /sez/.

k *Shined* usually means 'polished'. We say *I've **shined** my shoes*, but *The sun **shone***.

l *Sped* usually expresses movement.
> *The driver jumped in the car and **sped** off.*
> But we say *speeded up* (= went faster).
> *Once on the motorway, we soon **speeded** up.*

m Alternative forms such as *burned*/*burnt* and *learned*/*learnt* are both possible in British English. But the irregular forms such as *burnt* and *learnt* are less usual in America.

287 Special participle forms

Compare these sentences.

Have + participle: *A ship had **sunk** off the coast a century before.*

Participle + noun: *We heard stories of **sunken** ships and hidden treasure.*
Sink has a past participle *sunk*, which is used to form perfect tenses (*had sunk*). It also has a special form *sunken* that is mostly used before a noun (*a sunken ship, a sunken garden*) or to talk about a person's appearance.

*He had **sunken** eyes./His eyes were **sunken**.*

Here are some more examples of verbs which have two different participle forms.

bless
*Fortunately the event was **blessed** with good weather.* /blest/
*When the rain came, it was a **blessed** relief.* /'blesɪd/

drink
*The men had **drunk** too much.*
*There was a **drunken** argument.*

learn
*I've **learned** something useful from the lecture.* /lɜːnd/
*The king loved the company of wise and **learned** men.* /'lɜːnɪd/

melt
*The ice had **melted**.*
*The **molten** metal is poured into a mould.*

prove
*The technology has **proved** to be reliable.*
*We are using **proven** technology.* /'prəʊvən/ or /'pruːvən/

Weak forms and short forms

288 Introduction

When we are speaking slowly and deliberately, or when we give extra emphasis to a word, then we use the strong form of the word.

I ᴀᴍ sorry.

ᴀᴍ = /æm/

In writing we use the full form *am* to represent this pronunciation.

In speech we often join *I* and *am* together and use the weak form.

I'm sorry.

'm = /m/

In writing we can use the short form *'m* to represent this pronunciation.

	Strong	Weak
Spoken	/æm/	/m/
	Full	Short
Written	*am*	*'m*

A number of grammatical words have weak forms, such as auxiliary verbs, pronouns, and prepositions, e.g. *have, you, of.* Words with short forms are auxiliary verbs and *not.* For lists of the forms, > 289–290.

289 Weak forms → Audio

A Some grammatical words have weak forms in unstressed syllables.

We've finished for the moment.

Here *'ve* = /v/ and *for* = /fə(r)/.

But when such words are stressed, we use strong forms.

*Have you finished? ~ Yes, we **have**.*

Here *have* = /hæv/. A verb in a short answer is stressed.

In this example *for* is stressed.

What are you looking for?

Here *for* = /fɔː/. A preposition at the end of a question is often stressed.

We also use strong forms when speaking slowly, deliberately, or emphatically. > 288

B These are the main weak forms and their pronunciation.

a /ə/	*me* /mi/
am /əm/ or /m/	*must* /məst/ or /məs/
an /ən/	*not* /nt/
and /ənd/, /ən/, or /n/	*of* /əv/ or /v/
are /ə(r)/	*shall* /ʃəl/ or /ʃl/
as /əz/	*she* /ʃi/
at /ət/	*should* /ʃəd/ or /ʃd/
be /bi/	*some* /səm/ or /sm/> 172D
been /bɪn/	*than* /ðən/
can /kən/ or /kn/	*that* /ðət/ > Note
could /kəd/	*the* /ðə/ or /ði/ > 151
do /du/ or /də/	*them* /ðəm/ or /əm/
for /fə(r)/	*there* /ðə(r)/ > 35A Note
from /frəm/	*to* /tʊ/ or /tə/
had /həd/, /əd/, or /d/	*was* /wəz/
has /həz/, /əz/, or /z/	*we* /wi/
have /həv/, /əv/, or /v/	*were* /wə(r)/
he /hi/ or /i/	*will* /l/
her /hə(r)/ or /ə(r)/	*would* /wəd/, /əd/, or /d/
him /ɪm/	*you* /jʊ/ or /jə(r)/
his /ɪz/	*your* /jə(r)/
is /z/	

NOTE

That can have a weak form when it is a conjunction or relative pronoun.
I know **that** / ðət / it's true.
As a demonstrative, it does not have a weak form.
I've read **that** / ðæt / book.

290 Short forms

A We often use short forms in informal writing, such as in this advertisement.
*Fit a gas wall heater and you'll stop shivering. It'll warm up your bathroom so quickly you **won't** need a towel. It fits snugly and safely on the wall. And, because it's gas, it's easy to control and very economical.*

When writing a short form, we miss out part of a word and use an apostrophe instead. We say *it's* instead of *it is*. We do not leave a space before the apostrophe.

The short form corresponds to the spoken weak form: /ɪtz/ instead of /ɪt ɪz/. We use short forms in informal writing and to represent speech – in a filmscript or play, for example. Full forms are used in more formal writing.

We cannot use a short form of a verb when it would be stressed in speech.

*Is gas easy to use? ∼ Of course it **is**.*

But we can use unstressed *n't* at the end of a sentence.

*Is gas expensive? ∼ No, it **isn't**.*

B These are the main short forms.

Short form	Long form		
aren't	are not	*she's*	she is/she has
can't	cannot	*shouldn't*	should not
couldn't	could not	*that's*	that is/that has
daren't	dare not > 83	*there'd*	there had/there would > 35
didn't	did not	*there'll*	there will > 35
doesn't	does not	*there's*	there is/there has > 35
don't	do not	*they'd*	they had/they would
hadn't	had not	*they'll*	they will
hasn't	has not	*they're*	they are
haven't	have not	*they've*	they have
he'd	he had/he would	*wasn't*	was not
he'll	he will	*we'd*	we had/we would
he's	he is/he has	*we'll*	we will/we shall
here's	here is > 34C	*we're*	we are
how's	how is/how has	*we've*	we have
I'd	I had/I would	*weren't*	were not
I'll	I will/I shall	*what'll*	what will
I'm	I am	*what's*	what is/what has
I've	I have	*when's*	when is
isn't	is not	*where's*	where is/where has
it'll	it will	*who'd*	who had/who would
it's	it is/it has	*who'll*	who will
let's	let us > 11F	*who's*	who is/who has
mightn't	might not	*won't*	will not
mustn't	must not	*wouldn't*	would not
needn't	need not	*you'd*	you had/you would
oughtn't	ought not	*you'll*	you will
shan't	shall not	*you're*	you are
she'd	she had/she would	*you've*	you have
she'll	she will		

We can also use a short form with a noun.

If your bathroom's cold, a gas heater'll soon warm it up.

But this is less common than with a pronoun.

TIP

Do not confuse the short form *it's* with the possessive *its*. > 164B

*It's now that the tree starts to lose **its** leaves.*

NOTE
There is a non-standard short form *ain't*.
That ain't right. (= That isn't right.)
Ain't can mean 'am not', 'is not', 'are not', 'has not', or 'have not'.

C The form *'s* can mean *is* or *has*.
It's a big house. It's got five bedrooms.
(= It **is** a big house. It **has** got five bedrooms.)

And the form *'d* can mean *had* or *would*.
If you'd thought about it, you'd have realized.
(= If you **had** thought about it, you **would** have realized.)

There are two different ways we can shorten *is not* and *are not*.
It is not working. = *It isn't working./It's not working.*
We are not ready. = *We aren't ready./We're not ready.*
Both short forms are possible, although *it's not* and *we're not* are
more frequent.

There are also two possibilities with *will, have, has,* and *had.*
It will not take long. = *It won't take long./It'll not take long.*
You have not signed it. = *You haven't signed it./You've not signed it.*
Won't, haven't, hasn't, and *hadn't* are more usual than *'ll not, 've not,* etc.

NOTE
In Standard English *I am not* has only one short form: *I'm not.*

Glossary

abstract noun An abstract noun refers to an idea or a quality, something that we cannot see or touch, e.g. *science, excitement, strength*. The opposite is a concrete noun.

action verb a verb that refers to something happening, e.g. *do, walk, eat, speak*. ▶ 51A The opposite is a state verb.

active An active sentence has a verb like *stole* or *are cleaning*. *Someone **stole** my coat* and *We're **cleaning** the windows* are active, but *My coat was stolen* and *The windows are being cleaned* are passive. ▶ 86

active participle (or **present participle**) the ing-form of a verb used after *be* in the continuous, e.g. *I was **working***, and in other structures, e.g. *He lay on the bed **reading**.* ▶ 121

adding relative clause (or **non-defining/non-identifying relative clause**) a relative clause with commas around it that adds extra information, e.g. *Bernard, **who was feeling unwell**, left early*, but which does not identify which one is meant. ▶ 269

adjective An adjective is a word like *big, new, special*, or *famous*, often used to describe something. ▶ 181 It can come before a noun, e.g. *a **nice** day*, or after *be*, e.g. *That's **nice**.* ▶ 182

adjective phrase An adjective phrase is either an adjective on its own, e.g. *tall, hopeful*, or an adjective with an adverb of degree, e.g. *quite tall, very hopeful*.

adverb In the sentence *The time passed **slowly***, the word *slowly* is an adverb. Adverbs are words like *easily, there, sometimes, quite*, and *possibly*. They express ideas such as how, when or where something happens, or how true something is.

adverbial The adverb *late*, the phrase *in a hurry*, and the clause *because I was cold* all function as adverbials in these sentences: *The show started **late**; We did everything **in a hurry**; I put a coat on **because I was cold***. Adverbials express ideas such as when, how, or why something happens. ▶ 189

adverbial clause In the sentence *I'll phone you **when I get home***, the clause *when I get home* functions as an adverbial. ▶ 237 Compare *I'll phone you **later**.*

adverb particle see particle

adverb phrase An adverb phrase is either an adverb on its own, e.g. *carefully, often*, or an adverb which is modified by an adverb of degree, e.g. *very carefully, more often*.

affirmative see positive

agent The agent is who or what is doing the action. In an active sentence it is usually the subject, e.g. ***Tom** won the game*. In a passive sentence there is sometimes an agent in a phrase with *by*, e.g. *The game was won by **Tom**.*

agreement (or **concord**) the choice of the correct singular or plural verb form after a subject, e.g. *My ear **hurts***, but *My ears **hurt**.*

apostrophe In the phrase *my friend's flat*, there is an apostrophe between *friend* and *-s*. *Friend's* is the possessive form of the noun *friend*. ▶ 132 We also use an apostrophe in a short form, e.g. *I'm, you're*.

apposition In sentences such as ***The next day, Thursday**, was fine and dry* and ***My cousin Maria** gave it to me*, the two noun phrases are in apposition; they both have the same grammatical function and both mean the same thing.

article *A/an* and *the*. *A/an* is the indefinite article, and *the* is the definite article. ▶ 150

aspect Aspects are elements in the tense system which can combine with the present or the past. A verb can have continuous aspect (e.g. *is **walking**, was **looking***), perfect aspect (e.g. *has **walked**, had **looked***) or both (e.g. *have been **waiting**).

attributive An adjective in attributive position is before a noun, e.g. *a **cold** day*. But in the sentence *The day was **cold***, the adjective is in **predicative** position.

auxiliary verb The auxiliary verbs are *be*, *have*, and *do* (▶ 64) and the modal verbs, also called 'modal auxiliary verbs', such as *can*, *must*, and *should* (▶ 70). An auxiliary verb can combine with an ordinary verb, e.g. *I **am** trying, we **have** finished, **did** you remember?, he **can** swim, we **must** hurry.*

bare infinitive an infinitive without *to*, e.g. *I might **go** out, they made us **wait**.* ▶ 110

base form The base form of a verb is the form without an ending. We use it in the imperative, e.g. *Please **stop** it*, in the present simple, e.g. *I **get** off here*, or as a bare infinitive, e.g. *I heard you **come** in.*

capital letter A capital letter is a big letter, e.g. A, B, C, used at the beginning of a sentence or a name.

cardinal number a number such as *one, two, three*; compare ordinal number

causative The sentence *I **had** my hair cut* shows the causative use of *have* because it means 'I caused someone to cut my hair.'

classify When we classify something, we say what kind it is, e.g. *a **sports** car* (a kind of car), *a machine **that washes bottles*** (a kind of machine).

classifying relative clause a relative clause that tells us what kind is meant, e.g. *software **that protects your computer against viruses**.* ▶ 267B

clause A clause usually has a subject and a verb. The sentence *We stayed at home* is a single main clause. The sentence *We stayed at home because it rained* has two clauses. *We stayed at home* is the main clause, and *because it rained* is the sub-clause. A sub-clause with an infinitive or ing-form often has no subject, e.g. *I went out **to get some fresh air**; I can't help **worrying**.* ▶ 227

cleft sentence a structure with *it* or *what* used to emphasize part of the sentence, e.g. *It was yesterday I phoned you; What I saw was definitely a ghost.* ▶ 38D–E

collective noun see group noun

colon We can use a colon before an explanation, e.g. *I came by coach: it's much cheaper than the train.*

comma We use commas in a list, e.g. *tall, dark, and handsome*, or to separate off a clause or phrase, e.g. *The following weekend, something strange happened.*

comment adverbial an adverbial that makes a comment on what we say, e.g. *Incredibly, we slept through the noise.* ▶ 201

common noun see proper noun

comparative a form with *-er* or *more* used to make a comparison, e.g. *older, more famous, more efficiently.* ▶ 203–204

comparison Comparison involves forms used to compare one thing with another, e.g. *older, more useful, longest, most easily, as safe as.* ▶ 203–207

complement A complement is a noun phrase, e.g. *the boss*, or an adjective phrase, e.g. *unhappy*, in a sentence such as *You're **the boss*** or *He looked **unhappy**.* These are 'subject complements'; they follow a linking verb such as *be* and they relate to the subject of the sentence (*you, he*). See also object complement.

compound a word made up of other words, e.g. *bookshop* (book + shop), *good-looking* (good + looking), *something* (some + thing).

concession A clause of concession (or **concessive clause**) has a conjunction, e.g. *although, despite*, or *even though*: ***Although it was warm**, I was shivering.*

concord see agreement

concrete noun A concrete noun refers to something we can see or touch, e.g. *bottle, grass, man, shop.* The opposite is an **abstract noun.**

conditional clause a clause expressing a condition, e.g. ***If you need a lift**, I can give you one. We'd have won **if we'd kept our cool**.* ▶ 243; see also type 1/2/3 conditional

conditional form/tense A verb form with *would* such as *would go* or *would take* is sometimes called a conditional form or conditional tense.

conditional sentence a sentence with a conditional clause, usually a clause with *if*, e.g. *If we're late, we'll be in trouble.* ▶ 243

conjunction a word such as *and*, *but*, *because*, *when*, or *that*, which links two clauses, e.g. *I believe **that** it's true.*

connective clause a type of relative clause that says what happens next, e.g. *I bumped into a young woman, **who swore at me.*** ▶ 267E

connector A connector is a word used to link two clauses or sentences. It can be a conjunction, e.g. *You're crazy, **but** I like you*, or a linking adverbial, e.g. *I can't find the map. **Anyway**, I know the way.*

consonant see vowel

context The context of a sentence is the words that come before it or the situation in which it occurs.

continuous (or **progressive**) a verb form with *be* and an active participle, e.g. *The film **is starting** now; We've **been waiting** for you; I expect to **be working.***

continuous infinitive A continuous to-infinitive is *to be* + ing-form, e.g. *I'm supposed **to be relaxing.*** The infinitive is sometimes without *to*, e.g. *I should **be relaxing.***

contraction see short form

co-ordinate clause Two clauses linked by a conjunction such as *and*, *but*, or *or* are co-ordinate clauses, e.g. ***It was ten past nine** and I was late.* ▶ 227A
A co-ordinate clause is not part of another clause. See also main clause.

copular verb see linking verb

countable noun A countable noun can be either singular or plural and can be used with *a/an*, e.g. *a **bag**, three **hours**, some **trees.*** ▶ 137 See also uncountable noun.

dangling participle see hanging participle

dash We can use a dash to separate off part of a sentence, e.g. *I almost decided to quit – but I didn't.*

declarative A declarative sentence has the form of a statement, with the subject before the verb.

defining relative clause see identifying relative clause

definite *My friend Jack* is a definite person: I know exactly who I mean. *Someone* is indefinite because it doesn't say which person is meant.

definite article the word *the* ▶ 150

degree An adverb of degree is a word like *very*, *quite*, or *hardly*. ▶ 196

demonstrative *This*, *that*, *these*, and *those* are demonstrative determiners or pronouns. ▶ 165

dependent clause same as **sub-clause**; see main clause

determiner a word that can come before a noun to form a noun phrase, e.g. ***a** photo, **the** result, **my** old friend, **this** week.*

direct object see object

direct speech We use direct speech when we report someone's words by quoting them, e.g. *She said, '**I never want to see you again.'*** ▶ 258 See also indirect speech.

echo question a question which asks for information to be repeated, e.g. *She's gone to Vladivostock. ∼ **Where has she gone?*** ▶ 21A

echo tag (or **reply question**) a short question form expressing interest, e.g. *I play chess. ∼ Oh, **do you?*** ▶ 21B

ellipsis leaving out words when the meaning is clear without them, e.g. *I haven't seen the film, but Kate has*, meaning *but Kate has seen the film.*

emphasis/emphasize/emphatic Emphasis is drawing special attention to a word or phrase and making it more important. ▶ 38 We can use extra stress, special word order, or a special structure, e.g. *What he did was **run away.***

emphatic form We use the emphatic form of a verb to emphasize a positive or a negative, e.g. *I DID remind you. We CAN'T go back now.* ▶ 38C

emphatic pronoun a pronoun such as *myself* or *themselves* used to emphasize a noun phrase, e.g. *The Queen **herself** visited the scene.* ▶ 177E

emphatic stress speaking a word with extra force in order to draw attention to it, e.g. *I said LEFT, not right.* ▶ 38B

empty subject In the sentence ***It** was raining, it* is an empty subject. In the sentence ***There** was an argument, there* is an empty subject. It has no real meaning, but we use it because the sentence needs a subject. ▶ 35–36

ending The word *dogs* has the plural ending *-s*; the word *walking* has the ending *-ing*.

end position When an adverbial comes at the end of a clause, after a verb or a verb + object, it is in end position, e.g. *He repeated the words **slowly**.* ▶ 190F

exception see rule

exclamation a special structure with *how* or *what*, e.g. *What a waste!* or any sentence spoken with emphasis and feeling, e.g. *Quick!* ▶ 12

exclamation mark We write an exclamation mark at the end of an exclamation, e.g. *How awful! Look out!*

finite A finite verb is one that is in the present or past tense, e.g. *goes, waited, was coming, have seen*, or one that has a modal verb, e.g. *will be, can carry*. It can be the verb in a simple one-clause sentence, e.g. *She **goes** to college*, called a finite clause. A non-finite verb is an infinitive, gerund or participle, e.g. *She wants **to go** to college. I saw her **going** to college*; The clauses *to go to college* and *going to college* are non-finite clauses.

first conditional see type 1 conditional

first person see person

formal We speak in a more formal style to strangers than we do to our friends. We use formal language to be polite, or on official occasions. A business letter is more formal than a letter to a friend. *I am afraid I have no information* is more formal than *Sorry, I don't know.*

frequency An adverbial of frequency tells us how often, e.g. *always, usually, sometimes.* ▶ 195

fronting putting a word or phrase at the beginning of a clause to make it more prominent, e.g. ***Very carefully** they laid the patient on a stretcher.* ▶ 34

front position When an adverbial comes at the beginning of a clause, it is in front position, e.g. ***Luckily** we were just in time.* ▶ 190B

full form see short form

full stop We put a full stop at the end of a written sentence.

future continuous a verb form with *will be* + ing-form, e.g. *I **will be leaving** soon.* ▶ 60

future perfect a verb form with *will have* + past participle, e.g. *We **will have saved** enough money soon.* ▶ 61A

future perfect continuous a verb form with *will have been* + ing-form, e.g. *He **will have been working** here for twenty years.* ▶ 61B

future tense The use of *will* + verb in a sentence such as *Tomorrow **will be** wet and windy* is sometimes called the future tense.

gender Some words show differences between male/masculine, female/feminine, and non-personal/neuter, e.g. *he, she*, and *it*. *Waiter* is masculine, and *waitress* is feminine.

generalization The statement *Cats are nice* is a generalization; it is about all cats and not a specific one.

genitive see possessive form

gerund the ing-form of a verb used like a noun, e.g. ***Sailing** is fun; I've given up smoking.* ▶ 111

gerund clause a clause with a gerund as its verb, e.g. *Running a business isn't easy*; *I like sitting outside*. ▶ 112

gradable A gradable adjective expresses a quality which can exist in different degrees. *Busy, soft,* and *dirty* are gradable because something can be *a bit dirty, rather dirty, very dirty*, and so on. An ungradable adjective such as *brilliant, impossible*, or *enormous* does not go with *a bit, rather,* or *very*. ▶ 186

group noun (or **collective noun**) a noun referring to a group, e.g. *audience, class, gang, team*. ▶ 149

hanging participle (or **dangling participle**) In the sentence *Looking out of the window, my friend was cycling past*, the verb *looking* is a hanging participle. The understood subject of looking (*myself*) is not the same as the subject of the main clause (*my friend*). ▶ 122B Note

hyphen In the number *twenty-five* there is a hyphen between *twenty* and *five*. A hyphen joins two words.

identifying relative clause (or **defining relative clause**) a relative clause that says which one is meant, e.g. *That's the man who lives next door*, where *who lives next door* tells us which man is meant. ▶ 267A

idiom/idiomatic An idiom is a group of words which together have a meaning that is different from the meanings of the individual words, e.g. *come off* (= succeed), *make up your mind* (= decide).

imperative the base form of the verb used to give orders, express good wishes, and so on, e.g. *Wait there. Have a good time*. ▶ 11

indefinite see definite

indefinite article the word *a* or *an* ▶ 150

indirect object see object

indirect question *How much does this cost?* is a direct question. In an indirect question we put the question in a sub-clause, e.g. *Could you tell me how much this costs?* ▶ 17

indirect speech (or **reported speech**) We use indirect speech when we report in our own words what someone said, e.g. *She told me she never wanted to see me again*, rather than quoting the words '*I never want to see you again*.' ▶ 258B

infinitive The infinitive is the base form of the verb, e.g. *They let us stay the night*. We often use it with *to*, e.g. *They invited us to stay the night*. ▶ 97 We often use a to-infinitive after a verb or adjective, e.g. *I hope to get a job*; *It's good to talk*. A to-infinitive can also express purpose, e.g. *I came here to see you*.

infinitive clause a clause with an infinitive as its verb, e.g. *They asked me to open both my suitcases*; *You'll need to work hard*. ▶ 98

informal We use an informal style in everyday conversation and when we e-mail or text a friend. *Can you do it right away?* is more informal than *I would be grateful if you could attend to the matter immediately*. See also formal.

ing-form An ing-form is the form of a verb ending in *-ing*, e.g. *seeing, making, flying*. It can be a gerund, e.g. *Moving house is quite stressful*, or an active participle, e.g. *I'll be moving house on that day*.

intensifier a word that strengthens the meaning of another, e.g. *so stupid, very cold* ▶ 196

interrogative An interrogative sentence has the form of a question, e.g. *Have you finished?* Interrogative words are question words, e.g. *what, how*.

intonation the rise and fall of the voice in speech

intransitive verb An intransitive verb cannot have an object, e.g. *The parcel has arrived*. It can have an adverbial after it, e.g. *Let's go to the park*; *The police appeared eventually*.

inversion/invert Inversion means changing the order of two things. To form the question *Has the play started?* from the statement *The play has started*, we invert the subject (*the play*) and the auxiliary verb (*has*).

inverted commas see quotes

irregular see regular

linking adverbial an adverbial such as *also, otherwise*, or *nevertheless* that relates to the previous clause or sentence, e.g. *She felt furious.* **Nevertheless,** *she managed not to show it.* ▶ 202

linking verb (or **copular verb**) a verb such as *be, seem, become*, or *look* that can have a complement, e.g. *It **was** a great party*; *Everything **seems** fine.*

literary A literary style is a formal written style typical of literature. It may contain some unusual or old-fashioned words and structures.

main clause A main clause has a subject and a verb, e.g. *I phoned yesterday.* A sentence has at least one main clause. It can also have more than one, e.g. *I phoned yesterday, but you didn't answer.* A main clause can also have a sub-clause. In the sentence *I woke up when the alarm went off*, the main clause is *I woke up*, and the sub-clause is *when the alarm went off.* In the sentence *To be on time, I had to get up early*, the main clause is *I had to get up early*, and *to be on time* is a sub-clause. A main clause can stand on its own, but a sub-clause cannot. A sub-clause functions as part of the main clause. For example, it can be the object of the main clause, e.g. *I knew **that you were away***, or it can be an adverbial, e.g. *I phoned you yesterday **because I wanted a chat.*** ▶ 227A–B

main verb The main verb is the verb which follows the subject in a main clause, e.g. *I **like** classical music*; *Hearing a knock, he **jumped** up*; *They **will expect** us to be on time.* The main verb is in the present or past tense or has a modal verb.

manner An adverbial of manner says how something happens, e.g. *He looked at me **sadly.*** ▶ 193

mid position An adverbial is in mid position when it comes in the middle of a sentence, usually after an auxiliary verb, e.g. *I was **just** writing a note*, but before an ordinary verb, e.g. *I **just** wrote everything down.* ▶ 190C–E

mixed conditional a conditional sentence which is a combination of two different types, e.g. *If you hadn't lost the map, we would know where we are.* (type 3 condition and type 2 main clause) ▶ 247C

modal verb (or **modal auxiliary verb**) The modal verbs are *can, could, must, need, should, ought, may, might, will, would*, and *shall*, e.g. *I **can** drive*; *We **should** support the idea.* A modal verb always has the same form. ▶ 70

modifier/modify In the phrase *a **narrow** street*, the adjective *narrow* is a modifier. It modifies the noun *street.* It changes our idea of the street by giving more information about it. Other kinds of modifiers are nouns, e.g. *a **golf** ball*, adverbials, e.g. *They stopped **suddenly***, and prepositional phrases, e.g. *a man **in uniform.***

nationality word a word formed from the name of a country which can be used as an adjective, e.g. *the **German** economy*, or to refer to people, e.g. *the **Americans** in our group.*

negative A negative sentence has *not* or *n't*, e.g. *I'm **not** ready*, or a negative word such as *never* or *nothing.* ▶ 10

neutral A neutral style is neither formal nor informal; it is between the two extremes.

nominalization expressing the meaning of a clause in a noun phrase, e.g. *they are enthusiastic* → *their **enthusiasm*** ▶ 257

nominal relative clause a relative clause beginning with *what*, e.g. *This is **what I bought*** ▶ 272, or with *whoever, whatever*, etc, e.g. *I'll eat **whatever there is** in the fridge.* ▶ 273 and functioning like a noun phrase

non-finite see finite

non-defining relative clause see adding relative clause

non-identifying relative clause see adding relative clause

noun a word such as *desk, apple,* or *information* which can follow the word *the.* ▶ 130

noun clause A noun clause is a clause that functions like a noun phrase. It can be the subject, e,g, *What actually happened came as a complete surprise,* the object. e.g. *We suspected that it was a trick,* the complement, e.g. *The problem is we're lost,* or the object of a preposition, e.g. *I'm worried about whether I made a good impression.* ▶ 252

noun phrase A noun phrase can be the subject, object or complement of a sentence, e.g. *The bus is late; I could hear music; It was a lovely holiday.* It can also come after a preposition, e.g. *It was in my pocket.* It can be a noun on its own (*music*), but it usually has a determiner (*the, a, my*), and it can have an adjective (*lovely*). A noun phrase can also be a pronoun, e.g. *I've been looking for you.*

object In the sentence *He was wearing a sweater,* the noun phrase *the sweater* is the object or direct object. The object usually comes after the verb. In the sentence *They gave the children presents,* the noun phrase *presents* is the direct object, and *the children* is the indirect object. The indirect object typically refers to the person receiving something. ▶ 6A See also prepositional object.

object complement In a sentence such as *They voted her their leader* or *The quarrel made Tom miserable,* the object complement is a noun phrase, e.g. *their leader,* or an adjective phrase, e.g. *miserable.* These complements relate to the object of the sentence (*her, Tom*). ▶ 5D

object pronoun *I* and *she* are subject pronouns; *me* and *her* are object pronouns. ▶ 175B

ordinal number a number such as *first, second, third.*

ordinary verb (or **full verb** or **lexical verb**) a verb such as *bring, offer, remember,* or *stay,* any verb which is not an auxiliary verb

pair noun a plural noun which refers to something made of two parts, e.g. *jeans, scissors, trousers* ▶ 148

participle A participle is a verb form such as *turning, turned,* or *having turned* ▶ 121 See also active participle, passive participle, past participle, perfect participle.

participle clause a clause with a participle as its verb, e.g. *Arriving home, I found the front door open; We saw a ship launched by the Queen.* ▶ 122

particle (or **adverb particle**) an adverb which is part of a phrasal verb, e.g. *look up, turn down, run away,* ▶ 217A

passive A passive sentence has a verb form with *be* and a passive participle, e.g. *My coat was stolen. The windows are being cleaned.* ▶ 86 Compare the active sentences *Someone stole my coat* and *We're cleaning the windows.*

passive gerund a verb form with *being* + passive participle, e.g. *I hate being stared at.* ▶ 95

passive infinitive A passive to-infinitive is a verb form with *to be* + passive participle, e.g. *Something needs to be done.* ▶ 95 The infinitive is sometimes without *to,* e.g. *Nothing can be done.*

passive ing-form A passive ing-form is a verb form with *being* + passive participle. It can be a passive gerund, e.g. *No one likes being made to look foolish.* ▶ 95 It can also be a continuous passive participle, e.g. *We watched the building being knocked down.*

passive participle A passive participle is a verb form such as *cleaned* or *broken,* the same form as the past participle. It is used after *be* in the passive, e.g. *The room was cleaned,* and in other structures, e.g. *I stepped on a broken bottle.* ▶ 121

passive to-infinitive a verb form with *to be* + passive participle, e.g. *I asked **to be** excused.* ▶ 95

past continuous (or **past progressive**) a verb form with the past of *be* and an ing-form, e.g. *It **was raining** at the time.* ▶ 47

past participle A past participle is a verb form such as *arrived* or *known*, the same form as the passive participle. It is used after *have* in the perfect, e.g. *They have **arrived**; How long has he **known**?* ▶ 121

past perfect a verb form with *had* and a past participle, e.g. *I **had seen** the film before.* ▶ 49

past perfect continuous (or **past perfect progressive**) a verb form with *had been* and an ing-form, e.g. *I saw that it **had been raining**.* ▶ 50

past progressive see past continuous

past simple (or **simple past**) the past tense without an auxiliary, e.g. *The train **stopped**; I **wrote** a letter.* ▶ 43

perception see verb of perception

perfect a verb form with *have* + past participle, e.g. *The game **has started**; If only I **had known**; I regret **having opened** my mouth.*

perfect conditional A verb form such as *would have left* or *would have seen* is sometimes called a perfect conditional.

perfect gerund a verb form with *having* + past participle, e.g. *He denied **having taken** the money.* ▶ 111B

perfect infinitive A perfect to-infinitive is a verb form with *to have* + past participle, e.g. *I hope **to have finished** by then.* ▶ 97B The infinitive is sometimes without *to*, e.g. *We might **have finished** by then.*

perfect participle a verb form with *having* + past participle, e.g. ***Having paid** the bill, we left.* ▶ 121B

perfect to-infinitive a verb form with *to have* + past participle, e.g. *It would be good **to have done** all these jobs by the weekend.* ▶ 97B

performative verb When we say *I agree* to express agreement, we are using a performative verb. Others are *apologize, promise, refuse,* and *suggest.* ▶ 9

person First person relates to the speaker (*I, we*). Second person relates to the person spoken to (*you*). Third person relates to other people and things (*he, she, it, they*).

personal pronoun words such as *I, me, you,* and *she* ▶ 175

phrasal verb a verb + adverb combination, e.g. *I **got up** early; Did you **turn off** the heating?* ▶ 217A

phrase A phrase is a word or group of words that functions as part of a clause. In the sentence *My friend is leaving on Friday,* the noun phrase *my friend* functions as the subject, and the prepositional phrase *on Friday* functions as an adverbial. ▶ 3–5

plural A plural form means more than one. Compare the singular *That tree is very old* (one tree) and the plural *Those trees are very old* (more than one tree).

positive (or **affirmative**) *I'm ready* is a positive sentence, and *I'm not ready* is negative.

possessive a form expressing the idea of something belonging to someone, or a similar connection, e.g. *That's **my** chair; **Whose** idea was it?; I'd love **Diana's** job.*

possessive determiner (or **possessive adjective**) the words *my, your, his, her, its, our,* and *their* used before a noun, e.g. ***my** flat, **her** name* ▶ 164

possessive form (or **genitive**) The possessive form of a noun is a noun with an apostrophe such as *Adam's room* or *a dogs' home,* often used to express the idea that something belongs to someone. ▶ 132

possessive pronoun the words *mine, yours, his, hers, ours,* and *theirs,* e.g. *These photos are **mine**.* ▶ 164

postmodifier a word, phrase, or clause that modifies the word it follows, e.g. *the people **outside**, the shop **on the corner**, a game **you play on the beach***

predicative An adjective in predicative position comes after a linking verb such as *be*, e.g. *The room was small*. But in the sentence *It was a small room*, the adjective is before the noun in **attributive** position.

prefix A prefix is something we put at the beginning of a word to change the meaning. The word *subway* has the prefix *sub-* before *way*. The word *unhappy* has the prefix *un-* before *happy*.

premodifier a word or phrase that modifies the word that comes after it, e.g. *a red dress, a carefully prepared speech*

preposition A preposition is a word like *on, to, by,* or *with*. It is usually followed by a noun phrase, e.g. *on the water, to the left.* ▶ 208

prepositional object the object of a preposition, e.g. *behind the sofa, on your bike*

prepositional phrase A prepositional phrase is a preposition + noun phrase, e.g. *in the studio, from Australia*, or a preposition + adverb, e.g. *since then*. It often functions as an adverbial, e.g. *I've got an interview on Thursday*.

prepositional verb a verb + preposition combination, e.g. *Look at this photo; Did you pay for your drink?* ▶ 217B

present continuous (or **present progressive**) a verb form with the present of *be* and an ing-form, e.g. *Everyone is waiting for you.* ▶ 41

present participle see active participle

present perfect a verb form with the present of *have* and a past participle, e.g. *Nothing has changed.* ▶ 44

present perfect continuous (or **present perfect progressive**) a verb form with the present of *have + been* + ing-form, e.g. *She has been working all day.* ▶ 48

present perfect simple the present perfect, e.g. *I have written it*, as distinct from the present perfect continuous, e.g. *I have been writing it*.

present progressive see present continuous

present simple (or **simple present**) the present tense without an auxiliary, e.g. *I like this song; He sells computers.* ▶ 40

progressive see continuous

pronoun A pronoun is a word that functions like a noun phrase, e.g. *you* (personal pronoun), *ourselves* (reflexive/emphatic pronoun), *theirs* (possessive pronoun), *which* (relative pronoun).

pronounce/pronunciation Correct pronunciation is speaking something with the correct sounds.

proper noun A proper noun is a name, e.g. *Jessica, New York*. It begins with a capital letter and does not normally have a determiner such as *a* or *the*. Other nouns are **common nouns**, e.g. *table, business, mistake, treatment*.

punctuation marks such as a full stop or comma used to divide sentences, clauses or phrases.

quantifier A quantifier is a word that says how many or how much, e.g. *all the books, some milk, half of the students, enough money*. It usually comes before a noun.

question A question is a request for information which usually involves inversion of subject and auxiliary, e.g. *Have you bought a ticket? Where are we going?* ▶ 13–15

question mark We write a question mark at the end of a question, e.g. *Are you sure?*

question phrase a phrase with *what* or *how* at the beginning of a question, e.g. *What time is it? How long will you be?* ▶ 16C

question tag a short question added to the end of a statement, e.g. *That was nice, wasn't it?* ▶ 20

question word the words *who, what, which, whose, where, when, why,* and *how* ▶ 15

quotes/quotation marks (or **inverted commas**) When we report the words someone said, we put quotes before and after the words, e.g. *'It's not my fault,' she said.*

reflexive pronoun a pronoun such as *myself* or *themselves* which refers to the subject, e.g. *He blamed **himself** for the accident.* ▶ 177

regular A regular form is the same as most others; it follows the normal pattern. The verb *call* has a regular past tense *called*, but the verb *sing* has an irregular past tense *sang*. ▶ 285 Regular noun plurals end in *-s/-es*, but *men, women,* and *children* are irregular plurals. ▶ 281

relative adverb the words *where, when,* and *why* in a relative clause, e.g. *the hotel **where** we stayed* ▶ 271

relative clause a clause that comes after a noun and identifies what is meant or adds information, e.g. *the woman **who called yesterday**.* ▶ 266

relative pronoun a word such as *who, which,* or *that* in a relative clause, e.g. *the person **who** started the argument, a job **that** I have to do.* ▶ 266

reply question see echo tag

reported speech see indirect speech

reporting verb see verb of reporting

rule A grammatical rule is a statement of how a language works. For example, there is a rule that in English we form a noun plural by adding *-s* or *-es* to the singular, e.g. *car* → *cars, bus* → *buses*. This rule applies to almost all countable nouns in English, but there are a few exceptions, words which do not follow the rule, e.g. *man* → **men**.

s-form the form of a verb with *-s* or *-es* added in the simple present third person singular, e.g. *The office **opens** at nine.*

second conditional see type 2 conditional

second person see person

semi-colon In this sentence there is a semi-colon between the two clauses: *It was very late; I was ready for bed.*

sentence A sentence can be a statement, e.g. *I waited for you*, a question, e.g. *Did you wait for me?*, an imperative, e.g. *Wait for me*, or an exclamation, e.g. *How silly!* ▶ 7 It consists of one or more clauses, e.g. *I waited for you*, or *I waited for you, but you didn't come.* A written sentence begins with a capital letter and ends with a full stop (.), a question mark (?), or an exclamation mark (!).

short answer an answer where the words after the auxiliary are left out because they are understood in the context, e.g. *Have you heard the news? ~ **Yes, I have**,* meaning *Yes, I have heard the news.*

short form (or **contraction**) Some words can be written in a full form or a short form, e.g. *We **have*** or *we**'ve***. In the short form we miss out part of the word and write an apostrophe instead.

short question a question where the words after the auxiliary or after the question word are left out because they are understood in the context, e.g. *My tutor told me to rewrite the essay. ~ And **have you?** ~ No, but I'm going to. ~ Well, **when?***

sibilant Sibilant sounds are /s/, /z/, /ʃ/, /ʒ/, /tʃ/, and /dʒ/, as in the words *see, zoo, show, vision, chair,* and *just*.

simple The simple tenses are the present simple, e.g. *It **arrives***, and the past simple, e.g. *It **arrived***. Sometimes a perfect tense is called 'simple' meaning 'non-continuous'; *I **have done** it* is present perfect simple, and *I **have been doing** it* is present perfect continuous.

simple future The use of *will* + verb in a sentence such as *Tomorrow **will be** wet and windy* is sometimes called the simple future.

simple past see past simple

simple present see present simple

singular A singular form means one only. Compare the singular *That **tree is** very old* (one tree) and the plural *Those **trees are** very old* (more than one tree).

specific We are being specific when we mean a particular one. *The First World War* is a specific war, but if we say *War is a terrible thing*, we are talking about war in general.

spelling If you spell a word correctly, you write it with the correct letters.

split infinitive a to-infinitive with an adverb between *to* and the verb, e.g. *I want **to completely forget** about it.* ▶ 98A Note

standard Standard English is the kind of English used in education and in serious newspapers and generally considered correct. *I'm not telling you* is standard; *I ain't telling you* is non-standard.

state verb (or **stative verb**) a verb that expresses a meaning such as being, having an opinion, or thinking rather than doing, e.g. *exist, believe, know, include.* ▶ 51A The opposite is an action verb.

statement A statement is a sentence which gives information. *I like it here* is a statement, but *Do you like it here?* is a question. ▶ 7

stative verb see state verb

stress When we stress a word or syllable, we make it sound more prominent. The word *apple* /ˈæpl/ is stressed on the first syllable, and *again* /əˈgen/ is stressed on the second syllable.

strong form see weak form

structure The structure of a sentence is the way the different parts are arranged to form the whole. The sentence *My friend has won the lottery* has this structure: subject (*my friend*) + verb (*has won*) + object (*the lottery*). The phrase *my friend* has this structure: determiner (*my*) + noun (*friend*).

sub-clause (or **subordinate clause**) see main clause

subject In the sentence *The ship sails in an hour*, the noun phrase *the ship* is the subject. In a statement the subject comes before the verb. ▶ 4

subject complement see complement

subject pronoun *I* and *she* are subject pronouns; *me* and *her* are object pronouns. ▶ 175B

subjunctive The subjunctive is the base form of a verb. We can use it in rather formal English in some contexts, e.g. *We propose that the money **be** made available.* ▶ 231

subordinate clause (or **sub-clause**) see main clause

suffix A suffix is something we put on the end of a word. If we add the suffix -*ly* to the adjective *calm*, we form the adverb *calmly*; if we add the suffix -*ment* to the verb *move*, we form the noun *movement*.

superlative a form with -*est* or *most* used to make a comparison, e.g. *oldest, most famous, most efficiently.* ▶ 203–204

syllable The word *important* has three syllables: *im por tant.*

tag see question tag

tag question a sentence with a question tag, e.g. *It's true, isn't it?*

tense a form of the verb which shows whether we are talking about the present, e.g. *I play, he knows, we are*, or the past, e.g. *I played, he knew, we were*. The various combinations of tense and aspect can also be called tenses, e.g. *I have played* is the present perfect tense. ▶ 39

third conditional see type 3 conditional

third person see person

to-infinitive a form like *to go, to miss* or *to open*; see also infinitive

to-infinitive clause see infinitive clause

transitive verb a verb that has an object, e.g. *We **enjoyed** the meal; The postman **brings** the letters.*

truth adverbial a word or phrase which expresses the speaker's view of the truth of a statement, e.g. *There's **certainly** a problem; It went OK **on the whole**.* ▶ 200

type 0 conditional a conditional sentence with the present simple in both clauses expressing the idea that one thing follows automatically from another, e.g. *If you click on the icon, the file opens.* ▶ 244

type 1 conditional a conditional sentence with *if* ... + present ... + *will/can* etc, expressing an open condition, e.g. *If you drop that, it'll break.* ▶ 245

type 2 conditional a conditional sentence with *if* ... + past ... + *would/could* etc, expressing an unreal or theoretical condition, e.g. *If I had a car, the journey would be a lot easier.* ▶ 246

type 3 conditional a conditional sentence with *if* ... + past perfect ... + *would/could* etc + perfect, expressing an unreal condition in the past, e.g. *If I had left two minutes earlier, I would have caught the bus.* ▶ 247

uncountable noun An uncountable noun cannot have *a/an* in front of it and has no plural form, e.g. *gold, petrol, music.* ▶ 137

ungradable see gradable

verb In the sentence *The parcel **arrived** yesterday*, the word *arrived* is a verb. Verbs are words like *make, talk, expect, carry, discover*. There are also the auxiliary verbs *be, have*, and *do* and modal verbs, e.g. *can, should*.

verb of perception a verb whose meaning is to do with how we are aware of things around us, e.g. *see, hear, feel, smell*.

verb of reporting (or **reporting verb**) a verb used to report what someone says or thinks, e.g. *say, tell, think, answer, promise.* ▶ 259

verb phrase A verb phrase is a word or group of words that functions as a verb, e.g. *You **look** tired; We **watched** the game; Someone **is coming**; Lucy **did fail** her exam; I **can play** the piano; You **must have known***. There is always an ordinary verb, e.g. *look, watched, coming, fail, play*, and there may also be an auxiliary verb, e.g. *is, did, have*, or a modal verb, e.g. *can, must*.

viewpoint adverbial An adverbial which expresses the aspect or point of view from which we are looking at a situation is a viewpoint adverbial, e.g. *Things don't look too good **weather-wise**.* ▶ 199

voiced/voiceless The difference in pronunciation between *came* and *game* is that *came* begins with voiceless /k/, and *game* begins with voiced /g/. The consonant sounds in these words are voiceless: *play, take, call, sea, shop, cheese, four, thin*. These consonant sounds are voiced: *bag, down, good, zoo, jam, very, this, long, right, many, now, sang*. All vowel sounds are voiced, e.g. *dog, seem, boat*.

vowel The letters *a, e, i, o*, and *u* are vowels. The other letters are consonants.

weak form Some words can be spoken in two different ways: we use a strong form when they are stressed and a weak form when they are unstressed. The modal verb *can* has a strong form /kæn/ and a weak form /kən/ or /kn/.

wh-clause a noun clause beginning with a question word, e.g. *I know **what you did***, or with *if* or *whether*, e.g. *No one cares **whether it's true or not**.* ▶ 252

wh-question a question that begins with a question word, e.g. ***What** did you say?; **Where** can we park?* ▶ 15

word class a type of word such as a noun, adjective or preposition ▶ 1

yes/no question a question that begins with an auxiliary verb and can be answered *yes* or *no*, e.g. ***Am I late?** ~ No, not very; **Did you enjoy the show?** ~ Yes, it was great.* ▶ 14A

yes/no short answer an answer such as *Yes, it is* or *No, they didn't* ▶ 19B

zero conditional see type 0 conditional

Index

References are to section numbers. Terms followed by an asterisk (*) appear in the glossary. Keywords are in italics and grammatical categories in capital letters. Examples of grammatical points are given in italics within brackets.